BAKING ACROSS AMERICA

Arthur L. Meyer

Baking across America

Drawings by John A. Wilson

UNIVERSITY OF TEXAS PRESS
AUSTIN

REQUESTS FOR PERMISSION TO REPRODUCE MATERIAL FROM THIS WORK
SHOULD BE SENT TO PERMISSIONS, UNIVERSITY OF TEXAS PRESS,
BOX 7819, AUSTIN, TX 78713-7819.
♾ THE PAPER USED IN THIS PUBLICATION MEETS THE MINIMUM REQUIREMENTS
OF AMERICAN NATIONAL STANDARD FOR INFORMATION SCIENCES
—PERMANENCE OF PAPER FOR PRINTED LIBRARY MATERIALS, ANSI Z39.48-1984.

LIBRARY OF CONGRESS CATALOGING-IN-PUBLICATION DATA

Meyer, Arthur L.
    Baking across America / by Arthur L. Meyer ; drawings by John A.
Wilson.
        p.   cm.
    Includes bibliographical references and index.
    ISBN 0-292-75216-4 (hardcover : alk. paper).—ISBN 0-292-75222-9
(pbk. : alk. paper)
    1. Baking. 2. Cookery, American. I. Title.
TX763.M475 1998
641.8'15'0973—dc21   98-15165

This book is dedicated to the memory of my dad,
who showed me how to butter my bread
and taught me right from wrong.

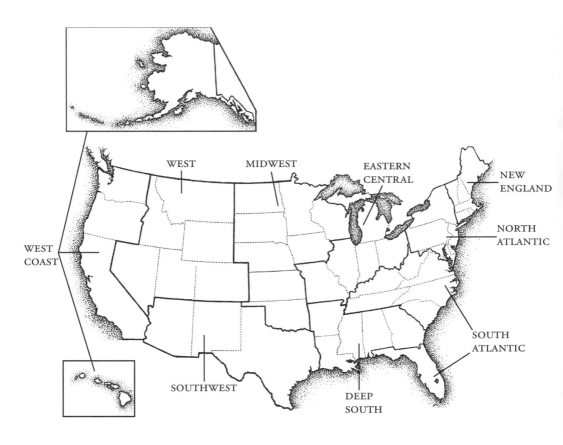

WEST   MIDWEST   EASTERN CENTRAL   NEW ENGLAND

WEST COAST

NORTH ATLANTIC

SOUTH ATLANTIC

SOUTHWEST

DEEP SOUTH

CONTENTS

FOREWORD

$\int$

Baking is rapidly becoming a lost art. It is no longer being passed down from generation to generation as busy schedules and the two-income requirement for most households necessitate the use of convenience foods. I suppose that baking is one of the first time-consuming tasks to go. This is unfortunate, as it is a marvelous way to spend time at home. It gives the house a wonderful smell and it can involve the whole family in a creative (and tasty) pastime. Many bakers find baking therapeutic. Kneading bread dough releases anxiety; creating cakes, pies, and tarts sets your right brain free! My generation seems to be the one responsible for not passing on the baking tradition, and I'm worried that the next generation will think that bread comes from a supermarket and cookies from a box.

Many good cooks and professional chefs are intimidated by baking. It has a reputation for potential failure that other cooking forms do not possess. Accurate measurement of ingredients and temperatures leads to success in baking. There is not a lot of room for approximating; exploration and experimentation should follow strict guidelines. My grandmother violated all that I just mentioned. A pinch of this and a handful of that and . . . voilà! . . . a perfect dough for her apple cake. The closest she came to a measuring device was a porcelain coffee cup she used for scooping flour from a canister.

While researching recipes that were the foundation for our American style of baking, I came across instructions like these:

> Take as much creame and newe milk as you please & put it to as much runnit as will make it come; then break yʳ curd very small & put to it 6 eggs and season it with sugar, mace, cloves, & a little salt; & put in as much grated bread as will make it up into little loaves about yᵉ bigness of halfe penney loaves. then wash them over with melted butter & put them on buttered papers. when they are well baked in yᵉ oven, cut them up on yᵉ top, & put into them melted butter, rosewater, & sugar beaten together, & soe serve them up.

This recipe for Cheese Loaues is taken from Martha Washington's *Booke of Cookery,* a manuscript "curiously copied by an unknown Hand" that was in Mrs. Washington's possession in the late eighteenth century. It is believed that many of the receipts (recipes) date from the seventeenth century and therefore represent some of the earliest recipes in use by colonial Americans.

With directions like these and the way my grandmother baked, how in the world did baking ever get a reputation for requiring accurate measurement?

I hope with this book to rekindle interest in home baking. Home-baked goods are economical and superior to store bought. Baking is a wonderful way to spend the precious time we have with our children, family, and friends. One of my earliest (and fondest) memories of my mother involves helping her measure ingredients for a cake. I would stand on a stool and she would show me how to carefully level a measuring cup full of flour with the back of a butter knife.

So, turn on your oven, invite your friends and family into the kitchen, get right in there with your hands, and try some of the recipes that follow. Don't be intimidated. Experience is the best teacher. And besides, you get to eat your mistakes!

PART ONE

A Brief History

INTRODUCTION

To TRACE THE TRADITION
of baking in America is to observe its development and its technologies in a more universal sense. Baking, and cookery in general, did not change much until the mid-1600's. A new method of leavening was developed in America in the mid-eighteenth century that would simplify the baking process. By the end of the nineteenth century, yeast had been standardized. Bakers no longer had to use the leftovers of the brewing process or "proof" the leavening. The oven changed from a metal reflector placed in front of coals in the hearth to a stand-alone stove with fairly accurate temperature control.

Of considerable importance was the change in the flavorings of foods from the Middle Ages to the beginning of the eighteenth century. It was common practice in medieval cookery to include sweet ingredients in most savory and meat dishes. As cookery became more sophisticated in the 1600's, sweet flavors migrated to cakes and other baked desserts.

The settlement of America by so many diverse cultures led to the melding of their cooking traditions and provided us with a rich mosaic of what would become our own recipes for baked goods. While the first truly American cookbook published was *American Cookery 1796* by Amelia Simmons, early-seventeenth-century English and European settlers and traders brought their traditional methods and recipes. *The Accomplisht Cook, or the Art and Mystery of Cookery* by Robert May, first published in 1660 in London, was popular among colonists, as was *The Compleat Housewife; or, Accomplished Gentlewoman's Companion* by Eliza Smith, first published in 1728. It is interesting to note that the fifth edition (1732) of Eliza Smith's book was the first cookbook to be published in America.

While it is accepted that the major influence in American cookery as a whole came from England, baking seems to have come from a variety of cultural influences. American baking is a composite of the baking of England and of most European countries. By 1626 New Amsterdam was a permanent Dutch settlement, and by 1643 it was the most diverse of the new colonies, with eighteen languages spoken. The Swedes settled the Bergen area in 1638 and established New Sweden on the Delaware River, soon to be Pennsylvania. The Quakers and Mennonites founded Germantown in 1683, two years after Charles II granted the land to William Penn. The French Huguenots settled in upstate New York in the 1640's. The English arrived in 1607 and established Jamestown in 1619. The *Mayflower* landing in 1620 led to colonies that proved to be quite influential in building a true American style of cookery. Native Americans provided the colonists with local ingredients such as corn and squash and farming techniques that helped develop the baking style and baked goods associated with colonial America. Today, New England serves up a unique regional cuisine. The other great influence in American cookery originated in Virginia. In 1699 Middle Plantation changed to Williamsburg and became its capital. Traditional cooking methods have survived through the preservation of this great settlement as Colonial Williamsburg.

From the 1750's through the early nineteenth century, American baking began to assume its own identity. Jonny cakes, gems (muffins), drop biscuits, griddlecakes, cornbread, and mince pie became part of the uniquely American repertoire along with pandowdies, steamed puddings, Indian pudding, flummeries, grunts, and duffs. By the end of the nineteenth century, immigrants from Eastern Europe, Central Europe, and the British Isles were bringing their baking specialties to be absorbed into the American baking tradition. Such breads as pumpernickel rye, bagels and bialys, English muffins and tea biscuits, scones, and even our humble (and much-maligned) white bread have become the mainstay of the American bread diet.

Apple pie has become a symbol for America but is not an American creation. It *is* an excellent example, however, of how recipes from Europe and England have been adapted and assimilated into the American repertoire. Gervase Markham, in *The English Housewife* (ca. 1620), gives a recipe (most probably sixteenth century) for a "pippin pie." That recipe directs the baker to

> take of the fairest and best pippins, and pare them and make a hole in the top of them; then prick in each hole a clove or two, then put them into the coffin, then break in whole sticks of cinnamon, and slices of orange peels and dates, and on the top of every pippin a little piece of sweet butter: then fill the coffin and cover the pippins over with sugar; then close up the pie and bake it, as you bake pies of the like nature, and when it is baked anoint the lid over with store of sweet butter, and then strew sugar upon it a good thickness, and set it into the oven again for a little space, as whilst the meat is in dishing up, and then serve it.

This recipe's similarity to a modern American apple pie is striking. The use of cinnamon and cloves as traditional apple pie spices along with applying a top crust sprinkled with sugar is very much in line with modern recipes. A *coffin* is an empty, unbaked pie crust. *Pippin* can be traced to the fifteenth century, derived from the French *pépin*, meaning a good apple for baking.

Not all pies are derived from earlier recipes, but the concept of the pie is very English. Manuscripts dating to the eleventh century mention pies, and it seems that the English were willing to bake almost anything in a pie shell. Pumpkin pie, pecan pie, and the various custard pies are, however, American variations on the theme.

We think of cookies as traditionally American, and there are variations that most certainly are, but the cookie comes to us from the Dutch. Cookies can be traced to the earliest Dutch settlements in New York (New Amsterdam). The word *cookie* is derived from *koekje,* which means "little cake." Wooden molds for forming cookies—mistakenly categorized as butter molds when first discovered—are found in museums and private collections. Cookie cutters were fashioned in the late seventeenth century, but the time-honored tradition of using a drinking glass as a cutter predates these tools, as illustrated in the following recipe for a "little cake" from Martha Washington's *A Booke of Sweetmeats*:

> Take two pounds of flower, & one pound of sugar, and ye youlks of 2 eggs, & a spoonful of sack, & a spoonful of rosewater, and make it up into paste with melted butter, & roule it out pritty thin, & cut them with a beer glass, & put them on plates & set them in an oven meanly hot with ye stone downe.

Any discussion of traditional American cookies must include the chocolate chip variety. Created by a Mrs. Wakefield in the 1930's, this cookie became known as the Toll House cookie, as she and her husband ran an inn built in 1709 in Whitman, Massachusetts, known as the Toll House Inn. As is the case with most great inventions, Mrs. Wakefield did not set out to make the cookie in its present form. After cutting a bar of chocolate into bits and adding them to a cookie dough, she was surprised that the pieces of chocolate didn't melt into the dough, but kept their integrity throughout the baking process and remained soft and creamy after cooling. The Nestlé Company started to make a semisweet chocolate bar sometime in the 1930s that was specially scored to make it easier for bakers to make this cookie and eventually produced the first chocolate chips, expressly for this cookie recipe!

LEAVENINGS AND FLAVORINGS

Leavenings I N ORDER FOR BREAD to rise
and to have a fine texture, some form of leavening must be introduced. The same is true for cakes and biscuits. The word *leaven* dates
from the fourteenth century and derives from the Middle English
levain, "to raise." Historically, leavening has usually been associated
with the use of a sour starter rather than other yeast preparations.

The process of fermentation is linked to the action of yeast, a
microscopic fungus that tends to aid in the chemical breakdown of
carbohydrates (starches and sugars) and forms carbon dioxide gas. It
is this expanding gas that causes bread dough to "rise." Fermentation
was known to the ancient Jews, Babylonians, and Egyptians.

Baking and brewing have always been intimately related, and
grains were fermented well before recorded history. In *The New
World Guide to Beer,* Michael Jackson, noted beer authority, cites the
work of anthropologist E. Huber. In *Bier und Bierbereitung bei den*

Volkernder Urzeit (Beer and beer making from the people of ancient times) Dr. Huber describes a process by which the ancient Egyptians crumbled leavened bread into water to make beer.

The relationship between baking and brewing is also seen quite clearly if we examine the methods of leavening used in colonial America. One of the first yeast-type leavenings used in America was brought from England and was known as "barm." In *The English Housewife,* Gervase Markham's recipe entitled "Of baking manchets" instructs the baker to do the following:

> first your meal, being ground upon black stones if it be possible, which makes the whitest flour, and bolted through the finest bolting [sifting] cloth . . . and, opening the flower hollow in the midst, put into it of the best ale barm.

Barm is the foam formed at the top of fermenting malt liquors and contains active yeasts. The word is derived from the Middle English *berme.* This term is not often used in the cookbooks of colonial America; I believe it is replaced with the term "ale yeast," as seen in Martha Washington's recipe for "A Butterd Loafe" from *Booke of Cookery:*

> Take 4 quarts of milke, put runnit to it, & whey it, & hang y^r curd up in a cloth to dreyne for an houre or 2. then take 10 eggs & leave out 3 of ye whites, y^n take a little ginger, a pinte of ale yeast, as much fine flower as will make it up to a loafe.

In Eliza Smith's *The Compleat Housewife,* a recipe for plain buns begins with

> Take two pounds of fine flour, a pint of Ale-yeast; put a little Sack in the Yeast, and three Eggs beaten . . .

Occasionally the ale itself was added as a leavening agent. Also from the *Booke of Cookery,* this recipe for Pancakes Another Way illustrates this technique:

> Take a quart of ale and warm, then mingle with it 4 or 5 eggs well beaten, a little flower, a nutmeg grated, a little rosewater, a quarter of a pinte of sacke . . .

Another popular form of yeast leavening related to brewing was referred to as "emptins" in colonial America. This by-product of brewing was found at the bottom of beer barrels, hence the name. Once obtained from the barrel, emptins could be propagated much as sourdough starters are. In *American Cookery 1796,* Amelia Simmons provides us with a recipe:

> Take a handful of hops and about three quarts of water, let it boil about fifteen minutes, then make a thickening as you do for starch, strain the liquor, when cold put a little emptins to work them, they will keep well cork'd in a bottle five or six weeks.

Another interesting reference to emptins comes from the kitchen manuscripts of the Van Rensselaer family of Pennsylvania. In *Selected Receipts of a Van Rensselaer Family 1785–1835* a recipe for Very Common Snook-Kill Dough Nuts calls for the following:

> 1 pint of Molasses, 1 do [ditto, i.e., 1 pint, in this case] Lard, 1 pint milk and 1 do Emptins, the milk and lard warmed together as much flour as they will take.

It is interesting to note that barm and emptins relate to the brewing of beer. By the mid-1700's it was well known in the brewing industry that some brewer's yeast rose to the top of the fermentation tank while other yeast sank to the bottom. It was believed that different yeasts were involved, but by the mid-1800's it had become clear that the same strain of Saccharomycetacea was somehow involved. To this day European brewers distinguish between top-fermented and bottom-fermented beers as "ales" and "lagers," respectively.

Many eighteenth-century bread recipes call for "good yeast," which was a sour starter passed on from household to household and even from generation to generation. In Martha Washington's *Booke of Cookery* the recipe for White Bread states the following:

> Take 3 quarters of a peck of fine flower, & strow salt in as much as will season it. y^n heat as much milke as will season it luke warm, & hould it high when you poure it on to make it light. & mingle wth y^r milke 4 or 5 spoonfuls of good yeast. worke y^r paste well, & y^n let it ly a rising by the fire.

As with all starters, attention must be paid to keep the colony well fed, and most books alert the cook to this fact.

Not all yeast preparations were liquids. It was recognized that if yeast could be dried, it would store well with minimum fuss and little attention. There were several forms of dried yeast in colonial America. The Dutch had their *rivvels,* known by other bakers as *rubs.* A hard yeast much like our modern compressed cake was also prepared. A recipe for drying yeast can be found in *The Art of Cookery*

Made Plain and Easy by Hannah Glasse, first published in London in 1796:

> When you have yeast in plenty, take a quantity of it, stir and work it well with a whisk until it becomes liquid and thin, then get a large wooden platter, cooler, or tub, clean and dry, and with a soft brush, lay a thin layer of the yeast on the tub, and turn the mouth downwards that no dust may fall upon it, but so that the air may get under to dry it. When that coat is very dry, then lay on another coat and let it dry and so go on . . . When you have occasion to make use of this yeast cut a piece off, and lay it in warm water.

By the end of the nineteenth century, a standardized form of yeast was available commercially and revolutionized both the home baking of bread and the rapidly expanding bread industry.

A new way to introduce carbon dioxide into a batter or dough without using yeast came around 1750 in the form of "pearl ash." Pearl ash is a salt (potassium carbonate [K_2CO_3]) formed in wood and other plant ashes. When heated, it decomposes to carbon dioxide and water. It can be considered to be the first "baking powder" and is chemically related to baking soda, or sodium bicarbonate ($NaHCO_3$).

Amelia Simmons was the first to use pearl ash in a published recipe for baked goods and should be given credit for her inventiveness. Her recipe for Molasses Gingerbread using this "baking powder" is found in *American Cookery 1796*:

> One tablespoon of cinnamon, some coriander or allspice, put to four teaspoons pearl ash, dissolved in half pint water, four pound flour, one quart molasses, four ounces butter, (if in summer rub in the butter, if in winter, warm the butter and molasses and pour to the spiced flour,) knead well 'till stiff, the more the better, the lighter and whiter it will be; bake brisk fifteen minutes; don't scorch; before it is put in, wash it with whites and sugar beat together.

By 1800 a second "baking powder" had been introduced. Called *saleratus,* it is related to pearl ash and is known chemically as potassium bicarbonate ($KHCO_3$). Finally, the sodium salt was introduced and baking soda, sodium bicarbonate, became the chemical leavening agent of choice. There was initial resistance to these leavening agents as they were not considered to be natural additives, but by the 1850's they had gained wide acceptance as a modern convenience.

In order for these chemical leavening agents to work effectively, some type of acidic ingredient has to be present in the recipe. The final improvement came with the development of what we know as baking powder—a mixture of soda with an acidic ingredient included in the dry mixture, thereby eliminating the need to add an additional acidic ingredient to a recipe.

Cakes require some form of leavening as well, but their delicate flavor should rule out the use of strong-tasting yeast preparations. Early recipes for cakes, however, regularly call for their use. The use of beaten eggs or separated and beaten whites folded into the cake batter also provided the expanding gas necessary for leavening to occur, but in this case the gas was air rather than carbon dioxide. Beating egg whites was no simple task in the early eighteenth century, as the first whips were often bunches of twigs held together. Beating required laborious hand mixing to achieve the proper consistency, as instructed in one of Hannah Glasse's recipes for Pound Cake:

> Take a pound of butter, beat it in an earthen pan with your hand till it is like a fine thick cream, then have ready, twelve eggs, but half the whites, beat them up with the butter, a pound of flour beat in it, a pound of sugar, and a few caraways; beat all together for an hour with your hand, or a great wooden spoon, butter a pan and put it in, and then bake it an hour in a quick oven.

Flavorings   To THE EXPERIENCED dessert baker, two of the most important flavors are vanilla and chocolate. Neither was available to the colonial American baker! The dominant flavoring extract in early cookbook recipes was rose water. Vanilla seems to have replaced it sometime in the mid-nineteenth century. Orange flower water is cited occasionally, but climate (both in England and the Colonies) dictated the more available rosebush as the practical source of plant material to extract.

Vanilla is the fermented pod of the orchid *Vanilla planifolia* and *Vanilla fragrans.* An epiphyte, this orchid receives its food and water from the air rather than from soil (much as a bromeliad does). The Aztecs called the plant *thilxochitl* and had used the vanilla bean for centuries before Hernando Cortez's arrival in what is now Mexico in 1519. Cortez used the Spanish word for little sheath (*vainilla*) to describe the pods he took back to Europe. The first cookbook to mention vanilla is *The Virginia Housewife* by Mary Randolph, published in 1824. While some historians believe that this is Thomas Jefferson's recipe for vanilla ice cream (described later), it does differ in several ways:

> Boil a vanilla bean in a quart of rich milk until it has imparted the flavour sufficiently; then take it out, and mix with the milk, eight eggs, yelks and whites, beaten well; let it boil a little longer— make it very sweet, for much of the sugar is lost in the freezing.

By the time *Seventy-Five Receipts for Pastry, Cakes, and Sweetmeats,* by Eliza Leslie, was published in 1828, the use of vanilla had become more commonplace and was being used in the form of the split bean that had been chopped into pieces. By mid-century, in Leslie's *New Receipts for Cooking,* tincture of vanilla and vanilla syrup were being used as the flavoring of choice in many desserts.

As well, wine and brandy were two popular additions to cake and cookie batters. Amelia Simmons calls for "a gill of rose-water and a gill of wine" in her Plain Cake. The *gill* is a volume measure equal to ¼ pint (½ cup). For A Cake in the Spanish Way, Hannah Glasse calls for "four spoonfuls of orange water" and for her Bride Cake a "half pint of brandy."

Sack (or *sacke*) represents a category of wine from Spain, most probably a dry sherry, and is used in many recipes. Martha Washington calls for "a pinte of sack, & as much Ale" in a recipe entitled "To Make an Excellent Cake."

In addition to liquid flavorings, spices are found in most dessert recipes. Cinnamon, nutmeg, ginger, cloves, mace, and coriander are the spices of choice. A recipe from Martha Washington's *A Booke of Sweetmeats* for the often-copied Shrowsbury Cakes illustrates this style of flavoring a dessert:

> Take 4 quarts of flower, 3 pounds of butter, & breake it in little pieces, & work them well together. then take a pownd & halfe of powder sugar, half an ounce of cinamon, a little cloves & mace, 3 whites of eggs, a little rosewater and sack, & work it up with warme creame, & soe bake it.

Plumb Cake appears in many of the cookbooks I have cited, and I must include this version from the Van Rensselaer family's manuscript, if only because of the quantities of ingredients called for in a single cake. Interestingly, no instructions are given:

> 7 pounds Flour, 7 do Butter, 7 do Sugar, 6 do Raisons, 6 do Citron, 16 do Currants, 70 eggs, 2 ounces Cloves, 2 do Cinnamon, 2 do Ginger, 1 do Mace, 2 do Nutmegs, 1 quart Rose-water, 1 do Brandy.

The first American recipe I have found to use vanilla was penned by none other than Thomas Jefferson, our third president, and is also the first recipe I have found for ice cream in America. The recipe was brought here from France in the 1780's:

> 2 bottles of good cream, 6 yolks of eggs, ½ pound sugar, mix the yolks and sugar, put the cream on a fire in a casserole first putting in a stick of vanilla.

In many ways chocolate's history in America is related to that of vanilla. Montezuma introduced Cortez to the drink *xocolatl* (*chocolatl*), a popular Aztec beverage made from the fermented pod of the cacao tree. Unlike our modern hot chocolate or chocolate milk, *xocolatl* was prepared as a bitter, red beverage, unsweetened and drunk for its stimulant properties, much as coffee is enjoyed today. In Europe sugar and vanilla were added to make a delicious beverage that became the rage in France. The Dutch brought this beverage to New Amsterdam in the 1600's, and many households had a chocolate pot for preparing it.

It was in Dorchester, Massachusetts, in 1765, that the first solid chocolate was milled by James Hannon. It soon became a staple of the American pantry. Hannon was financially supported by James Baker, who eventually took over from him. The Walter Baker Company was established by James's grandson. Soon, Baker's chocolate was appearing everywhere. The famous German chocolate cake is made from a type of chocolate formulated in 1852 by the Baker Company. It is a sweet, smooth chocolate bar named for a friend and employee named Samuel German, who helped in the formulation.

In 1828 the Dutch perfected a method of removing the cocoa butter from the chocolate to make a dry cocoa powder, a pantry staple that no modern dessert baker could manage without. By the 1870's the Swiss had developed a product called milk chocolate, which became very popular as a chocolate that could be eaten as a snack or treat.

The first cookbook recipe I could locate that refers to the use of solid chocolate is from Mary Randolph's *The Virginia Housewife,* the same cookbook that first refers to vanilla. The recipe is for chocolate cream and instructs the cook to

> scrape a quarter pound of chocolate very fine, put it in a quart of milk, boil it till the chocolate is dissolved, stirring it continuously; thicken with six eggs.

The first chocolate cake recipe that I could find is for Chocolate Pound Cake. From the ingredients used, this Shaker recipe probably dates from around 1860. The three significant ingredients are "2 tablespoons shaved chocolate, ½ cup cocoa and 1 teaspoon vanilla." By 1896, when Fannie Farmer's *Boston Cooking-School Cook Book* was published, chocolate had become a very popular ingredient in cakes.

FROM HEARTH TO STOVE

Baking requires an enclosed space and dry heat over a fairly long period of time. The temperature inside the space should be controlled, as different baked goods require specific temperatures and baking times: breads, for example, require a very hot oven; cakes need more moderate heat.

Providing these conditions was no simple task in the seventeenth-century kitchen. The main cooking area was the hearth. It consisted of a large chimney that protruded out three or four feet into the kitchen, serving as a hood to catch the sparks and grease from cooking. Around the chimney was built the fireplace, a great structure from four to ten feet wide, usually the full height of the ceiling. Typically made of stone in New England or brick in the South, the hearth radiated heat and became the main source of warmth for the house-hold. Rock ledges were sometimes built on the sides of the hearth to provide benches on which family and honored guests could warm themselves. A fire was built on the floor of the hearth and all cooking, including baking, was done using coals from the fire. In order to increase the efficiency of the hearth, a large cast iron plate, often elaborately decorated, was placed on the back wall.

Climate dictated that many homes in the South build separate (but usually attached) buildings to house the hearth, while inclusion of the hearth in the home was the best choice for the colder regions of the North.

The first apparatus developed for baking bread was the "Dutch oven," or reflector oven, a metal box open on one face and rounded on the other. The idea was to place the oven on the hearth floor with the open end facing the back of the hearth. The food to be baked was placed inside and coals were piled on the rounded back and all around the sides. A small trapdoor was built into the top to allow the baker to peek in to see if the food was done without disturbing the coals and embers.

This must have been a wonderful device. Before the introduction of the Dutch oven, breads were baked directly in the fire, as described by Catherine Beecher in *Miss Beecher's Domestic Receipt Book* in a recipe for Pilgrim Cake:

> Rub two spoonfuls of butter into a quart of flour, and wet it to dough with cold water. Rake open a place in the hottest part of the hearth, roll out the dough into a cake an inch thick, flour it well both sides, and lay it on hot ashes. Cover it with hot ashes, and then with coals. When cooked, wipe off the ashes, and it will be very sweet and good.

A smaller version of the Dutch oven was in use throughout colonial America during the eighteenth century. In *The Seasonal Hearth: The Woman at Home in Early America,* Adelaide Hechtlinger provides us with a letter from a first Pilgrim to a friend in England:

> Mistress White and Mistress Tilley each brought from Leyden, in Holland, what some people call a roasting kitchen, and you can think of nothing more convenient . . . It is nearly a yard long, and it stands so high as to take all the heat from the fire which would otherwise be thrown into the room . . . We often borrow Mistress Tilley hers, and father has promised to send by the first ship that comes to this harbour for one that shall be our very own.

Another improved way to bake from the coals at the base of the hearth was to use a "spider," a cast iron pan with a lid. It had a very long handle and three legs. Some of the coals were separated from the main fire and the spider was placed on top.

Many of these baking pans had concave lids so that coals could be placed on the top of the pan as well. Cornbreads were usually baked in a spider, while wheat and rye breads and pies were baked in the Dutch oven.

An early improvement to the hearth was the "beehive" oven, appearing around 1700. It was built into the side wall of the hearth and a moveable door—first made of wood, then improved with a metal version—was placed in front of the opening. A fire was built in the oven to heat the interior bricks, then the ashes were swept out. Directions for building a good fire and properly heating the oven can be found in *The Pocumtuc Housewife,* dated 1805:

> Some people consider it economical to heat Ovens with faggots, brush and light stuff. Hard wood heats quicker and hotter. Take four foot wood split fine, and pile it criss-cross so as to nearly fill the oven, and keep putting in. A Roaring fire for an hour or more is usually enough. The top and sides will at first be covered with black soot. See that it is all burned off. Rake the coals over the bottom of the Oven and let them lie a minute. Then sweep it out clean. If you can hold your hand inside while you count forty, it is about right for flour bread; to count twenty is right for rye or Indian. If it is too hot, wet an old broom two or three times and turn it around near the top of the oven till it dries.

Other than the preceding directions for cooling off a too-hot oven, there was no way to regulate the oven's temperature. Foods were baked in a constantly changing oven. For this reason, women did all of their baking, usually a week's worth, over a twenty-four-hour period. Planning was critical to take advantage of the oven's changing heat. When the oven was hottest, breads were baked. Pies were baked next, followed by custards and puddings. Just before retiring for the night, a pot of beans or apples were placed in the oven and baked overnight, to extract the very last heat of the oven. As you can imagine, this was extremely hard, hot, and often dangerous work, as the oven faced the hearth and the clothing of the day was a long dress, which could easily catch fire.

In 1750 an improved beehive oven was placed at the front of the hearth, away from the coals and embers. The improved beehive oven required new tools to manage the food going in and coming out. One type of "peel" had a flat paddle and a long handle and was used to place breads in the back of the oven and to remove baked breads. Bread was baked directly on the oven base. To remove pies, a peel with a shorter handle was used. By the nineteenth century interesting devices such as the pie lifter and the pie hook were used to manage pies in the oven.

Recipes rarely contained directions for baking and, when instructions were included, they were usually sparse and varied considerably. Martha Washington's Buttered Loaf has the following instruction: "When it is well baked, cut it up." No directions are given for baking time or temperature. In her White Bread recipe, however, the following details are given:

> . . . rising by the fire. y^r oven will be hoted in about an houre & halfe. y^n shut it up a quarter of an houre, in wch space make up y^r loaves & y^n set them in ye oven. an houre & halfe will bake them.

In *American Cookery 1796* Amelia Simmons' directions are more varied, although many of her cake recipes, such as for Plain Cake, have no baking instructions whatsoever:

> Nine pounds of flour, 3 pounds of sugar, 3 pounds of butter, 1 quart emptins, 1 quart milk, 9 eggs, 1 ounce spice, 1 gill of rose-water, 1 gill of wine.

For a bread pudding she instructs, "bake three quarters of an hour, middling oven." She also uses "slow oven," "quick oven," "light oven," "bake quick," "bake slowly," "bake fast," "bake brisk," and "bake quick in a well heat oven" to describe oven temperature. In *A Colonial Plantation Cookbook: The Receipt Book of Harriott Pinckney Horry, 1770*, the author's instructions read: "the Oven must not be two hott," and in a recipe for Egg Pyes, she warns that "it should be baked in a pretty hot oven" when making biscuit. Gervase Markham instructs us to "bake [manchets, that is, white bread] with a gentle heat" when baking manchets and "then bake [cheat bread] with an indifferent good heat."

The earliest stoves were meant to produce heat for the home and were not intended for cooking. As early as AD 25, the Chinese were producing cast iron stoves, but they did not become popular in Europe until the 1400's. Before then the word *stove* meant a room of the house, without doors, that was heated to warm the entire house.

Stove manufacture was one of the American colonies' earliest industries. By 1647 stoves of German design, known as jamb stoves, were being manufactured in Massachusetts. They were placed in the existing fireplace to increase heating efficiency. A hole was cut out of the back of the hearth so that part of the stove protruded into the room behind the kitchen.

By 1700 the French were experimenting with closed fireplaces and the Dutch had designed a box stove, neither of which became popular. By the mid-1700's the Dutch design, known as the six-plate stove, was being manufactured with small cutouts in the top to accommodate cooking vessels and a small oven below.

Benjamin Franklin made many improvements to the stove and fireplace. In 1744 he designed a way to control air flow to the stove by using sliding doors, and in 1745 he invented a workable enclosed fireplace. His designs were much more efficient than previous ones, and his stoves were small enough to move into the room. In 1771 Franklin invented a stove that used bituminous coal, with a downdraft system that consumed its own smoke.

It was not until the end of the nineteenth century, when the kitchen stove and range were "perfected," that recipes could specify oven temperatures and fairly precise baking times. Count Rumford (who was born in Massachusetts in 1753 but who was in the British State Department during the revolutionary war) designed the first range in 1798. A range is a stove meant exclusively for cooking. Other improvements followed, and by 1835 there were self-feeding stoves and stoves that used anthracite coal. As early as 1823 advertisements for "improved cooking stoves" appeared.

The cooking stove did not receive immediate acclaim. These early designs were not much better at temperature regulation than the hearth and the beehive oven. As well, people preferred the taste of foods cooked in the hearth. The 1841 edition of Catherine Beecher and Harriet Beecher Stowe's *The American Woman's Home* does not mention cooking stoves at all, but they finally included them in the 1869 edition.

Over time, the safety factor, convenience, economy, and controllability of the range would win out over the open fireplace. In the 1840's natural gas was becoming available to homes and stoves were being adapted to its use. An 1896 advertisement by Smith & Anthony Co. claimed that "Hub ranges are perfectly adjusted cookers—great fuel and time savers—thoroughly dependable—and the best cooks and cooking schools use them because they are. Why don't you?" The electric range made its first appearance in 1914 and continues to be improved. We also have the convection oven, in which a fan forces the heated air throughout the oven, reducing hot and cold spots and dramatically reducing cooking times.

BREADS

Bread has always been a staple of the diet. It appears that bread was baked at least 10,000 years ago. The Egyptians were baking leavened bread by 2500 BC and had developed the use of yeast starters. The Greeks, in fact, referred to the Egyptians as *Artophagoi* (bread eaters).

Rich in nutrients, protein, complex carbohydrates, and fiber, bread is an almost perfect food. It is easy to digest for all but the gluten intolerant, is satisfying, and it can be made from a variety of indigenous grains. Wheat flour, however, is superior to all others for making a fine loaf.

Grain is composed of three parts. The process of milling separates the endosperm, the part that makes white flour, from the germ and the bran. The Romans invented the milling process and were, therefore, the first to produce a white bread.

The endosperm makes up between 75 and 80 percent of the weight of the grain, and the quality of the flour may be described by its "extraction rate." A flour at 80 percent extraction is nearly pure white flour; at 100 percent, it is a whole wheat flour.

After the endosperm is separated from the other parts, it is finely ground and sieved to produce particles of varying size. The finest particles produce the best white bread. By the thirteenth century, England was producing fine wheat flours by the process of "bolting," that is, passing the ground flour through a series of fine-meshed pieces of cloth. The word *bolt,* derived from the Middle English *bulten,* means "to sift."

The type of bread a person ate in England throughout the Middle Ages and until the beginning of the eighteenth century was a function of social station. The finely milled white flours were made into the manchet, the white bread of the wealthy. According to the fourteenth-century manuscript *Curye on Inglysch,* the best-quality flour was referred to as *mayne,* and manchet may be a combination of *mayne* and *cheat* (loaf). In Gervase Markham's recipe for baking manchets, he instructs:

> . . . first your meal, being ground upon black stones if it be possible, which makes the whitest flour, and bolted through the finest bolting cloth . . .

In the next recipe, for baking cheat bread, he directs the baker:

> To bake the best cheat bread, which is also simply of wheat only, you shall, after your meal is dressed and bolted through a more coarse bolter than was used for your manchets . . .

His description of the design of a proper bake house states that "in your bake-house you shall have a fair bolting house with large pipes to bolt meal in."

Martha Washington does not use the word *manchet* in her *Booke of Cookery,* but there is one recipe for White Bread that states "Take 3 quarters of a peck of fine flower," and another for French Bread, which does not specify the quality of the flour—"Take a gallon of flowre." Her French bread recipe resembles the manchet more than the white bread in its use of ale yeast for leavening; the white bread recipe calls for good yeast (starter). Starter was never used in a proper manchet. The French bread recipe does differ from Markham's manchet in the use of "new milke heated"; Markham's recipe calls for water as the only liquid. In *The Virginia Housewife* by Mary Randolph there is a recipe simply titled "To Make Bread." It appears to be quite similar to the manchet in that no milk is called for and a quality to the flour is specified:

> When you find the barrel of flour a good one, empty it into a chest or box made for the purpose, with a lid that will shut close; it keeps much better in this manner than when packed in a barrel, and even improves by lying lightly; sift the quantity you intend to make up, put into a bowl three quarters of a pint of cold water to each quart of flour, with a large spoonful of yeast, and a little salt, to every quart; stir into it just as much of the flour as will make a thin batter, put half the remaining flour in the bottom of a tin kettle, pout the batter on it, and cover it with the other half; stop it close, and set it where it can have a moderate degree of warmth. When it has risen well, turn it into a bowl, work in the dry flour and knead it some minutes, return it to the kettle, stop it, and give it moderate heat. In the morning work it a little, make it into rolls, and bake it.

It is interesting to note that the specified form of the bread is not a loaf, but individual rolls. According to Karen Hess in Mary Randolph's *The Virginia Housewife* (1985: p. 260), "The upper-class origins of so many Virginia colonists may account for this historic preference for individual loaves; great loaves were associated with peasants and the poor."

All of the bread recipes mentioned so far require wheat flour, a scarce commodity in seventeenth-century New England. While some wheat was grown in Plymouth, it wasn't until the Ohio River Valley and western New York state were settled in the late 1700's that enough wheat was grown to make it economical to use in home baking. The introduction of cornmeal to our first settlers by the Native Americans sparked a variety of uniquely American baked goods, however. Corn that had been ground into meal was known as Indian meal, and sometimes it was just referred to as "Indian." Not having the gluten proteins found in wheat, cornmeal cannot support the fine network structure provided by the action of yeast that wheat flour doughs can, and the simplest recipes that use cornmeal have no leavening. They may be considered to be batter breads, mixed, usually with a spoon, to a consistency much thinner than a wheat bread dough.

The first of these batter breads were simply cornmeal, water, and salt spread onto a board and placed vertically in front of the hearth fire or fashioned into small cakes and baked on the floor of the fireplace. The Ash Cake is an example of a cornmeal bread baked on the fireplace floor. This recipe is from *North Carolina and Old Salem Cookery* as printed in *Fireside Cooks & Black Kettle Recipes* by Doris E. Farrington:

> Mix 2 cups cornmeal and 1 teaspoon salt. Add enough hot water to make a dough. Let stand an hour or more. With the hands, shape into cakes about an inch thick. Lay on hot hearth stones near the fire until the outside crusts up a little. Then cover with hot ashes and bake at least a half hour or until well browned. Brush off ashes with a cloth. Split with slabs of butter and eat hot.

This recipe is quite similar to Catherine Beecher's Pilgrim Cake, p. 16, except that cornmeal is substituted for wheat flour.

The Hoe Cake was a cornmeal batter spread onto the back of a garden hoe and placed in front of the fire. This recipe appears in Amelia Simmons' *American Cookery 1796*:

> Scald 1 pint of milk and put to 3 pints of indian meal, and half a pint of flour—bake before the fire. Or scald with milk two thirds of the indian meal, or wet two thirds with boiling water, add salt, molasses and shortening, work up with cold water pretty stiff, and bake as above.

To lighten the cornmeal batter, eggs were added. Amelia Simmons' recipe for Indian Slapjack shows us that the batter could be cooked in a variety of ways:

> One quart of milk, 1 pint of indian meal, 4 eggs, 4 spoons of flour, little salt, beat together, baked on griddles, or fry in a dry pan, or baked in a pan which was rub'd with suet, lard or butter.

In *The Virginia Housewife* Mary Randolph provides us with a recipe for Batter Bread:

> Take six spoonfuls of flour and three of corn meal, with a little salt; sift them and make a thin batter with flour, eggs, and a sufficient quantity of rich milk; bake in little tin moulds in a quick oven.

One of the most common corn breads of colonial New England was the journey cake, or jonny (johnny, johny) cake. Much speculation surrounds its name. It was well known that corn breads did not become stale as easily as wheat breads, so they were the food of choice when traveling, hence the name "journey" cake. A popular belief is that "jonny" represents the New England pronunciation of *journey.* Other people, including Karen Hess, suppose that it might be an Indian or English name for a baked or fried cake that sounded like the word *journey.* Either way, the bread's popularity helped spread the recipe to the southern states, where it became known as "pone." Amelia Simmons refers to her recipe for Hoe Cake as Johny Cake or Hoe Cake. In Farrington's *Fireside Cooks & Black Kettle Recipes,* a recipe for Journey Cake is given and dated as a "17th century recipe," although no specific manuscript is cited:

> Sift one quart of Indian meal into a pan; make a hole in the middle and pour in a pint of warm water, adding one teaspoonful of salt; with a spoon mix the meal and water gradually into a soft dough; stir it very briskly for a quarter of an hour or more, till it becomes light and spongy; then spread the dough smooth and evenly on a straight flat board (a piece of the head of a flour barrel will serve for this purpose); place the board nearly upright before an open fire, and put an iron against the back to support it; bake it well; when done, cut it in squares; send it hot to table, split and buttered.

One of the few early corn bread recipes to include yeast is from Randolph's *The Virginia Housewife* and is titled Corn Meal Bread:

> Rub a piece of butter the size of an egg into a pint of corn meal, make a batter with two eggs and some new milk, add a spoonful of yeast, set it by the fire an hour to rise, butter little pans and bake it.

In another recipe from that cookbook, Miss Randolph offers this advice for batter cakes: "When eggs cannot be procured, yeast makes a good substitute."

Occasionally (such as in the recipe for Batter Bread) cornmeal was mixed with other grains, including wheat, rye, or oats. Benjamin Franklin provides instructions for dealing with mixed-grain bread in "To Make Bread with Maize Flour Mixed with Wheat Flour":

> Maize Flour takes longer to bake well than Wheat Flour; so that if mixed together cold, then fermented and cooked, the Wheat part will be well baked whilst the Maize Part will remain uncooked. To remedy this inconvenience, We boil one Pot of Water with a little

Salt added and whilst the Water boils with one Hand we throw into it a little Maize Flour and with the other Hand stir it into the boiling Water that must be kept on the Fire, and this Operation shall be repeated with a little Flour each time, until the Mush is so thick it can hardly be stirred with the Stick. Then, after leaving it a little longer on the Fire, until the last Handful has done boiling, it is taken off, then the Mush is poured into the Kneading Trough where it must be thoroughly mixed and kneaded with a Quantity of Wheat Flour sufficient to make a Dough thick enough to make Bread, and some Yeast, or Leaven, to make it rise; and after the necessary Time it is shaped into Loaves, and then put in the Oven.

Another popular colonial bread that utilized mixed grains was called thirded bread, or rye, Injun' & wheat flour bread, a bread comprising mostly wheat flour, with a small amount of rye and cornmeal added. A most unusual, but very common, bread in seventeenth-century New England was a bread known as Ryaninjun, "made of equal parts of rye flour and corn meal mixed with milk, sweetened with stewed pumpkin, and raised with homemade yeast," according to Hilde Gabriel Lee in *Taste of the States* (p. 10).

The history of baking would not be complete without mention of the adventuresome pioneer settlers of Oregon and California in the mid-1800's. In an observer's account of Mormon travelers to Salt Lake using the Platte River route, it is written that "they learned to make butter on a march by the dashing of the wagon, and so nicely to calculate the working of the barm in the jolting heats that, as soon as the halt, as an oven could be dug in the hillside and heated, their well-kneaded loaf was ready for baking, and produced good leavened bread for supper" (*Nebraska Pioneer Cookbook*, p. 4). Permanent settlers established the Nebraska Territory in 1854 along the Platte River route. By the 1860's homestead laws were in effect and the sod house period, as it was known, began. These settlers built their homes right out of the soil that they farmed, hence the name.

According to Kay Graber in the *Nebraska Pioneer Cookbook* (p. 27), "One of the first items that a homesteader installed in his soddy was a stove. A common early type used both for cooking and heating was designed to burn hay—hence the name, the hay burner—although corn cobs and buffalo and cow chips were also frequently used as fuel."

Yeast was not always available to the pioneers and settlers, and it was common practice to use baking sodas. One of the most original

American breads to be developed was salt-rising bread, made when the baker ran out of yeast:

> Take about half a gallon of warm water; add to it salt, soda and sugar, of each a lump about as large as an ordinary pea. A spoonful of corn improves it if convenient, though not necessary; stir in flour to the consistency of thick batter. A vessel holding about a gallon is most convenient and it should be placed in a larger vessel and surrounded with warm water, and kept warm for four or five hours, when it will have become light, perhaps filling the vessel. If while it was kept in a warm place there should any water rise on it pour it off. Now that it is light get your flour into the kneading pan. Take about a pint of scalding water and scald part of the flour; then add enough cold water to cool the scalded flour; now add your rising and knead until smooth, but do not make it so stiff as for hop yeast bread. When the dough has become smooth mold and put in your baking pans, and keep in a warm place to rise. When ready to bake it will require a hotter fire than yeast bread. When baked wrap in a wet cloth and set away to cool.

Not everyone was a fan of salt-rising bread, and the most outspoken opponent of it was Catherine Beecher, the famous women's rights activist and cookbook author of the mid-nineteenth century. In *The American Woman's Home* (1869) she writes:

> There is, however, one species of yeast, much used in some parts of the country, against which protest should be made. It is called salt-risings, or milk-risings. . . . It has, however, when kept, some characteristics which remind us of the terms in which our old English Bible describes the effect of keeping the manna of the ancient Israelites, which we are informed, in words more explicit than agreeable, "stank, and bread worms." If salt-rising bread does not fulfill the whole of this unpleasant description, it certainly does emphatically a part of it. The smell which it has in baking, and when more than a day old, suggests the inquiry, whether it is the saccharine or the putrid fermentation which it is raised.

I imagine that we will not find salt-rising bread recipes in any of Miss Beecher's cookbooks!

The pioneers used corn meal, rye and graham flours quite often for producing breads and many of these recipes did not require yeast, a difficult commodity to maintain while in the process of traveling or settling. The following recipes (all from *Nebraska Pioneer*

Cookbook) show the sharing of very old New England recipes well into nineteenth-century Nebraska. The first is for Rye and Indian Loaves:

> (First rate—the real Yankee loaf.) Scald two quarts of Indian meal, and when cold add one quart unbolted rye flour, three quarters of a pint molasses, one tablespoon salt, and water enough to make a stiff sponge or batter. Pour into deep iron pots or kettles and bake in a slow oven for three or four hours. If in a brick oven, leave it over night. A standard bread in New England, eaten both hot and cold.

The next recipe is for Pumpkin Indian Loaf:

> Scald one quart of Indian meal and stir in one pint stewed pumpkin, mashed fine, or sifted; add one teaspoonful salt, one quarter pint molasses, mixing to a stiff batter. Bake in deep iron dishes as rye and Indian loaves, above.

Finally, an interesting recipe (with some interesting advice) for Yeast Corn Bread:

> Three pints of meal, and one of rye or Graham flour, two tablespoonfuls of sugar and one teaspoon of salt. One yeast cake softened in warm water. This should be mixed with warm water to a dough just compact enough not to run, and then be put in a deep pan, and left by the fire until it rises about one forth higher than when mixed. Bake in a moderate oven five hours. This makes a thick crust upon the top which is to be lifted off, and the remainder to be eaten warm. Slice and heat in a steamer for breakfast. The crusts are to be softened in warm water, and crumbled fine for the wetting of the next loaf, and the cook will be surprised to find the second experiment far superior to the first.

Graham flour, named after Sylvester Graham, an advocate of healthful living, vegetarianism, and temperance in the early 1800s, is whole wheat flour that has been ground extremely fine to the consistency of white flour.

PIES AND PASTES

ENGLAND IS THE historical home of the pie. Manuscripts dating to the eleventh century contain recipes for savory pies, usually meats baked in a crust. By the sixteenth century pies that contained fruits exclusively were being developed.

Many of the early recipes for pie doughs were not intended to be eaten, as they baked to an impenetrable encasement. The filling was eaten from this "container." Sometimes the filling itself was not meant to be eaten. "Spectacle" food, meant to surprise and entertain the guests, was an important part of the Medieval feast. A famous nursery rhyme notes "four and twenty blackbirds baked in a pie." The birds were not actually baked into the pie; an empty pie crust was baked and just before presentation, the live birds were placed inside. At tableside the crust was carefully cut into and the birds escaped, fluttering in all directions, much to the amusement of the guests.

Frogs and turtles were commonly used as well. The idea of the inedible crust was considered aristocratic and wasteful by early American colonists, and they soon dropped the practice.

The English Housewife was one of the colonists' favorite cookbooks, and Gervase Markham provides the cook with the following advice: "Next to these already rehearsed, our English housewife must be skilled in pastry . . . and how to handle and coumpound such pastes." In his book he follows with a series of recipes, one of which is for rye paste:

> To speak then of the mixture and kneading of pastes, you shall understand that your rye paste would be kneaded only with hot water and a little butter, or sweet seam [probably something like crème fraiche, clotted cream, or double cream] and rye flour very finely sifted, and it would be made tough and stiff that it may stand well in the raising, for the coffin thereof must be very deep.

"Raising" here does not refer to the rising action of a yeast dough, but is intended to mean that the dough will be baked "blind," that is, unfilled, and needs to stand high without falling so that it may be filled after baking. The term "coffin" is derived from the Greek *cophinos*, which means basket. Markham continues:

> your coarse wheat crust would be kneaded with hot water, or mutton broth and good store of butter, and the paste made stiff and tough because that coffin must be deep also; your fine wheat crust must be kneaded with as much butter as water, and the paste made reasonable lithe and gentle, into which you must put three or four eggs or more according to the quantity you blend together, for they will give it a sufficient stiffening.

Puff paste, an extremely delicate and fine paste for sweets, comprises many thin layers of buttery pastry. According to Karen Hess' notes in Martha Washington's *Booke of Cookery,* the use of puff paste can be traced to fifteenth-century Tuscany and was probably brought to France through the Medici marriage; it appears to have gotten the name "puffe-paste" around the turn of the seventeenth century. Markham provides us with an early recipe:

> Now for the making of puff paste of the best kind, you shall take the finest wheat flour after it hath been a little baked in a pot in the oven, and blend it well with eggs, whites and yolks all together, after the paste is well kneaded, roll out a part thereof as thin as

you please, and then spread cold sweet butter over the same, then upon the same butter roll another leaf of paste as before; and spread it with butter also; and thus roll leaf upon leaf with butter between till it be as thick as you think good . . . There be some that to this paste use sugar, but it is certain it will hinder the rising thereof; and therefore when your puffed paste is baked, you shall dissolve sugar into rose-water, and drop it into the paste as much as it will by any means receive, and then set it a little while in the oven after and it will be sweet enough.

Martha Washington's recipe for puff paste differs from Markham's in many ways and starts to approximate the modern method of making puff paste, incorporating as it does some butter into the dough as it is being rolled initially. Only egg whites are used:

Take a quartern of ye purest flowre & 3 pound of butter; work ye butter in little rouls & lay them in cold spring water all night. y^n mix ye flowre up with egg whites & a little cold water; make it as stiff as you can. work it well & roule out in a square, pritty thin sheete; take a trencher & clame it & spread it pritty thin on ye paste, strowe a little flowre on it, y^n clap it together and roule it out again. y^n spread on some more butter as before, & soe continue till all ye butter be work'd up, & strow flowre every time you roule out y^r paste. If you have egg whites enough to wet y^r flower, you need not use any water at all.

In America's first cookbook, Amelia Simmons provides us with no fewer than six recipes for puff paste (for tarts). As with most of the recipes from *American Cookery 1796,* the instructions are quite brief and some would consider them inadequate unless previously demonstrated to the cook. The first is probably the most detailed:

No. 1 Rub one pound of butter into one pound of flour, whip 2 whites and add with cold water, and one yolk; make into paste, roll in, in six or seven times, one pound of butter, flouring it each roll. This is good for any small thing.

A shorter recipe with fewer directions is No. 3:

To any quantity of flour, rub in three fourth of its weight of butter, (twelve eggs to the peck) rub in one third or half, and roll in the rest.

Finally, Hannah Glasse gives a recipe that is very close to a modern recipe:

Take a quarter of a peck of flour, rub fine half a pound of butter, a little salt, make it up into a light paste with cold water, just stiff enough to work it well up; then roll it out, and stick pieces of butter all over, and strew a little flour, roll it up, and roll it out again; and do so nine or ten times, till you have rolled in a pound and a half of butter. This crust is mostly used for all sorts of pies.

It is surprising to learn that as early as the 1730's cooking schools were established to teach pastry techniques to housewives in New York. According to Louise Conway Beldon in *The Festive Tradition: Table Decoration and Desserts in America, 1650–1900,* Martha Gazley advertised her classes in pastry making in the *New York Gazette* in 1731. An advertisement in the *South Carolina Gazette* in 1741 told of pastry classes at reasonable rates, taught by Peter Perkin. In these courses several types of pastes were demonstrated, such as the raised paste, puff paste, and pastes for tarts and pies.

Pies were a favorite of colonists all along the eastern coast. There were berry pies, especially blueberry in Maine, mincemeat pies all across New England, and apple pies made from fresh, dried, and sauced apples found throughout the colonies. Peach pies were a favorite of the Pennsylvania Quakers, who used fruit from trees brought to the area from Florida and presumably introduced in Florida by the Spaniards in the 1500's. The Pennsylvania Dutch from Germany, including the Amish and the Mennonites, were great innovators as well as lovers of pies. Shoo fly pie, schnitz pie, and funeral (raisin) pie came from the large, outdoor communal ovens that were almost seven feet wide inside, as they were in Germany. Custard pies from the South made their way all along the eastern seaboard.

One of the earliest pies made in America was the mincemeat, or minced, pie. This pie was much loved in England and made its way to the colonies with our first settlers. A bit of controversy seems to surround the mincemeat pie, as told by Hilde Gabriel Lee in *Tastes of the States* (p. 11):

> Shortly after the Puritans settled Boston, they banned Christmas mincemeat pie. The pie was baked in a dish that had come to symbolize the Christ Child's manger, and the spices used in the pie had come to represent the gifts of the Wise Men. The Puritans considered these symbols sacrilegious and passed laws not only outlawing the pie but also all Christmas celebrations.

With such an exciting history behind the pie, we must examine several of the recipes used in the Colonies. Since Martha Washington's cookbook contains recipes mostly from England, her recipe for Mincd Pies from her *Booke of Cookery* is an excellent starting point:

> Take to 4 pounds of ye flesh of a legg of veale, or neats tongues, 4 pounds of beef suet, 2 pounds of raysons stoned and shread, 3 pounds of currans, halfe a pound or more of sugar, 3 quarters of an ounce of nutmegg, & cinnamon, beaten, halfe a dosin apples shread, some rosewater, a quarter of a pinte of muskadine or sack, some candied orringe, leamon & citron pill minced, shread y^r meat & suet very fine & mingle all together, for plaine mincd pies, leave out ye fruit & put in blanched almonds minced small.

There is no instruction for baking and no indication of what type of paste to use. Amelia Simmons' recipe for Minced Pie of Beef has both baking directions and a specified paste:

> Four pounds of boiled beef, chopped fine, and salted; six pound of raw apple chopped also, one pound beef suet, one quart of Wine or rich sweet cyder, one ounce mace, and cinnamon, a nutmeg, two pounds raisins, bake in paste No 3, three fourths of an hour.

The apple pie has come to symbolize America and there are several interesting versions that have all of the modern attributes we have come to expect. In the introduction I give an early English recipe for pippin pie, and here is a recipe by Hannah Glasse from *The Art of Cookery Made Plain and Easy* for Apple Pie:

> Make a good puff-paste crust, lay some round the sides of the dish, pare and quarter your apples and take out the cores, lay a row of apples thick, throw in half the sugar you design for your pie, mince a little lemon peel fine, throw over, and squeeze a little lemon over them, then a few cloves, here and there one, then the rest of your apples and the rest of your sugar; you must sweeten to your palate, and squeeze a little more lemon; boil the peelings of the apples and the cores in some fair water with a blade of mace, till it is very good; strain it and boil the syrup with a little sugar till there is but very little and good, pour it into your pie, put on your upper crust and bake it. You may put in a little quince or marmalade (if you please).

In Amelia Simmons' cookbook two versions are given, one that starts with apples that have been cooked and the other a more traditional version. First is the recipe for Apple Pie:

> Stew and strain the apples, to every three pints, grate the peal of fresh lemon, add cinnamon, mace, rose-water and sugar to your taste—and bake in paste No. 3.

A Buttered Apple Pie is the more expected recipe in that the apples are not cooked first. Interestingly, the pie is baked for a while before any spices are added:

> Pare, quarter and core tart apples, lay in paste No. 3, cover with the same; bake half an hour, when drawn, gently raise the top crust, add sugar, butter, cinnamon, mace, wine or rose-water q:s [i.e., to fill to a certain mark]:

Included in her first recipe are ideas for other fruit pies, another American tradition:

> Every species of fruit such as peas, plums raspberries, black berries may be only sweetened, without spice—and bake in paste No. 3.

Early-nineteenth-century Shakers were so fond of pies that special ovens were used for their baking exclusively. These special-purpose communal ovens were quite large. One ingenious oven contained rotating racks that could hold sixty pies, each one easily removed as the racks were rotated to the front of the oven. According to Walter Muir Whitehill in *The Best of Shaker Cooking,* this oven was in use in the Canterbury Shaker kitchen. He gives a recipe for Shaker Apple Pie (p. 253):

> Slice apples [3 cups peeled sliced sour apples] into mixing bowl and add [⅔ cup] maple or white sugar, [1 tablespoon] cream and [1 tablespoon] rose water, and mix thoroughly so that the rose water will be distributed evenly. Line the pie dish with favorite pastry. Fill with apple mixture and cover with top crust in which a few small vents have been slashed for steam to escape. Flute the edges well to keep juice from escaping. Bake in a moderate 350° F oven for 50 minutes.

By the 1830's ovens were beginning to be equipped with thermometers and cooking temperatures could be specified for the first time. This recipe also includes instructions for steam vents and for fluting the edge of the top crust.

The Shakers were also lovers of berry pies, and the baker is told that "few things are more acceptable than the blackberry pie. It takes 2 quarts of berries to make a good pie." In the *Nebraska Pioneer Cookbook* a recipe for Dried Apple Pie is given. It was common for the Pennsylvania Dutch to use dried fruit in pies (such as Schnitz Pie), and this recipe illustrates the migration of recipes carried by the pioneers of the mid–nineteenth century:

Wash the fruit thoroughly, soak over night in water enough to cover. In the morning, stew slowly, until nearly done, in the same water. Sweeten to taste. The crust, both upper and under, should be rolled thin; a thick crust to a fruit pie is undesireable.

Apparently not every pioneer was a fan of this pie, as this ditty from the cookbook attests:

> Spit in my ears
> and tell me lies
> but give me no
> dried apple pies.

While not mentioned in earlier recipes, it was common practice by the 1750's to decorate and seal the edge of pies by using a pie wheel, and examples of wrought iron devices can be found in museums. Pies were also decorated with leaves and other shapes cut from pie dough as well as rolled strings of dough to make bows and other fancy designs.

A truly American pie is the pumpkin pie. Introduced by the Native Americans to the Pilgrims, the pumpkin became a staple of the settlers' diet, and incorporating this indigenous squash into a pie must have seemed natural. One of the earliest published recipes that uses pumpkin in a dessert is a recipe for Pumpion Pye from *The Gentlewoman's Companion* by Hannah Woolley (1673):

> Take a pound of Pumpion and slice it; a handful of Thyme, a little Rosemary, sweet Marjoram snipped off the stalks, chop them small; then take Cinnamon, Nutmeg, Pepper and a few Cloves, all beaten; also ten Eggs, and beat them all together, with as much Sugar as you shall think Sufficient. Then fry them like a pancake, and being fried, let them stand till they are cold. Then fill your Pye after this manner: Take Apples, sliced thin round ways, and lay a layer of the pancake, and another of the Apples, with currants between the layers. Be sure you put in a good amount of sweet Butter before you close it. When the Pye is baked, take six yolks of Eggs, some White-wine or verjuice [pressed, unfermented grape juice], and make a caudle thereof, but not too thick; cut up the lid and put it in, and stir them well together, and so serve it up.

The English had a tradition of cooking puddings and custards, and the pumpkin was easily adapted to the English recipes brought with them to America. Puddings were even served at the first Thanksgiving meal. A recipe for pumpkin pudding in Mary Randolph's *The Virginia Housewife* certainly sounds like a modern recipe for a pumpkin pie:

> Stew a fine sweet pumpkin till soft and dry, rub it through a sieve, mix with the pulp six eggs quite light, a quarter of a pound of butter, half a pint of new milk, some pounded ginger and nutmeg, a wine glass of brandy, and sugar to your taste. Should it be too liquid, stew it a little drier, put a paste round the edges, and in the bottom of a shallow dish or plate—pour in the mixture, cut some bits of paste, twist them, and lay them across the top, and bake it nicely.

In *American Cookery 1796* Amelia Simmons places her recipes for pumpkin pie under puddings as well. The recipes are titled Pompkin Pie.

> No. 1. One quart stewed and strained [pumpkin], 3 pints cream, 9 beaten eggs, sugar, mace, nutmeg and ginger, laid into paste No. 7 or 3, and with a dough spur, cross and chequer it, and baked in dishes three quarters of an hour.

> No. 2. One quart of milk, 1 pint pumpkin, 4 eggs, molasses, allspice and ginger in a crust, bake 1 hour.

A recipe for Pumpkin Pie is found in Margaret Hooker's *Early American Cookery* "Compiled from Old and Reliable Sources":

> Take out the seeds and pare the Pumpkin; Stew and Strain it through a Colander. Take two Quarts of scalded Milk and eight Eggs and stir your Pumpkin into it; sweeten it with Sugar or Molasses to your Taste. Salt this Batter and season with Ginger, Cinnamon, or grated Lemon Peel to your Mind. Bake with a bottom Crust.

CAKES AND COOKIES

Cakes   A SLICE OF CHOCOLATE
cake with a glass of milk seems as American as "apple pie" and might
very well be. The term "cake" had several meanings in the cookbooks
popular with our Founding Fathers and Mothers. As used by the Pilgrims, "cake" usually applied to unsweetened breads, such as Hoe
Cake or Plank Cake, and referred to the shape of the final product.

None of the recipes I've examined is quite like the ones
we are now familiar with, and chocolate did not make its way into
baked goods until the latter half of the nineteenth century. Some of
the earliest recipes for dessert-type cakes were actually sweet, yeast-

type breads, often with candied or dried fruits added. Little cakes were cookies or something similar, usually "crunchy and" with no leavening and few eggs. Some cakes resembled our modern butter cake or pound cake.

The term "cake" was also used by Martha Washington in *A Booke of Sweetmeats* to describe a variety of fruit pastes that were shaped into patties and allowed to dry in the sun. Examples include Cakes of Orringes, Apricot Cakes, Clear Cakes, Violet Cakes, Cakes of Roses, and Hunny Combe Cakes.

Making cakes in colonial times was no easy matter. Sugar came in lumps or cones and needed to be pounded fine and meticulously sieved to obtain a finely granulated product. Spices, which were common flavorings, also needed much work to become the finely powdered ingredients needed for an acceptable final result. Almonds had to be blanched, skinned, dried, and pounded; other nuts required much work as well. Mixing, beating, and creaming were laborious tasks done by hand that could last for an hour or more.

When all of the preparation was done, the baking of the cake was the next challenge. Irregularly heated ovens with no temperature control were always a problem, resulting in variable baking times. Many of the early recipes (sometimes calling for up to seventy eggs!) produced amazingly large cakes by modern standards and were certainly cumbersome to move in and out of the oven. It wasn't until the nineteenth century that cakes were baked in layers to speed up baking times and ease the effort required for handling. Elizabeth Raffald gives advice on the making of cakes in *The Experienced English Housekeeper:* "be sure that you get the things ready before you begin"; "beat your eggs well, and don't leave them till you have finished the cakes . . . If your cakes are to have butter in, take care you beat it to a fine cream before you put in your sugar." As to the baking of cakes, Mrs. Raffald advises when baking plum, seed, or rice cakes, "Bake them in wood garths [wooden rings or pans made of wood], for if you bake them in either pot or tin, they burn the outside of the cakes, and confine them so that the heat cannot penetrate into the middle of your cake, and prevents it from rising." Finally, on oven management she advises, "bake all kinds of cake in a good oven, according to the size of your cake, and follow the instructions of your receipt, for though care hath been taken to weigh and measure every article belonging to every kind of cake, yet the management and the oven must be left to the maker's care."

Martha Washington provides us with a recipe for A Great Cake, demonstrating the use of yeast as the leavening and producing a cake that is more like a sweet, rich bread:

> Take a peck of flowre & put to it 10 eggs beaten; take out 3 of yᵉ whites, put in nutmegg, cinamond, cloves, & mace of each a quarter of an ounce; a full quart of Ale barme, & mingle with yᵉ flowre two pound of fresh butter. when it is allmoste kneaded, put 6 spoonfuls of hot water to it, & 10 pound of currans, & halfe a pownd of sugar beaten, let it ly a while by yᵉ fire to rise & then bake it.

There are two additional recipes for Great Cake in *A Booke of Sweet-meats*. They vary slightly in proportion and quantity of basic ingredients, but the second recipe includes a quart of cream and 12 spoonfuls of rosewater. Karen Hess notes that this version is similar to very old recipes for wedding cake. The only other recipe provided by Martha Washington for a large cake is An Excellent Cake:

> Take a peck of flowre, 10 eggs beaten, 2 nutmegg, A quatern of cloves and mace, 2 pound & halfe of fresh butter, one pound of sugar, 6 pound of currans, wash, dry, and pick them very well. then take halfe a pownd of candyed orring, leamon, & citron pill, & mince it small. & make a possit with good cream, halfe a pinte of sack, & as much Ale. & put halfe of yʳ butter into yᵉ possit & yᵉ other halfe with some good ale barme. put it in to yᵉ flowre & break it in, into small bits, & strow in some rose water, juice of leamond, & sack as you mingle and knead up.

In *The Art of Cookery Made Plain and Easy*, Hannah Glasse offers a recipe for A Fine Seed or Saffron Cake:

> You must take a quarter of a peck of fine flour, a pound and a half of butter, three ounces of carraway-seeds, six eggs beat well, a quarter of an ounce of cloves and mace beat together very fine, a penny-worth of cinnamon beat, a pound of sugar, a pennyworth of rose water, a pennyworth of saffron, a pint and a half of yeast, and a quart of milk; mix it all together lightly with your hands thus: first boil your milk and butter, then skim off the butter and mix with your flour, and a little of the milk, stir the yeast into the rest and strain it, mix it with the flour, put in your seed and spices, rose-water, tincture of saffron, sugar, and eggs; beat it all up well with your hands lightly, and bake it in a hoop or pan, but be sure to butter the pan well; it will take an hour and a half in a quick oven.

You may leave out the seed if you choose it, and I think it rather better without it; but that you may do as you like.

In her recipes for cakes, Mrs. Glasse usually refers to a hoop to bake the cake in, as it provided a shaping form for the cake. No mention of a cake pan or hoop is found in Martha Washington's recipes, and it is believed that her cakes were hand formed and placed directly on the hearth to be baked as a bread.

Hannah Glasse provides a recipe for icing a Great Cake, although she does not provide a recipe for the cake itself. The recipe is quite interesting:

Take the whites of twenty-four eggs, and a pound of double refined sugar beat and sifted fine; mix both together in a deep earthen pan, and with a whisk, whisk it well for two or three hours, till it looks white and thick; then with a thin broad board, or a bunch of feathers, spread it all over the top and sides of the cake; set it at a proper distance before a good clear fire, and keep turning it continually for fear of its changing colour; but a cool oven is best, and an hour will harden it: you may perfume the icing with what perfume you please.

Most of Amelia Simmons' recipes for cakes are yeast-risen types, such as Plain Cake:

Nine pounds of flour, 3 pounds of sugar, 3 pounds of butter, 1 quart emptins, 1 quart milk, 9 eggs, 1 ounce of spice, 1 gill of rose-water, 1 gill of wine.

Also found in *American Cookery 1796* is a recipe for Rich Cake:

Rub 2 pound of butter into 5 pound of flour, add 15 eggs (not much beaten) 1 pint of emptins, 1 pint of wine, knead up stiff like biscuit, cover well and put by and let rise over night. To 2 and a half pound raisins, add 1 gill brandy, to soak over night, or if new half an hour in the morning, add them with 1 gill rose-water and 2 and a half pound of loaf sugar, 1 ounce cinnamon, work well and bake as loaf cake, No. 1.

In *The Virginia Housewife* Mary Randolph provides us with a recipe for Risen Cake:

Take three pounds of flour, one and a half [pounds of] pounded sugar, a tea-spoonful of cloves, one of [mace] and one of ginger, all finely powdered-pas[sed] whole through a sieve, put to it four spoonsful o[f good] yeast; and twelve eggs—mix it up well and [illegible text] sufficiently soft, add a little milk; make it up at [illegible text] and set it to rise—when well risen, knead in[to it] pound of butter, and two gills of brandy; have [illegible text] two pounds of raisins stoned, mix all well tog[ether] pour it into a mould of proper size, and bake it [illegible text] oven heated as for bread; let it stand till thoro[ughly] done, and do not take it from the mould until [ ] cold.

Election Day Cake was served at evening celebrations of our new nation's most patriotic day. Its title reflects the patriotism displayed by the bakers living in an independent America. This cake was sold outside the polling places and was often made in rather large dimensions. Amelia Simmons included a recipe in the second edition of *American Cookery 1796* that called for 120 cups of flour and 14 pounds of sugar. The Van Rensselaer manuscripts offer a smaller version called Election Cake:

> 4 Quarts flour, 1 ¾ lb Butter, 2 lb Sugar, 2 eggs, 3 pints milk, 1 do Wine, 1 gill Rose water, 3 gills yeast (emptins), 1 oz cinnamon.

Recipes for pound cake abound in the early colonial cookbooks. The technique used for making these cakes is the standard method of cake making today and involves the creaming of butter with sugar and the incorporation of eggs into the mixture. Martha Washington's recipe entitled "To Make Excellent Curran Cakes," from *A Booke of Sweetmeats,* is an early pound cake version, although she does not call it that. The butter is creamed, eggs are incorporated, and no yeast is used:

> Take 2 pound of butter & wash it in rose water, casting ye water out. then take 2 pound of flowre & 2 pound of sugar. mix ye flowre & sugar together, deviding it into 2 parts, & putting in some into a dredging box. & shake it into a trey till halfe be shaked in, beating ye butter all ye while with y^r hand. y^n take 6 eggs to a pound of sugar & flowre (takeing out 2 of ye whites), 6 spoonefulls of rose water, some mace beaten, y^n put in ye other halfe of ye sugar & flowre, and 2 pound of currans, picked and rubbed very clean. y^n butter y^r panns & fill them halfe full, & set them in a moderate oven.

In principle a pound cake should have a pound of each basic ingredient. It would certainly be an easy recipe to remember and Amelia Simmons provides us with a classic version in *American Cookery 1796:*

> One pound sugar, one pound butter, one pound flour, one pound
> or ten eggs, rose-water one gill, spices to your taste, watch it well,
> it will bake in a slow oven in 15 minutes.

Another version of pound cake requires the separation of eggs, with
the beaten whites folded in separately, another modern cake-making
technique. In *Selected Receipts of a Van Rensselaer Family 1785–1835* we
find a recipe for Pound Cake that illustrates this technique:

> Beat 1 lb Butter to a cream & mix it with the yolks and whites of
> 8 eggs beaten apart, have warm by the fire 1 lb of flour, the same
> of sifted sugar mix them a few cloves a little nutmeg & cinnamon
> in fine powder together then by degrees work the dry ingredients
> with the butter & eggs, when well beaten add a glass of wine. It
> requires one hours beating, butter the pans & bake it 1 hour in a
> quick oven.

American Cookery 1796 offers a similar recipe called Another (called)
Pound Cake:

> Work three quarters of a pound butter, one pound of good sugar,
> till very white, whip ten whites to a foam, add the yolks and beat
> together, add one spoon rose water, 2 of brandy, and put the whole
> to one and a quarter of a pound flour, if yet too soft add flour and
> bake slowly.

A recipe from Mrs. Elizabeth Goodfellow of the Goodfellow Cooking
School in Philadelphia for Indian Pound Cake comes from Eliza Leslie's *Seventy Five Receipts, for Pastry, Cakes, and Sweetmeats*. According
to William Woys Weaver, in *Thirty Five Receipts from "The Larder
Invaded"* (p. 32), most of the recipes from Miss Leslie's cookbook were
derived from the notebook she kept while attending Mrs. Goodfellow's school. In this recipe cornmeal is used, reflecting Mrs. Goodfellow's advocacy of the use of American ingredients:

> Eight eggs, one pint of powdered sugar, one pint of Indian meal,
> sifted and a half a pint of wheat flour, half pound of butter, one
> nutmeg grated—and a teaspoonful of cinnamon, a glass of mixed
> wine and brandy. Stir the butter and sugar to a cream. Beat the
> eggs very light. Stir the meal and eggs, alternately, into the butter
> and sugar. Add the spice and liquor. Stir all well. Butter a tin pan,
> put in the mixture, and bake it in a moderate oven. This cake
> should be eaten while fresh.

Kids of all ages love cupcakes, and Amelia Simmons offers the only
recipe I've been able to find. Her recipe is called A Light Cake to Bake

in Small Cups and is found below her pound cake recipe. Note the use of yeast (emptins):

> Half a pound sugar, half a pound butter, rubbed into two pounds flour, one glass wine, one do. rose water, two do emptins, a nutmeg, cinnamon and currants.

A recipe titled "Cup Cake" is found in *Selected Receipts of a Van Rensselaer Family 1785-1835,* but the title refers to the measurements, rather than to the baking container, that is, individual cups:

> 4½ Tea cups Flour, 2 do Sugar, 1 do Butter, 1 do Cream, 2 eggs a little pearlash & spice.

An interesting variation on the pound cake is found in the Van Rensselaer manuscript. Molasses Pound Cake is similar to a soft gingerbread:

> 2½ lb flour, 1½ lb butter, ¾ lb sugar, one quart molasses, 12 eggs, ginger & other spices, fruit if you wish & a little pearlash.

Finally, I include a patriotically named Federal Cake, also from the Van Rensselaer manuscripts, in the pound cake category:

> One lb of Flour, ½ lb Butter, ¾ lb Sugar, Four Eggs[,] 2 Teacups full of cream, one glass Wine & Brandy, one lb fruit, one nutmeg.

Sponge cake is a type of cake made without fat (butter, shortening, etc.) and its texture is derived from the separate beating of the whites and the yolks of eggs. Doris Farrington gives two recipes in *Fireside Cooks & Black Kettle Recipes.* The first is called Sponge Cake. No specific manuscript is cited, but she refers to it as a "Mid-18th-century recipe":

> One Pd of sugar—nine eggs—the weight of four eggs in flour, beat the yolks—and whites separate; mix the Sugar and Eggs together before you add the flour.

The second recipe is called Monticello Sponge Cake, cited as coming from "Martha Jefferson—circa 1790." According to Miss Farrington, "Jefferson insisted that this cake be constantly on hand to serve with his favorite wine." Thomas Jefferson was quite the oenophile. (Recently, three bottles of Jefferson's 1800 Madeira were sold at auction for over $20,000.)

> One dozen eggs, whites and yolks beaten separately; one pint of sugar; one pint of flour; juice and grated rind of one lemon; mix yolks, sugar, flour, and lemon. Add Whites. This is a good cake.

In *Selected Receipts of a Van Rensselaer Family 1785–1835,* a recipe for Sponge Cake provides detailed instructions:

> The weight of eleven Eggs in Sugar sifted. The weight of six eggs in flour sifted[,] the grated rinds of two lemons & the juice of one to be added to the mixture when ready for the oven.
>
> Separate carefully the whites from the yolks, after beating the yolks briskly add to them by degrees the sugar then the whites which must be beaten to a thick froth & lastly the flour must be stirred in quickly in small quantities then the lemon added & put into a quick oven[,] bake one hour.

The cider cake is a very American cake. I found one recipe in *Whistler's Mother's Cook Book,* a collection of recipes by Anna McNeill Whistler, better known as Whistler's mother, and collected by Margaret F. MacDonald:

> 2 lb flour, 1 lb sugar, 1 lb raisins, 1 pint Cider, 2 teaspoons full of pearlash, spices and other flavors to your taste.

A similar recipe for Cider Cake is given in Farrington's *Fireside Cooks & Black Kettle Recipes* and originates from a cookbook manuscript of Elizabeth Humbler, circa 1760:

> One and a half pound of flour, ¾ of a pound of Butter, ¾'s of Sugar, 4 eggs, pint of Cider, large spoonful of pearlash with spice to the taste.

The addition of spices to basic cake recipes increased the variety of cakes enjoyed by early Americans; one of the most popular was gingerbread. It took on many forms, baked soft as a cake and hard as cookies. Its origin appears to be medieval. Medieval recipes produced a hard, cookielike product that fell into the category of medicine rather than food. It is believed that the more familiar soft, cakelike gingerbread is an American invention, probably brought about by the use of pearl ash (see p. 10).

Common to both types is the use of molasses, known as treacle in Europe. Molasses is a by-product of sugar refining and is the syrup left after the sugar crystals have been removed from the cane juice. One of the earliest recipes in use in America for a gingerbread is from Martha Washington's *Booke of Cookery.* The name of the recipe is interesting because it doesn't use the word *gingerbread* and because of its length: To Make Pepper Cakes That Will Keep Good in Yᵉ House for a Quarter or Halfe a Year:

Take treakle 4 pound, fine wheat flowre halfe a peck. beat ginger
2 ounces, corriander seeds 2 ounces, carraway and annyseeds of
each an ounce, suckets slyced in small pieces a pretty quantety,
powder of orring pills one ounce, work all these into paste, and let
it ly 2 or 3 hours after, make it up into what fashions you please in
pritty large cakes about an intch and a halfe thick at moste, or
rather an intch will be thick enough, wash your cakes over with a
little oyle and treacle mixt together before you set them into y^e
oven, then set them in after household bread & though they be
hard baked, they will give againe, when you have occasion to use
it, slyce and serve it up.

Martha Washington includes several other recipes for gingerbread,
but they are very old recipes that call for the use of bread crumbs or
crumbled bread, similar to those in fourteenth-century manuscripts.
In *The Art of Cookery Made Plain and Easy,* Hannah Glasse offers "To
Make Gingerbread":

Take three quarts of fine flour, two ounces of beaten ginger, a
quarter of an ounce of nutmeg, cloves, and mace beat fine, but
most of the last; mix all together, three quarters of a pound of fine
sugar, two pounds of treacle, let it over the fire, but do not let it
boil; three quarters of a pound of butter melted into the treacle,
and some candied lemon and orange peel cut fine; mix all these
together well: an hour will bake it in a quick oven.

No eggs are used in this recipe and there is no leavening. Amelia
Simmons published several recipes for gingerbread that are more
cakelike and use both eggs and pearlash. A recipe for her Molasses
Gingerbread is given on p. 10 to illustrate the first use of pearl ash I
could find in a published recipe. A recipe for Gingerbread Cakes is
more like our modern version, though it lacks the addition of molasses (or honey):

No. 1. Three pounds of flour, a grated nutmeg, two ounces ginger,
one pound sugar, three small spoons pearl ash dissolved in cream,
one pound butter, four eggs, knead it stiff, shape it to your fancy,
bake 15 minutes.

No. 2. is titled Soft Gingerbread to be Baked in Pans:

Rub three pounds of sugar, two pounds of butter, into four pounds
of flour, add 20 eggs, 4 ounces ginger, 4 spoons rose-water, bake
as No. 1.

In *Whistler's Mother's Cook Book* there are four recipes for gingerbread; two are very close to modern recipes in their inclusion of molasses, eggs, and pearlash. The first is called simply Gingerbread:

> 6 eggs, a pound of sugar, a pint of Molasses made luke warm, with a pound of butter melted, ginger to your taste add flour untill the mixture is a stiff batter and three teaspoons of dissolved pearlash, and ½ pint of milk or Buttermilk.

The second recipe is called Children's Gingerbread. Note the absence of flour in the recipe (I suppose it was assumed that the baker would add enough to make a stiff batter):

> 3 Pint of Molasses & 2½ pint of cyder, 3 tea-spoonsful dissolved pearlash, 3 large spoons ginger, 1½ pounds of Butter mix to a stiff batter — bake in a large loaf slowly.

The last category of cake types represented in early American cookbooks is the sponge cake. There is no mention of this type of cake by either Martha Washington or Amelia Simmons, but Mary Randolph provides us with one in *The Virginia Housewife*, called Spunge Cake or Savoy Cake:

> Take twelve fresh eggs, put them in a scale, and balance them with sugar; take out half, and balance the other half with flour; separate the whites from the yelks, whip them up very light, then mix them, and sift in, first sugar, then flour, till both are exhausted; add some grated lemon peel; bake them in paper cases or little tin moulds.

When baked in small moulds, this product could be called ladyfingers and was quite popular, used much the same way as we use them today. Mrs. Randolph also includes a recipe for Naples Biscuit, another lady-finger-type cake:

> Beat twelve eggs, add to them one pound of flour, and one of powdered sugar; continue to beat all together till perfectly light; bake in long pans, four inches wide, with divisions; so that each cake, when done, will be four inches long and one and a half wide.

The Van Rensselaer manuscripts offer a recipe entitled Sponge Cake:

> The weight of eleven eggs in Sugar sifted. The weight of six eggs in flour sifted the grated rinds of two lemons & the juice of one to be added to the mixture when ready for the oven.
> Separate carefully the whites from the yolks, after beating the yolks briskly add to them by degrees the sugar then the whites

which must be beaten to a thick froth & lastly the flour must be stirred in quickly in small quantities then the lemon added & put it in a quick oven[,] bake one hour.

Cookies   Recipes for little cakes are quite common in the early cookbooks and usually represent what we now call "cookies." The early American cookbooks also call cookies "biscuits" and "jumbals." Martha Washington provides us with an early recipe, English in origin, for Shrowsbury Cakes:

> Mix a pound of searced [finely pulverized] sugar & a pound of flowre well together. then beat & searce some sinamon, nutmegg, & ginger, & put in 2 egg youlks. worke all these to a paste with sweet butter, & roule it about halfe an intch thick. cut them round, & flowre yʳ papers, & soe bake them. and when they looke Ised over, they are enough.

Amelia Simmons includes a recipe in *American Cookery 1796* entitled Shrewsbury Cake:

> One pound butter, three quarters of a pound sugar, a little mace, four eggs mixed and beat with your hand, till very light, put the composition to one pound flour, roll into small cakes—bake with a light oven.

Mary Randolph's *The Virginia Housewife* also includes a recipe for Shrewsbury Cakes:

> Mix a pound of sugar, with two pounds of flour, and a large spoonful of pounded coriander seeds; sift them, add three quarters of a pound of melted butter, six eggs and a gill of brandy; knead it well, roll it thin, cut it in shapes, and bake without discolouring it.

While apparently quite popular in the eighteenth and early nineteenth centuries, this cookie did not survive into the twentieth century.

Recipes for biscuits abound in the early cookbooks, and the term represents several different types of cookies and baked goods. In modern terms, a biscuit is not a sweet, but a bread, usually associated with southern cooking. The word is probably French in origin, from *bescuit,* which means twice-cooked bread. Baking twice gives the cookie a very dry, crunchy texture without burning. Martha Washington's *A Booke of Sweetmeats* offers two recipes for Biskit Bread, one for Biskit, and one for French Biskit, for which I provide the recipe:

> Take halfe A peck of fine flowre and bake it in ye oven, then mingle with it A quarter of a pound of annyseeds. then make it up with as hot water as you can, & 5 or 6 eggs. knead it into paste as you doe for manchets, then make it into a longe roule & soe bake it. and when it is a day ould, pare it and slyce it, & sugar it with powder sugar. then bake it again for an houre. after that, take it out, & when you see it is dry, hard, & cold, y^n take double refined sugar beaten & searced, & rub it well with your hand over every slyce of your biskit, & it will keep it white as any flowre on ye outsides. then box them up & they will keep 2 or 3 years.

Another recipe in the style of the Italian biscotto is found in Hannah Glasse's *The Art of Cookery Made Plain and Easy* and is titled "To Make Common Biscuits"

> Beat up six eggs, with a spoonful of rose-water and a spoonful of sack; then add a pound of fine powdered sugar, and a pound of flour; mix them into the eggs by degrees, and an ounce of coriander seeds; mix all well together, shape them on white thin paper, or tin moulds, in any form you please; beat the white of an egg, with a feather rub them over, and dust fine sugar over them; set them in an oven moderately heated, when you have done with the oven, if you have no stove to dry them in, put them in the oven again, and let them stand all night to dry.

A recipe for Drop-Biscuits is given just before the previous recipe and is quite similar in baking technique. The batter is a bit thinner and the dough is dropped on floured sheets of tin.

The recipes for Butter Biscuit found in Amelia Simmons' *American Cookery 1796* do not resemble the previous recipes for biscuits. No sugar is added and they are not twice baked to dry them out. They begin to resemble the traditional southern biscuit. Note the use of emptins:

One pint each milk and emptins, laid into flour, in sponge; next morning add one pound butter melted, not hot, and knead into as much flour as will another pint of warmed milk, be of sufficient consistence to make soft—some melt the butter in the milk.

The beaten biscuit is another early form of the southern biscuit, and a fine example is found in Margaret Hooker's *Early American Cookery or Yᵉ Gentlewoman's Housewifery:*

Warm one tablespoonful of Lard or butter in equal quantities of Milk and water, as much as will make a quart of Flour a very Stiff dough. Beat the dough for thirty Minutes with an Axe or rolling Pin. Work it very Smooth. Roll it Thin and cut it into round Biscuits, and prick full of Holes. About six minutes will Bake them.

Another beaten biscuit is called Apoquiniminc Cakes in *The Virginia Housewife:*

Put a little salt, one egg beaten, and four ounces of butter, in a quart of flour; make it into a paste with new milk, beat it for half an hour with a pestle, roll the paste thin, and cut it into round cakes; bake them on a gridiron and be careful not to burn them.

Having briefly digressed into the realm of biscuits (which are so much a part of American baking) we should return to the cookie (also an important part of American baking!). Amelia Simmons provides us with a recipe for Cookies:

One pound sugar boiled slowly in half pint water, scum well and cool, add two teaspoons pearl ash dissolved in milk, then two and half pounds flour, rub in 4 ounces butter, and two large spoons of finely powdered coriander seed, wet with above; make rolls half an inch thick and cut to the shape you please; bake fifteen or twenty minutes in a slack oven—good three weeks.

Christmas cookies are a significant part of modern holiday baking, and Amelia Simmons offers a recipe for Another Christmas Cookey (interestingly, she gives no other recipes for Christmas cookies):

To three pound flour, sprinkle a tea cup of fine powdered coriander seed, rub in one pound butter, and one and half pound sugar, dissolve three teaspoonfuls of pearl ash in a tea cup of milk, knead all together well, roll three quarters of an inch thick, and cut or stamp into shape and size you please, bake slowly fifteen or twenty minutes; tho' hard and dry at first, if put into an earthen pot, and dry cellar, or damp room. they will be finer, softer and better when six months old.

A rather brief recipe in the Van Rensselaer manuscript is titled Tea Cookjes:

½ lb butt ¾ Sugar 1 tea cup water as much flour as it will take.

By the beginning of the twentieth century all forms of cookies were being developed in America. Cookies with chocolate added or peanuts and raisins, and bars and brownies were (and still are) being eaten by children of all ages.

PART TWO

Recipes by Region

INTRODUCTION

Within the map:
WEST   MIDWEST   EASTERN CENTRAL   NEW ENGLAND

NORTH ATLANTIC

WEST COAST

SOUTH ATLANTIC

SOUTHWEST   DEEP SOUTH

W̲E ARE SO BLESSED in America. Fertile land, relatively clean air and water, and the richness of the numerous cultures that have been woven into our landscape provide a broad base for the development of an American style of baking. The geography, geology, and hydrology of our continent have allowed regional specialties and styles to develop. Would it surprise you to learn that Buttermilk Cracklin' Bread is from an Appalachian cookbook or that Pineapple-Macadamia Nut Bread is baked in Hawaii? How about Peanut Butter Pie from Georgia or Amish Shoo Fly Pie from Pennsylvania? There's Italian Cheese Cake from New York and Festival Orange Cheesecake from Florida.

I have divided America into nine regions and tried to select recipes that represent the style or unique character of each region. I struggled to limit the number of recipes to about seven hundred. With fifty states and four categories of baked goods to cover, I reviewed almost three hundred regional cookbooks, many from church groups publishing their parish's favorite recipes, and Junior League–type cookbooks. The cookbooks date from the 1890's to the 1990's. Some had been typed on a trusty Smith-Corona and were spiral bound; others were quite professional. My favorite cookbook of them all is a charming small book titled *Out of Vermont Kitchens* that was compiled by Trinity Mission of Trinity Church in Rutland, Vermont, in conjunction with the Women's Service League of St. Paul's Church in Burlington. I have a copy of the eighteenth printing (1947) of this apparently perennial favorite, originally published in 1939. Each recipe is in the handwriting of the submitting baker and is illustrated by the baker as well. I am reprinting a page so that you can share in its pure American "hominess" and sincerity.

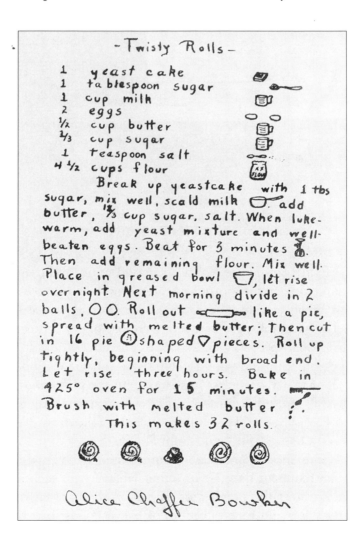

THE NAMES of regional baked goods are as fascinating and unique as the items themselves. There's a Lazy Cake from Connecticut, a Harvest Moon Glow Cake from Mississippi, and Chocolate "Wacky" Cake from Indiana. There are recipes adapted to the hard times experienced in the depression era of the 1930's—Poor Man's Cake from Iowa and my personal favorite, Butterless, Eggless, Milkless Cake from Oklahoma.

Ease in preparation is another popular theme—the One, Two, Three, Four Cake from Massachusetts; Hurry Up Cake from New Jersey; Mix-in-the-Pan Cake from Texas; Easy-Do Cake from Wyoming; and One Cup Cake from Kansas.

Only America would have desserts named after popular soft drinks! I'm sure the European pastry world would cringe over recipes such as Aunt Caroline's Coca-Cola Cake from Ohio, Dr. Pepper Chocolate Cake from South Carolina, or Alva T.'s 7-Up Cake, a Texas favorite. They are delicious and truly American in character.

The names of America's cookies are so colorful that it's hard to believe that we did not actually invent the cookie. A cookbook from Tennessee offers us Billy Goat Cookies while one from Colorado has Strike It Rich Bars. My favorite is a recipe for Grandmother Smith's Shin-Plasters, a New Hampshire cookie.

The recipes in this book are edited originals. These are not my recipes; they are your recipes, the recipes of your parents, grandparents, and our ancestors before them. I resisted the temptation to change ingredients to modernize the recipes. Lard is one of those ingredients that I've left in when originally called for, in spite of the health issues conjured up by its use. Should you want to substitute, you will need 25 percent more butter or margarine. Vegetable shortening and oil are equivalent to lard, so use the same amount. No substitutions for regional ingredients are given, as the purpose of the book is to provide recipes that are region-specific and special. Be warned that you will need banana yuccas if you want to make a Banana Yucca Pie and marionberries for Marionberry Cheesecake!

Some of the recipes from cookbooks of the 1920's and the 1930's contain recipes that are written as though they came from America's earliest cookbooks. It would be hard to tell whether the following recipe for White Cake came from Amelia Simmons' *American Cookery 1796* or from the *Marion Cook Book,* which was published in 1921:

Whites of five eggs, two cupfuls of sugar, two cupfuls of flour, one cupful of cornstarch, one cupful of butter, level teaspoon of baking powder, one cupful of sweet milk.

Baking directions were often omitted in early American cookbooks, and this trend seems to have continued well into the twentieth century. When directions do appear in recipes from the *Marion Cook Book*, they can be quite brief, as in early books. A recipe for Fruit Cake directs the cook to "bake [the cake] three hours." There is no mention of oven temperature. When the cookbook gives any temperature-related directions, it tells the baker to "bake [the item] in a moderate oven," "in a very slow oven," or "in a quick oven." The most complete directions in the cookbook are "beat well, bake in layers and put together with plain icing," in the recipe for Walnut Cake.

I've taken the diverse writing styles and recipe formats from seventy cookbooks representing the fifty states and unified them. I hope I have faithfully reproduced the spirit of the recipes while taking a little liberty in adding instructions for clarity. The nine regions of the United States and the states they encompass (see map, on page 53) are as follows:

New England	Maine, New Hampshire, Vermont, Massachusetts, Rhode Island, and Connecticut
North Atlantic	New York, New Jersey, Delaware, Pennsylvania, and Maryland, plus Washington, D.C.
South Atlantic	Virginia, North Carolina, South Carolina, West Virginia, Kentucky, Tennessee, and Florida
Deep South	Georgia, Alabama, Mississippi, Arkansas, and Louisiana
Eastern Central	Ohio, Indiana, Michigan, Illinois, and Missouri
Midwest	Wisconsin, Minnesota, North Dakota, South Dakota, Nebraska, Iowa, Kansas, and Oklahoma
Southwest	Texas, New Mexico, and Arizona
West	Montana, Wyoming, Colorado, Idaho, Utah, and Nevada
West Coast	Washington, Oregon, California, Alaska, and Hawaii.

Baked goods are divided into the following categories:

Breads

Yeast Breads
Quick Breads
Coffee Cakes, Sweet Yeast Breads and Buns,
    and Gingerbreads
Cornmeal Breads
Muffins, Tea Biscuits, and Scones
Rolls and Pretzels
Biscuits and Crackers
Bread Puddings

Pies

Fruit and Berry Pies
Custard and Egg Pies
Chiffon and Cream Pies
Nut and Chocolate Pies
Special Pies
Cobblers, Crisps, and Tarts

Cakes

Butter, Shortening, and Oil Cakes
    White Cakes
    Chocolate Cakes
    Spice, Nut, and Fruit Cakes
Sponge and Yeast Cakes
Tortes and Special Cakes
Cheesecakes
Cupcakes
Roll Cakes

Cookies

Drop and Shaped Cookies
Roll, Slice, and Cut Cookies
Bars and Brownies

As you leaf through the recipes that follow, you will notice that not all categories are represented in each geographical region. For example, recipes for pretzels, a bread subcategory, appear in this book only in the North Atlantic region. The influence of the German settlers in the region (the Pennsylvania Dutch, for example) accounts for the number of pretzel recipes found in its cookbooks. Cookbooks from other regions rarely mention pretzels at all.

The Northeast (the New England and North Atlantic regions) reflects the recipes of our founders more than any other area. Many of the recipes here have the original names from sixteenth-, seventeenth-, and eighteenth-century cookbooks cited in the earlier chapters of this book. There are many gingerbread recipes, bread recipes that include cornmeal, and recipes with names like "gems." Molasses is a popular ingredient in many categories.

As we move down the coast to the South Atlantic region, muffins and corn products are more frequently mentioned in cookbooks. Deep South recipes incorporate sweet potatoes, grits, and hominy into bread recipes, as well as peanuts (and peanut butter). Cream and buttermilk are mentioned more often, and cracklin's are everywhere!

The Eastern Central region offers a more straightforward style of bread. Grains predominate, especially oats, wheat berries, and rye. Dried herbs and dairy products are used frequently, and cracker recipes show up in this region's cookbooks. The Midwest recipes include bread starters, and coffee cake and buns dominate as sweet bread recipes, probably a result of the strong presence of Scandinavian settlers.

Regionally specific ingredients, including some derived from produce not grown in other parts of the country, characterize the recipes of the Southwest—green chiles and jalapeños, pecans and blue cornmeal among them. Spanish and Native American contributions to the food culture are apparent in many of the cookbooks.

The West has a very simple approach to bread. The cookbooks contain lots of camping and "outdoors"-type breads and rolls. Many breads are made from wheat flour, but mixed-grain breads are not uncommon. Sometimes nuts (usually walnuts) and dried fruits appear in the recipes.

Like the Southwest, the West Coast features ingredients special to the region in its recipes, in this case because of its varied microclimates and the tropical influence of Hawaii and Mexico. Pineapples, mangoes, and macadamia nuts find their way into bread recipes, as do apples, berries, and hazelnuts from the Northwest. Sourdoughs are very popular, particularly in Alaska and the Bay Area of California. Alaska's vast mineral wealth drew many of the California gold rushers north to a colder clime, and the sourdough represents an obvious food connection between the two areas.

Pies, too, show regional distinctions. In New England, colonial names persist: pandowdies and grunts. Cobblers abound, made primarily with blueberries and apples. It was difficult to find chocolate pies in these cookbooks, so the subcategory is left out of the region. A few custard pies are offered, but not of the variety to follow from other regions. Pumpkin pie has maintained a place among New England recipes as a holdover from colonial times.

In the North Atlantic region, custard pies and egg-based pies are seen more frequently; dried fruit accompanies many of them. Strawberries appear in South Atlantic recipes, along with other indigenous berries. Custard pies proliferate, and sweet potatoes make their way into pies. Peach pies and pies with pecans are first seen in the Deep South, and molasses is a common ingredient in many of the subcategory recipes of the region.

The Eastern Central region developed mock pies and other cracker pies (recall the appearance of cracker recipes in the bread section). Cream pies are favored here as well.

We find few unique fruit pies in the Midwest. Apple pie, popular everywhere, and cherry and rhubarb are regional favorites. Squash pies are mentioned frequently in the cookbooks, including the ubiquitous pumpkin.

The Southwest's unusual produce comes into play once again to make its pie offerings highly regional. Piñons (pine nuts) and banana yucca are frequent in recipes, along with pecans and peaches.

The pies of the West seem to feature liquors and liqueurs, such as rum and crème de menthe. Rather than fruit pies, fruit juice pies are offered. There are not many custard pies that are in any way unique to the West.

Ingredients for pies are again very regional on the West Coast: cherries, pears, and hazelnuts from the Northwest as well as the tropical fruits of Hawaii and California. Coconut is found in a variety of pie types, and chiffon pies of mango, guava, and passionfruit make their appearance.

Returning to the Northeast, and turning to the cakes of the region, we find that the recipes reflect, as we've come to expect, those of the colonial era. Seed cake and cider cake are classics. Also of interest is the use of many spices, just as in the old recipes of New England. Surprisingly, recipes for yeast-risen cakes, the first of type of sweet cake baked in the colonies, are now few. Sponge and yeast cakes do appear in the North Atlantic region, as do some classic chocolate cakes. Cakes with apples and applesauce or with pears are frequent in Northeastern cookbooks. Cheesecakes make a strong showing as well.

The South Atlantic region has a variety of jam and jelly cakes, like the jelly roll. More unusual chocolate cakes appear, using syrups and soft drinks as additions to basic recipes. White cakes dominate in the South, along with "gooey" chocolate cakes such as Mississippi Mud and varieties that use marshmallows.

Cooks in the Eastern Central region include more dairy in recipes, and a unique type of cake emerges, the pie-filling cake. Fruit cakes are abundant, and chocolate cakes tend toward the unusual, particularly in their inclusion of beets and sauerkraut as ingredients. The Midwest shows less variety, and white and yellow cake seem to dominate the selection in many cookbooks. Spices and fruits are often part of these recipes.

The recipes of the Southwest, which so often take advantage of ingredients peculiar to the region, are a bit more "mainstream" when it comes to cakes. Candy bars and chocolate chips are frequently added, but some recipes exhibit a decided Hispanic flair. There is no getting away from such regional ingredients as piñons and pecans—and coriander as the spice.

The proportion of cakes among baking recipes is lower in the West than in other regions, and these recipes seem to be borrowed (e.g., Black Forest Cake). In general, bakers in the West like nuts and spices in their cakes.

Surprisingly, yeast cakes make their strongest showing on the West Coast, and vegetables such as zucchini and carrots appear as cake ingredients in many of the cookbooks I examined. But, again, regional produce is favored by bakers, especially the nuts and fruits of the Northwest and the tropical varieties from Hawaii and California, including pineapple and coconut.

It's a good thing I did not try to divide America into cookie-based regions. Cookies are everyone's favorite, and cookie recipes spread quickly throughout the states to provide a more homogenous category of baked goods than breads, pies, or cakes. There are some noteworthy geographical differences though. The Northeast features maple as a sweetener. While this should not come as a surprise considering the vast stands of sugar maples in New England, not much in the way of maple is found in the region's other baked goods. Molasses and spice flavors dominate, and gingerbread-type cookies are quite popular. We see more refrigerator and cut cookies in the North Atlantic; the South Atlantic introduces oats, dried fruits, and some nuts. Peanuts and peanut butter are frequent additions to the cookies of the Deep South.

Coconut and unusual add-ins, such as chow mein noodles and crispy rice cereals, are common in recipes from the Eastern Central region. Sorghum is used in the Midwest, and many recipes call for oats. We even find potato chips in Midwest cookie recipes.

Piñon and aniseed add a special flavor to the cookies of the Southwest, as do the Mexican names attached to them. Look for these colorful Western names and the copious use of nuts in cookies from the West. Once again, the West Coast provides the cookies that utilize produce from its own region. Hazelnuts and zucchini and other vegetables are added to basic doughs, and the Asian influence is apparent in the addition of sesame seeds and almond flavoring.

Join me now in a baking tour across the United States. And remember, you can eat the souvenirs of this road trip!

Breads

Breads

Shredded Wheat Bread

MAINE

Adapted from Roux, *What's Cooking Down in Maine*

2 cups boiling water	2 large Shredded Wheat
2 tablespoons shortening	biscuits
2 teaspoons salt	1 tablespoon dry yeast
⅓ cup molasses	¼ cup warm water
	5 cups flour

1. Place the boiling water, shortening, salt, and molasses in a mixing bowl. Crumble in the Shredded Wheat.
2. Dissolve the yeast in the warm water and add to the Shredded Wheat mixture, followed by the flour.
3. Turn out on a floured board and knead for 8 minutes.
4. Allow the bread to rise for about 2 hours in a buttered bowl. Punch it down and let it rise again for 1 hour. Allow the dough to rest for 10 minutes.
5. Divide the dough in half and place in two 8-inch ungreased loaf pans.
6. Bake at 400° for 45–50 minutes.

Great-Aunt Jessie Sanborn's Graham Bread

NEW HAMPSHIRE

Adapted from Berquist, *The High Maples Farm Cookbook*

2 cups milk	½ cup butter
½ cup light cream	1 teaspoon salt
1 package dry yeast	½ cup dark molasses
½ teaspoon sugar	2 cups all-purpose flour
½ cup lukewarm water	5½ cups graham flour

1. Scald the milk with the cream.
2. Dissolve the yeast and sugar in the water.
3. Add the butter, salt, and molasses to the hot milk. Cool to lukewarm and add the yeast mixture.
4. Mix in the all-purpose flour a little at a time. Add 1 cup of the graham flour and beat to form a smooth batter. Allow the dough to rise for an hour.
5. Stir in the remaining graham flour. Knead gently to form a smooth dough. Allow to rise until doubled in bulk.
6. Divide the dough in half and place into greased loaf pans. Allow to rise until doubled in bulk.
7. Bake at 375° for 45–50 minutes, or until done.

Mrs. Johnson's Oatmeal Bread

NEW HAMPSHIRE
Adapted from Berquist, *The High Maples Farm Cookbook*

2 cups boiling water	⅓ cup molasses
1 cup quick-cooking oats	½ cup butter
1 package dry yeast	1 teaspoon salt
1 teaspoon sugar	8 cups sifted all-purpose
¼ cup lukewarm water	flour
1 cup scalding-hot milk	

1. Pour the boiling water over the oats and allow to cool to lukewarm.
2. Dissolve the dry yeast and the sugar in the lukewarm water.
3. Mix the hot milk, molasses, butter, and salt together. Cool to lukewarm. Stir in the oatmeal mixture and the yeast mixture.
4. Add 2 cups of the sifted flour and beat until smooth. Cover and leave in a warm place for 45 minutes.
5. Stir in the remaining flour, a little at a time. Mix to form a smooth dough. Allow to rise until doubled in bulk. Punch down and allow to rise again.
6. Knead the dough lightly until smooth and elastic. Form into 3 loaves and place in buttered loaf pans. Allow to rise until doubled in bulk.
7. Bake at 375° for 45–50 minutes, or until the loaves are done.

Date Bread

VERMONT
Adapted from *Out of Vermont Kitchens*

1½ cups boiling water	2 teaspoons baking soda
1 cup dates, chopped	1 teaspoon salt
1 cup malt cereal, uncooked	1 egg, beaten
¾ cup sugar	1 tablespoon butter, melted
1½ cups flour	

1. Pour the boiling water over the chopped dates and malt cereal and let stand 20 minutes.
2. Sift the sugar, flour, baking soda, and salt together. Stir into the date mixture. Add the egg and butter.
3. Beat well and place in 2 greased bread tins.
4. Bake at 350° for 45–50 minutes.

COFFEE CAKES, SWEET YEAST BUNS, AND GINGERBREADS

Lill's Blueberry Gingerbread

MAINE
Adapted from Roux, *What's Cooking Down in Maine*

½ cup shortening
1 cup sugar
1 egg
1 teaspoon baking soda
1 cup sour milk or buttermilk
2 cups sifted flour

½ teaspoon ginger
1 teaspoon cinnamon
½ teaspoon salt
3 tablespoons molasses
1 cup blueberries
3 tablespoons sugar

1. Cream the shortening with the sugar. Add the egg and mix well.
2. Stir the baking soda into the sour milk or buttermilk.
3. Sift the flour, ginger, cinnamon, and salt together. Add to the creamed mixture alternately with the sour milk or buttermilk. Add the molasses.
4. Add the blueberries and pour the batter into a greased and floured 9-by-9-inch pan. Sprinkle the 3 tablespoons of sugar over the batter.
5. Bake at 350° for 50 minutes to 1 hour.

Maple Sugar Gingerbread

VERMONT
Adapted from Pixley, *Vermont Country Cooking*

1 teaspoon ginger
½ teaspoon salt
1 teaspoon baking soda
2 cups flour

1 egg, beaten
1 cup sour cream
1 cup maple syrup

1. Sift the ginger, salt, baking soda, and flour together.
2. Mix the egg, sour cream, and maple syrup together.
3. Combine the two mixtures to form a smooth batter.
4. Bake in a greased and floured 8-inch square pan at 350° for 20 minutes.

COFFEE CAKES, SWEET YEAST BUNS, AND GINGERBREADS

Sticky Buns

VERMONT
Adapted from Out of Vermont Kitchens

1 cup raisins	4–6 cups flour
1 quart milk	2 eggs
2 tablespoons sugar	1 tablespoon cinnamon
1 tablespoon shortening	3 tablespoons sugar, divided
1½ tablespoons yeast	½ cup maple syrup
½ teaspoon salt	

1. Soak the raisins in warm water until soft. Drain.
2. Warm the milk; stir in the sugar and the shortening.
3. Dissolve the yeast in a little warm water. Add the salt and then enough flour to make a soft dough.
4. Add the drained raisins to the dough.
5. Add the eggs, cinnamon, and 2 tablespoons of the sugar. Mix together, stirring well.
6. Let the dough rise until doubled.
7. Roll to 1-inch thickness and cut out buns with 3-inch round cutter.
8. Place the buns in a 10-inch-by-14-inch rectangular pan and allow to rise again.
9. Bake at 375° until golden.
10. Add the remaining 1 tablespoon sugar to the maple syrup and cook until it threads. Brush over buns while they are still hot from the oven.

Molasses Gunjee

MAINE
Adapted from Roux, What's Cooking Down in Maine

1 cup molasses	1 teaspoon salt
½ cup sugar	2 cups flour
¼ cup shortening, melted	1 heaping teaspoon baking
1 egg	soda
1 teaspoon ginger	1 cup boiling water

1. Mix the first 6 ingredients together until well blended. Add the flour.
2. Dissolve the baking soda in the boiling water and fold into the batter until smooth. The batter will be quite thin.
3. Pour into a greased and floured 9-inch square cake pan.
4. Bake at 350° for 25–30 minutes.

COFFEE CAKES, SWEET YEAST BUNS, AND GINGERBREADS

Maple Coffee Cake

NEW HAMPSHIRE

Adapted from Berquist, *The High Maples Farm Cookbook*

Cake:

2 cups all-purpose flour	½ cup soft maple sugar
½ teaspoon salt	½ cup softened butter
2 teaspoons baking powder	1 large egg, beaten
¼ teaspoon nutmeg	½ cup milk
¼ teaspoon cinnamon	½ cup broken nut meats

Topping:

3 tablespoons soft maple sugar	¼ teaspoon cinnamon
	¼ teaspoon nutmeg
3 tablespoons flour	¼ cup broken nut meats
¼ cup cold butter, cut into bits	

1. Sift the flour, salt, baking powder, nutmeg, and cinnamon together.
2. Cream the maple sugar and the softened butter until light. Add the egg.
3. Add the flour mixture alternately with the milk. Mix until a smooth batter is formed. Add ½ cup nut meats to batter.
4. Spread the dough in a greased 9-inch square baking pan.
5. Make the topping by rubbing together all the topping ingredients except the nuts. Drop this mixture by spoonfuls over the batter and sprinkle on the remaining nut meats.
6. Bake at 350° for 45 minutes. Cut into squares while hot.

COFFEE CAKES, SWEET YEAST BUNS, AND GINGERBREADS

Grandmother Smith's Gingerbread

NEW HAMPSHIRE
Adapted from Berquist, *The High Maples Farm Cookbook*

2½ cups all-purpose flour	½ cup sugar
½ teaspoon cream of tartar	2 large eggs
½ teaspoon nutmeg	¾ teaspoon baking soda
¾ teaspoon ginger	1 cup buttermilk
½ cup softened butter	1 cup dark molasses

1. Sift the flour, cream of tartar, nutmeg, and ginger together.
2. Cream the butter and the sugar together until light and fluffy. Add the eggs and beat thoroughly.
3. Dissolve the baking soda in the buttermilk and stir this into the creamed mixture. Stir in the molasses.
4. Add the flour mixture and mix until the batter is smooth. Pour the batter into a greased deep 9-inch square pan.
5. Bake at 350° for 30 minutes, or until the gingerbread is done.

CORNMEAL BREADS

Indian Meal Bannock

RHODE ISLAND
Adapted from Dyer, *The Newport Cookbook*

3 eggs, separated	½ teaspoon salt
2 cups milk	1 tablespoon butter, room
1 cup cornmeal	temperature

1. Beat the egg yolks until frothy.
2. Beat the whites until they are stiff but not dry.
3. Heat the milk until it steams. Pour it over the cornmeal in a large bowl. Add the salt and the butter and stir until the butter has melted.
4. Stir in the egg yolks and fold in the egg whites. Pour this mixture into a well-greased 2-quart baking dish.
5. Bake at 375° until firm, about 30 minutes.

Vermont Johnny Cake

VERMONT

Adapted from Pixley, *Vermont Country Cooking*

4 cups boiling water	1 teaspoon salt
1 cup cornmeal	2 tablespoons melted butter

1. Pour the boiling water over the cornmeal, stirring constantly, to form a thin batter.
2. Stir in the salt and pour into an ungreased 8-inch square baking dish. Pour the melted butter over the top.
3. Bake at 425° for 10 minutes.

Steamed Brown Bread

MAINE

Adapted from Roux, *What's Cooking Down in Maine*

4 cups white cornmeal	1 teaspoon baking powder
2 cups flour	4 cups sour milk
¼ teaspoon salt	1 cup molasses

1. Sift the cornmeal, flour, and salt together.
2. Dissolve the baking powder in a little of the sour milk and add it to the flour mixture. Add the molasses and the remaining sour milk and mix well.
3. Pour the batter into a well-greased covered can.
4. Steam in a 325° oven in a pan half full of water for 4 hours.

"Grandma used quart-sized lard pails."

CORNMEAL BREADS

Ellen's Custard Corncake

NEW HAMPSHIRE
Adapted from Berquist, *The High Maples Farm Cookbook*

1 cup yellow cornmeal, stone ground if available	3 teaspoons baking powder
½ cup all-purpose flour	1⅓ cups milk
⅓ cup sugar	2 tablespoons melted butter
½ teaspoon salt	1 egg
	1⅓ cups light cream

1. Sift the cornmeal, flour, sugar, salt, and baking powder together.
2. Add the milk and the melted butter and stir to form a smooth batter. Pour the batter into a greased 9-by-13-inch pan. Allow to stand for 15 minutes.
3. Beat the egg and cream until frothy. Carefully pour this mixture in a thin stream over the batter. Allow to stand for a minute or so.
4. Bake at 450° for 10 minutes. Reduce the heat to 350° and bake for 40 minutes.

Uncle Charlie's Lumbermill Johnnycake

NEW HAMPSHIRE
Adapted from Berquist, *The High Maples Farm Cookbook*

¾ cup all-purpose flour	½ teaspoon baking soda
¾ cup yellow cornmeal	2 cups buttermilk
⅓ cup sugar	2 tablespoons vegetable oil
1 teaspoon salt	

1. Sift the flour, cornmeal, sugar, salt, and baking soda together. Stir in the buttermilk and the vegetable oil. Mix to form a smooth batter. Pour the batter into a greased 8-inch square pan.
2. Bake at 375° for 25–30 minutes, or until lightly browned.

Six Good Muffins

CONNECTICUT

Adapted from *The Neighborhood Cook Book*

1 cup flour	1 rounded teaspoon sugar
1 level teaspoon baking powder	1 heaping teaspoon butter
	1 egg, well beaten
pinch salt	½ cup milk

1. Sift the flour, baking powder, and salt together. Add the sugar, butter, egg, and milk. Stir gently.
2. Pour into greased muffin tins.
3. Bake at 400° for 10 minutes.

Filled Bran Tea Biscuits

CONNECTICUT

Adapted from *The Neighborhood Cook Book*

Filling:

1 cup dates, cut in pieces	¼ cup water
1 cup light brown sugar	

Biscuits:

⅔ cup butter	½ teaspoon salt
¾ cup light brown sugar	⅓ teaspoon baking soda
1 egg, beaten	½ teaspoon baking powder
1¼ cups bran	½ cup sour milk or
1½ cups flour	buttermilk

1. Prepare the filling by cooking the ingredients together in the top of a double boiler until thickened. Allow to cool.
2. For the biscuits, cream the butter and brown sugar until fluffy. Add the beaten egg.
3. Mix the bran with the flour and the rest of the dry ingredients. Add this mixture to the butter mixture alternately with the sour milk or buttermilk.
4. Drop teaspoons about 3 inches apart onto an ungreased cookie sheet. Flatten with a knife.
5. Place a generous helping of filling on each biscuit and cover with another biscuit.
6. Bake at 400° for 8 minutes.

Sweet Mincemeat Tea Biscuits

RHODE ISLAND
Adapted from Dyer, *The Newport Cookbook*

9	ounces mincemeat	3	eggs, well beaten
3	tablespoons water	3	cups flour
½	cup butter, softened	1	cup chopped walnuts
⅓	cup shortening	1	teaspoon baking soda
1½	cups sugar	½	teaspoon nutmeg

1. Stir the mincemeat with the water and set aside.
2. Cream the butter and shortening with the sugar. Add the eggs and beat well.
3. Add 1½ cups of the flour and blend to form a smooth batter. Stir in the mincemeat.
4. Mix the remaining 1½ cups flour with the walnuts, baking soda, and nutmeg. Add to the batter and blend.
5. Roll out to ½-inch thickness and cut into 2-inch rounds.
6. Place the rounds on an ungreased baking sheet and bake at 375° until golden.

Graham Muffins

VERMONT
Adapted from *Out of Vermont Kitchens*

1	cup sour milk	2	tablespoons shortening, melted
1	teaspoon baking soda		
2	tablespoons sugar	1	cup graham flour
		¼	cup white flour

1. Mix ingredients in the order given. Distribute batter into 8 greased or paper-lined muffin cups.
2. Bake at 400° for 25 minutes.

Cream Scones

VERMONT

Adapted from Pixley, *Vermont Country Cooking*

1⅓ cups flour
¼ teaspoon salt
1 heaping teaspoon baking
   powder

1 cup light cream

1. Sift the flour with the salt and baking powder. Stir in the cream.
2. Bake as scones, dropping from a spoon on a hot griddle, or as muffins at 400° for 10 minutes.

"They are excellent for tea."

Blueberry Muffins

MAINE

Adapted from Roux, *What's Cooking Down in Maine*

2 cups sifted flour
3 teaspoons baking powder
⅓ cup sugar
¾ teaspoon salt

1 egg, beaten
¾ cup milk
¼ cup shortening, melted
1 cup blueberries

1. Mix and sift the dry ingredients.
2. Mix the egg, milk, and melted shortening together and add to the dry ingredients. Mix briefly and add the blueberries.
3. Fill greased muffin tins two-thirds full.
4. Bake at 425° for 20–25 minutes.

MUFFINS, TEA BISCUITS, AND SCONES

Apple Cream Muffins

NEW HAMPSHIRE
Adapted from Berquist, *The High Maples Farm Cookbook*

1¾ cups all-purpose flour	¼ cup salad oil
½ cup sugar	½ cup heavy cream
¾ teaspoon cream of tartar	2 apples, peeled, cored, and
½ teaspoon baking soda	diced
½ teaspoon salt	¼ cup sugar
1 large egg	½ teaspoon cinnamon

1. Sift the flour, sugar, cream of tartar, baking soda, and salt together.
2. Whisk the egg, oil, and cream together. Add the flour mixture and stir just until blended. Fold in the apples.
3. Fill greased muffin tins ⅔ full with the batter. Sprinkle lightly with the sugar mixed with the cinnamon.
4. Bake at 425° for 15 minutes, or until the muffins are firm to the touch.

Graham Gems

MASSACHUSETTS
Adapted from *Boston Chapter, No. 28 Order of Eastern Star Cook Book*

1 cup sour milk	¼ cup sugar
1 cup graham flour	1 teaspoon baking soda

1. Mix all ingredients together in a bowl gently until just incorporated.
2. Bake in 6 ungreased muffin tins at 400° for 10 minutes, or until firm to the touch in center.

Crusty Rolls

MASSACHUSETTS

Adapted from *Boston Chapter, No. 28 Order of Eastern Star Cook Book*

1 cup milk	2 tablespoons shortening
½ yeast cake	1 egg, well beaten
½ cup lukewarm water	2 tablespoons sugar
1½ cups flour	2½ cups flour
1 teaspoon salt	salted butter, melted

1. Scald the milk and allow to cool.
2. Dissolve the yeast cake in the warm water and add it, along with the 1½ cups flour, the salt, and the shortening. Beat well, cover, and allow to rise overnight.
3. Add the egg, sugar, and the 2½ cups flour. Let rise until double in bulk.
4. Roll to ¾-inch thickness and cut with round or oval cutter. Allow to rise, then brush with melted salted butter. Place in an ungreased pan 1 inch apart.
5. Bake at 400° for about 15 minutes.

Twisty Rolls

VERMONT

Adapted from *Out of Vermont Kitchens*

1 yeast cake	1 teaspoon salt
1 tablespoon sugar	2 eggs, well beaten
1 cup milk	4½ cups flour
½ cup butter	butter, melted
⅔ cup sugar	

1. Break up the yeast cake with the 1 tablespoon sugar and mix together well.
2. Scald the milk. Add the butter, ⅔ cup sugar, and the salt to the milk.
3. When the milk mixture is lukewarm, add the yeast and well-beaten eggs.
4. Beat for 3 minutes. Add the flour and mix well.
5. Place in a greased bowl and let rise overnight in the refrigerator.
6. Divide the dough into 2 balls. Roll each ball out in a thin circle. Spread each circle with melted butter and cut each into 16 pie-shaped pieces.
7. Roll each triangle up tightly, beginning with the broad end. Let rise 3 hours.
8. Bake at 425° for 15 minutes. Brush with melted butter.

Maple Breakfast Rolls

VERMONT

Adapted from Pixley, *Vermont Country Cooking*

1   egg
½   cup milk
½   cup cream
3   teaspoons granulated
      maple sugar

1–2   cups flour
3   teaspoons baking powder
½   teaspoon salt

1. Mix the egg, milk, cream, and maple sugar together.
2. Add enough flour, the baking powder, and the salt to make a batter "as thick as griddle cake batter."
3. Bake in greased muffin tins at 400° until done, about 10 minutes.

Dewey Rolls

VERMONT

Adapted from Pixley, *Vermont Country Cooking*

1⅓   cups flour
2   teaspoons baking powder
⅓   cup sugar
½   teaspoon salt

2   eggs, beaten
½   cup milk
4   tablespoons melted butter

1. Sift the dry ingredients together.
2. Add the eggs, milk, and melted butter. Stir to form a smooth batter. Pour into small ungreased muffin rings.
3. Bake at 400° for 10 minutes, or until done.

Butterscotch Bread Pudding

MAINE

Adapted from Roux, *What's Cooking Down in Maine*

1   cup light brown sugar
4   slices buttered bread, cubed
3   eggs

2   cups milk
1   teaspoon vanilla
½   teaspoon salt

1. Put the brown sugar and the bread in the top of a double boiler.
2. Beat the eggs and add the milk, vanilla, and salt to them. Pour this over the bread mixture. Cook over simmering water 5 minutes to warm the mixture.
3. Pour the batter into an ungreased 2-quart baking dish and set it in a pan half filled with hot water.
4. Bake it at 350° for one hour. Do not stir.

Federal Bread

MARYLAND
Adapted from *Tested Maryland Recipes*

1½	pounds flour	½	teacup yeast
1	pint milk	3	eggs
2	ounces butter		salt

1. Mix all of the ingredients together. Stir well to form a smooth dough.
2. Place the dough in an ungreased 8-inch baking pan and allow to rise until doubled in bulk.
3. Bake at 350° for 45 minutes, or until done.

Zucchini Bread

NEW JERSEY
Adapted from *Chicken Foot Soup and Other Recipes from the Pine Barrens*

3	eggs	1	teaspoon baking soda
¾	cup honey	1	teaspoon baking powder
¾	cup light brown sugar	½	teaspoon salt
½	cup vegetable oil	¾	teaspoon ground ginger
3	cups peeled, grated, and squeezed zucchini	2	cups white flour
		2	cups whole wheat flour
1	teaspoon cinnamon		

1. Beat the eggs with the honey, brown sugar, and oil to blend. Stir in the zucchini.
2. Sift the cinnamon, baking soda, baking powder, salt, ginger, white flour, and whole wheat flour together. Stir this into the zucchini mixture, a little at a time, until well blended. Pour the batter into two ungreased 8-inch loaf pans.
3. Bake at 350° for 1 hour, or until a knife comes out clean.

Pumpkin Bread

NEW JERSEY

Adapted from *Chicken Foot Soup and Other Recipes from the Pine Barrens*

2 cups flour	1 cup cooked pumpkin
2 teaspoons baking powder	1 cup sugar
½ teaspoon baking soda	½ cup milk
½ teaspoon salt	2 eggs
1 teaspoon cinnamon	¼ cup softened butter
½ teaspoon nutmeg	1 cup chopped nuts

1. Sift the flour, leavenings, and spices together. Stir in the remaining ingredients in the order given. Mix well.
2. Pour the batter into 2 greased and floured 8-inch loaf pans.
3. Bake at 350° for about 1 hour.

Carrot Bread

NEW JERSEY

Adapted from *Chicken Foot Soup and Other Recipes from the Pine Barrens*

¾ cup flour	¾ cup olive oil
¾ cup whole wheat flour	2 eggs
⅛ teaspoon salt	1 cup honey, warmed
½ teaspoon cinnamon	1 cup grated carrots
1 teaspoon baking soda	¾ cup chopped nuts
1 teaspoon baking powder	

1. Sift the flours, salt, cinnamon, baking soda, and baking powder together.
2. Add the oil and eggs and blend until smooth. Add the warmed honey and stir well.
3. Mix in the carrots and nuts and pour the batter into a greased 10-inch loaf pan.
4. Bake at 350° for 45–50 minutes.

Cheddar, Bacon, and Olive Bread

NEW YORK

Adapted from *A Library of Favorite Recipes from New York State*

2½	cups flour	1	cup cheddar cheese, grated
2½	tablespoons sugar	1	egg
2	teaspoons baking powder	1	cup buttermilk
½	teaspoon baking soda	1	teaspoon Worcestershire
1	teaspoon salt		sauce
1	teaspoon dry mustard	5	slices bacon, cooked and
	generous pinch ground		crumbled
	cayenne pepper	1	cup pitted ripe olives,
¼	cup margarine, softened		coarsely chopped

1. Mix the dry ingredients together. Cut in the margarine with a fork until the mixture resembles coarse meal. Stir in the grated cheese.
2. Combine the egg, buttermilk, and Worcestershire sauce. Make a well in the flour mixture and pour in the liquid; mix until just moistened. Stir in the bacon and olives.
3. Turn the batter into a greased 8- or 9-inch loaf pan.
4. Bake at 375° for 40 minutes.

Oatmeal Ribbon Loaf

DELAWARE

Adapted from *Winterthur's Culinary Collection*

2	tablespoons shortening	1	teaspoon cinnamon
1½	cups all-purpose flour	1	cup oatmeal
½	cup sugar	1	egg
2	teaspoons baking powder	⅔	cup orange juice
⅓	teaspoon baking soda	⅓	cup water
½	teaspoon salt	1	cup raisins

1. Melt and cool the shortening.
2. Mix the first 6 dry ingredients. Stir in the oatmeal and egg and beat well.
3. Add the cooled shortening to the oatmeal mixture.
4. Combine the orange juice and water and add to the batter. Mix well.
5. Pour half the batter into a greased loaf pan, sprinkle with the raisins, then pour in the remaining batter.
6. Bake at 350° for 40–50 minutes.

Philadelphia Cinnamon Buns

PENNSYLVANIA

Adapted from Reed, *The Philadelphia Cook Book of Town and Country*

Cake:

1	cake yeast	½	cup sugar
¼	cup lukewarm water	¼	cup melted butter
1	cup scalded milk, cooled to lukewarm	½	teaspoon salt
		2	egg yolks
4	cups flour, sifted		butter, melted

Filling:

6	tablespoons light brown sugar	2	teaspoons cinnamon
		½	cup raisins

Pan:

	melted butter	¾	cup dark corn syrup
1	pound light brown sugar		

1. Dissolve the yeast in the warm water and add it to the lukewarm milk.
2. Stir in 2 cups of sifted flour and allow the mixture to stand for about 20 minutes.
3. Add the sugar, ¼ cup melted butter, salt, and egg yolks. Mix well. Stir in enough additional flour to make a soft dough.
4. Knead for 10 minutes. Cover and allow to rise until doubled in bulk.
5. Divide the dough in 2 pieces. Roll each piece into a ¼-inch thickness, 15-by-10 inches. Brush the surface with melted butter.
6. To make the filling, mix the brown sugar, cinnamon, and raisins together and spread over the dough. Roll up jelly-roll fashion and cut into slices 1½ inches thick.
7. To prepare the pan, grease a deep 3-quart baking dish with melted butter. Sprinkle it generously with the brown sugar and pour the corn syrup over. Place the buns close together in the pan. Brush them with additional melted butter and allow them to rise until light.
8. Bake at 325° for 45 minutes. Remove the buns from the pan immediately.

Easy Sour Cream Coffee Cake

NEW YORK

Adapted from *A Library of Favorite Recipes from New York State*

Cake:

½ cup soft butter
1 cup sugar
2 eggs
1 teaspoon vanilla
2 cups flour

1 teaspoon baking powder
¼ teaspoon salt
1¼ teaspoons baking soda
½ pint sour cream

Filling:

½ cup ground walnuts
1 teaspoon cinnamon

¼ cup sugar

1. Cream the butter and sugar. Add the eggs, one at a time, and beat well. Add the vanilla.
2. Add the flour, baking powder, salt, and baking soda. Mix well. Add the sour cream and beat for 1 minute.
3. Pour half of the batter into a greased tube pan.
4. Stir all the filling ingredients together. Sprinkle half of the filling mixture on the cake in the tube pan. Add the remaining batter and top with the remaining filling mixture. Lightly mix the top filling into the batter.
5. Bake at 350° for 45–55 minutes.

COFFEE CAKES AND SWEET YEAST BUNS

Rhubarb Coffee Cake

NEW YORK

Adapted from *A Library of Favorite Recipes from New York State*

1½ cups light brown sugar	2 cups flour
½ cup shortening	1 teaspoon baking soda
1 egg	½ teaspoon salt
1 cup sour cream	1½ cups raw rhubarb, cut into ½-inch pieces

Topping:

½ cup sugar	½ tablespoon butter, melted
½ cup chopped walnuts	1 teaspoon cinnamon

1. Mix the brown sugar and shortening together. Beat 1 minute. Add the egg and sour cream.
2. Sift the flour, baking soda, and salt together and mix into the liquids a bit at a time, forming a smooth batter. Fold in the rhubarb. Pour into a 9-by-13-inch greased and floured pan.
3. Prepare the topping by mixing all the ingredients. Sprinkle this on top of the coffee cake.
4. Bake at 350° for 45 minutes, or until just done.

CORNMEAL BREADS

Maryland Rice Bread

MARYLAND

Adapted from *Tested Maryland Recipes*

⅛ teaspoon salt	1 pint milk
2 cups cooked white rice, cooled	1 cup cornmeal
1 tablespoon lard or butter	3 eggs, separated butter

1. Stir the lard or butter and salt into the cooked rice.
2. Mix the milk, cornmeal, and egg yolks together. Add the rice mixture to the milk mixture and stir in the egg whites. Pour the batter into a buttered 8-inch square baking dish.
3. Bake at 400° until set, about 20 minutes.

Onion Shortbread

DELAWARE

Adapted from *Winterthur's Culinary Collection*

1	large onion, sliced thin		several dashes Tabasco
¼	cup butter	1	17-ounce can cream-style
12	ounces cornmeal		corn
¼	teaspoon salt	1	cup sour cream
2	teaspoons baking soda	¼	teaspoon dill seed
1	egg, beaten	1	cup sharp cheddar cheese,
⅓	cup milk		grated

1. Preheat the oven to 425°.
2. Sauté the onions in the butter until translucent. Set aside.
3. Mix the cornmeal with the salt and baking soda. Mix the egg, milk, Tabasco, and corn.
4. Combine the 2 mixtures and stir to form a batter. Pour into a buttered 8-inch square pan.
5. Combine the sour cream, dill seed, sautéed onions, and half the cheddar cheese. Spread over the batter. Sprinkle with the remaining cheese.
6. Bake at 425° for 25–30 minutes. Serve warm.

Indian Muffins

NEW JERSEY

Adapted from *Chicken Foot Soup and Other Recipes from the Pine Barrens*

1	egg	2	heaping tablespoons
1	teaspoon melted lard, cooled		cornmeal
		2	teaspoons baking powder
½	cup evaporated milk	1½	cups flour
½	cup water		

1. Whisk the egg and mix it with the lard, evaporated milk, and water.
2. Sift the dry ingredients together and add them to the egg mixture. Mix briefly to form a smooth batter.
3. Bake in greased muffin tins at 450° for about 20 minutes.

Plunkets

PENNSYLVANIA

Adapted from Reed, *The Philadelphia Cook Book of Town and Country*

8	ounces butter	2	cups rice flour
2	cups powdered sugar	1	teaspoon vanilla
4	eggs, separated		sugar

1. Cream the butter with the sugar until light. Add the egg yolks and beat until smooth.
2. Beat the egg whites until stiff and fold them into the creamed mixture. Stir in the rice flour. Add the vanilla and beat until light. Pour the batter into greased small muffin tins.
3. Bake at 350° for 20 minutes. Dust the tops with sugar.

Bread Crumb Muffins

MARYLAND

Adapted from *Tested Maryland Recipes*

2	cups unseasoned bread crumbs	2	cups flour
2	cups milk	1	teaspoon baking soda
2	eggs, separated	2	teaspoons cream of tartar

1. Soak the bread crumbs in the milk until soft. Add the egg yolks.
2. Sift the flour with the baking soda.
3. Beat the eggs whites until foamy. Add the cream of tartar and beat until stiff peaks form.
4. Stir the flour mixture into the bread crumb mixture. Fold in the egg whites to form a smooth batter.
5. Bake in greased muffin pans at 400° for 10 minutes, or until set.

Apple Muffins

NEW YORK

Adapted from Wilson, *American Cooking: The Eastern Heartland*

2	cups unsifted flour	1	cup sour cream
4	teaspoons baking powder	3	medium cooking apples,
¼	teaspoon baking soda		peeled, cored, and finely
½	teaspoon ground mace		chopped (about 1 cup)
½	teaspoon salt	1	medium cooking apple,
4	tablespoons butter,		unpeeled, cored, and cut
	softened		lengthwise into ⅛-inch
¼	cup sugar		thick slices
2	eggs		

1. Sift the flour, baking powder, baking soda, mace, and salt together.
2. Cream the butter and the sugar together until the mixture is light and fluffy. Beat in the eggs, one at a time.
3. Stir about 1 cup of the flour mixture into the butter, then beat in ½ cup of the sour cream. Repeat and stir until the batter is smooth.
4. Stir in the chopped apples and spoon the batter into buttered and floured muffin cups, filling each cup halfway. Insert a slice of apple, peel side up, into the top of each muffin.
5. Bake at 400° for 15–20 minutes, or until the muffins are brown.

ROLLS AND PRETZELS

Popovers

NEW JERSEY

Adapted from *Chicken Foot Soup and Other Recipes from the Pine Barrens*

1	cup milk	1	cup flour
¼	teaspoon salt	2	eggs

1. Mix the ingredients together in the order given.
2. Pour the batter into greased popover cups (or muffin tins), filling each halfway.
3. Place the pan in a cold oven, turn the heat to 450°, and bake for 35 minutes.

ROLLS AND PRETZELS

Bagels

NEW YORK
Meyer family recipe

1	tablespoon dry yeast	3–4 cups bread flour
2¼	cups warm water	1 tablespoon gluten powder
3	tablespoons shortening	1 tablespoon malt powder
1	tablespoon salt	egg white, beaten
1	tablespoon sugar	¼ cup sugar

1. Dissolve the yeast in ¼ cup of the warm water. Stir in the shortening, salt, and sugar. Add the remaining water and stir to blend.
2. Mix 3 cups of the flour with the gluten and malt. Add this to the liquid mixture and beat until smooth. Continue to beat for 5 minutes.
3. Add additional flour to form a soft, smooth dough. Knead for 5 minutes.
4. Allow the dough to rise until doubled in bulk. Punch down and divide the dough into 12 portions.
5. Roll each portion into a rope about 8 inches in length. Form each rope into a circle, pinching the ends to seal each bagel.
6. Brush each bagel with egg white and carefully slip them into a large pot of simmering water to which ¼ cup of sugar has been added. Do not crowd them.
7. Remove the bagels from the water when they have risen completely and are firm. Allow them to dry for a minute. Brush them again with egg white and place the bagels on a baking sheet.
8. Place the baking sheets in a 500° oven and immediately lower the heat to 425°. Bake for 20–25 minutes.

Whizzer Rolls

PENNSYLVANIA
Adapted from *Choice Recipes*

1 cake yeast	½ cup milk, scalded
¼ cup lukewarm water	2 eggs
¼ cup shortening	2 cups sifted flour
1 tablespoon sugar	3 tablespoons melted butter
¾ teaspoon salt	

1. Soften the yeast in the water. Stir to dissolve.
2. Stir the shortening, sugar, and salt into the hot milk. Allow to cool to lukewarm.
3. Add the eggs, yeast mixture, and flour. Beat vigorously for several minutes. Cover and allow to rise for about 1 hour.
4. Spoon into greased muffin tins, filling halfway. Let them rise until double in bulk.
5. Pour ½ teaspoon of melted butter over each roll.
6. Bake at 375° degrees for 20 minutes.

Soft Pretzels

PENNSYLVANIA
Adapted from Lestz, *The Pennsylvania Dutch Cookbook*

1 envelope yeast	2 tablespoons butter, softened
1¼ cups warm water	
¼ teaspoon sugar	4 cups water
2 teaspoons salt	4 teaspoons baking soda
4–5 cups flour	2 tablespoons coarse salt

1. Dissolve the yeast in ¼ cup warm water. Add the additional cup of warm water and the sugar. Add the salt and mix.
2. Beat in enough flour to make a stiff dough. Knead for 10 minutes (until dough is elastic) and place in a bowl. Spread the dough with the 2 tablespoons butter, cover, and let rise for 45 minutes, or until doubled in bulk.
3. Punch down and shape pretzels into sticks or twists.
4. Bring 4 cups of water to a boil with the baking soda. Drop 3 pretzels in at a time and boil for 1 minute, or until they float to the surface. Remove and drain.
5. Place the pretzels on a buttered cookie sheet and sprinkle with coarse salt.
6. Bake at 475° for about 12 minutes, or until golden brown. Allow to cool on a wire rack.

Rye Pretzels

NEW YORK

Adapted from *A Library of Favorite Recipes from New York State*

1 package active dry yeast	1 teaspoon salt
1½ cups warm water	4 – 4¾ cups rye flour
1 tablespoon malted milk powder	1 tablespoon caraway seeds
1 tablespoon molasses	coarse or kosher salt

1. Dissolve the yeast in the water. Add the malted milk powder, molasses, and salt. Stir in enough rye flour to form a smooth dough and the caraway seeds. Knead until smooth, about 5 minutes.
2. Cut into 12 portions. Roll each into a rope 15 inches long. Shape into pretzels.
3. Place the pretzels on a greased baking sheet. Mist with water. Sprinkle with coarse or kosher salt.
4. Bake at 425° for 25 minutes, or until golden brown.

Buttermilk Soda Biscuits

PENNSYLVANIA

Adapted from Reed, *The Philadelphia Cook Book of Town and Country*

1¾ cups bread flour	½ teaspoon baking soda
1 teaspoon salt	¾ cup buttermilk
3 teaspoons baking powder	4 tablespoons melted butter

1. Sift the flour, salt, baking powder, and baking soda together.
2. Add the buttermilk to the melted butter and stir this liquid into the dry ingredients. Mix to form a soft, smooth dough.
3. Roll the dough out to ½-inch thickness. Cut with a small biscuit cutter and place on a greased baking sheet.
4. Bake at 450° for about 12 minutes.

Maryland Biscuit

MARYLAND
Adapted from *Tested Maryland Recipes*

3	pounds flour	1	pint water
½	pound lard	2	teaspoons salt

1. Mix all of the ingredients. Beat hard until the dough "blisters," about 10 minutes.
2. Pat the dough into an ungreased 8-inch square cake pan or roll and cut into 3-inch circles.
3. Bake at 425° for 20 minutes.

Split Potato Biscuit

MARYLAND
Adapted from *Tested Maryland Recipes*

2	large white potatoes, boiled and sieved	2	eggs, well beaten
½	cup lard	1	cup milk
½	cup butter	½	cake yeast, crumbled
⅛	teaspoon salt	1	tablespoon sugar
		6	cups flour

1. While the potatoes are still warm, stir in the lard and butter. Stir in the salt and eggs.
2. Add the milk, yeast cake, sugar, and 4 cups of flour. Allow to rise until doubled in bulk.
3. Add the remaining flour and knead for 5 minutes. Allow to rise 30 minutes.
4. Roll the dough thin and cut with a 2-inch biscuit cutter. Place half of the biscuits on an ungreased baking sheet and stack the other half on the first layer. Allow to rise 30 minutes.
5. Bake at 400° until golden brown.

BISCUITS

Shortcake Soda Biscuits

PENNSYLVANIA
Adapted from Lestz, *The Pennsylvania Dutch Cookbook*

2	cups sifted all-purpose flour	½	teaspoons salt
½	teaspoon baking soda	4	tablespoons shortening
		¾	cup buttermilk

1. Mix the flour, baking soda, and salt together. Cut in the shortening as for pie dough.
2. Add enough buttermilk to the crumbs to make a soft dough. Knead lightly a few times. Roll or pat out to ½-inch thickness. Cut into squares.
3. Bake on a greased cookie sheet at 475° for 12 minutes, or until brown.

South Atlantic

YEAST BREADS

Sally Lunn

VIRGINIA
Adapted from *The Junior League Cook Book*

2	eggs	4	cups flour
1	tablespoon sugar	1	cup milk
2	tablespoons lard	½	cup yeast starter
2	tablespoons butter		

1. Beat the eggs lightly. Add the sugar, lard, and butter and beat for 2 minutes.
2. Mix in the flour and milk. Beat in the yeast starter. Allow to rise for 4 hours.
3. Pour the dough into an 8-inch square pan and allow it to rise for 2 hours.
4. Bake at 400° for 40 minutes, or until done.

Editor's note: See the recipe for Everlasting Starter, p. 137.

Crusty Cuban Bread

FLORIDA

Adapted from Nickerson, *Florida Cookbook*

6½ cups flour
2 packages dry yeast
2 cups water

2 tablespoons sugar
2 teaspoons salt

1. Mix 2 cups of the flour and the yeast together.
2. Heat the water, sugar, and salt until warm to the touch, about 120°.
3. Add this to the flour mixture. Beat until smooth, about 3 minutes.
4. Stir in enough additional flour to make a stiff dough. Knead for 10 minutes, or until the dough becomes smooth and quite elastic. Allow to rise for 45 minutes.
5. Divide the dough into thirds. Roll each third into a rectangle about 10-by-13 inches. Roll each rectangle into a long cylinder and press the ends together. Fold the ends under the loaf.
6. Place the cylinders seam side down on an ungreased baking sheet. Make small diagonal cuts across the top of each loaf with a sharp knife. Brush each loaf with water. Allow to rise in a warm place for about 20 minutes.
7. Starting the loaves in a cold oven, turn to heat to 400° and bake for 45 minutes. Remove them from the oven to cool. Maintain the oven temperature.
8. Return the loaves to the oven for 10 minutes.

Onion Casserole Bread

NORTH CAROLINA

Adapted from *Pass the Plate*

1 cup milk
¼ cup sugar
2 teaspoons salt
¼ cup margarine
2 tablespoons dry yeast

½ cup lukewarm water
1 egg
4½ cups flour
1 16-ounce can french fried onion rings, crushed

1. Scald the milk. Add the sugar, salt, and margarine. Allow to cool.
2. Dissolve the yeast in the lukewarm water. Add the milk mixture, the egg, and 3 cups of flour. Beat until smooth.
3. Add the remaining flour. Cover and allow to rise 1 hour.
4. Add the onion rings and mix well. Pour into two greased 3-quart casseroles.
5. Bake at 350° for 40 minutes, or until breads pull away from the sides of the pans.

Aunt Roberta's Dilly Bread

NORTH CAROLINA
Adapted from *Pass the Plate*

2½–3 cups flour
  2 tablespoons sugar
  1 tablespoon dehydrated onion
  2 teaspoons dill seed
1¼ teaspoons coarse salt
  ¼ teaspoon baking soda
  1 envelope dry yeast

½ cup creamed cottage cheese
¼ cup water
  1 tablespoon butter or margarine
  1 egg
    melted butter
    coarse salt

1. Combine 1½ cups of the flour with the sugar, onion, dill seed, salt, baking soda, and yeast.
2. In a saucepan heat the cottage cheese with the water and butter until the butter melts and the mixture is warm.
3. Add the egg and the cottage cheese mixture to the dry ingredients. Blend until smooth, about 3 minutes.
4. Stir in enough of the remaining flour to form a stiff dough. Knead until smooth. Cover and allow to rise until doubled, about 1 hour.
5. Stir down the dough and place it in a well-greased 8-inch round casserole pan. Allow to rise until light, about a half hour.
6. Bake at 350° for 35–40 minutes, or until golden brown.
7. Brush with melted butter and sprinkle with coarse salt, if desired.

English Muffin Bread

SOUTH CAROLINA
Adapted from *A Taste of South Carolina*

3–4 cups self-rising flour
2 packages dry yeast
¼ cup sugar
1¼ cups very hot tap water

½ cup oil
2 eggs
cornmeal

1. Mix 3½ cups flour, the yeast, and the sugar in a large bowl. Add the very hot water and mix until the sugar dissolves. Beat until smooth.
2. Blend in the oil and eggs. Add enough of the remaining flour to make a stiff batter. Beat until the batter is smooth and elastic, about 2 minutes.
3. Cover and let rise in a warm place until light and bubbly, about 1 hour. Punch down.
4. Divide the dough into 3 well-greased and cornmeal-dusted 1-pound coffee cans. Cover and let rise in a warm place until doubled, about 40 minutes.
5. Bake at 375° for 15–20 minutes, or until done.

Buttermilk Bread

TENNESSEE
Adapted from Dalsass, *Miss Mary's Down-Home Cooking*

1 package active dry yeast
½ cup warm water
⅓ cup sugar
2 teaspoons salt
1 teaspoon baking soda

2 cups buttermilk
4 ounces butter
1 egg
7–8 cups flour

1. In a large bowl, dissolve the yeast in the warm water. Add the sugar, salt, and baking soda.
2. In a saucepan, heat the buttermilk with the butter until the buttermilk is quite warm. Add this to the yeast mixture, along with the egg and 1 cup of flour. Beat well.
3. Stir in enough additional flour, about 1 cup at a time, to make a firm dough. Knead, adding more flour if necessary, until the dough is stiff and elastic.
4. Place the dough in a greased bowl and allow it to rise until doubled in bulk. Turn the dough onto a floured surface and knead briefly.
5. Divide the dough in half and shape each half into a loaf. Place each in a greased 9-by-5-inch loaf pan. Cover and let rise until doubled.
6. Bake at 400° for 10 minutes. Lower the heat to 350° and bake 35 minutes longer, or until loaves are golden brown.

Sunday Hot Bread

VIRGINIA

Adapted from *The Junior League Cook Book*

¾ cup sugar	1½ cups bread flour
2 tablespoons butter	3 teaspoons baking powder
¼ teaspoon salt	2 tablespoons light brown
1 egg, beaten	sugar
¾ cup milk	1 teaspoon cinnamon
1 teaspoon lemon extract	

1. Cream the sugar and butter together. Add the salt and the egg and mix well. Stir in the milk and lemon extract.
2. Sift the flour with the baking powder and beat into the creamed mixture.
3. Pour the batter into 2 greased 8-inch cake pans and sprinkle with a mixture of the brown sugar and cinnamon.
4. Bake at 400° for 20–25 minutes.

Orange Marmalade Nut Bread

SOUTH CAROLINA

Adapted from *The South Carolina Cook Book*

3 cups sifted pastry flour	1 cup sweet milk
3 teaspoons baking powder	½ cup walnut meats, chopped
½ teaspoon salt	1 teaspoon grated orange
4 tablespoons sugar	peel
1 egg, beaten	½ cup orange marmalade
2 tablespoons melted shortening	

1. Sift the first four ingredients together.
2. Add the remaining ingredients in the order given. Stir well to form a smooth batter.
3. Pour the batter into a well-greased loaf pan and allow to stand for 10 minutes.
4. Bake at 350° for 1 hour.

Ogontz Cinnamon Buns

VIRGINIA
Adapted from *The Junior League Cook Book*

½ cup sugar	4–6 cups flour
4 ounces butter	2 ounces melted butter
3 eggs	¼ cup currants
⅛ teaspoon salt	2 tablespoons light brown
2 cups water	sugar
1 tablespoon dry yeast	2 teaspoons cinnamon

1. Cream the sugar and butter together. Beat in the eggs, salt, water, and yeast.
2. Add enough flour to make a soft bread dough. Knead for 5 minutes and refrigerate overnight.
3. Roll out the dough to ¼-inch thickness. Spread the dough with the melted butter, add the currants, brown sugar, and cinnamon.
4. Roll the dough up like a jelly roll and cut into 1½-inch pieces.
5. Place the rolls in a well-greased pan and allow them to rise for about 1 hour.
6. Bake at 350° for about 1 hour.

Mayonnaise Corn Bread

WEST VIRGINIA
Adapted from *The Foxfire Book of Appalachian Cookery*

1 cup self-rising cornmeal	1 egg
1 cup self-rising flour	1 tablespoon mayonnaise
½ cup milk	

1. Mix all of the ingredients together. Beat until smooth.
2. Pour the batter into a greased cast iron skillet and bake at 450° until done.

Buttermilk Cracklin Bread

KENTUCKY

Adapted from *The Foxfire Book of Appalachian Cookery*

2 cups cornmeal	½ teaspoon baking powder
2 teaspoons salt	1 cup buttermilk
1 teaspoon baking soda	½ cup cracklins

1. Mix the cornmeal, salt, baking soda, and baking powder together. Stir in the buttermilk to form a smooth batter.
2. Mix in the cracklins. Add a little warm water if the batter is too dry.
3. Bake in a greased 8-inch square pan at 425° for ½ hour, or until brown.

"Granny Gibson told us: 'You can put cracklins in it. That's what I like—cracklin bread. You know when you kill a hog you've got all kinds of fat and stuff. You have to cut it up and put it on the stove and cook it out to make your lard. You have to keep it stirred, and it'll fry down to the cracklins. That's where your cracklins comes in at. Put them in with your corn bread whenever you go to cook it. That makes it good.'"

Good Old-Fashioned Corn Lightbread

APPALACHIA

Adapted from *The Foxfire Book of Appalachian Cookery*

4 cups cornmeal mush or leftover grits	¾ cup sugar
½ teaspoon salt	¾ cup lard
	cornmeal

1. Cook the cornmeal mush until done. Stir in the salt.
2. Remove the mush from the heat and add cold water until it's cool enough to the touch to not burn.
3. Stir in the sugar, lard, and enough cornmeal to make a thick batter. Allow the batter to stand overnight, unrefrigerated, until it ferments.
4. Bake in a well-greased 8-inch cast iron skillet at 350° until golden brown.

Corn Pones

KENTUCKY

Adapted from *The Foxfire Book of Appalachian Cookery*

2 cups cornmeal	1 tablespoon lard
1 teaspoon baking powder	milk
½ teaspoon salt	

1. Mix the cornmeal, baking powder, and salt together.
2. Add the lard and enough milk to form a smooth batter. Drop by tablespoonfuls onto a greased baking sheet.
3. Bake at 400° for 8–10 minutes.
4. Alternately, bake in an 8-inch square greased baking dish until set and golden on the edges and cut into squares for serving.

Spoon Bread

VIRGINIA

Adapted from *The Junior League Cook Book*

1 cup cornmeal	2 eggs
2 cups warm water	2 teaspoons salt
1 cup milk	1 tablespoon butter

1. Mix the cornmeal with the water and cook over medium heat, stirring constantly, for 3 minutes. Remove from the heat.
2. Add the milk beaten with the eggs, then the salt and butter.
3. Pour the batter into a greased 8-inch square pan.
4. Bake at 425° for 25 minutes, or until well browned.

"Serve in baking pan."

CORNMEAL BREADS

Batter Bread

VIRGINIA

Adapted from *The Junior League Cook Book*

2 eggs	1 cup cold cooked rice
2 cups milk	1 tablespoon melted butter
1 teaspoon baking powder	cornmeal
½ teaspoon salt	

1. Beat the eggs very lightly. Stir in the milk.
2. Mix the baking powder and salt with the rice. Beat in the butter. Stir in the egg/milk mixture.
3. Add enough cornmeal to make a very soft batter. Pour the batter into a greased 8-inch square baking pan.
4. Bake at 425° for 40 minutes.

Grits Bread

VIRGINIA

Adapted from *The Junior League Cook Book*

1 cup cooked hominy grits	1 tablespoon butter, softened
½ cup flour	milk
½ teaspoon baking powder	1 egg, separated

1. Mix the hominy grits with the flour and baking powder. Stir in the butter.
2. Add enough milk to make a stiff batter. Stir in the egg yolk.
3. Whip the egg white stiff and fold it into the dough. Pour the batter into a greased 8-inch loaf pan.
4. Bake at 375° until set, about 20 minutes.

Cornmeal Cakes

VIRGINIA

Adapted from *The Junior League Cook Book*

1 egg	1 teaspoon salt
12 fluid ounces sour milk	1 teaspoon baking soda
2 cups cornmeal	1 tablespoon melted lard

1. Beat the egg lightly and add the sour milk.
2. Sift the cornmeal, salt, and baking soda into the milk mixture. Stir in the lard.
3. Drop by tablespoonfuls onto a greased baking sheet.
4. Bake at 425° for 5 minutes.

Florida Spoon Bread or Baked Grits

FLORIDA
Adapted from Nickerson, *Florida Cookbook*

½ cup grits (regular, not quick-cooking)	2 eggs, beaten
	2 cups milk
½ teaspoon salt	1 cup white cornmeal
2 tablespoons butter	

1. Cook the grits and salt according to package directions.
2. Stir in the butter, eggs, and milk. Slowly add the cornmeal, stirring constantly. Beat until smooth. Pour the batter into a buttered 6-quart casserole dish.
3. Bake at 400° for 45 minutes, or until a knife inserted in the center comes out clean.

Old Fashioned Southern Egg Bread

SOUTH CAROLINA
Adapted from *The South Carolina Cook Book*

2 cups water-ground cornmeal	½ cup shortening
	2 cups milk
3 level tablespoons sugar	2 eggs, well beaten
1 level teaspoon salt	1 tablespoon baking powder

1. Sift the cornmeal, sugar, and salt together.
2. Melt the shortening in an 8-inch square pan. Add this slowly to the cornmeal mixture, alternating with the milk. Beat hard for 1 minute.
3. Add the eggs and the baking powder. Stir to form a smooth batter.
4. Bake at 350° for 20–30 minutes.

CORNMEAL BREADS

Owendaw

TENNESSEE

Adapted from Dalsass, *Miss Mary's Down-Home Cooking*

2	cups cooked grits, hot	2	cups milk
3	tablespoons butter	1	cup cornmeal
4	eggs	½	teaspoon salt

1. Mix the hot cooked grits with the butter.
2. Beat the eggs well and add them to the grits.
3. Stir in the milk gradually. Add the cornmeal and salt. Add a little more milk if the batter seems too thick.
4. Bake in a greased deep casserole at 350° for 45–60 minutes.

MUFFINS AND TEA BISCUITS

Honey Tea Cakes

WEST VIRGINIA

Adapted from *The Foxfire Book of Appalachian Cookery*

2	cups flour	2	eggs
½	teaspoon baking soda	1	cup honey
1	teaspoon baking powder	1	cup sour cream
½	teaspoon salt	1	teaspoon lemon juice

1. Sift the dry ingredients together.
2. Beat the eggs and honey together until blended.
3. Add the sour cream and lemon juice to the egg mixture and add this to the dry ingredients. Mix to form a smooth batter.
4. Spoon the batter into greased muffin tins.
5. Bake at 350° for 15–20 minutes.

Green Corn Gems

VIRGINIA

Adapted from *The Junior League Cook Book*

2 cups golden bantam corn, cut from cob	2 cups flour
¼ cup milk (½ cup if corn is dry)	3 teaspoons baking powder
	1 teaspoon salt
2 eggs	⅛ teaspoon pepper

1. Chop the corn coarsely. Add the milk and eggs and blend well.
2. Sift the flour, baking powder, salt, and pepper together. Add this to the liquid mixture. Blend until smooth.
3. Pour the batter into hot greased muffin tins.
4. Bake at 400° for about 25 minutes.

Beer Muffins

SOUTH CAROLINA

Adapted from *A Taste of South Carolina*

4 cups biscuit mix	1 can beer
2 tablespoons sugar	

1. Mix all ingredients and beat 30 seconds.
2. Fill hot greased muffin tins two-thirds full.
3. Bake at 400° for about 15 minutes.

Rice Muffins

VIRGINIA

Adapted from the *Marion Cook Book*

1 cup milk	½ teaspoon salt
2 eggs, beaten	1 tablespoon sugar
5 tablespoons butter, melted	1 tablespoon baking powder
1 cup cooked rice, cooled	1½ cups all-purpose flour

1. Mix the milk, eggs, and butter together. Stir in the rice.
2. Sift the dry ingredients and stir into the rice mixture to make a soft batter.
3. Drop spoonfuls into hot, well-buttered muffin tins.
4. Bake at 400° for 20 minutes.

Cream Ginger Gems

VIRGINIA
Adapted from the *Marion Cook Book*

1 cup sour cream	½ teaspoon cinnamon
½ cup sugar	1 teaspoon baking soda
½ cup molasses	2 cups all-purpose flour
2 eggs, beaten	½ teaspoon salt
½ teaspoon ground ginger	

1. Mix the sour cream, sugar, molasses, and eggs.
2. Sift the dry ingredients and stir into the liquids to form a smooth batter.
3. Bake at 375° for 15 minutes, or until browned.

ROLLS

Potato Refrigerator Rolls

APPALACHIA
Adapted from *The Foxfire Book of Appalachian Cookery*

1 cup milk, scalded	1 package dry yeast
½ cup sugar	½ cup lukewarm water
⅔ cup shortening	2 eggs, well beaten
1 teaspoon salt	5½–6 cups sifted flour
1 cup mashed potatoes, cooled	melted butter

1. Mix the scalded milk with the sugar, shortening, salt, and mashed potatoes. Stir together and allow the mixture to cool.
2. Dissolve the yeast in the lukewarm water and add it to the cooled potato mixture.
3. Beat in the eggs and enough flour to make a smooth, soft dough. Cover and refrigerate overnight or up to a week.
4. Form the dough into small rolls. Place them in a greased baking pan and brush them with melted butter. Allow the rolls to rise until doubled in bulk.
5. Bake at 400° for 15–20 minutes, or until lightly browned.

Girvin Rolls

VIRGINIA

Adapted from *The Junior League Cook Book*

2 tablespoons lard	2 eggs
2 tablespoons butter	1 cake yeast
2 tablespoons sugar	1 teaspoon warm water
1 tablespoon salt	6 cups flour
2 cups milk	pecan halves or pieces

1. Heat the lard, butter, sugar, and salt in the milk until the fats are melted and the sugar is dissolved. Allow to cool slightly.
2. Beat the eggs and add them to the milk.
3. Dissolve the yeast in the warm water and add it to the milk.
4. Stir in the flour and beat until smooth. Allow the batter to rise for 45 minutes.
5. Spoon tablespoonfuls into ungreased muffin rings on baking sheets. Place pecans on each.
6. Bake at 400° for 8–10 minutes.

Rich Dinner Rolls

NORTH CAROLINA

Adapted from *Pass the Plate*

1 cup milk	½ cup warm water
¼ cup sugar	1 tablespoon dry yeast
1 teaspoon salt	2 eggs, beaten
¼ cup margarine	5¼ cups unsifted flour

1. Scald the milk. Stir in the sugar, salt, and margarine. Mix until the margarine dissolves. Cool to lukewarm.
2. To the warm water add the yeast. Stir until dissolved.
3. Add the milk mixture, eggs, and 2 cups of flour to the yeast. Beat until smooth.
4. Stir in enough of the remaining flour to make a soft dough. Knead until smooth and elastic, about 8 minutes. Cover and allow to rise in warm place for about 30 minutes.
5. Punch the dough down and divide it into 3 equal pieces. Form each piece into a 9-inch-long roll. Cut each roll into 9 equal pieces and form into smooth balls.
6. Place the rolls into 3 greased round cake pans. Cover and let rise until doubled in bulk, about 30 minutes. Brush lightly with melted margarine.
7. Bake at 375° for 15–20 minutes.

Crescent Rolls

NORTH CAROLINA
Adapted from *Pass the Plate*

2 packages dry yeast	1½ cups boiling water
½ cup warm water	1 teaspoon salt
¾ cup vegetable shortening	2 eggs
1 tablespoon sugar	6 cups sifted flour

1. Dissolve the yeast in the warm water and allow to rest 5 minutes.
2. Place the shortening and sugar in a mixing bowl. Pour in the boiling water. Mix at low speed to combine and dissolve the sugar and shortening. Cool to 150° and add the salt and eggs. Beat 1 minute.
3. When the shortening mixture has cooled to 110°, add the yeast.
4. Add the sifted flour 1 cup at a time, mixing well after each addition. Knead until smooth. Allow to rise in a warm place until double in volume.
5. Divide the dough into 4 equal parts. Roll each into a 14-inch circle. Cut each circle into quarters. Divide each quarter into 3 equal pie-shaped pieces. Start at the wide end and roll each piece toward the point.
6. Curve each roll into a crescent shape and lay it on a well-greased baking sheet and let rise 30 minutes, covered.
7. Bake at 375° for 15 minutes, or until nicely browned.

Tender Crisp Rolls

SOUTH CAROLINA
Adapted from *The South Carolina Cook Book*

½ cup granulated sugar, divided	1 teaspoon salt
¼ cup lukewarm water	1 tablespoon shortening
1 cake yeast	1 egg, well beaten
1 cup hot water	4 cups all-purpose flour

1. Dissolve 1 tablespoon of the sugar in the lukewarm water. Stir in the yeast.
2. Combine the hot water with the salt, the remaining sugar, and the shortening.
3. When lukewarm, add the yeast mixture and the well-beaten egg.
4. Add 2 cups of flour and blend well. Add enough of the remaining flour (or more) to form a soft, elastic dough. Knead for 2 minutes. Cover and refrigerate for 2 hours.
5. When ready to use, shape into rolls and allow to rise 2 hours.
6. Bake on a greased baking sheet at 425° until golden brown, about 12–15 minutes.

Mayonnaise Biscuits

WEST VIRGINIA
Adapted from *The Foxfire Book of Appalachian Cookery*

2 cups flour   water
2 tablespoons mayonnaise

1. Sift the flour. Stir in the mayonnaise and enough water to make a moist dough.
2. Roll out the dough and cut into rounds. Place them on a greased baking sheet.
3. Bake at 400° for 15 minutes.

Angel Flake Biscuits

APPALACHIA
Adapted from *The Foxfire Book of Appalachian Cookery*

1 package dry yeast   1 teaspoon baking soda
2 tablespoons lukewarm   ¼ cup sugar
  water   1 teaspoon salt
5 cups sifted flour   1 cup shortening
3 teaspoons baking powder   2 cups buttermilk

1. Dissolve the yeast in the water.
2. Sift the dry ingredients together. Cut in the shortening with a pastry knife.
3. Add the dissolved yeast and the buttermilk and knead to form a smooth dough.
4. Roll the dough to a ¼-inch thickness and cut 2-inch circles with a biscuit cutter.
5. Fold each circle in half and place the biscuits on a greased baking sheet.
6. Bake at 400° for 12 minutes.

Beaten Biscuits

VIRGINIA

Adapted from *The Junior League Cook Book*

1	quart flour	2	teaspoons salt
1	kitchen spoon lard		water

1. Mix the flour, lard, and salt together. Add enough water to make a stiff dough.
2. Beat the dough for half an hour.
3. Roll the dough out and cut into 2-inch rounds with a biscuit cutter. Place the biscuits onto an ungreased baking sheet.
4. Bake at 450° until nicely browned.

"Riz" Biscuits

TENNESSEE

Adapted from Dalsass, *Miss Mary's Down-Home Cooking*

1	package active dry yeast	½	teaspoon salt
1	cup warm buttermilk	½	cup lard or solid vegetable
½	teaspoon baking soda		shortening
2½	cups flour	2	tablespoons melted butter
2	tablespoons sugar		or margarine

1. Dissolve the yeast in the warm buttermilk. Stir in the baking soda.
2. In a large bowl, stir the flour, sugar, and salt together. Cut in the lard or shortening with a pastry cutter until the mixture is like coarse meal. Add the yeast mixture and stir well.
3. Roll out to about ½-inch thickness on a floured surface. Brush with the melted butter or margarine.
4. Cut into 2-inch rounds with a biscuit cutter and place almost touching, buttered side down, on a greased baking sheet. Brush the tops with butter. Cover lightly with plastic wrap and let rise for 1 hour.
5. Bake the biscuits at 425° until lightly browned, about 25 minutes.

"Serve immediately with butter or gravy."

Dill Bread

ARKANSAS
Adapted from Marshall, *Cooking Across the South*

¾ cup sour cream	2 tablespoons shortening
1 package dry yeast	1 egg, beaten
¼ cup warm water	1 tablespoon dill seed
2 tablespoons sugar	1 tablespoon dill weed
1 teaspoon salt	2¼ cups all-purpose flour

1. Heat the sour cream over low heat until lukewarm.
2. Dissolve the yeast in the warm water. Stir in the sour cream, sugar, salt, shortening, egg, dill seed, dill weed, and 1½ cups of the flour. Beat until smooth. Beat in more flour if dough is too sticky.
3. Allow the dough to rise for 30 minutes. Punch the dough down and divide it into 2 greased 9-inch loaf pans. Allow the dough to rise until doubled in bulk.
4. Bake at 350° for about 1 hour, or until golden brown.

St. James Bread

ALABAMA
Adapted from *Gulf City Cook Book*

2 teaspoons granular yeast	2 eggs, separated
2 cups flour	2 cups milk
2 tablespoons sugar	2 tablespoons lard, melted

1. Mix the yeast with the flour.
2. Beat the sugar and the eggs yolks together until pale.
3. Whip the egg whites until stiff and add them to the yolk mixture, folding to incorporate.
4. Add the flour mixture in thirds, alternating with the milk. Stir in the melted lard.
5. Pour the batter into greased muffin tins.
6. Bake at 400° until done, about 15 minutes.

"Very nice."

Barmbrack

GEORGIA

Adapted from DeBolt, *Savannah Sampler Cookbook*

4 cups flour	¼ cup milk, tepid
½ teaspoon ground nutmeg	2 eggs, well beaten, divided
⅛ teaspoon salt	1½ cups raisins
2 tablespoons butter	1 cup currants
1 package active dry yeast	⅓ cup chopped candied fruit
2 tablespoons sugar, divided	peel

1. Sift the flour, nutmeg, and salt together. Rub the butter into the flour.
2. Mix the yeast with a teaspoon of the sugar. Add the rest of the sugar to the flour mixture and mix well.
3. Add the milk to the yeast, followed by most of the well-beaten eggs; reserve a little of the eggs for the glaze.
4. Beat the liquid into the butter mixture until the batter is stiff but elastic.
5. Fold in the raisins, currants, and fruit peel. Turn into a buttered 8-inch cake pan. Allow to rise until doubled in bulk, about an hour. Brush the top of the loaf with the reserved eggs.
6. Bake at 400° for approximately 1 hour, or until a skewer "thrust in the cake" comes out clean.

Emma R. Law's Peasant Bread

GEORGIA

Adapted from DeBolt, *Savannah Sampler Cookbook*

3½ cups warm water	⅔ cup nonfat dry milk
3 packages active dry yeast	⅓ cup vegetable oil
2 tablespoons salt	8–9 cups flour
⅓ cup sugar	

1. Pour the warm water over the yeast and stir until the yeast is dissolved. Stir in the salt, sugar, and dry milk powder.
2. Add the oil and gradually beat in the flour until the dough is smooth. Allow to rise until doubled in bulk.
3. Beat down and divide into 5 oiled 6-inch round pans. Allow to rise a second time.
4. Bake at 375° for 40–45 minutes, until loaves are golden brown and shrink slightly from the pans.

Anadama Bread

GEORGIA

Adapted from DeBolt, *Savannah Sampler Cookbook*

7–8 cups flour	⅓ cup butter, softened
1¼ cups yellow cornmeal	2¼ cups very warm water
1½ teaspoons salt	⅔ cup molasses
2 packages (2 tablespoons) dry yeast	

1. Mix the flour, cornmeal, salt, and dry yeast in a large bowl. Add the butter and mix.
2. Add the warm water and molasses. Work into a stiff dough, adding more flour if necessary.
3. Knead until smooth and elastic, about 8–10 minutes. Let rise until doubled.
4. Punch down and divide dough in half. Roll each half out into a rectangle approximately 14-by-9 inches. Shape into loaves. Place into ungreased 9-inch bread loaf pans. Allow to double in bulk.
5. Bake at 375° for 45 minutes. Cool on wire racks.

Louisiana Honey Bread

LOUISIANA

Adapted from Hawkins and Hawkins, *The American Regional Cookbook*

2 cups flour	½ teaspoon cinnamon
1 teaspoon baking soda	1 cup milk
1 teaspoon baking powder	1 cup honey
1 teaspoon salt	1 egg, slightly beaten
1 teaspoon powdered ginger	

1. Sift the dry ingredients together.
2. Stir in the milk, honey, and egg. Beat for 30 seconds. Pour the batter into a buttered loaf pan.
3. Bake at 375° for 45 minutes.

Banana Bread

MISSISSIPPI

Adapted from *Tunica County Tasty Treats*

3½ cups flour	½ cup buttermilk
1½ cups sugar	3 mashed bananas
½ teaspoon baking soda	½ cup raisins
½ teaspoon baking powder	1½ cups pecans
½ cup shortening	

1. Sift the dry ingredients together and cut in the shortening.
2. Stir in the buttermilk, bananas, raisins, and pecans.
3. Pour the batter into a greased 9-inch loaf pan.
4. Bake at 350° for 30 minutes, or until a tester comes out clean from the center.

Southern Sweet Potato Bread

GEORGIA

Adapted from DeBolt, *Savannah Sampler Cookbook*

4 tablespoons butter	1 teaspoon grated orange rind
½ cup light brown sugar, firmly packed	2 cups sifted self-rising flour
2 eggs, beaten	¼ teaspoon nutmeg
1 cup mashed, cooked sweet potatoes, cooled	¼ teaspoon allspice
3 tablespoons milk	½ cup chopped pecans

1. Cream the butter until fluffy. Add the brown sugar and beat until light.
2. Add the eggs, sweet potatoes, milk, and orange rind. Mix well.
3. Add the flour, nutmeg, allspice, and pecans to the sweet potato mixture. Mix thoroughly until smooth. Pour the batter into a greased 9-inch loaf pan.
4. Bake at 350° for 45–50 minutes.

Isle of Hope Cinnamon Bread

GEORGIA

Adapted from DeBolt, *Savannah Sampler Cookbook*

Cake:

6–7 cups unsifted flour	½ cup sugar
6 tablespoons sugar	2 teaspoons ground
1½ teaspoons salt	cinnamon
2 packages active dry yeast	3 tablespoons butter or mar-
1 cup milk	garine, melted
¾ cup water	1 egg white, slightly beaten
⅓ cup butter or margarine	
3 eggs, room temperature	

Isle of Hope crumb topping:

⅓ cup unsifted flour	1 teaspoon ground cinnamon
⅓ cup light brown sugar, firmly packed	3 tablespoons butter or margarine, room temperature

1. Mix 2 cups of the flour, the sugar, salt, and dry yeast together.
2. Combine the milk, water, and ⅓ cup of butter or margarine in a saucepan. Heat on low until the liquids are very warm.
3. Gradually add the warm liquids to the dry ingredients, scraping the bowl occasionally.
4. Add the eggs and ½ cup of flour. Beat for 2 minutes. Stir in enough additional flour to make a stiff dough.
5. Knead until smooth and elastic, about 8–10 minutes. Cover and allow to rise in a warm place, until doubled in bulk.
6. Combine the ½ cup sugar and the cinnamon.
7. Punch the dough down and divide in half. Roll each half to a 14-by-9-inch rectangle. Brush lightly with the 3 tablespoons melted butter or margarine. Sprinkle each with half of the cinnamon-sugar mixture.
8. Tightly roll the dough as for a jelly roll and shape into 2 loaves. Place in 2 oiled 9-inch loaf pans. Allow to rise until doubled in bulk. Brush the loaves with the egg white.
9. Prepare the topping by mixing all the ingredients to form a crumbly mixture. Top the loaves.
10. Bake at 350° until golden, about 45 minutes.

COFFEE CAKES AND GINGERBREADS

Wesley Gingerbread

GEORGIA

Adapted from DeBolt, *Savannah Sampler Cookbook*

½	cup vegetable shortening	⅓	cup orange juice
½	cup light brown sugar, firmly packed	3	cups sifted flour
		2	teaspoons ginger
1	tablespoon grated orange peel	1	teaspoon cinnamon
		1	teaspoon baking soda
3	eggs	1	teaspoon baking powder
1	cup dark molasses	1	teaspoon salt
¾	cup hot water	1	teaspoon nutmeg
2	teaspoons instant coffee powder	½	cup currants
		½	cup finely chopped pecans

1. Cream the shortening, brown sugar, orange peel, and eggs together.
2. Beat in the molasses, hot water, coffee powder, and orange juice.
3. Sift the dry ingredients together, then add them to the batter. Beat until smooth.
4. Stir in the currants and pecans. Pour into a greased and floured 13-by-9-inch pan.
5. Bake at 350° for 40–45 minutes.

CORNMEAL BREADS

Baked Grits

MISSISSIPPI

Adapted from *Tunica County Tasty Treats*

1	cup cooked grits, cooled and mashed	1	tablespoon flour
		1	tablespoon butter
1½	cups milk	1	teaspoon salt
2	eggs		

1. Mix all of the ingredients together. Pour the batter into a greased 8-inch square pan.
2. Bake at 300° in a pan of water for 30 minutes, or until set.

Dixie Corn Sticks

GEORGIA

Adapted from DeBolt, *Savannah Sampler Cookbook*

1 scant cup sifted yellow cornmeal	1 egg, beaten
2 tablespoons flour	1 teaspoon sugar
½ teaspoon salt	2 tablespoons vegetable oil
2 teaspoons baking powder	½ cup milk

1. Sift the cornmeal, flour, salt, and baking powder together.
2. Beat the egg, sugar, oil, and milk together. Pour into the dry ingredients. Stir quickly. Do not overmix.
3. Pour the batter into corn stick molds oiled halfway up.
4. Bake at 400° for 15–17 minutes, or until the sticks are shrinking from the pans.

Spoon Bread with Grits

GEORGIA

Adapted from DeBolt, *Savannah Sampler Cookbook*

2 tablespoons butter, softened	1 cup milk
1 cup cooked grits	½ teaspoon salt
2 eggs, well beaten	½ cup sifted white cornmeal

1. Stir the butter into the grits.
2. Mix the eggs, milk, and salt together. Add some of the grits and stir. Pour this mixture into the grits and stir to combine.
3. Mix in the cornmeal to form a smooth batter. Pour into a buttered, deep casserole.
4. Bake at 375° for 30 minutes.

Hominy Muffins

GEORGIA

Adapted from DeBolt, *Savannah Sampler Cookbook*

2 cups fine hominy [white cornmeal], boiled and cold	2 tablespoons white sugar
3 cups sour milk	3 eggs, beaten well
½ cup melted butter	1 teaspoon soda dissolved in 2 tablespoons hot water
2 teaspoons salt	1 large cup flour

1. Beat the hominy briskly. Stir in the sour milk, butter, salt, and sugar.
2. Add the eggs, soda mixture, and flour. Stir to incorporate. Do not overmix.
3. Pour into greased muffin pans.
4. Bake at 400° until done, about 10 minutes.

Shortenin' Bread

GEORGIA

Adapted from DeBolt, *Savannah Sampler Cookbook*

4 cups sifted flour	1 pound butter, at room temperature
1 cup light brown sugar	

1. Sift the flour with the brown sugar. Rub the butter into the mixture with the back of a spoon until well blended.
2. Gently roll out. Cut into desired shapes and sizes.
3. Bake on ungreased cookie sheets at 350° for about 25 minutes. Cool on racks.

Lela Bell's Everlasting Rolls

MISSISSIPPI

Adapted from *Tunica County Tasty Treats*

1	cake yeast	1	egg
½	cup sugar, divided	1	teaspoon salt
2½	cups warm water	9	cups flour
½	cup oil		

1. Dissolve the yeast and 1 teaspoon of the sugar in ½ cup of the warm water. Allow to stand for 20 minutes.
2. Stir in the oil, the remaining sugar, the egg, salt, and the remaining warm water. Beat in the flour to form a smooth dough. Refrigerate until needed.
3. Roll the dough thin and shape into rolls. Allow the rolls to rise for 1 hour.
4. Bake at 375° until nicely browned, about 20 minutes.

Peanut Butter Biscuits

GEORGIA

Adapted from DeBolt, *Savannah Sampler Cookbook*

⅔	cup milk	2	cups packaged biscuit mix
¼	cup smooth peanut butter	3	slices cooked and crumbled bacon

1. Beat the milk and peanut butter until smooth and well blended.
2. Combine the biscuit mix and bacon. Stir lightly. Add the milk and peanut butter mixture and stir until dough just clings together.
3. Knead the dough gently a few times.
4. Pat the dough out to about ¾-inch thickness on a floured board or a smooth, clean surface and cut into 2-inch rounds.
5. Bake on an ungreased cookie sheet at 400° for 10–12 minutes, or until lightly browned.

Savannah Cream Biscuits

GEORGIA
Adapted from DeBolt, *Savannah Sampler Cookbook*

3 teaspoons baking powder	2 cups sifted flour
¾ teaspoon salt	1 cup heavy cream

1. Sift the dry ingredients together.
2. Whip the cream until it is very thick. Fold it into the dry ingredients.
3. Knead the dough for 1 minute. Roll to a thickness of ¼-inch. Cut with a floured 2-inch cutter and place on a lightly buttered cookie sheet.
4. Bake at 400° for 10–12 minutes, or until golden brown.

Buttermilk Biscuits

MISSISSIPPI
Adapted from *Tunica County Tasty Treats*

4 cups flour, divided	2 teaspoons salt
½ teaspoon baking soda	½ cup shortening
2 teaspoons baking powder	2 cups buttermilk

1. Sift the dry ingredients together, reserving ½ cup of the flour.
2. Cut in the shortening with a pastry knife. Stir in the buttermilk gradually.
3. Sift the reserved flour over the dough and knead thoroughly. Roll the dough out and cut into 2-inch circles. Place the biscuits into an ungreased baking pan.
4. Bake at 450° for 15 minutes, until golden brown.

Cheese Biscuits

MISSISSIPPI

Adapted from *Tunica County Tasty Treats*

1	cup flour	½	cup butter
1	cup grated sharp [cheddar] cheese		dash cayenne
		1	teaspoon salt

1. Toss the flour and cheese together. Cut in the butter and add the cayenne and salt. Knead this into a dough and roll out to ½-inch thickness.
2. Cut into 2-inch biscuits and place them on an ungreased baking sheet.
3. Bake at 450° until brown, about 10 minutes.

"The perfect compliment for fruit salad."

Bread Pudding with Whiskey Sauce

LOUISIANA

Adapted from Feibleman, *American Cooking: Creole and Acadian*

Bread pudding:

12	ounces stale french bread, cubed	2	cups sugar
1	quart milk	½	cup raisins
3	eggs	2	tablespoons vanilla extract

Sauce:

8	tablespoons butter	1	egg
1	cup sugar	½	cup bourbon

1. Soften the bread by pouring the milk over the cubes, allowing the milk to soak in. When the bread is softened, crumble it into small bits and continue to soak until all of the milk is absorbed.
2. Beat the eggs and the sugar together until the mixture is smooth. Stir in the raisins and the vanilla. Pour the egg mixture over the bread and stir to combine.
3. Pour the bread pudding evenly into a 13-by-9-by-2-inch buttered pan. Set the pan in a shallow roasting pan filled with 1 inch of hot water.
4. Bake at 350° for 1 hour, or until a knife inserted in the center comes out clean.
5. Prepare the sauce by melting the butter in the top of a double boiler. Stir in the sugar and egg. Cook, stirring constantly, until the sugar dissolves completely and the mixture thickens. Let the sauce cool to room temperature before stirring in the bourbon.

Pioneer Bread

INDIANA

Adapted from *The Hoosier Cookbook*

½ cup yellow cornmeal	2 teaspoons salt
⅓ cup cold water	2 cups tomato juice
1 cup boiling water	2 packages dry yeast
4 tablespoons vegetable oil	10 cups flour
4 tablespoons molasses	

1. Stir the cornmeal into the cold water. Add this mixture to the boiling water, stirring constantly while boiling for 5 minutes.
2. Add the vegetable oil, molasses, and salt to the cornmeal. Set aside to cool to lukewarm.
3. Heat the tomato juice to lukewarm; add the dry yeast and stir until dissolved.
4. Combine the tomato juice mixture with the cornmeal mixture. Stir in 4 cups of the flour until smooth.
5. Knead the remaining 6 cups of flour into the batter. Set the dough in a warm place until doubled in bulk. Punch down and let rest 15 minutes.
6. Grease 3 bread pans with shortening. Divide the bread dough into 3 equal portions. Let the dough rise again until doubled in size.
7. Bake at 325° for 30 minutes, or until done.

Beer Bread

INDIANA

Adapted from *The Hoosier Cookbook*

¼ cup very warm water	1½ tablespoons salt
3 tablespoons dry yeast	6–8 cups flour
2¾ cups warm beer	5 tablespoons oil
¼ cup sugar	

1. Combine the water and yeast. Add the warm beer, sugar, and salt. Stir to dissolve the yeast.
2. Beat in 3–4 cups flour. Add the oil, then knead in 3–4 cups more flour to form a smooth dough.
3. Knead 5–10 minutes, cover and let rise 45 minutes, or until doubled.
4. Punch down, divide, and place in 2 greased 9-by-5-inch loaf pans. Let rise for 30 minutes.
5. Bake at 375° for 35–40 minutes.

Oatmeal Yeast Bread

INDIANA

Adapted from *The Hoosier Cookbook*

½	package dry yeast	2	tablespoons shortening
½	cup warm water	2	cups milk, scalded
¼	cup light brown sugar, packed	2	cups quick oats
1	tablespoon salt	5½	cups sifted flour

1. Dissolve the yeast in the warm water.
2. Add the sugar, salt, and shortening to the scalded milk. Cool. Stir in the yeast liquid.
3. Add the oats and flour. Let stand 10 minutes.
4. Knead until smooth and elastic. Let rise until doubled in bulk.
5. Shape into 2 loaves and place in 2 greased 5-by-9-by-3-inch loaf pans. Let rise until almost to the top of the pans.
6. Bake at 350° for 40 minutes, or until browned on top.

Herb Sour Cream Bread

INDIANA

Adapted from *The Hoosier Cookbook*

½	cup warm water	½	teaspoon marjoram leaves
2	packages dry yeast	½	teaspoon oregano
1	cup warm sour cream	½	teaspoon thyme
6	tablespoons margarine	2	eggs, beaten and at room
⅓	cup sugar		temperature
2	teaspoons salt	3¾–4¾	cups flour, unsifted

1. Measure the warm water into a large, warm bowl. Sprinkle in the yeast and stir until dissolved.
2. Add the sour cream, margarine, sugar, salt, marjoram, oregano, thyme, and eggs.
3. Beat in 3 cups of the flour until well blended. Stir in enough additional flour to make a soft dough.
4. Cover and let rise in a warm place until the dough has doubled in bulk, then punch down.
5. Turn into 2 greased 1-quart casserole dishes. Cover and let rise until doubled in bulk.
6. Bake at 375° for about 35 minutes.

Egg Bread

ILLINOIS

Adapted from Linsenmeyer, *Cooking Plain*

2 yeast cakes, crumbled (or 2 packages dry yeast)
½ cup lukewarm water
2⅔ cups whole milk
4 ounces butter, softened

1½ tablespoons sugar
1½ teaspoons salt
2 eggs, beaten
8 cups flour
softened butter

1. Dissolve the yeast in the lukewarm water.
2. Scald the milk (do not boil). Stir in the butter, sugar, and salt. Set aside until cooled to lukewarm.
3. Add the eggs and yeast and blend well. Add the flour gradually, beating constantly.
4. Cover the bowl with a clean cloth and set in a warm, draft-free place until doubled in bulk.
5. Punch down the dough and divide into halves.
6. Shape each piece into a loaf and place into ungreased 10-by-4-inch loaf pans.
7. Cover the pans, set in a warm place, and let rise again until doubled in bulk.
8. Bake at 375° for 50 minutes, or until bread has shrunk away from the sides of the pan. Brush the tops with soft butter.

Welsh Raisin Bread

ILLINOIS
Adapted from Linsenmeyer, *Cooking Plain*

5½ cups flour	6 tablespoons water
¾ cup sugar	6 tablespoons butter
½ teaspoon salt	1 egg
¼ teaspoon cinnamon	1 cup raisins
¼ teaspoon nutmeg	1 cup currants
1½ packages dry yeast	½ cup chopped candied peel
1½ cups milk	

1. Combine 1¼ cups of the flour, the sugar, salt, cinnamon, nutmeg, and yeast.
2. Mix the milk, water, and butter in a large saucepan over low heat until lukewarm.
3. Gradually add the dry ingredients and beat hard for about 3 minutes.
4. Add the egg and ¾ cup flour or more if needed to make a thick batter. Beat for 3 minutes longer.
5. Stir in the raisins, currants, candied peel, and enough additional flour to form a soft dough. Knead until smooth and elastic.
6. Allow the dough to rise until doubled in bulk (about an hour).
7. Punch down, knead lightly, and divide into halves. Shape into loaves and place into 2 greased loaf pans. Let rise until doubled in bulk.
8. Bake at 375° for 45 minutes, or until loaves sound hollow when tapped lightly.

Maple Wheaten Bread

OHIO

Adapted from Macmillan, *In a Shaker Kitchen*

1 package active dry yeast	4 cups whole wheat flour
3 tablespoons warmed pure maple syrup, divided	1 cup warm milk 2 tablespoons butter, melted
1 cup warm water	and cooled plus extra for
1½ cups white flour	glazing
½ tablespoon salt	

1. Put the yeast and ½ tablespoon of the maple syrup in ¼ cup of the warm water in a small bowl. Let the yeast soak 1 minute, then whisk with a fork to dissolve the yeast.
2. Sift the white flour and salt into a large bowl. Add the whole wheat flour and stir to mix. Make a well in the center and pour in the yeast mixture, milk, butter, and remaining maple syrup and water.
3. Mix the liquid ingredients in the well, then gradually draw in the flour.
4. Continue mixing to make a soft dough, adding more white flour if the dough feels too wet.
5. Turn the dough onto a floured surface and knead until smooth and elastic, about 10 minutes.
6. Shape the dough into a ball. Cover and let rise until doubled in bulk, about 1½ hours.
7. Gently punch the dough to deflate it and fold the sides to the center. Knead again for 2–3 minutes, then divide the dough in half and shape into loaves, tucking the ends under.
8. Put into greased 8½- or 9-inch loaf pans. Let rise in a warm place 30–45 minutes.
9. Bake at 400° until well risen and browned, about 45–50 minutes.

Minnie's Sage Bread

OHIO
Adapted from DuSablon, *Cincinnati Recipe Treasury*

1	cup milk	1	tablespoon sage leaves
3	tablespoons lard or shortening	2	tablespoons dried onions
3	tablespoons sugar	2	packages dry yeast
1	teaspoon salt	1	cup warm water
		4	cups white flour

1. Scald the milk. Add the lard, sugar, salt, sage, and onions. Set aside to cool.
2. Dissolve the yeast in the warm water and add it to the cooled mixture.
3. Add the flour and beat well. Knead for 3–5 minutes. Set aside to rise until doubled.
4. Divide the dough and place in greased loaf pans and let rise again for about 1 hour.
5. Bake at 375° for 35–40 minutes for large pans, 20–25 minutes for small pans.

Hobo Bread

INDIANA
Adapted from *The Hoosier Cookbook*

2	cups boiling water	⅛	teaspoon salt
2	cups raisins	2	eggs, well beaten
4	teaspoons baking soda	4	cups flour
½	cup salad oil	1	cup black walnuts
1½	cups sugar		

1. Combine the water, raisins, and baking soda. Allow to cool and refrigerate overnight.
2. Add the remaining ingredients. Stir to form a smooth batter.
3. Grease three 1-pound coffee cans well. Distribute the batter in the cans.
4. Bake at 350° for 1 hour. Cool on a rack. Remove bread when cold.
5. Wash the cans thoroughly.
6. Return the breads to the cans and store for a week in the refrigerator.

Spanish Nut Loaf

INDIANA

Adapted from *The Hoosier Cookbook*

1¾	cups flour	⅔	cup nuts, chopped
1	teaspoon cinnamon	2	eggs
3	teaspoons baking powder	½	cup milk
¼	teaspoon salt	½	cup butter, melted
1	cup sugar		

1. Sift the dry ingredients into a bowl. Add the nuts.
2. Separate the eggs, beating the whites until stiff.
3. Beat the egg yolks and milk. Add the melted butter.
4. Add the milk mixture to the dry ingredients and mix well. Fold in the beaten egg whites.
5. Baked in a greased 8½-by-4½ loaf pan at 350° for 1 hour.

Herb and Cheese Bread

OHIO

Adapted from Macmillan, *In a Shaker Kitchen*

1½	cups all-purpose flour	1	cup grated sharp cheddar cheese, divided
2	teaspoons baking powder		
½	teaspoon baking soda	½	tablespoon dry sage, crumbled
½	teaspoon salt		
½	cup graham or whole wheat flour	1	teaspoon dried dill
		1	cup buttermilk

1. Sift the all-purpose flour, baking powder, baking soda, and salt into a bowl.
2. Add the graham or whole wheat flour, ¾ cup of the cheese, and the herbs.
3. Stir to mix.
4. Add enough buttermilk to mix a soft dough.
5. Form the dough gently into a bolster shape and put it in a buttered 8½-by-4½-inch loaf pan. Sprinkle the remaining cheese over the top.
6. Bake at 350° until golden brown and a skewer inserted in the center comes out clean, about 60 minutes.

Irish Soda Bread

ILLINOIS
Adapted from Linsenmeyer, *Cooking Plain*

4 cups flour   1 teaspoon baking soda
½ teaspoon salt   1½ cups buttermilk

1. Sift the dry ingredients together in a large bowl, making a well in the center.
2. Add the buttermilk to the well and mix quickly with a wooden spoon to form a stiff dough.
3. Knead on a floured board until the dough is smooth and elastic. Flatten into a circle about 1½-inches thick.
4. Cut a deep cross in the center and bake on a floured baking sheet at 425° for 30–35 minutes.

Lincoln Logs

INDIANA
Adapted from *The Hoosier Cookbook*

Dough:

4–5 cups unsifted flour
½ cup sugar
1½ teaspoons salt
2 packages active dry yeast

½ cup milk
½ cup water
¼ cup margarine
2 eggs, room temperature

Filling:

1 8-ounce package cream cheese, softened

¼ cup sugar
1 egg yolk

Browned butter frosting:

1 cup powdered sugar
1 teaspoon vanilla

1½ tablespoons milk
⅛ cup browned butter

1. Prepare the dough by thoroughly mixing 1¼ cups of the flour, the ½ cup sugar, salt, and dry yeast.
2. Combine the milk, water, and margarine in a saucepan. Heat over low heat until the liquids are warm. The margarine does not need to melt.
3. Gradually add the liquids to the dry ingredients and beat 2 minutes, scraping the bowl occasionally.
4. Add the eggs and ½ cup of the remaining flour to make a thick batter. Beat at high speed for 2 minutes, scraping the bowl occasionally.
5. Stir in enough additional flour to make a soft dough. Turn onto a lightly floured board and knead until smooth and elastic.
6. Let rise in a warm place until doubled in bulk.
7. Prepare the filling by beating the cream cheese with the ¼ cup sugar until light and fluffy. Blend in the egg yolk.
8. Punch the dough down and turn onto a lightly floured board. Divide it in half.
9. Roll each piece of dough into a 10-by-14-inch rectangle. Spread each with half of the filling. Roll up like a jelly roll and seal the edges by pinching.
10. Place the rolls on a greased baking sheet. Cut slits three quarters through the logs at 1-inch intervals. Let rise in warm place until doubled in bulk.
11. Bake at 350° for 20–25 minutes, or until done. Remove from baking sheets and cool.
12. Prepare the frosting by mixing the powdered sugar, vanilla, milk, and browned butter together. Beat 1 minute. Spread on the bread.

Holiday Stollen

ILLINOIS
Adapted from Linsenmeyer, *Cooking Plain*

4   cups milk
3   cups sugar
4   yeast cakes or packages of
      dry yeast
9   cups flour
1   teaspoon salt
5   eggs, beaten
1½ pounds raisins, chopped

½   pound candied cherries or
1¼ pounds mixed fruit,
      chopped coarsely
¾   pound citron
      grated rind of 2 lemons
2   teaspoons almond extract
1   pound butter, melted

1. Scald the milk and cool to lukewarm. Add the sugar and stir until dissolved.
2. Pour out ½ cup of the milk mixture and partially dissolve the yeast in it, then stir this into the rest of the milk until completely dissolved.
3. Add the flour, 1 cup at a time, then the salt, and beat for 5 minutes.
4. Let rise for about 1 hour, or until doubled in bulk. Punch down.
5. Stir in the beaten eggs, fruit, lemon rind, almond extract, and melted butter. Add more flour if necessary, to make a stiff dough. Allow to rise 3 hours.
6. Turn onto a floured board and divide into 8 portions.
7. Shape into loaves, place in ungreased baking pans, and allow to rise for 1 hour.
8. Bake at 375° for about 1 hour.

Fresh Corn Corn Bread

INDIANA
Adapted from *The Hoosier Cookbook*

1   cup flour
1   cup cornmeal
½   teaspoon baking soda
1   tablespoon sugar
2   eggs
      salt

1   cup fresh corn, cut from
      the cob
1   cup buttermilk
½   cup water
¼   cup shortening, melted

1. Sift the flour, cornmeal, baking soda, salt, and sugar together.
2. Stir in the eggs, fresh corn, buttermilk, and water. Mix until smooth. Stir in the shortening.
3. Pour the batter into a hot, greased 9-inch square baking pan and bake at 425° for 30 to 35 minutes or until done.

Breakfast Muffins

OHIO

Adapted from DuSablon, *Cincinnati Recipe Treasury*

1–1½ cups milk or fruit juice	½ teaspoon salt
½ cup salad oil	½ cup wheat germ
¼ cup honey or maple syrup	½ cup raisins
1 egg	¼ cup chopped nuts
3 cups flour	1 apple, grated
1 tablespoon baking powder	

1. Beat the milk or juice, oil, honey, and egg together.
2. Sift the flour, baking powder, and salt into the liquid ingredients. Add the wheat germ, raisins, nuts, and apple. Stir only to moisten.
3. Spoon the batter into greased muffin tins.
4. Bake at 350° for 20 minutes.

Spice Apple Muffins

INDIANA

Adapted from *The Hoosier Cookbook*

Muffins:

¼ cup shortening	½ teaspoon salt
½ cup sugar	½ teaspoon cinnamon
1 egg	½ cup milk
1½ cups flour	1 cup apple, grated
1 tablespoon baking powder	

Topping:

⅓ cup light brown sugar	⅓ cup nuts, finely chopped
½ teaspoon cinnamon	

1. For the muffins, cream the shortening and sugar. Add the egg and blend well.
2. Sift the flour, baking powder, salt, and cinnamon together.
3. Alternately add the milk and the flour mixture to the shortening mixture. Fold in the apple.
4. Fill muffin cups half full.
5. Make the topping by mixing the brown sugar, cinnamon, and nuts. Top each muffin with topping mixture.
6. Bake at 350° for approximately 30 minutes.

Makes 18 muffins

Shredded Wheat and All-Bran Muffins

INDIANA

Adapted from *The Hoosier Cookbook*

2 large or 3 small Shredded Wheat biscuits	1⅓ cups shortening
	1¼ cups sugar
¼ cup raisins (or more)	2 eggs
1 cup boiling water	2½ cups flour, unsifted
	½ cup All-Bran cereal

1. Crumble the Shredded Wheat biscuits and toss with the raisins. Add the boiling water, let stand, and allow to cool.
2. Add the shortening and the sugar and beat 1 minute. Add the eggs.
3. Stir in the flour and All-Bran carefully until just barely mixed together. Drop into greased muffin pans.
4. Bake at 350° for 30 minutes, or until done.

Whipped Cream Biscuits

OHIO

Adapted from Macmillan, *In a Shaker Kitchen*

2 cups flour	pinch sugar
1 tablespoon baking powder	1¼ cups heavy cream
½ teaspoon salt	butter, melted

1. Sift the flour, baking powder, salt, and sugar together.
2. Whip the cream until it is thick but not stiff. Add to the dry ingredients and mix together lightly to make a soft dough.
3. Turn the dough onto a lightly floured surface and pat or roll out to ½-inch thickness. Cut out rounds using a floured 2- or 3-inch cutter.
4. Arrange the biscuits on an ungreased baking sheet and brush the tops with melted butter.
5. Bake the biscuits at 425° for 15 minutes, or until they are risen and golden brown.

Homemade Crackers

ILLINOIS
Adapted from Linsenmeyer, *Cooking Plain*

4 cups flour	¼ cup butter
2 tablespoons sugar	1 cup milk (or less)
1 teaspoon salt	

1. Sift the dry ingredients together.
2. Blend the butter into the flour mixture with 2 knives until the mixture looks mealy.
3. Stir in sufficient milk to form a stiff dough.
4. Roll out to about ¼-inch thick on a lightly floured board and cut into squares with a sharp knife. Prick holes about ¼ inch apart with the tines of a fork and brush the surface with milk. Place the crackers on an ungreased baking sheet.
5. Bake at 425° for 15–18 minutes, or until lightly browned.

Yields about 5 dozen

"Extra good when served hot from the oven."

Cloud Biscuits

INDIANA
Adapted from *The Hoosier Cookbook*

2 cups flour	½ cup shortening
1 tablespoon sugar	1 egg
4 teaspoons baking powder	⅔ cup milk
½ teaspoon salt	

1. Sift the dry ingredients together. Cut in the shortening until the mixture resembles coarse crumbs.
2. Combine the egg and milk and add to the flour mixture. Stir until the dough follows the fork around the bowl.
3. Turn out on a lightly floured surface and knead gently with the heel of the hand about 20 times. Roll out and cut with a biscuit cutter and place on a greased baking sheet.
4. Bake at 450° for 15 minutes.

Shaker Bread Pudding

OHIO
Adapted from Macmillan, *In a Shaker Kitchen*

Pudding:

2½	cups milk	5	cups slightly stale bread without crusts, cut in cubes
4	tablespoons butter		
½	cup sugar	¼	cup dried cherries
1	teaspoon grated lemon zest	3	eggs, beaten
1	teaspoon pure vanilla extract	¼	cup chopped toasted pecans
½	teaspoon ground cinnamon		

Sauce:

1	cup packed dark brown sugar	½	cup butter
		¼	cup heavy cream

1. Combine the milk, butter, and sugar in a heavy saucepan and heat to dissolve the sugar. Stir in the lemon zest, vanilla, and cinnamon.
2. Add the bread cubes and cherries and stir to mix. Let soak 20 minutes.
3. Stir the eggs into the bread mixture. Add the pecans and pour into a buttered shallow baking dish.
4. Bake the pudding at 350° until it is set and golden brown on top, about 40 minutes.
5. To prepare the sauce, combine the sugar and butter in a heavy saucepan and heat gently. Stir to melt the butter and dissolve the sugar. Bring it to a boil, then carefully stir in the cream.

White Bread (Brot)

KANSAS

Adapted from *The Centennial Treasury of Recipes*

1 cake yeast	2 tablespoons lard, melted
1 tablespoon sugar	1 tablespoon salt
3 cups warm water, divided	4–6 cups bread flour

1. Dissolve the yeast and sugar in ½ cup of the warm water. Add the remaining water, the lard, and the salt.
2. Stir in half of the flour to form a smooth paste. Add enough of the remaining flour to form a smooth, firm dough. Knead for 10 minutes. Allow to rise until doubled in bulk.
3. Punch down the dough and allow to rise again. Repeat once more.
4. Form the dough into 2 balls. Allow them to rest for 10 minutes, form each into a loaf, and place them into ungreased loaf pans to rise until doubled in bulk.
5. Bake at 350° for about 1 hour.

Wisconsin Beer Bread

WISCONSIN

Adapted from Hawkins and Hawkins, *The American Regional Cookbook*

1½ cups beer	½ teaspoon sugar
1 package dry yeast	1 teaspoon salt
4 cups flour, sifted	

1. Heat the beer to lukewarm and stir in the yeast to dissolve.
2. Stir in half of the flour and allow to rise until doubled in bulk.
3. Add the remaining flour, sugar, and salt. Knead the dough until it is smooth. Allow the dough to rise until doubled in bulk.
4. Place the dough into an ungreased 9-inch loaf pan and allow to rise for 1 hour more.
5. Bake at 375° for about 1 hour, or until golden brown.

Whole Wheat Bread

WISCONSIN
Adapted from *"The Four Hundred" Cook Book*

2 cakes compressed yeast	3 tablespoons sugar
1 cup warm water	1 teaspoon salt
1½ cups white flour	6–7 cups whole wheat flour
3 cups whey	softened butter
½ teaspoon baking soda	

1. Mix a sponge by adding the yeast to the warm water and white flour. Let stand overnight.
2. When the sponge is very light, add the whey, baking soda, sugar, and salt.
3. Stir in whole wheat flour—enough to make a stiff batter—and turn into well-greased bread tins, which should be only half full.
4. Allow to rise slowly for 3 hours to double in bulk.
5. Bake at 350° for 1 ½ hours.
6. Butter the tops of the loaves as they cool.

Editor's note: You may be able to find whey in a health food store.

Modern Manna Yeast Bread

IOWA
Adapted from *How Iowa Cooks*

½ cup milk, scalded	1 tablespoon dry yeast
3 tablespoons shortening	1½ cups warm water
2 teaspoons salt	5½ cups flour
3 tablespoons sugar	

1. Combine the scalded milk with the shortening, salt, and sugar. Cool to lukewarm.
2. Dissolve the yeast in the warm water. Add to the milk mixture.
3. Beat in 3 cups of flour to develop the gluten. Add the remaining flour to form a soft dough. Knead 8–10 minutes. Allow to rise in a covered bowl until doubled in bulk.
4. Divide and shape into 2 loaves. Place them into greased loaf pans. Allow to double in bulk.
5. Bake at 400° for 30 minutes.

"The family will think you are special if they are greeted by the smell of freshly baked bread."

Everlasting Starter

KANSAS
Adapted from *The Centennial Treasury of Recipes*

½ cup sugar   ¼ cup water
¼ cup milk   ½ cup flour

1. Mix the ingredients together to form a smooth batter. Add more
   flour if necessary to make it spongy.
2. Allow to stand, at room temperature, 2 days, covered with a porous
   cloth.
3. Refrigerate.
4. After each use, sprinkle a little sugar on it.
5. Reserve 1 cup to "feed" and propagate.

Onion Bread

IOWA
Adapted from *How Iowa Cooks*

1 tablespoon dry yeast   1 tablespoon butter
¼ cup warm water   2 tablespoons dill seed
1 cup creamed cottage cheese   1 teaspoon salt
2 tablespoons sugar   ¼ teaspoon baking soda
1 tablespoon minced dehy-   1 egg
   drated onion   2¼–2½ cups flour

1. Sprinkle the yeast over the warm water.
2. Heat the cottage cheese to lukewarm. Combine in a mixing bowl
   with the sugar, onion, butter, dill seed, salt, baking soda, egg,
   and the yeast mixture.
3. Add flour, in portions, to form a stiff dough, beating well after each
   addition. A little more flour may have to be added. Dough may
   be kneaded lightly if desired.
4. Cover and let rise until doubled in bulk.
5. Punch dough down and turn into a well-greased 2-quart dish. Let
   rise until doubled in bulk.
6. Bake at 350° for 40 minutes.

Pawpaw Bread

KANSAS

Adapted from Carey and Naas, *The Kansas Cookbook*

⅓ cup shortening
¾ cup sugar
2 eggs
1¾ cups all-purpose flour
1 teaspoon baking powder
½ teaspoon baking soda

½ teaspoon salt
¼ teaspoon cinnamon
¼ teaspoon ginger
¼ teaspoon nutmeg
1 cup pawpaws, peeled, seeded, and mashed

1. Cream the shortening and sugar together until light and fluffy. Add the eggs and mix well.
2. Sift the dry ingredients together. Add them in thirds, alternating with the mashed pawpaws, to the creamed mixture.
3. Pour the batter into a greased 9-inch loaf pan.
4. Bake at 350° for 45–50 minutes, or until an inserted toothpick comes out clean.

St. Paul Poor Man's Brown Bread

MINNESOTA

Adapted from Kreidberg, *Food on the Frontier*

1 heaping cup corn flour
1 heaping cup rye flour
1 heaping cup graham flour
2 cups molasses
2 cups milk

1 cup buttermilk
2 teaspoons baking soda
1 teaspoon salt
1 tablespoon water

1. Sift the flours together.
2. Mix the molasses with the milk and buttermilk.
3. Dissolve the baking soda and salt in 1 tablespoon water and add it to the milk mixture. Stir in the flours to form a smooth batter.
4. Pour the batter into a 9-inch loaf pan set in a pan of water.
5. Bake at 300° for 1 hour, or until set.

Olive Nut Bread

IOWA

Adapted from *How Iowa Cooks*

2½ cups cake flour	½ cup chopped nuts
¾ teaspoon salt	1 cup stuffed olives, chopped
4 teaspoons baking powder	1 egg, well beaten
½ cup sugar	1 cup milk

1. Sift the dry ingredients together. Add the nuts and olives.
2. Combine the egg and milk. Add to the dry ingredients and mix only enough to moisten the flour. Turn into a greased 9-by-5-by-3-inch loaf pan.
3. Bake at 350° for 45 minutes.

COFFEE CAKES AND SWEET YEAST BUNS

Swedish Coffee Cake (Karevei)

KANSAS

Adapted from *The Centennial Treasury of Recipes*

2 cakes or 2 packages yeast	2¾ cups sugar
3 cups warm water	5 eggs, well beaten
4½ pounds flour	2 teaspoons salt
1½ cups cream, scalded	2 pounds powdered sugar
½ cup butter	milk

1. Dissolve the yeast in the warm water. Stir in 4 cups of the flour to form a smooth dough. Allow to rise until spongy.
2. To the warm cream add the butter and sugar. Stir to melt the butter. Allow to cool.
3. Add the cream mixture, eggs, and salt to the sponge and mix well. Add enough of the remaining flour to make a soft dough and knead well.
4. Allow the dough to rise until doubled in bulk, punch it down, and allow it to rise again.
5. Divide the dough into 6 portions. Place them into ungreased 8-inch cake pans and allow to rise again.
6. Bake at 350° for about 30 minutes.
7. When cool, frost with an icing made from the powdered sugar combined with enough milk to form a soft glaze.

"They were usually decorated with corn candy" in the early 1900s.

Kolaches

KANSAS
Adapted from *The Centennial Treasury of Recipes*

½ cup butter	2 cakes yeast
½ cup sugar	¾ cup warm water
1 teaspoon salt	4 cups flour
2 eggs	8 tablespoons fruit preserves

1. Cream the butter with the sugar until light and fluffy. Add the salt and eggs and beat until smooth.
2. Dissolve the yeast in the warm water. Stir in 1½ cups of the flour. Add the remaining flour, stir to form a smooth dough, and allow to rise for 1 ½ hours.
3. Punch the dough down and divide it into 24 pieces. Allow the pieces to rest for 10 minutes.
4. Form each piece into a ball and place them on a greased baking sheet.
5. Make a depression in the center of each and fill with your favorite preserves. Allow the buns to rise until light.
6. Bake at 350° for 12–15 minutes, or until nicely browned.

Hot-Cross Buns

OKLAHOMA
Adapted from Wilhelm, *Smidgen of Honey*

½ cup shortening	4–5 cups white flour (enough to
1 cup scalded milk	make a medium stiff dough)
¾ teaspoon salt	2 egg yolks
½ cup sugar	raisins (optional)
1 yeast cake	1 egg white
½ cup warm water	plain frosting

1. Add the salt, sugar, and shortening to the scalded milk. Stir to incorporate.
2. When lukewarm, add the yeast dissolved in the warm water and 1½ cups of flour. Beat well and let rise until very light.
3. Add the egg yolks and the remaining flour. Knead lightly and let rise until doubled in bulk. (A cup of raisins may be added to the dough.)
4. To make the buns, roll out the dough to 1-inch thick and cut into rounds. Set them close together in a greased pan and allow them to rise.
5. Glaze the surface of each bun with a little egg white diluted with water. With a sharp knife, cut a cross on the top of each bun.
6. Bake at 350° for about 20 minutes.
7. Just before removing them from the oven, brush them with sugar and water. Fill the cross with plain frosting.

Sour Cream Coffee Cake

IOWA

Adapted from *How Iowa Cooks*

Cake:

4	ounces butter, softened	1	teaspoon baking soda
1	cup sugar, divided	1	teaspoon baking powder
2	eggs	1	teaspoon salt
1	cup sour cream	1	teaspoon vanilla
2	cups sifted all-purpose flour		

Topping:

½	cup sugar	¼	cup ground nuts (pecans or
½	cup light brown sugar		walnuts)
1	teaspoon cinnamon		

1. For the cake, cream the butter with the sugar. Add the eggs and sour cream. Beat until smooth.
2. Sift the flour, baking soda, baking powder, and salt together. Add to the creamed mixture.
3. Add the vanilla and mix to form a smooth batter.
4. Make the topping by mixing together ½ cup sugar, the brown sugar, cinnamon, and nuts.
5. Add half the batter to a greased 7-inch loaf pan. Add the topping and fill with the remaining batter.
6. Bake at 350° for 35–40 minutes, or until done.

Corn Lunn

MINNESOTA

Adapted from Kreidberg, *Food on the Frontier*

¾	cup butter	3	teaspoons baking powder
¾	cup sugar	1	teaspoon salt
4	eggs	1½	cups cornmeal
1½	cups sifted flour	1	cup milk

1. Cream the butter and sugar together until smooth and light. Add the eggs, one at a time, beating well after each addition.
2. Sift the flour with the baking powder and salt. Stir this into the creamed mixture. Add the cornmeal and the milk and stir to form a smooth batter.
3. Bake in a greased 8-inch square pan at 350° for 40 minutes, or until set.

Huckleberry Muffins

NORTH DAKOTA
Adapted from Hawkins and Hawkins, *The American Regional Cookbook*

3	cups flour	1	egg
3	teaspoons baking powder	5	tablespoons melted butter
4	tablespoons sugar	1	cup huckleberries
½	teaspoon salt	2	tablespoons sugar
1	cup milk		

1. Sift the flour, baking powder, sugar, and salt together.
2. Whisk the milk and egg together and stir into the dry ingredients to form a smooth batter. Add the butter and fold in the huckleberries, which have been tossed with the remaining 2 tablespoons of sugar.
3. Pour the batter into buttered muffin tins two-thirds full.
4. Bake at 400° for 15–20 minutes.

Nanny's Cornmeal Rolls

KANSAS
Adapted from *The Centennial Treasury of Recipes*

1½	cups sifted flour	1	egg, beaten
¾	cup cornmeal	½	cup milk
3	teaspoons baking powder	2	tablespoons butter,
1	teaspoon salt		softened
3	tablespoons lard or butter		

1. Sift the flour, cornmeal, baking powder, and salt together. Cut in the lard or butter.
2. Combine the beaten egg and milk and stir this into the flour mixture.
3. Roll out onto a floured board and cut into biscuits with a cutter. Spread each biscuit with softened butter and fold like Parker House rolls.
4. Bake at 450° for 12–15 minutes.

Mennonite Buns

KANSAS
Adapted from *The Centennial Treasury of Recipes*

1 package dry yeast
2 tablespoons sugar
2 cups warm water
2 cups potato water

2 tablespoons salt
12 cups flour
2 tablespoons shortening

1. Dissolve the yeast and sugar in the warm water. Add the potato water and the salt. Allow to stand for 10 minutes.
2. Add enough flour to make a sponge. Cover and allow to rise until foamy.
3. Add the shortening and knead in the remaining flour. Allow to rise until doubled in bulk. Punch the dough down and allow to rise again.
4. Pinch off small balls of dough and shape into buns. Place them, touching, on greased baking pans. Allow the buns to rise until doubled in bulk.
5. Bake at 350° for 15–20 minutes.

"Serve while fresh!"

Salad Rolls

WISCONSIN
Adapted from *"The Four Hundred" Cook Book*

½ cake compressed yeast
2 tablespoons warm water
½ cup milk
2 tablespoons sugar
¼ teaspoon salt

3¾ cups flour
2 tablespoons melted butter
1 egg, well beaten
rind of ½ lemon, grated

1. Dissolve the yeast cake in the warm water.
2. Scald the milk and add the sugar, salt, yeast mixture, and ¾ cup of the flour.
3. Let rise, then add the butter, egg, and lemon rind.
4. Add the remaining flour and knead until smooth. Allow to rise until doubled in bulk.
5. Roll to ½-inch thickness. Shape with a biscuit cutter, place close together in ungreased rectangular pans, and allow to rise again.
6. Bake at 375° until golden brown.

Butterhorn Rolls

IOWA

Adapted from *How Iowa Cooks*

2 tablespoons dry yeast	½ cup sugar
1 cup lukewarm water	2 eggs, beaten
⅔ cup shortening	7 cups flour
1 cup hot water	softened butter or
2 teaspoons salt	margarine

1. Dissolve the yeast in the lukewarm water.
2. Melt the shortening in the hot water and cool.
3. Combine the two mixtures and add the salt, sugar, and the eggs.
4. Add 3 cups flour and beat well with a mixer. Stir in the remaining flour with a spoon. This will be a "really soft dough." Refrigerate 1 hour.
5. Roll out like a pie dough and cut it in wedges. Roll up each triangle from its large end. Place them on a greased sheet pan and allow to rise until "real light."
6. Brush with butter or margarine, then bake at 375° for 15 minutes.

Soy Biscuits

NORTH DAKOTA

Adapted from Hawkins and Hawkins, *The American Regional Cookbook*

¼ cup soy flour	½ teaspoon salt
¼ cup white flour	¾ cup milk
1 cup whole wheat flour	3 tablespoons vegetable oil

1. Mix all of the ingredients together, beating enough to form a soft dough.
2. Roll the dough out on a floured board or other smooth surface to a thickness of ½ inch and cut into biscuits. Place the biscuits onto an oiled cookie sheet.
3. Bake at 425° for 10–15 minutes, or until golden.

Indian Bear Paw Bread

NEW MEXICO
Adapted from Butel, *Woman's Day Book of New Mexican Cooking*

2	cups hot water	2	packages(tablespoons)
2	teaspoons lard		dry yeast
1	teaspoon honey	½	cup warm water
½	teaspoon salt	10	cups all-purpose flour

1. Combine the hot water, lard, honey, and salt in a large mixing bowl. Stir to melt the lard.
2. Dissolve the yeast in the ½ cup warm water. Add the yeast to the cooled liquid mixture.
3. Add 8 cups of the flour, 1 cup at a time, beating well after each addition. Knead in the remaining 2 cups of flour on a work surface. Work until smooth and elastic, about 10 minutes.
4. Allow the dough to rise until doubled. Punch down and knead for 3 minutes.
5. Divide the dough into fourths and make an 8-inch round from each quarter.
6. Fold each circle almost in half. Make two cuts into the dough, from the outer edge to halfway to the junction of the top and bottom halves. This will make the bear paw shape. Allow the paws to rise until doubled.
7. Bake about 1 hour in a preheated 350° oven. Add a pan of water to the oven, if desired.

Wild Sage Bread

ARIZONA

Adapted from Hawkins and Hawkins, *The American Regional Cookbook*

1	package dry yeast	1	teaspoon salt
¼	cup warm water	¼	teaspoon baking soda
1	cup cottage cheese	2½	cups flour
1	egg		butter, melted
1	tablespoon melted lard		piñons (pine nuts), crushed
1	tablespoon sugar		and roasted
2	teaspoons crushed dried wild sage		

1. Dissolve the yeast in the warm water.
2. Beat the cottage cheese and egg together until smooth. Add the melted lard, sugar, and yeast. Stir in the sage, salt, and baking soda.
3. Add the flour in portions, beating vigorously after each addition until a stiff dough is formed. Allow the dough to rise until doubled in bulk.
4. Punch the dough down and knead for 1 minute. Place the dough into a buttered loaf pan and allow to rise for 40 minutes.
5. Bake at 350° for 50 minutes. Brush the top with melted butter and sprinkle with crushed, roasted piñons.

Adobe Hornos

NEW MEXICO

Adapted from Dent, *The Feast of Santa Fe*

2	teaspoons active dry yeast	1½	cups unbleached white flour
1	teaspoon sugar	2	teaspoons salt, divided
1	cup warm water	2	tablespoons hot water
1	cup whole wheat flour		

1. Dissolve the yeast and sugar in the warm water and allow to proof for 10 minutes.
2. Add both flours and 1 teaspoon of the salt to the yeast and beat for 2 minutes. Add additional white flour, if necessary, to form a soft dough. Allow the dough to rise until doubled in bulk, about 1½ hours.
3. Pat the dough into an ungreased 8-by-12-inch pan. Dissolve the remaining salt in the hot water and brush this glaze over the dough. Allow to rise for 30 minutes.
4. Bake at 375° until done, about 20 minutes.

Pecan Bread

TEXAS
Adapted from Coleman and Coleman, *The Texas Cookbook*

4 cups flour	¾ cup sugar
4 teaspoons baking powder	1 egg
1 cup chopped pecans	1½ cup milk
½ cup raisins	

1. Sift the flour and baking powder together. Divide in 2 portions and toss the pecans and raisins in one of the portions.
2. Beat the sugar, egg, and milk together thoroughly.
3. Add the other half of the sifted flour to the milk mixture and then the portion containing the pecans and the raisins. Stir to form a smooth dough. Knead 2 minutes.
4. Shape the mixture into 2 loaves and allow them to rise is greased loaf pans for about 20 minutes.
5. Bake at 350° for 1 hour.

Bachelor's Bread

ARIZONA
Adapted from Weiner, *Arizona Territorial Cookbook*

2 cups sour milk	1 egg, beaten
1 heaping teaspoon baking soda	2 tablespoons butter or lard
¼ teaspoon salt	½ cup all-purpose flour
2 tablespoons sugar	cornmeal and graham flour, as needed

1. To the sour milk add the baking soda, salt, sugar, butter or lard, egg, and all-purpose flour.
2. Add equal parts of cornmeal and graham flour to make a stiff batter.
3. Bake at 350° for 40 minutes. Serve hot.

Panhandle Brown Bread

TEXAS

Adapted from Ross, *Nanny's Texas Table*

1 cup coarse yellow cornmeal	1 cup sour milk or
1 cup all-purpose flour	buttermilk
2 cups whole wheat flour	1 cup milk
1 cup raisins	1 tablespoon baking soda
1 tablespoon salt	1 tablespoon hot water
2 cups molasses	

1. Mix the cornmeal, both flours, raisins, and salt together.
2. Add the molasses and both milks. Dissolve the baking soda in the hot water and add it. Mix thoroughly.
3. Generously butter three 1-quart pudding molds or coffee cans, plus 3 pieces of aluminum foil large enough to cover the top of the mold.
4. Fill the pudding molds three-fourths full. Cover each with the foil and secure with string.
5. Fit a large pot with a rack. Add 1 inch of water and bring it to a boil. Place the molds on the rack to steam, covered, for 3 hours. Add water as necessary.
6. Unmold and bake at 350° for 20 minutes.

Texas Stollen

TEXAS

Adapted from Shenton et al., *American Cooking: The Melting Pot*

Dough:

1 package active dry yeast	8 tablespoons butter, cut into bits
½ teaspoon plus 1½ cups sugar	8 tablespoons butter, softened
¼ cup lukewarm water	4 teaspoons cinnamon
4–4½ cups all-purpose flour	1 cup seedless raisins
1 tablespoon salt	1 egg, lightly beaten with
2 eggs	1 tablespoon milk
¾ cup lukewarm milk	

Frosting:

2 cups powdered sugar	5–6 tablespoons cold water

1. Dissolve the yeast and the ½ teaspoon sugar in the warm water. Let the mixture stand for 2–3 minutes. Stir to dissolve the yeast. Allow to stand for 5–8 minutes.
2. Combine 4 cups of the flour, ½ cup of the remaining sugar, and the salt in a bowl, making a well in the center. Pour in the yeast mixture, add the eggs, ¾ cup of warm milk, and the 8 tablespoons butter bits. Gradually incorporate the dry ingredients into the liquid.
3. Gather the dough into a ball and knead 2 minutes. Add additional flour until the dough is no longer sticky. Continue to knead for 10 minutes.
4. Butter a deep bowl with 2 tablespoons of the softened butter and place the dough in it to rise, covered, until the dough has doubled in volume. Punch it down and set it to rise again for another 30–45 minutes.
5. Roll out the dough to a rectangle measuring 20 inches long and 15 inches wide. Spread the surface of the dough with the remaining 6 tablespoons of softened butter, then sprinkle it evenly with the remaining cup of sugar and the cinnamon. Scatter the raisins evenly over the top.
7. Starting at one of the long sides, roll up the dough, jelly-roll fashion, into a cylinder. Transfer the cylinder to a buttered baking sheet and bring together the ends of the dough to make a ring.
8. With a sharp knife, cut two thirds of the way through the ring, from its outer edge inward, at 1-inch intervals, gently turning each pastry cut to its right to reveal the filling. Drape the ring with a kitchen towel and set it to rise until it doubles in volume.

9. Beat the egg and milk together and, with a pastry brush, coat the surface of the coffee ring with the mixture.
10. Bake at 375° for 25–30 minutes, or until it is golden brown.
11. Prepare the frosting by placing the powdered sugar in a large bowl and gradually beating in the water, 1 tablespoon at a time. Beat the frosting until smooth. While the cake is still warm, spoon the frosting over the top, letting it run down the sides.

Dime Ginger Bread

ARIZONA
Adapted from Weiner, *Arizona Territorial Cookbook*

1 ounce butter	1 teaspoon ginger
½ pint molasses	1 teaspoon baking soda
1 teaspoon cloves	½ pint boiling water
1 teaspoon cinnamon	2 cups flour

1. Melt the butter. Add it to the molasses and spices.
2. Dissolve the baking soda in the boiling water. Mix with the molasses and lightly stir in the flour.
3. Line a cake pan with buttered paper. Pour in the batter (which will be very thin).
4. Bake it at 350° for ½ hour.

Pan de los Tres Reyes

NEW MEXICO
Adapted from Cameron, *The Best from New Mexico Kitchens*

1 cup butter or margarine	4 tablespoons candied orange peel, chopped
¾ cup sugar	3 cups flour
3 eggs	1 teaspoon cinnamon
¼ cup milk	¼ teaspoon allspice
¾ cup golden raisins	4 tablespoons chopped almonds
¾ cup currants	1 bean
4 tablespoons citron, chopped	

1. Cream the butter and sugar until fluffy. Beat in the eggs one at a time. Add the milk and beat thoroughly.
2. Coat the raisins, currants, citron, and orange peel with a little of the flour. Sift the rest of the flour and spices into the batter. Fold in until blended.
3. Add the fruits and nuts and mix well. Stir in the bean. Turn into a greased and floured ring mold.
4. Bake at 275° for 2 hours.

"The person who gets the bean in his slice is the king or queen of the festivities and is especially blessed."

Molletes (Sweet Saffron Rolls)

NEW MEXICO
Adapted from Dent, *The Feast of Santa Fe*

1 package active dry yeast	3 cups unbleached white
1 tablespoon sugar	flour, plus ½ cup more
½ cup warm water	flour if needed to stiffen
½ cup butter	the dough
2–3 saffron threads	½ teaspoon salt
3 eggs	1 egg yolk
½ cup sugar	1 teaspoon water

1. Dissolve the yeast and sugar in the warm water. Allow to stand for a few minutes to proof.
2. Melt the butter in a small skillet, let it foam, and add the saffron threads. Remove the skillet from the heat and allow it to cool.
3. Beat the eggs briefly and add the melted butter. Stir to incorporate.
4. Mix the flour, salt, and sugar together. Pour in the yeast and egg-saffron mixtures. Beat to form a smooth dough. Allow to rise until doubled in bulk.
5. Form the dough into small rolls and place them on an ungreased baking sheet. Allow the rolls to double in bulk, covered.
6. Beat the egg yolk into the water and brush the rolls with this glaze.
7. Bake at 375° for 20 minutes, or until the rolls are nicely browned.

New Mexico Spoon Bread

Adapted from Cameron, *The Best from New Mexico Kitchens*

NEW MEXICO

1 can cream-style corn	1 teaspoon baking powder
¾ cup milk	1 teaspoon salt
⅓ cup melted shortening	1 teaspoon sugar (optional)
1½ cups cornmeal	1 4-ounce can chopped green
2 eggs, slightly beaten	chiles
½ teaspoon baking soda	1½ cups grated cheddar cheese

1. Mix all the ingredients except the chiles and cheese.
2. Pour half the batter in a greased 9-by-9-inch pan, sprinkle with half the cheese and half the chile.
3. Add the remaining batter and top with the remaining cheese and chiles.
4. Bake at 400° for 45 minutes.

"We think a little minced onion added to the batter would be good, too."

Piki (Indian Paper Bread)

NEW MEXICO
Adapted from Dent, *The Feast of Santa Fe*

5 tablespoons masa harina	⅛ teaspoon salt
2 tablespoons cornstarch	1 cup hot water

1. Mix the masa, cornstarch, and salt together.
2. Add the hot water, all at once, and beat the batter for a few seconds until it is smooth.
3. Using a pastry brush, spread the batter in circles of about 4 inches on a nonstick baking sheet.
4. Bake at 400° for 3–5 minutes, or until the breads are browned on the edges.

New Mexico Blue Cornbread

NEW MEXICO
Adapted from Dent, *The Feast of Santa Fe*

½ cup unsalted butter or margarine, melted	2 teaspoons baking powder
	½ teaspoon baking soda
1 cup blue cornmeal	1 large egg
⅓ cup whole wheat flour	1 teaspoon salt
⅔ cup unbleached white flour	1⅓ cups buttermilk

1. Mix all of the ingredients except the buttermilk together.
2. Pour in the buttermilk and stir to form a smooth batter, about 2 minutes. Pour the batter into a 9-inch buttered cake pan.
3. Bake at 375° for 15–20 minutes.

Jalepeno Corn Sticks

TEXAS

Adapted from Ross, *Nanny's Texas Table*

¾	cup all-purpose flour	3	tablespoons butter, melted
1½	cups yellow cornmeal	2	fresh jalepeno peppers
2	tablespoons sugar		seeded, deveined, and
1	teaspoon salt		minced
1	tablespoon baking powder	½	teaspoon baking soda
2	eggs, beaten	1½	cups warm buttermilk

1. Stir the flour, cornmeal, sugar, salt, and baking powder together.
2. Stir in the eggs, butter, and jalepeno peppers. Add the baking soda and stir in the buttermilk; mix thoroughly.
3. Pour into greased corn-stick molds or 3-inch tins.
4. Bake at 425° for 15–20 minutes, or until golden.

Apache Rolls

ARIZONA

Adapted from Hawkins and Hawkins, *The American Regional Cookbook*

1	cup white cornmeal	1	cup boiling water
1	cup yellow cornmeal	½	cup heated buffalo fat (or
1	teaspoon salt		bacon drippings)
½	teaspoon cayenne		green corn husks

1. Mix the dry ingredients together. Moisten with the water and stir in the buffalo fat.
2. Form into small rolls. Wrap each roll in a corn husk.
3. Bake at 350° for 1 hour.

Cornmeal Rolls

TEXAS

Adapted from Ross, *Nanny's Texas Table*

1½	cups all-purpose flour	4	tablespoons vegetable
¾	cup coarse cornmeal		shortening
4	teaspoons baking powder	1	egg
1	teaspoon salt	¾	cup buttermilk
¼	teaspoon baking soda		softened butter

1. Sift the dry ingredients together. Cut in the shortening.
2. Beat the egg with the buttermilk and stir into the dry ingredients, forming a smooth dough. Knead lightly on a floured board.
3. Roll ½-inch thick and cut with a large biscuit cutter. Make a crease just off center on each round.
4. Brush each with butter and fold the smaller part over, as for a Parker House roll.
5. Bake at 450° for 12–14 minutes, or until golden.

Mashed Potato Rolls

TEXAS

Adapted from Ross, *Nanny's Texas Table*

2	cups milk	½	cup warm water
2	tablespoons butter	½	cup sugar
1	cup cooked mashed pota-	1	egg, well beaten
	toes, cooled	1	tablespoon salt
1	package yeast	7–8	cups all-purpose flour

1. Scald the milk. Add the butter to melt. When lukewarm, add the potatoes.
2. Dissolve the yeast in the warm water and add it, along with the sugar, egg, and salt, to the milk mixture. Mix well.
3. Place most of the flour in a large bowl. Stir in the milk mixture and combine until smooth. Add more flour as necessary to make a stiff dough.
4. Place the dough in a greased bowl, cover with plastic wrap, and refrigerate 24 hours.
5. Roll out ⅓-inch thick, cut with a 3-inch biscuit cutter, shape into Parker House rolls, and let rise until doubled.
6. Bake on ungreased cookie sheets at 425° for 12–15 minutes, or until well browned.
7. Use within 5 days.

Bolillos

NEW MEXICO

Adapted from Butel, *Woman's Day Book of New Mexican Cooking*

½	package (½ tablespoon) dry yeast	½	teaspoon salt
¾	cup warm water	3	cups all-purpose flour
1	teaspoon sugar	1	egg white
		1	tablespoon water

1. Dissolve the yeast in the warm water. Add the sugar and allow to stand 5 minutes.
2. Add the salt and 1 cup flour to the yeast mixture. Stir to a uniform paste. Add the remaining flour (possibly less) to form a dough. Knead until smooth and elastic, 5–10 minutes.
3. Allow to rise until doubled in bulk, about 1 hour. Punch down and allow to rise again.
4. Divide the dough in half, and each half into sixths. Shape each piece into an oval. Pull and twist the ends slightly.
5. Place the rolls on an ungreased baking sheet about 2 inches apart. Cut a ¼-inch-deep slit in each, lengthwise.
6. Mix the egg white with the water and brush the tops of the rolls with this wash.
7. Bake in a preheated 400° oven for 15 minutes. Remove from the oven for 10 minutes. Return to the oven and bake 15–20 minutes more, or until lightly browned.

Sourdough Biscuits

TEXAS
Adapted from Coleman and Coleman, *The Texas Cookbook*

2 tablespoons grated potato	water
4–6 cups flour	grease

1. Combine the grated potato, 2 cups of flour, and enough water to make a thin batter. Pour into a gallon jar and allow to ferment for 24 hours.
2. Mix in enough flour to the starter to form a smooth dough that can be rolled out.
3. Cover the bottom of a warm skillet with grease. Cut out the biscuits, dip them in the grease on both sides, and place them on baking sheets.
4. Bake at 375° for 10–12 minutes.

Cowboy Biscuits

TEXAS
Adapted from Ross, *Nanny's Texas Table*

1 cup all-purpose flour	1½ tablespoons solid vegetable
2 teaspoons baking powder	shortening
½ tablespoon sugar	⅓ cup milk
¼ teaspoon salt	vegetable oil for frying
1½ tablespoons butter	

1. In a bowl sift the flour with the baking powder, sugar, and salt. Cut in the butter and shortening until the mixture resembles coarse meal.
2. Stir the milk into the mixture with a fork, using just enough milk to make a soft dough. Turn the dough out onto a well-floured board and knead gently for half a minute.
3. Either divide the dough into 8 portions, roll into balls, and flatten to ½-inch thickness, or roll out to ½-inch thickness and cut into biscuits with a 2-inch or 2½-inch biscuit cutter.
4. Heat 1 inch of oil in a large heavy skillet. Drop the biscuits into the hot oil and fry for 4–5 minutes, turning once halfway through the cooking time. (The biscuits can be baked at 425° for 10 minutes, if preferred.)

Lottie's Biscuits

TEXAS

Adapted from Ross, *Nanny's Texas Table*

4	cups sifted all-purpose flour	6	tablespoons butter
8	teaspoons baking powder	6	tablespoons solid vegetable shortening
2	tablespoons sugar	1½	cup milk
1½	teaspoons salt		

1. In a bowl sift the flour with the baking powder, sugar, and salt.
2. Cut in the butter and the shortening until the mixture resembles coarse meal.
3. Stir the milk in with a fork, using just enough milk to make a soft dough. Turn the dough out onto a floured board and knead gently for 30 seconds.
4. Roll the dough out to ½-inch thickness and cut with 2½-inch biscuit cutter. Place on an ungreased cookie sheet.
5. Bake at 450° for 10–15 minutes, until a "light butterscotch color."

Panocha

NEW MEXICO

Adapted from Cameron, *The Best from New Mexico Kitchens*

4	cups panocha flour	2	cones piloncillo (Mexican brown sugar) or 1 cup light brown sugar
2	cups sifted white flour		
½	teaspoon salt		
6	cups warm water		

1. In a large ovenproof bowl, mix the panocha flour, sifted white flour, and salt. Slowly stir in the water until the mixture is very soft.
2. Add the shaved piloncillo or brown sugar and mix until completely dissolved. Pat dough into mounds.
3. Bake at 350° for 1½ hours. Panocha is done when it turns a dark brown and is thick in consistency. Serve with cream or ice cream.

Mormon Rye Bread

UTAH
Adapted from *American Cooking: The Great West*

1	package active dry yeast	¼	cup honey
1	teaspoon granulated sugar	½	cup vegetable shortening,
1	cup lukewarm water		cut into ½-inch bits,
1	cup rye flour		softened
2⅓–3	cups unsifted all-purpose flour	2	tablespoons butter, softened
¼	cup dark brown sugar	1	egg beaten lightly with 1
1	teaspoon salt		tablespoon milk

1. Dissolve the yeast and sugar in ¼ cup of the warm water. Allow to stand for 10 minutes.
2. Mix the rye flour, 2 cups of all-purpose flour, the brown sugar, and salt together.
3. To the yeast mixture add the remaining warm water, the honey, and the vegetable shortening bits. Beat in the flour mixture until a smooth ball forms.
4. Knead in additional flour to form a soft, elastic dough, about 10 minutes. Cover and allow to rise until it has doubled in volume.
5. Punch the dough down, shape it into a loaf, and place it into a 9-inch loaf pan that has been greased with the 2 tablespoons butter to rise for about 45 minutes, or until it has doubled in volume. Brush the loaf with the egg mixed with milk.
6. Bake at 375° for 30–35 minutes, or until the top is golden brown.

Graham Bread

COLORADO
Adapted from *Pioneer Potluck*

1	cake yeast	5	tablespoons molasses
¼	cup lukewarm water	1½	teaspoons salt
2½	cups milk, scalded and cooled	3	tablespoons melted butter
		4½	cups graham flour

1. Dissolve the yeast cake in the warm water.
2. Mix the milk, molasses, salt, and butter. Add the yeast mixture.
3. Add the flour and make a stiff batter. Let rise about 2 hours.
4. Punch the dough down and place it into an ungreased bread or loaf pan (2 small loaves or 1 large). Let rise 1 hour.
5. Bake at 375° for 1 hour.

Stone Ground Whole Wheat Bread

WYOMING

Adapted from *Cooking in Wyoming*

1	egg	½	cup water
1	teaspoon salt	1	package dry yeast
2	tablespoons honey or	⅓	cup warm water
	molasses	3	cups unsifted whole wheat
1	tablespoon salad oil		flour
½	cup evaporated milk		

1. Beat the egg slightly in a large mixing bowl. Add the salt, honey or molasses, salad oil, and the evaporated milk diluted with the ½ cup water.
2. Dissolve the yeast in the warm water and add it to the liquid mixture. Stir in the whole wheat flour, beating until the dough is smooth. Cover with a cloth and allow to rise to double in size.
3. Knead on a floured bread board until the dough is smooth. Shape and place into an oiled loaf pan.
4. Let rise only a very short time, not quite doubled in volume.
5. Bake at 315° for 40 minutes, or when the loaf sounds hollow when tapped with finger.

Molasses Wheat Bread

COLORADO

Adapted from *Nuggets: Recipes Good as Gold*

2	cups water	1	tablespoon salt
3	tablespoons shortening	2½	cups whole wheat flour
¼	cup light molasses	2	packages dry yeast
½	cup nonfat dry milk	2½	cups flour

1. Combine the water, shortening, molasses, milk powder, salt, and 1 cup of the whole wheat flour. Add the yeast and beat for 1 minute.
2. Add the remaining whole wheat flour. Beat for 3 minutes.
3. Work in enough white flour to make a soft dough and knead for 6 minutes. Cover and let rise until doubled.
4. Punch down. Knead for 30 seconds and divide dough in half.
5. Place the dough in 2 greased 8-inch loaf pans. Cover and let rise until almost doubled.
6. Bake at 375° for 30–35 minutes.

Onion Braid Bread

COLORADO

Adapted from *Nuggets: Recipes Good as Gold*

2	packages dry yeast	1	teaspoon salt
1	envelope dry onion soup mix	1	egg
		⅓	cup shortening
⅓	cup sugar	6½	cups flour
2	tablespoons light molasses	2	cups hot water

1. Combine the yeast, soup mix, sugar, molasses, salt, egg, shortening, and 2 cups of the flour. Add the hot water and beat for 1 minute.
2. Mix in enough of the remaining flour to make a soft dough. Knead 8–10 minutes. Place in a greased bowl. Cover and let rise until doubled.
3. Punch down and divide dough into 9 equal parts. Roll each portion into a 14-inch strand.
4. On a baking sheet, braid 3 strands to make a loaf, tucking the ends under. Repeat for the 2 remaining loaves.
5. Cover and let rise until almost doubled.
6. Bake at 375° for 20–30 minutes.

Wheat Berry Batter Bread

COLORADO

Adapted from *Nuggets: Recipes Good as Gold*

½	cup wheat berries	1	cup warm water
1	quart water	1	teaspoon salt
2¼	cups flour	1	tablespoon butter, melted
1	tablespoon sugar		cornmeal
1	package dry yeast		

1. In a large saucepan, combine the wheat berries and 1 quart of water. Cover and let stand for 8 hours or boil 2 minutes and let stand for 1 hour.
2. Without draining the berries, bring them to a boil over high heat. Reduce the heat and simmer until tender, about 2 hours. Drain and cool.
3. Combine 1½ cups of flour, the sugar, the yeast, and the salt. Add the warm water. Beat for 3 minutes.
4. Add the wheat berries and the remaining ¾ cup flour. Cover and let rise until doubled.
5. Stir the dough down. Place it in a buttered 8-inch loaf pan coated with cornmeal.
6. Bake at 375° for 30 minutes.

Three-Flour Bread

COLORADO
Adapted from *Nuggets: Recipes Good as Gold*

2 packages dry yeast	½ cup light brown sugar
3½ cups white flour	3 tablespoons shortening
1½ cups whole wheat flour	2 tablespoons sugar
½ cup rye flour	2 teaspoons salt
2 cups milk	

1. Combine the yeast, 1 cup of the white flour, 1½ cups whole wheat flour, and ½ cup rye flour.
2. In a saucepan, heat the milk with the brown sugar, shortening, sugar, and salt. Stir until the shortening is melted and the mixture is warm, but not hot.
3. Add the liquid to the flour mixture. Beat for 3 minutes.
4. Add enough white flour to make a soft dough. Knead for 8 minutes. Cover and let rise until doubled.
5. Punch down, shape into 2 loaves, and place in greased 8-inch loaf pans. Allow to rise until doubled.
6. Bake at 375° for 30 minutes.

House Party Banana Bread

WYOMING
Adapted from *Cooking in Wyoming*

¼ cup shortening	1¼ cups flour
½ cup sugar	2 teaspoons baking powder
1 egg	½ teaspoon baking soda
1 cup All-Bran	½ teaspoon salt
1½ cups mashed banana	½ cup chopped nuts
1 teaspoon vanilla	

1. Blend the shortening and sugar thoroughly. Add the egg and beat well.
2. Stir in the All-Bran, bananas, and vanilla.
3. Stir in the dry ingredients, then add them to the shortening mixture with the nut meats. Stir only until combined. Spread in a well-greased loaf pan.
4. Bake at 350° for 1 hour, or until done.

Brazil Nut Loaf

WYOMING
Adapted from *Cooking in Wyoming*

4 eggs, separated	6 ounces white wine or
1 cup sugar	brandy
1 cup flour	½ teaspoon salt
1 teaspoon ground cloves	½ pound candied cherries
½ teaspoon nutmeg	2 cups pecans
1 teaspoon baking powder	2 cups Brazil nuts
½ teaspoon vanilla	1 pound dates

1. Beat the egg yolks, sugar, ¾ cup of the flour, the spices, baking powder, vanilla, wine or brandy, and salt together.
2. Flour the fruit and nuts with the remaining ¼ cup flour and add to mixture.
3. Beat the egg whites very stiff and fold in.
4. Grease and flour two 8-inch loaf pans. Pour the batter in.
5. Bake at 300° for 45–50 minutes.

Loquat Loaf

NEVADA
Adapted from *Nevada's Finest Western Cooking*

2 cups finely chopped, unpeeled, ripe loquats	3 large eggs
2 cups flour	½ cup cooking oil
1½ cups sugar	½ cup margarine, melted
1½ teaspoons ground cinnamon	½ cup coarsely chopped almonds, walnuts, or filberts
½ teaspoon allspice	½ cup plumped, drained raisins
2 teaspoons baking soda	½ cup grated coconut
½ teaspoon salt	
1 teaspoon vanilla extract	

1. Combine all of the ingredients in the order given. Mix to form a smooth batter.
2. Pour the batter into a greased 10-inch loaf pan and allow it to rest for 20 minutes.
3. Bake at 350° for 1 hour, or until the loaf is firm to the touch in the center.

Health Bread

COLORADO

Adapted from *Pioneer Potluck*

2	teaspoons baking soda	1	cup sugar
2	cups buttermilk	1	cup raisins
3½	cups white flour	1	cup molasses
3	cups bran	2	teaspoons shortening
1	teaspoon salt	1	egg

1. Dissolve the baking soda in the buttermilk.
2. Place all the dry ingredients in a bowl. Add the raisins, molasses, and buttermilk.
3. Add the shortening and the egg. Pour into 2 ungreased bread pans and let stand 20 minutes.
4. Bake at 325° for 1 hour.

Camping Bread

WYOMING

Adapted from *Cooking in Wyoming*

2	cups flour	2	tablespoons lard or butter
4	tablespoons baking powder	1	cup water
1	tablespoon salt		

1. Mix the flour, baking powder, and salt together. Rub in the lard, then the water. Mix well.
2. Bake in a greased cast iron skillet at 325° until the top is browned, about 20 minutes. (Can be baked over a slow campfire, but must be turned over to brown.)

Orehova Poteca (Walnut Bread)

WYOMING

Adapted from *Cooking in Wyoming*

Bread:

1	cake yeast	¼	pound butter, melted
⅔	cup lukewarm water	¾	tablespoon salt
6	cups flour	1	cup sugar
3	eggs	1	tablespoon lemon extract
1	cup milk, scalded		melted butter

Filling:

1	pound shelled walnuts	2	teaspoons vanilla
1	cup honey	2	teaspoons cinnamon
1	cup cream	½	teaspoon cloves
2	eggs, separated		

1. Dissolve the yeast in the lukewarm water. Mix in 1 cup flour. Set aside to rise at least 1 hour.
2. Beat the eggs well and add the scalded milk and melted butter. Add the egg mixture, the salt, sugar, and lemon extract to the yeast mixture, mixing well.
3. Add the remaining flour and knead lightly.
4. Brush the top with melted butter, cover, and set aside to double in bulk in a warm place.
5. Prepare the filling by grinding the nuts with a food processor.
6. Heat the honey and warm the cream.
7. Whip the egg whites stiff.
8. Mix the nuts with the honey, cream, and vanilla, and fold in the egg whites.
9. Beat the egg yolks, cinnamon, and cloves together.
10. Divide the dough into 2 parts. Take 1 part and roll out on a floured board or table top as thin as possible without breaking it.
11. Spread the egg yolk mixture over the entire surface of the dough.
12. Roll out the second piece of dough as thin as possible without breaking, then spread the remaining filling over the surface.
13. Roll as for a jelly roll. Cut the roll in half and place halves side by side in a well-greased oblong pan. Set aside in warm place to raise until double in bulk.
14. Bake at 350° for 30 minutes. Lower the heat to 325° and bake for another half hour.
15. When baked, leave the "potecas" in the pans for 15 minutes. Remove from pans and place on a rack to cool.

Editor's note: *Orehova* means "walnut"; *potecas* are a traditional Slovenian sweet.

Bread Spongecake

WYOMING
Adapted from *Cooking in Wyoming*

1 cup bread sponge	1 teaspoon nutmeg
1 cup sugar	2 eggs
1 cup currants	1 heaping cup flour
1 cup raisins, chopped	pinch salt
½ teaspoon cinnamon	nuts if desired
1 teaspoon cloves	

1. Bake as loaf cake 40–50 minutes.

Editor's note: Bread sponge is a starter. These are the original instructions. I would mix all ingredients together in a large bowl to form a smooth batter and bake at 350° for 30–40 minutes in a greased cake pan, or until the center of the cake is set.

Blueberry Boy Bait

COLORADO
Adapted from *Nuggets: Recipes Good as Gold*

2 cups flour	1 teaspoon salt
1½ cups sugar	1 cup milk
¾ cup shortening	1 teaspoon vanilla
2 teaspoons baking powder	1 pint fresh blueberries,
2 eggs, separated, room temperature	cleaned

1. Blend the flour, sugar, and shortening. Reserve ¾ cup of this mixture for topping.
2. To the flour mixture, add the baking powder, egg yolks, salt, milk, and vanilla. Stir to form a smooth batter.
3. Beat the egg whites stiff and fold into the batter.
4. Pour into a greased and floured 9-by-13-inch pan. Sprinkle with the blueberries and the reserved topping.
5. Bake at 350° for 35–45 minutes.

CORNMEAL BREAD

Mormon Johnnycake

UTAH
Adapted from *American Cooking: The Great West*

2 eggs
2 cups buttermilk
2 tablespoons honey
½ cup unsifted flour
1 teaspoon baking soda

1 teaspoon salt
2 cups yellow cornmeal
2 tablespoons butter, melted
   and cooled

1. Whisk the eggs until frothy. Beat in the buttermilk and honey. Stir in the flour, baking soda, and salt. Beat until smooth.
2. Beat in the cornmeal, about ½ cup at a time. Stir in the melted butter and pour the batter into a buttered 9-inch square baking dish.
3. Bake at 425° for 20 minutes, or until the cake pulls away from the sides of the dish and the top is brown and crusty.

MUFFINS

Caramel Pecan Oatmeal Muffins

WYOMING
Adapted from *Cooking in Wyoming*

½ cup light brown sugar
3 tablespoons softened butter
   pecan pieces or halves
¼ cup sugar
¼ cup shortening
1 egg

1 cup milk
1 cup flour
3 teaspoons baking powder
½ teaspoon salt
1 cup quick oatmeal

1. Mix the brown sugar and butter together until smooth. Spread the sugar mixture in the bottom of each cup of a greased muffin pan.
2. Arrange pecan pieces or halves on top of the sugar mixture.
3. Combine the remaining ingredients to make a batter and fill the cups two-thirds full.
4. Bake at 425° for 20 minutes.

Makes 12

Date Muffins

COLORADO

Adapted from *Nuggets: Recipes Good as Gold*

1	teaspoon baking soda	1	cup sugar
1	cup hot water	1½	cups flour
1	cup chopped dates	2	eggs, beaten
½	cup shortening	1	teaspoon salt

1. Dissolve the baking soda in the hot water. Add the dates and allow to soak until cool.
2. Combine the remaining ingredients. Stir in the date mixture.
3. Fill greased muffin tins two-thirds full.
4. Bake at 350° for 15–20 minutes.

Bess Truman's Bran Rolls

NEVADA

Adapted from *Nevada's Finest Western Cooking*

½	cup sugar	2	eggs, slightly beaten
⅔	cup shortening	2	cakes yeast
1	cup bran flakes	1	cup warm water
2	teaspoons salt	7	cups white flour
1	cup boiling water		

1. Mix the sugar, shortening, bran flakes, and salt together. Pour the boiling water over the mixture and stir until the sugar is dissolved and the shortening melted.
2. Mix the eggs with the yeast and warm water and stir to dissolve the yeast. Add this to the bran mixture.
3. Stir in enough of the flour to form a firm dough and knead until smooth. Refrigerate overnight.
4. Form the dough into 2-inch balls and shape into rolls. Place them on ungreased baking sheets and allow them to rise, covered, until doubled in bulk.
5. Bake at 400° for 15–20 minutes.

CRACKERS

Soda Crackers

COLORADO
Adapted from *Pioneer Potluck*

7	ounces flour	1	cup shortening
1	teaspoon salt	1	teaspoon baking soda
2	teaspoons cream of tartar	1½	teacups cold water

1. Mix the flour, salt, and cream of tartar. Rub in the shortening.
2. Dissolve the baking soda in the cold water. Mix all the ingredients. Roll out and cut into squares.
3. Bake at 400° degrees until crisp and golden on edges.

BREAD PUDDING

Pioneer Bread Pudding

WYOMING
Adapted from *Cooking in Wyoming*

2	cups bread crumbs	2	eggs, beaten
2	cups milk, scalded		dash of salt
3	tablespoons butter	1	cup raisins
¼	cup sugar	½	teaspoon vanilla

1. Mix all the ingredients together. Place in a buttered casserole dish.
2. Bake at 350° for 1 hour, or until a small knife comes out clean when it is inserted in the center of the pudding.

Deluxe Thick Sourdough Starter

ALASKA
Adapted from *Cooking Alaskan*

1 **package dry yeast**	4 **cups or more unsifted all-**
2¼ **cups warm water**	**purpose flour**
2 **tablespoons sugar**	

1. Dissolve the yeast in ¼ cup of the warm water. Place the remaining warm water, the dissolved yeast, and the sugar in a large jar or stone crock. Stir to dissolve. Add enough flour to form a stiff batter. Stir well.
2. Cover loosely and allow to stand in a warm room for 2 days, stirring down occasionally.
3. When removing starter from this jar, do so with a clean spoon.

Sourdough Potato Bread

ALASKA
Adapted from *Cooking Alaskan*

1 **package dry yeast**	¼ **cup melted margarine**
5¾ **cups unbleached flour**	2 **eggs**
¼ **cup sugar**	1 **cup starter (see Deluxe**
2 **teaspoons salt**	**Thick Sourdough Starter,**
2 **servings instant mashed**	**above)**
potato flakes	1 **egg white**
¾ **cup milk**	2 **tablespoons water**

1. Combine the yeast, 2 cups of the flour, the sugar, and salt.
2. Prepare two servings of instant mashed potatoes according to the directions on the package. Stir in the milk, melted margarine, eggs, and starter. Stir until blended.
3. Add the potato mixture to the yeast mixture. Beat 2 minutes. Add 1 cup of flour and beat 2 minutes longer.
4. Stir in the remaining flour to form a stiff dough. Knead for 8–10 minutes. Cover and allow to rise until doubled in bulk. Punch down and divide in half.
5. Shape the dough into balls, keeping any seams underneath. Allow to rise until almost doubled, about 45 minutes.
6. Cut ½-inch-deep slashes on top of the loaves. Brush the loaves with the egg white beaten with the water.
7. Bake at 350° for about 35 minutes, or until nicely browned.

Mashed Potato Starter

ALASKA
Adapted from *Cooking Alaskan*

2	medium potatoes	2	tablespoons sugar
4	cups water	2	cups flour

1. Boil the potatoes with skins on until they fall apart. Discard the skins and mash the potatoes in the water, making a puree. Cool.
2. Add 2 cups of this puree to a sourdough pot. Add the remaining ingredients. Beat until a smooth batter is formed. Cover and set aside in a warm place to ferment.
3. The starter can be used after 3 days, but is better if a week is allowed. After a week, add a little flour and sugar to ensure activity.

Hazelnut Rye Bread

OREGON
Adapted from Brooks, *Oregon's Cuisine of the Rain*

4	cups unbleached flour	1	tablespoon salt
2	cups rye flour	2¼	cups lukewarm water
2	tablespoons unsalted butter, melted	2	cups coarsely chopped roasted hazelnuts
2	tablespoons active dry yeast	2	large egg yolks, beaten
1	tablespoon molasses		

1. Mix the unbleached flour with the rye flour. Mix 3 cups of this with the melted butter, yeast, molasses, salt, and lukewarm water until well blended.
2. Gradually knead in the remaining 3 cups of flour mixture and the hazelnuts to form a dough. Knead until the dough is smooth and elastic, about 10 minutes.
3. Shape the dough into a smooth ball. Cover and allow to rise for 20 minutes. Punch the dough down and divide it into 2 equal portions. Shape each portion into a long loaf.
4. Place the loaves on a baking sheet lined with parchment paper. Cover and allow to rise for 30 minutes.
5. Brush the loaves with the beaten egg yolks.
6. Bake at 400° for about 30 minutes, or until the loaves sound hollow when tapped.

Monkey Bread

CALIFORNIA
Adapted from *The Los Angeles Times California Cookbook*

2	cups milk	2 packages dry yeast
2	tablespoons sugar	½ cup lukewarm water
2–3	teaspoons salt	6–7 cups flour
1	tablespoon shortening	8 ounces butter, melted

1. Scald the milk and add the sugar, salt, and shortening. Cool the mixture to lukewarm.
2. Stir the yeast into the lukewarm water until dissolved. Stir this into the cooled milk mixture.
3. Gradually add the flour to the milk mixture, mixing well. Knead until smooth and satiny.
4. Shape the dough into an 18-by-3-inch-long loaf. Brush the surface lightly with a little melted butter. Cover and allow to rise until doubled in bulk.
5. Cut the loaf crosswise into 32 slices and dip the slices into the melted butter. Place 8 slices each in two 9-inch tube pans. Add another layer of 8 slices to each pan. Allow to rise again until doubled in bulk.
6. Bake at 350° for about an hour, or until golden and crusty.

San Francisco Sourdough Bread

CALIFORNIA

Adapted from *American Cooking: The Great West*

Basic sourdough bread starter:

1	cup sourdough starter	¾	cup bread flour

Sourdough starter sponge:

4	ounces sourdough bread starter	1	cup bread flour
¼	cup warm water		

Sourdough bread dough:

5	ounces starter sponge	2–3	tablespoons yellow cornmeal
2	cups warm water		
7	cups bread flour	1	egg white
1	tablespoon salt	2	tablespoons water
¼	cup rice flour		

1. For the starter, mix the sourdough starter with 2 or 3 tablespoons of the bread flour and beat vigorously. Add the remaining bread flour, a little at a time, beating well after each addition. Gather the dough into a ball and allow to rest for 10 minutes. Allow the dough to rise for 8 hours.
2. For the sponge, cut off 4 ounces of the basic starter and knead for 2 minutes.
3. Break it into pieces and dissolve it in the ¼ cup warm water. Add ¼ cup of the bread flour and beat vigorously. Repeat until you have added the full cup of flour, beating well after each addition.
4. Knead the dough for 5–10 minutes, until it is smooth and elastic. Allow the dough to rest for 8–10 hours.
5. For the bread, break the sponge into pieces and dissolve them in the 2 cups warm water. Stir in ½ cup of the bread flour.
6. Add the salt and 5½ cups of flour, ½ cup at a time, mixing well after each addition.
7. Knead for 20 minutes, incorporating flour as needed to form a smooth, elastic dough that is not sticky. Allow the dough to rest for 1 hour.
8. Divide the dough in half and shape each into a round loaf. Place them on a rice-floured board to rise for 4 hours, covered. Keep the cover moist.

9. Transfer the loaves to a cornmeal-dusted peel, score them with a razor blade, and slide the loaves into a 425° oven, directly on a baking stone. Set a pan of hot water in the oven and bake for 15 minutes. Lower the heat to 375° and bake an additional 15 minutes.

10. Remove the loaves from the oven and brush them with the egg white, which has been beaten with the water. Return the loaves to the oven and continue to bake until golden brown and crisp on the surface, about 15 minutes.

Roman Bread

CALIFORNIA
Adapted from *The Los Angeles Times California Cookbook*

1 tablespoon sugar	½ teaspoon salt
1 package dry yeast	½ cup chopped onion
1½ cups lukewarm water	1 tablespoon olive oil
4 cups flour	1 tablespoon fresh rosemary

1. Add the sugar and yeast to the lukewarm water and stir until dissolved.
2. Add the flour, salt, and onion. Knead until smooth. Allow to rise until doubled in bulk.
3. Flatten the dough on a greased baking sheet to a round shape about 2 inches thick. Brush the top with oil. Allow to rise until doubled in bulk.
4. Sprinkle with the rosemary and bake at 400° for 30–35 minutes.

Squaw Bread

CALIFORNIA

Adapted from *The Los Angeles Times California Cookbook*

2 cups water	2½ cups unbleached all-purpose flour
⅓ cup oil	
¼ cup honey	3 cups whole wheat flour
¼ cup raisins	1½ cups rye flour
5 tablespoons light brown sugar, divided	½ cup instant nonfat milk powder
2 packages dry yeast	2½ teaspoons salt
¼ cup warm water	

1. Combine the water, oil, honey, raisins, and 4 tablespoons of the brown sugar in a blender. Blend to liquefy.
2. Soften the yeast in the warm water with the remaining tablespoon of brown sugar.
3. Sift 1 cup unbleached flour, 2 cups whole wheat flour, 1 cup rye flour, nonfat milk powder, and salt together. Add the blender mixture and yeast. Beat 2 minutes.
4. Gradually stir in enough of the remaining flours to make a soft dough. Knead until smooth and satiny, about 10–12 minutes. Cover and allow to rise until doubled in bulk. Punch down and let rest 10 minutes.
5. Shape into 4 round loaves. Cover and allow to rise until light and doubled in bulk.
6. Bake at 375° for 30–35 minutes.

Banana Macadamia Bread

HAWAII

Adapted from Toupin, *Hawaii Cookbook & Backyard Luau*

2	cups flour	¾	cup sugar
2½	teaspoons baking powder	2	large eggs
¼	teaspoon baking soda	1	cup mashed banana
¼	teaspoon salt	½	cup chopped macadamia
½	cup butter		nuts

1. Sift the flour, baking powder, baking soda, and salt together.
2. Cream the butter with the sugar until light and fluffy. Beat in the eggs.
3. Add the flour mixture in thirds, alternating with the banana pulp. Blend well after each addition. Fold in the nuts. Pour the batter into a buttered 9-inch loaf pan.
4. Bake at 350° for about an hour, or until firm to the touch in the center.

Date, Pecan, and Orange Bread

CALIFORNIA

Adapted from *American Cooking: The Great West*

8	ounces pitted dates cut into small bits	1	teaspoon baking soda
		½	teaspoon salt
½	cup finely chopped fresh orange peel	4	tablespoons butter, softened
½	cup pecan pieces	1	cup sugar
2	cups flour	1	egg
1	teaspoon baking powder	1	cup fresh orange juice

1. Toss the dates, pecans, and orange peel with a bit of the flour.
2. Sift the remaining flour, the baking powder, baking soda, and salt together.
3. Cream the butter and the sugar together until smooth and light. Beat in the egg.
4. Add the flour mixture in thirds, alternating with the orange juice. Beat well after each addition. Stir in the floured fruit and the nuts. Pour the batter into a greased and floured 9-inch loaf pan.
5. Bake at 350° for about an hour, or until a toothpick inserted in the center comes out clean.

Wenatchee Apple Bread

WASHINGTON

Adapted from *The Seattle Classic Cookbook*

Batter:

2 cups sifted flour	⅔ cup sugar
½ teaspoon baking soda	3 eggs, beaten
1 teaspoon baking powder	¼ cup applesauce
1 teaspoon salt	1 cup peeled and diced
½ teaspoon allspice	apples
½ teaspoon nutmeg	⅓ cup sour cream
1 teaspoon cinnamon	¼ cup chopped walnuts
¾ cup butter, melted	⅓ cup raisins

Topping:

½ cup applesauce	¼ teaspoon cinnamon
¼ cup firmly packed light brown sugar	

1. For the batter, sift the dry ingredients together.
2. Cream the butter and sugar until well blended. Stir in the eggs and add the applesauce, diced apples, sour cream, nuts, and raisins. Mix thoroughly.
3. Stir in the flour mixture and mix to form a smooth batter. Pour the batter into a greased 9-inch loaf pan.
4. Mix all of the topping ingredients together and spread on top of the batter.
5. Bake at 375° for 50 minutes.

Brown Bread Baked

OREGON

Adapted from *The Portland Woman's Exchange Cook Book, 1913*

1 egg, beaten	1 cup milk
½ cup light brown sugar	1 teaspoon salt
1 cup molasses	1½ cups white flour
3½ cups graham flour	3 teaspoons baking soda
2½ cups buttermilk	

1. Mix the egg, brown sugar, and molasses together. Stir in the graham flour to form a smooth batter. Stir in the buttermilk, milk, and salt.
2. Sift the white flour with the baking soda and resift over the batter. Beat to form a smooth dough. Pour the dough into two greased 9-inch loaf pans.
3. Bake at 350° for 45 minutes, or until done.

Apple-Cheddar Bread

OREGON

Adapted from Brooks, *Oregon's Cuisine of the Rain*

¼ pound unsalted butter, softened
½ cup granulated sugar
¼ cup dark brown sugar
2 large eggs
2 cups unbleached flour
1 teaspoon baking powder
1 teaspoon baking soda
½ teaspoon salt

½ teaspoon ground ginger
1 teaspoon ground cinnamon
1 cup finely chopped, un-peeled tart apple
¾ cup grated sharp Oregon cheddar cheese
¼ cup dried black currants
¼ cup chopped hazelnuts or walnuts

1. Cream the butter and both sugars until smooth and light. Beat in the eggs, one at a time, until thoroughly blended.
2. Sift the flour, baking powder, baking soda, salt, ginger, and cinnamon together. Mix one third of the flour mixture into the creamed mixture.
3. Stir the apples, cheese, currants, and nuts into the creamed mixture. Stir in the remaining flour mixture, mixing to form a smooth batter. Pour the batter into a greased 9-inch loaf pan.
4. Bake at 350° until set in the center, about 40 minutes.

Pineapple–Macadamia Nut Bread

CALIFORNIA

Adapted from *The Los Angeles Times California Cookbook*

4 eggs
1 cup sugar
½ cup oil
¾ cup pineapple juice
½ cup canned crushed pine-apple, with juice

1 tablespoon baking powder
3 cups flour
½ cup chopped macadamia nuts

1. Mix the eggs, sugar, oil, juice, and crushed pineapple together.
2. Sift the baking powder with the flour and mix into the pineapple mixture. Fold in the nuts. Pour into a greased, parchment-lined 9-inch loaf pan.
3. Bake at 350° for 50 minutes.

COFFEE CAKES AND SWEET YEAST BREADS AND BUNS

Alaska's Easter Sourdough Coffeecake

ALASKA

Adapted from *Cooking Alaskan*

4 cups sourdough starter	3 tablespoons butter, melted
⅔ cup fireweed honey	flour, as directed below
1 teaspoon salt	1 cup halved blanched almonds
1 envelope dry yeast	1 teaspoon grated lemon peel
¼ cup very warm water	6 eggs

1. Mix the starter, honey, and salt together.
2. Dissolve the yeast in the warm water. Add this to the starter mixture and mix well. Blend in the butter.
3. Add flour until the dough is as thick as can be hand beaten.
4. Add the almonds and lemon peel. Add the eggs and enough additional flour to form a soft dough that is not sticky. Knead 2 minutes.
5. Place the dough into a greased 9-inch square baking pan. Cover and allow to rise to double in bulk.
6. Glaze with melted butter and honey, if desired.
7. Bake at 425° until golden brown.

Merk's Coffee Cake

CALIFORNIA

Adapted from *The Los Angeles Times California Cookbook*

½ cup shortening	1 cup sour cream
¾ cup sugar	6 tablespoons butter,
1 teaspoon vanilla	softened
3 eggs	1 cup light brown sugar,
2 cups sifted flour	packed
1 teaspoon baking powder	2 teaspoons cinnamon
1 teaspoon baking soda	1 cup chopped nuts

1. Cream the shortening, sugar, and vanilla until light and fluffy. Add the eggs, one at a time, beating well after each addition.
2. Sift the flour, baking powder, and baking soda together. Add this to the creamed mixture alternately with the sour cream, blending well after each addition
3. Pour half the batter into a greased 10-inch tube pan lined with parchment paper.
4. Cream the softened butter with the brown sugar and cinnamon. Add the nuts and toss to make a crumbly mixture. Place half of this mixture over the dough in the pan. Add the remaining batter and top with the remaining nut mixture.
5. Bake at 350° for 30 – 40 minutes, or until cake springs back when lightly touched.

Sweet Potato Bread

CALIFORNIA

Adapted from *The Los Angeles Times California Cookbook*

1 pound sweet potatoes, peeled	2 teaspoons salt
2 cups sugar	6 eggs
2 packages dry yeast	½ cup butter or margarine, melted and cooled
¾ cup milk	8 cups flour

1. Boil the potatoes in water to cover until tender. Drain and reserve ½ cup of the potato water. Peel and mash the potatoes and measure 1 cup.
2. Combine 3 tablespoons of the sugar, the yeast, and the reserved potato water and stir until dissolved. Blend in the potatoes to form a smooth batter. Set aside to rise until doubled in bulk.
3. Scald the milk with the salt. Cool to lukewarm.
4. Beat the eggs. Add the remaining sugar to the eggs gradually while continuing to beat. Stir in the cooled butter.
5. Combine the yeast and egg mixtures. Blend thoroughly. Stir in 2 cups of flour then add the scalded milk. Beat until thoroughly blended. Add 2 more cups of flour and beat for 5 minutes.
6. Add the remaining flour gradually, kneading by hand when the dough becomes too stiff to beat. Knead for 10 minutes. Allow to rise until doubled in bulk.
7. Divide the dough into 4 portions and shape into round loaves on greased baking sheets. Allow to rise until doubled in bulk.
8. Bake at 350° degrees for 20 minutes, or until nicely browned.

COFFEE CAKES AND SWEET YEAST BREADS AND BUNS

Blueberry Crunch Coffee Cake

WASHINGTON
Adapted from *The Seattle Classic Cookbook*

Batter:

1	cup flour	⅓	cup vegetable oil
1½	teaspoons baking powder	½	cup milk
½	teaspoon salt	1	tablespoon lemon juice
⅓	cup sugar	1	cup blueberries
1	egg, well beaten		

Topping:

¼	cup flour	2	tablespoons butter
⅓	cup sugar	½	cup chopped walnuts
1	teaspoon cinnamon		

1. Sift the flour, baking powder, salt, and sugar together.
2. Beat the egg, vegetable oil, milk, and lemon juice together and add to the dry mixture. Mix until smooth.
3. Pour the batter into a greased 8-inch square pan and sprinkle with the blueberries.
4. Prepare the topping by mixing all the ingredients together until crumbly and sprinkle it over the blueberries.
5. Bake at 375° for 40 minutes. Cool slightly and cut into squares.

Huckleberry Cake

OREGON
Adapted from *The Portland Woman's Exchange Cook Book, 1913*

3	eggs	2½	cups flour
½	cup sugar	1	teaspoon baking powder
1	cup milk	1	pint huckleberries
3	tablespoons butter, melted		

1. Mix the eggs, sugar, milk, and melted butter together.
2. Sift the flour with the baking powder and add it to the liquid ingredients. Stir in the berries.
3. Bake in a greased shallow square pan at 375° for 10–15 minutes.

COFFEE CAKES AND SWEET YEAST BREADS AND BUNS

Polk Gulch Cinnamon Rolls

CALIFORNIA

Adapted from Berger and Custis, *Sumptuous Dining in Gaslight San Francisco 1875–1915*

2 cups biscuit dough	3 teaspoons cinnamon
3 tablespoons soft butter	½ teaspoon nutmeg
½ cup light brown sugar	

1. Roll out the biscuit dough to ¼-inch thickness. Spread it with the butter and sprinkle the sugar, cinnamon, and nutmeg over it.
2. Roll the dough up like a jelly roll and cut it in 1-inch-thick slices.
3. Bake the rolls in a well-greased pan at 450° for 15 minutes.

Pão Doce (Portuguese Sweet Bread)

HAWAII

Adapted from Toupin, *Hawaii Cookbook & Backyard Luau*

1 large potato	1 teaspoon salt
1 cup sugar	¼ cup butter, melted
1 package dry yeast	3 large eggs
¼ cup milk	4 cups flour

1. Boil the potato until soft. Reserve ¼ cup of the cooking water. Mash the potato and measure ½ cup of it.
2. Add 2 tablespoons of the sugar and the yeast to the lukewarm potato water. Stir to dissolve. Stir in the mashed potato and allow to stand until doubled in bulk.
3. Scald the milk. Add the salt and cool to lukewarm.
4. Mix the butter, eggs, and remaining sugar together. Beat this into the potato mixture. Add a portion of the flour followed by the milk mixture. Add additional flour to form a dough. Knead until smooth and elastic.
5. Allow the dough to rise until doubled in bulk. Punch down and from the dough into two balls. Set them on a greased baking sheet, cover them, and allow the breads to rise until doubled in bulk.
6. Bake at 350° for 35–45 minutes, or until nicely browned.

Blueberry Corn Bread

OREGON

Adapted from *Oregon's Cuisine of the Rain*

6 ounces butter	1 tablespoon baking powder
1 cup sugar	½ teaspoon salt
3 eggs	2 cups milk
1½ cups cornmeal	1 cup blueberries
2 cups flour	

1. Cream the butter with the sugar until light and fluffy. Beat in the eggs until blended. Stir in the cornmeal.
2. Sift the flour with the baking powder and salt and add this in thirds to the creamed mixture, alternating with the milk. Stir in the blueberries.
3. Pour the batter into a greased 10-inch square pan and bake at 375° for 40 to 50 minutes or until a tester comes out clean from the center.

Sourdough Granola Muffins

ALASKA

Adapted from *Cooking Alaskan*

1 cup sourdough starter	1 cup applesauce
½ cup milk	½ teaspoon salt
1 egg	1 teaspoon baking powder
¼ cup cooking oil	1½ cups whole wheat flour
½ cup honey	1 cup granola cereal

1. Measure the sourdough and add the next five ingredients. Mix well.
2. Add the salt, baking powder, and flour and mix gently. Fold in the granola. Do not overmix. Fill paper-lined muffin cups two-thirds full.
3. Bake at 400° for 15–20 minutes.

A good variation: Dredge ¾ cup of wild blueberries with flour and fold in with the granola.

Cranberry Muffins with Nutmeg Sugar

OREGON

Adapted from Brooks, *Oregon's Cuisine of the Rain*

1 cup cranberries, cleaned	¾ cup milk
½ cup powdered sugar	¼ cup vegetable shortening,
2 cups unbleached flour,	melted
sifted	1¼ tablespoons granulated
½ cup sugar	sugar
3 teaspoons baking powder	1¼ teaspoons freshly grated
¼ teaspoon salt	nutmeg
1 large egg	

1. Sprinkle the cranberries with the powdered sugar. Set aside.
2. Sift the flour, sugar, baking powder, and salt together. Gently beat the egg and stir in the milk and the melted shortening. Add to the dry ingredients. Do not overmix. Carefully fold in the cranberries.
3. Fill paper-lined muffin tins two-thirds full with the batter.
4. Bake at 400° until a toothpick inserted in the center of a muffin comes out clean, about 20 minutes.
5. When cool, sprinkle the muffins with the sugar mixed with nutmeg.

Huckleberry-Banana Muffins

OREGON

Adapted from Brooks, *Oregon's Cuisine of the Rain*

2 large ripe bananas, peeled and sliced	1 teaspoon vanilla extract
	1 cup fresh huckleberries
¼ pound unsalted butter, melted	2¼ cups unbleached flour
	2 teaspoons baking powder
1 cup light brown sugar	1 teaspoon ground cinnamon
2 large eggs, lightly beaten	½ teaspoon salt

1. Puree the bananas and measure 1 cup for use.
2. To the melted butter add the brown sugar, eggs, and banana puree. Mix well. Stir in the vanilla and berries.
3. Sift the flour, baking powder, cinnamon, and salt together. Gently stir in the berry mixture. Do not overmix.
4. Pour the batter into paper-lined muffin tins two-thirds full.
5. Bake at 350° for 25–30 minutes, or until muffins are firm to the touch in the center.

Ragamuffins (Bran Muffins)

WASHINGTON

Adapted from *The Seattle Classic Cookbook*

2	tablespoons baking soda	2	cups 40% Bran Flakes
2	cups boiling water	2	cups dates or raisins
1	cup butter	1	cup nuts
2	cups sugar	5	cups flour
4	eggs	1	tablespoon salt
4	cups All-Bran cereal	4	cups buttermilk

1. Dissolve the baking soda in the boiling water. Allow to cool.
2. Cream the butter with the sugar until light and fluffy. Add the eggs and the soda-water mixture and beat until smooth. Add the cereals, dates, and nuts.
3. Sift the flour and salt and add in thirds to the creamed mixture, alternating with the buttermilk. Mix to form a smooth batter. Pour into 2 greased muffin tins.
4. Bake at 400° for 20 minutes.

Wheat Germ Hamburger Buns

CALIFORNIA

Adapted from *American Cooking: The Great West*

2 packages active dry yeast	2 eggs
¼ cup sugar	8 tablespoons butter,
2 cups lukewarm water	softened
5–6 cups unsifted flour	1 egg, lightly beaten
1 cup wheat germ	1 tablespoon milk
⅔ cup dry milk solids	3 tablespoons sesame seeds
4 teaspoons salt	

1. Dissolve the yeast and a pinch of the sugar in ½ cup of the warm water. Allow the mixture to stand 10 minutes to proof.

2. Mix 5 cups of the flour, the remaining sugar, the wheat germ, dry milk solids, and salt together.

3. Add the remaining warm water to the yeast mixture and beat in the eggs.

4. Gradually beat in the flour mixture followed by the softened butter. Stir until the dough can be gathered into a soft ball. Knead in additional flour to form a smooth dough that is not sticky, about 10 minutes.

5. Allow the dough to rise until doubled in bulk. Punch the dough down and roll into a cylinder about 18 inches long. Cut the cylinder into 1-inch pieces and shape each piece into a bun about 3 inches in diameter. Place the buns 1½ inches apart on greased baking sheets and allow them to rise, covered, until doubled in bulk.

6. Brush the buns with the egg mixed with the milk and sprinkle each one with ½ teaspoon of sesame seeds.

7. Bake at 400° for 15 minutes, or until the hamburger buns are golden brown.

Boalotchkee (Russian Buns)

ALASKA
Adapted from *Cooking Alaskan*

1	pound butter	2	pounds flour
5	eggs	1	pound sugar
2	cups sour cream	1	egg yolk, beaten
¾	teaspoon baking soda	1	ounce chopped nuts

1. Cream the butter and eggs until light and fluffy.
2. Mix the sour cream and baking soda together. Combine this with the butter mixture.
3. Sift the flour and add the sugar. Add the egg mixture. Knead the dough for 10 minutes, until smooth and elastic.
4. Shape the dough into round buns and place them on a lightly oiled shallow pan. Brush with the beaten egg yolk and sprinkle with the chopped nuts.
5. Bake at 350° until done, about 20 minutes.

Conchas

CALIFORNIA
Adapted from *The Los Angeles Times California Cookbook*

3½–4 cups flour
¼ cup sugar
1 teaspoon salt
1 package dry yeast
10 ounces softened butter or margarine

⅔ cup very warm water
2 eggs, room temperature
½ cup honey
¾ cup chopped almonds

1. Mix ¾ cup of the flour, the sugar, salt, and undissolved yeast together. Add two ounces of the softened butter.
2. Add the warm water gradually and beat 2 minutes. Add the eggs and ½ cup of the flour. Beat 2 minutes.
3. Stir in enough additional flour to make a stiff dough and knead until smooth and elastic, about 5–10 minutes. Cover and allow to rise until doubled in bulk.
4. Divide the dough in halves. Roll half of dough to a 15-by-12-inch rectangle. Spread with 2 tablespoons of the softened butter. Fold in half and roll out again to a 15-by-12-inch rectangle. Repeat this process.
5. Cut dough lengthwise into six 1-inch strips. Fold each strip in half lengthwise and coil each into a round roll.
6. Repeat with the other half of the dough.
7. Allow the rolls to rise for 1 hour. Brush them with honey and sprinkle with the almonds.
8. Bake at 350° for 15–20 minutes, or until done.

Mush Biscuit

OREGON
Adapted from *The Portland Woman's Exchange Cook Book, 1913*

4 cups cooked cornmeal mush or grits, cold

½ cup melted butter
flour

1. Stir the cold cornmeal mush into the melted butter and mix thoroughly.
2. Form the mixture into thin, little biscuits, using just enough flour to prevent sticking. Place the biscuits on a greased baking sheet.
3. Bake at 400° for 10 minutes.

Ranch Wedgies

CALIFORNIA

Adapted from *The Los Angeles Times California Cookbook*

2 cups boiling water	2 tablespoons butter or
1¼ cups bulgur	margarine
½ cup light brown sugar,	2 packages dry yeast
packed	⅔ cup warm water
1 teaspoon salt	4½ cups flour

1. Pour the boiling water over the bulgur. Allow to stand for a minute, then stir in the brown sugar, salt, and butter or margarine. Cool to lukewarm.
2. Sprinkle the yeast over the warm water and stir to dissolve. Stir the yeast into the bulgur mixture. Stir in enough flour to make a sticky dough.
3. Knead the dough until smooth and elastic, about 10 minutes. Cover and allow to rise until doubled in bulk, about 1 hour.
4. Punch down and let rise again 30 minutes.
5. Divide dough into halves and pat each half into a well-greased 8-inch round cake pan. Cover and allow to rise slightly above the rims of the pans.
6. Bake at 350° for 1 hour, or until done. Allow to cool and cut into wedges.

BREAD PUDDING

Blueberry Sourdough Bread Pudding

OREGON

Adapted from Brooks, *Oregon's Cuisine of the Rain*

1 loaf sourdough bread	1 tablespoon vanilla extract
2 cups blueberries	1½ teaspoons ground cinna-
¼ pound unsalted butter,	mon, divided
melted and cooled	½ teaspoon freshly grated
4 large eggs	nutmeg
3 large egg yolks	¼ cup sugar
1 cup half-and-half	boiling water as needed
2 cups milk	heavy cream for serving
¾ cup sugar	

1. Cut about two thirds of the bread into 1-inch thick slices. Trim and cut into cubes.
2. Toss the blueberries with the bread cubes. Pour the cooled butter over the top and mix lightly. Fill a buttered 2-quart casserole with this mixture.
3. Whisk the whole eggs, egg yolks, half-and-half, milk, sugar, vanilla extract, ½ teaspoon of the cinnamon, and the nutmeg together. Pour this over the top of the bread and blueberries. Allow to stand for 15 minutes.
4. Toss the sugar with the remaining cinnamon and sprinkle the top of the bread pudding generously with this mixture. Place the casserole in a pan of hot water that comes up halfway.
5. Bake at 350° for an hour, or until set. Remove the dish and pan from the oven and allow the pudding to cool in the water bath. Serve with cream.

Pies

Pies

Esther's Old-Fashioned Rhubarb Pie

NEW HAMPSHIRE

Adapted from Berquist, *The High Maples Farm Cookbook*

6–8 stalks fresh strawberry rhubarb, washed and cut into
pieces
1 9-inch pie shell
2 tablespoons flour

1¼ cups sugar
2 tablespoons cold butter,
cut into pieces
1 top crust

1. Place the rhubarb in a saucepan and cover with cold water. Bring to the boil. Drain and allow to cool.
2. Measure 4 cups of cooked rhubarb and add it to the pie shell.
3. Mix the flour and sugar together and spread it on top of the rhubarb. Dot with the butter.
4. Add the top crust and crimp to seal.
5. Bake at 375° for 45 minutes.

Sadie Nason's Blueberry Pie

MAINE

Adapted from Roux, *What's Cooking Down in Maine*

Pie crust:

2 cups flour
½ teaspoon baking powder
1 cup shortening

½ teaspoon salt
½ cup milk

Filling:

1 quart blueberries
1 cup sugar
½ lemon, juice only

dash cinnamon
1 tablespoon butter
dabs of milk

1. To form the pie dough, knead the flour, baking powder, shortening, and salt together. Add portions of the milk gradually until a pie dough just forms.
2. Divide the dough in half and roll half the pastry out and line the bottom of a pie plate.
3. Mix the berries, sugar, lemon juice, cinnamon, and butter together. Fill the pie shell with this mixture.
4. Dab milk around the edge of the lower crust before putting on the top crust. Cut a steam vent in the top crust. Wash the crust with milk.
5. Bake at 375° for 20 minutes, or until bubbling through the steam vent.

FRUIT AND BERRY PIES

Green Apple Pie

NEW HAMPSHIRE
Adapted from Berquist, *The High Maples Farm Cookbook*

4 cups green apples, peeled, cored, and sliced	¼ teaspoon cinnamon
1 unbaked 9-inch pie shell	1 tablespoon butter
1 scant cup sugar	1 top crust
¼ teaspoon nutmeg	1 tablespoon heavy cream

1. Mound the apples in the center of the pie shell.
2. Mix the sugar, nutmeg, and cinnamon and sift onto the pie. Dot with the butter.
3. Cover with the top crust, crimping the edge to seal. Score the crust and brush generously with heavy cream.
4. Bake at 450° for 10 minutes, then reduce the heat to 350° for 35–45 minutes.

Green Tomato Mincemeat Pie

NEW HAMPSHIRE
Adapted from Berquist, *The High Maples Farm Cookbook*

5 cups hard green tomatoes	2 tablespoons cinnamon
4 cups apples, peeled and cored	1 tablespoon nutmeg
1 pound seedless raisins	4 tablespoons fresh lemon juice
1 cup beef suet, ground	2 unbaked 9-inch pie shells
1¼ cups cider vinegar	2 top crusts
1 tablespoon salt	1 tablespoon cream
2 pounds dark brown sugar	

1. Chop the tomatoes coarsely. Drain them and cover with cold water in a saucepan. Bring to a boil and cook 5 minutes. Drain.
2. Chop the apples coarsely. Add the tomatoes and the remaining ingredients (except the pie crusts and cream) and bring to a boil over medium heat. Reduce the heat and simmer for 2 hours, stirring occasionally to prevent burning.
3. When the filling has cooled slightly, add it to the pie shells. Cover each with a top crust. Score the tops and brush with cream.
4. Bake at 400° for 30 minutes, or until bubbling in the center.

Mary's Sour Cherry Pie

NEW HAMPSHIRE
Adapted from Berquist, *The High Maples Farm Cookbook*

4 cups sour cherries, pitted	2 tablespoons flour
1 unbaked 9-inch pie shell	¼ teaspoon cinnamon
1 cup sugar	1 top crust

1. Add the cherries to the pie shell.
2. Mix the sugar, flour, and cinnamon together and spread the mixture over the cherries. Cover with the top crust and score with a sharp knife.
3. Bake at 400° for 10 minutes. Reduce heat to 325° and bake for 45 minutes.

Beach Plum Pie

MASSACHUSETTS
Adapted from Hawkins, Havemeyer, and Havemeyer, *Nantucket and Other New England Cooking*

2 cups ripe beach plums, washed	1 grated rind of orange pastry for 9-inch pie
1½ cups sugar	sour cream

1. Remove pits from the beach plums. Add the sugar and orange rind.
2. Line a 9-inch pie pan with half of the pastry. Pour the plums into the pie pan. Cover with the top pastry, crimp the edges, and cut vents in the top.
3. Bake at 375° for 10 minutes. Reduce the heat to 325° and bake for 20–30 minutes longer, until juice bubbles out of the vents. Serve with sour cream.

CUSTARD AND EGG PIES

Sour Cream Pie

VERMONT

Adapted from *Out of Vermont Kitchens*

1　egg	1　teaspoon cinnamon
1½　cups light brown sugar	½　teaspoon cloves
1½　cups chopped raisins	½　teaspoon allspice
1　cup sour cream	½　teaspoon salt
1　teaspoon vinegar	1　unbaked pie shell

1. Prepare the pie filling by mixing the ingredients in the order given. Pour into the pie shell.
2. Bake at 425° for 10 minutes, then lower the heat to 350° and continue to bake until set.

Date Custard Pie

MASSACHUSETTS

Adapted from *Boston Chapter, No. 28 Order of Eastern Star Cook Book*

½　pound pitted dates	⅛　teaspoon salt
1　baked 9-inch pie shell	1　tablespoon sugar
2　cups milk	pinch nutmeg
2　eggs, well beaten	

1. Slice the dates in half and place them on the bottom of the pie shell.
2. Cook the milk, eggs, salt, sugar, and nutmeg together in the top of a double boiler to form a thick custard. Pour this over the dates.
3. Refrigerate 3 hours.

Raisin Cream Pie

MASSACHUSETTS

Adapted from *Boston Chapter, No. 28 Order of Eastern Star Cook Book*

1　cup raisins, coarsely chopped	2　egg yolks
	1　teaspoon vanilla
1　cup milk	1　baked 9-inch pie shell
¾　cup sugar	2　egg whites
1　tablespoon flour	

1. Mix the first 6 ingredients. Cook in the top of a double boiler until thickened. Pour into the baked pie shell.
2. Beat the egg whites stiff, but not dry. Top the pie with the meringue and brown in the oven at 400°.

Rum Pumpkin Meringue Pie

RHODE ISLAND
Adapted from Dyer, *The Newport Cookbook*

Filling:

3 egg yolks, lightly beaten	½ teaspoon cinnamon
¼ cup molasses	1 cup light cream
¾ cup sugar	2 cups cooked pumpkin
½ teaspoon salt	¼ cup dark rum
½ teaspoon ground ginger	1 unbaked 9-inch pie shell
½ teaspoon ground nutmeg	

Meringue:

3 egg whites	⅓ cup sugar
¼ teaspoon cream of tartar	1 tablespoon dark rum
¼ teaspoon salt	

1. Combine the egg yolks, molasses, and ¾ cup sugar. Whisk until the sugar has dissolved.
2. Add the salt, ginger, nutmeg, cinnamon, and cream.
3. Blend in the pumpkin, mixing well. Stir in the rum.
4. Pour the mixture into the pie shell and bake at 425° for 15 minutes. Lower the heat to 350° and continue to bake until the filling is set, about 30 minutes. Remove the pie from the oven and let stand at room temperature until cool.
5. To make the meringue, beat the egg whites until frothy. Add the cream of tartar and the salt and continue to beat until stiff but not dry.
6. Beat in the sugar a little at a time, beating well after each addition. Fold in the rum.
7. Spread the meringue evenly over the entire surface of the pie to the edge of the shell. Pull the meringue to form peaks.
8. Bake at 350° until the meringue is delicately browned, about 15 minutes.

CUSTARD AND EGG PIES

Pumpkin Pie

CONNECTICUT

Adapted from *The Neighborhood Cook Book*

1	pound cooked pumpkin	1	teaspoon salt
1	can evaporated milk	2	teaspoons cinnamon
1½	cups sugar	4	eggs
1	teaspoon ginger	1	unbaked 9-inch pie shell

1. Mix the pumpkin with the evaporated milk. Stir in the sugar, ginger, salt, and cinnamon.
2. Beat in the eggs and pour into the unbaked pie shell.
3. Bake at 400° for 30 minutes, or until set in the center.

CHIFFON AND CREAM PIES

Strawberry Cream Pie

CONNECTICUT

Adapted from *The Neighborhood Cook Book*

Filling:

1	tablespoon gelatin	1	teaspoon vanilla
3	tablespoons cold water	1	quart strawberries, halved
1½	pints cream	1	cup granulated sugar
½	cup powdered sugar	1	baked 9-inch pie shell

Glaze:

½	cup strawberries, mashed	½	teaspoon gelatin
¼	cup sugar	2	tablespoons water

1. Soak the 1 tablespoon gelatin in the 3 tablespoons cold water. Dissolve it over hot water.
2. Whip the cream stiff. Stir in the powdered sugar and vanilla. Fill the cooled pie shell and refrigerate.
3. Marinate the halved berries with the sugar. When the whipped cream is set, pour the berries over and glaze.
4. To make the glaze, add the mashed berries and the sugar to a non-reactive saucepan and bring to the boil. Add the gelatin, which has been softened in the water.
5. When the gelatin is dissolved, pour the glaze into a shallow pan and refrigerate until just set. Top the pie with this.
6. Refrigerate at least 3 hours.

Banana Cream Pie

CONNECTICUT

Adapted from *The Neighborhood Cook Book*

¾ cup sugar
⅓ cup flour
2 eggs
1 teaspoon salt
2 cups scalded milk

1 teaspoon vanilla
1 baked pie shell
3 bananas, sliced
2 cups whipped cream,
  sweetened

1. Mix the sugar, flour, eggs, and salt. Pour the milk in gradually and cook over moderate heat, stirring until thickened. Allow to cool, then add the vanilla.
2. Pour this into the baked pie shell. Top with sliced bananas and cover with whipped cream.

Grandmother Smith's Frosted Lemon Pie

NEW HAMPSHIRE

Adapted from Berquist, *The High Maples Farm Cookbook*

1¼ cups sugar
3 tablespoons flour
1 tablespoon cornstarch
¼ teaspoon salt
1 tablespoon softened butter
¼ cup lemon juice and pulp

2 tablespoons grated lemon
  peel
1 whole egg
3 eggs, separated
1 cup cold water
1 unbaked 9-inch pie shell

1. Combine 1 cup of the sugar with the flour, cornstarch, and salt. Add the butter and beat until light and smooth. Mix in the lemon juice and pulp and the lemon peel.
2. Add the whole egg, 3 egg yolks, and water. Mix gently and refrigerate until thoroughly chilled. Pour the filling into the pie shell.
3. Bake at 450° for 10 minutes. Reduce the heat to 325° and bake for 3 minutes, or until the custard is just set.
4. Beat the egg whites until foamy. Add the remaining ¼ cup sugar to the egg whites and beat until glossy but not dry.
5. Top the pie with the meringue and bake at 350° until the meringue is nicely browned.

COBBLERS AND TARTS

Blueberry Cobbler

MAINE

Adapted from Roux, *What's Cooking Down in Maine*

2	ounces butter	½	teaspoon salt
1	cup flour	2	cups blueberries
½	cup milk	1	cup sugar
2	teaspoons baking powder	1	cup boiling water
½	cup sugar		

1. Mix the first six ingredients together and spread the dough over the bottom of a well-buttered baking dish.
2. Place the blueberries on the dough, followed by the sugar and the boiling water.
3. Bake at 350° for 35–45 minutes. When done, the dough will be on top and the filling below.

Blueberry Buckle

MAINE

Adapted from Roux, *What's Cooking Down in Maine*

Dough:

½	cup shortening	½	teaspoon salt
½	cup sugar	2½	teaspoons baking powder
1	egg, beaten	½	cup milk
2	cups sifted flour		

Filling:

2½	cups blueberries	¼	teaspoon cinnamon
½	cup sugar	⅓	cup butter
½	cup flour		

1. Prepare the dough by creaming the shortening and sugar together. Add the beaten egg and mix well.
2. Mix and sift the flour, salt, and baking powder together and add this to the creamed mixture alternately with the milk. Spread this dough in an ungreased 8-inch square pan.
3. Spread the blueberries on top of the dough. Mix and sift the filling's dry ingredients together and cut in the butter. Spread this over the top of the blueberries.
4. Bake at 375° for about an hour.

Apple Grunt

MASSACHUSETTS

Adapted from Hawkins, Havemeyer, and Havemeyer, *Nantucket and Other New England Cooking*

2 tablespoons butter	¼ cup water
6 medium tart apples	1 cup flour
¼ cup molasses	½ tablespoon baking powder
¼ cup sugar	⅓ cup cream
½ teaspoon cinnamon	

1. Melt the butter in a skillet. Sauté the apples with the molasses, sugar, and cinnamon. Add the water and simmer a minute. Place in an ungreased small rectangular or 8-inch square pan.
2. Mix the flour with the baking powder and stir in the cream to form a biscuit dough. Drop tablespoons of batter on the apples.
3. Cover and bake in a 350° oven for 15 minutes.

Blueberry Pandowdy

MASSACHUSETTS

Adapted from Hawkins, Havemeyer, and Havemeyer, *Nantucket and Other New England Cooking*

1 quart blueberries	1 tablespoon sugar
1 cup sugar	½ teaspoon salt
½ teaspoon ground ginger	3 tablespoons butter
3 tablespoons butter	3 tablespoons solid vegetable
2 cups sifted all-purpose flour	shortening
4 teaspoons baking powder	¾ cup milk

1. Wash and pick over the blueberries. Sprinkle with the sugar and ginger. Dot with the butter.
2. Sift the flour, baking powder, sugar, and salt together. Cut in the 3 tablespoons butter and shortening. Add the milk and stir carefully to just mix together.
3. Roll the dough out to fit a greased 10-inch square baking pan.
4. Place the blueberries in the pan and top with the biscuit dough.
5. Bake at 350° for 30 minutes, or until biscuits are light brown.

COBBLERS AND TARTS

Great-Grandmother Smith's Apple Pandowdy

NEW HAMPSHIRE

Adapted from Berquist, *The High Maples Farm Cookbook*

4½ cups apples, peeled, cored, and sliced	½ teaspoon cinnamon
	½ teaspoon salt
2 tablespoons cold butter, cut into bits	¼ cup molasses
	1 recipe pie dough
⅓ cup sugar	2 tablespoons heavy cream
¼ teaspoon nutmeg	

1. Butter a 10-inch deep-dish pie plate and fill with the apples. Dot with the butter.
2. Mix the sugar, nutmeg, cinnamon, and salt together and spread over the apples. Drizzle on the molasses.
3. Roll the pie dough to ½-inch thickness and cover the pan. Spread with the cream. Prick the crust with a fork.
4. Bake at 375° for 1 hour.
5. To serve, cut the crust into the apple mixture.

Editor's note: To "dowdy" is to stir together.

Apple Potpie

MASSACHUSETTS

Adapted from Hawkins, Havemeyer, and Havemeyer, *Nantucket and Other New England Cooking*

1 recipe bread dough	1 cup molasses
1 teaspoon lard	1 cup water
6–8 apples, peeled and quartered	

1. Take the risen bread dough to make a top crust for a deep baking dish. Mix it with the teaspoon of lard and roll out to the size of the baking dish.
2. Put the quartered apples in the baking dish. Pour the molasses over the apples and add the water. Cover with the bread dough.
3. Bake at 350° for 35–40 minutes, until the crust is brown.

Banbury Tarts

MASSACHUSETTS

Adapted from Hawkins, Havemeyer, and Havemeyer, *Nantucket and Other New England Cooking*

½ recipe pie pastry
1 egg
1 cup sugar
1 cup raisins

1 tablespoon cornstarch stirred into 2 tablespoons water
2 tablespoons butter
1 lemon, juice and rind

1. Roll out the pastry ¼-inch thick. Cut into 6 squares 3-by-3 inches.
2. Mix the egg, sugar, raisins, cornstarch, and butter together. Add the lemon juice and grated lemon rind.
3. Place one sixth of the filling on a square of pastry. Fold the dough over to make a triangle, crimping all around. Place on a greased cookie sheet. Repeat with all the squares.
4. Bake at 400° for 10 minutes, then reduce the heat to 350°. Bake for an additional 15–20 minutes.

Newport Apple Slump

RHODE ISLAND

Adapted from Dyer, *The Newport Cookbook*

2 cups stone-ground white flour
1 teaspoon salt
1 cup sugar
⅓ cup butter
⅓ cup lard
¼ cup ice water
1 teaspoon vinegar

10–12 large crisp, tart apples, peeled, quartered, and cored
¼ teaspoon nutmeg
¼ teaspoon cinnamon
3 cups molasses
heavy cream

1. Sift the flour, salt, and sugar together. Cut in the butter and lard with a pastry cutter until the mixture resembles coarse meal.
2. Mix the water with the vinegar and add it, 1 tablespoon at a time, to the mixture. Mix lightly with a fork. Form the dough into a ball and roll out to 16-by-8-inches.
3. Line the bottom and sides of a deep 8-inch baking dish with the rolled out dough, letting the dough hang over the sides of the dish. Allow enough to fold over and cover the top of the dish completely.
4. Fill the dough-lined dish with the apples to about 1 inch of the rim. Sprinkle with the nutmeg and cinnamon and pour the molasses over the apples. Bring the overlapping dough over the top to cover.
5. Bake at 425° until bubbling and the crust is browned. Serve with heavy cream.

FRUIT AND BERRY PIES

Schnitz Pie

PENNSYLVANIA

Adapted from Lestz, *The Pennsylvania Dutch Cookbook*

1	pound dried apples (schnitz)	2	tablespoons cinnamon
	rind and juice of 1 orange		unbaked crust for 2-crust pie
2	cups sugar	1	tablespoon butter

1. Cover the apples with water and soak overnight.
2. Add the orange rind and juice and more water to the apples if necessary. Add all to a saucepan and boil until the apples are soft. Sieve through a colander, then add the sugar and cinnamon.
3. Pour the filling into the pie crust, dot the top with the butter, and cover with a top crust or lattice strips made from dough scraps.
4. Bake at 450° for 10 minutes. Reduce heat to 350° and bake for 30 additional minutes.

Strawberry Rhubarb Pie

NEW YORK

Adapted from *A Library of Favorite Recipes from New York State*

1⅓	cups sugar	1	unbaked pie shell
6	tablespoons flour	2	tablespoons butter
2½	cups rhubarb	1	top crust
2½	cups fresh or frozen strawberries		sugar

1. Mix the sugar and flour. Toss in the fruit and pour the filling into the unbaked pie shell. Dot with the butter and cover with the top crust. Cut vents with a knife. Sprinkle the crust with sugar.
2. Bake at 375° until crust is browned and juice begins to bubble through slits.

Funeral Pie

PENNSYLVANIA
Adapted from Lestz, *The Pennsylvania Dutch Cookbook*

1 cup raisins, washed	2 tablespoons grated lemon
1½ cups sugar	rind
4 tablespoons flour	juice of 1 lemon
1 egg, beaten well	pinch salt
	1 unbaked pie shell

1. Soak the raisins for 3 hours in water. Drain.
2. In a separate bowl, mix the sugar, flour, and egg. Add the lemon rind, lemon juice, salt, and raisins.
3. Cook the raisin filling in the top of a double boiler for 15 minutes, stirring occasionally.
4. Allow the mixture to cool. Pour it into a pie shell.
5. Cover the raisin filling with a lattice top made with leftover pie dough.
6. Bake the pie at 400° for 40 minutes, or until nicely browned.

Somersault Pie

PENNSYLVANIA
Adapted from *Choice Recipes*

Dough:

1 cup sugar	1¼ cups flour
¼ cup butter or lard	½ teaspoon baking soda
1 egg	1 unbaked pie shell
½ cup sour milk	

Filling:

½ cup molasses	1 teaspoon nutmeg
½ cup sugar	1 teaspoon cinnamon
1 egg	1 cup water
1 tablespoon flour	

1. Cream the sugar with the butter until light. Add the egg and milk. Beat until smooth.
2. Mix the flour and the baking soda and add to the creamed mixture. Form a dough and press it into the pie shell.
3. Combine all of the filling ingredients. Pour this over the dough and bake at 400° for 40 minutes, or until set.

Montgomery Pie

PENNSYLVANIA
Adapted from *Choice Recipes*

Batter:

1 cup sugar	1¼ cups flour
¼ cup shortening	1½ teaspoons baking powder
1 egg	2 unbaked pie shells
½ cup sweet milk	

Filling:

¼ cup sugar	1 tablespoon flour
½ cup molasses	1 cup cold water
1 egg	

1. Mix the sugar, shortening, and egg until smooth and light.
2. Add the milk and the flour mixed with the baking powder. Stir to form a smooth batter.
3. Stir all the ingredients together for the filling and pour this into the unbaked pie shells. Top with the batter.
4. Bake at 375° for 50 minutes.

Mother's Pumpkin Custard Pie

DELAWARE
Adapted from *Winterthur's Culinary Collection*

2 cups fresh pumpkin, mashed	½ cup sugar
1½ tablespoons butter	2 eggs
2 tablespoons all-purpose flour	1 cup milk
½ teaspoon nutmeg	1 9-inch pie shell, unbaked

1. Warm the pumpkin. Add the butter and stir until melted.
2. Mix the flour, nutmeg, and sugar. Stir into the warm pumpkin.
3. Beat the eggs and add the milk. Stir thoroughly into the pumpkin mixture. Pour the filling into a 9-inch pie shell.
4. Bake at 450° for 10 minutes. Reduce the heat to 375° and continue to bake about 30 minutes longer, or until set in the middle.

Sour Cream Raisin Pie

PENNSYLVANIA
Adapted from Lestz, *The Pennsylvania Dutch Cookbook*

1	tablespoon flour	2	eggs
½	teaspoon cinnamon	1½	cups sour cream
½	teaspoon nutmeg	1½	cups raisins
1	cup sugar	1	unbaked pie shell

1. Mix the flour, spices, and sugar together in a large mixing bowl.
2. Add the eggs, sour cream, and raisins. Stir until smooth.
3. Bake in an unbaked pie shell at 350° for about 30 minutes, or until done.

Union Pie

PENNSYLVANIA
Adapted from Lestz, *The Pennsylvania Dutch Cookbook*

2	cups sugar	1	teaspoon baking soda
4	tablespoons flour	1	cup buttermilk
1	teaspoon cinnamon	1	cup sour cream
2	eggs	1	unbaked pie shell
½	cup water		

1. Mix the sugar, flour, and cinnamon together. Add the eggs and water and mix well.
2. Dissolve the baking soda in a little buttermilk, add it and the remaining buttermilk and sour cream to the above mixture. Stir gently.
3. Bake in an unbaked pie shell at 350° until set in the center, or "an inserted silver knife comes out clean" (about 30 minutes).

CHIFFON AND CREAM PIES

Apple Chiffon Pie

NEW YORK

Adapted from Schultz, *As American as Apple Pie*

Crust:

1½ cups (about 60) ground gingersnaps

¼ cup powdered sugar

6 tablespoons unsalted butter, melted

Filling:

4 egg yolks

¼ cup sugar

1½ tablespoons cornstarch

¼ teaspoon vanilla

¾ cup milk, scalded

2 teaspoons lemon juice

¼ cup apricot preserves

½ cup light brown sugar

3 tablespoons light rum

3 green apples, peeled, cored, and sliced

1 envelope unflavored gelatin

¼ cup apple juice

½ cup heavy or whipping cream

1 tablespoon powdered sugar

3 egg whites

1. Toss the ground gingersnaps with the powdered sugar. Stir in the butter until well blended.
2. Press the mixture over the bottom and the sides of a 9-inch deep-dish pie plate.
3. Bake at 300° for 12 minutes. Allow to cool.
4. Mix the egg yolks with the sugar, cornstarch, vanilla, and scalded milk in the top of a double boiler. Cook, stirring constantly, until thick. Allow to cool and refrigerate until well chilled.
5. Mix the lemon juice, preserves, brown sugar, and rum in a nonreactive saucepan. Add the apples and bring to the boil. Cook over medium heat until syrupy, about 15 minutes. Puree the mixture and pass it through a sieve.
6. Mix the gelatin with the apple juice and allow it to soften. Warm the mixture to dissolve the gelatin.
7. Whisk in the apple puree. Allow to cool and refrigerate for 30 minutes. The gelatin should not be set.
8. Whip the cream with the powdered sugar until stiff.
9. Fold the cooled custard into the apple puree. Fold the whipped cream into this mixture. Refrigerate while whipping the egg whites stiff. Fold the egg whites into the filling.
10. Pour the filling into the baked crust and refrigerate thoroughly, at least 3 hours.

Lemon Sponge Pie

PENNSYLVANIA

Adapted from Lestz, *The Pennsylvania Dutch Cookbook*

1	cup sugar	¼	teaspoon salt
1	tablespoon flour	2	tablespoons butter, melted
3	egg yolks	3	egg whites
⅓	cup lemon juice, fresh	1	cup milk
¼	teaspoon grated lemon rind	1	unbaked pie shell

1. Blend the sugar with the flour. Add the egg yolks, lemon juice, lemon rind, salt, and butter.
2. Whip the egg whites to form soft peaks.
3. Fold the whites into the flour mixture, then add the milk. Pour this filling into an unbaked pie shell.
4. Bake at 350° for 20–30 minutes.

Tavern Rum Pie

DELAWARE

Adapted from *Winterthur's Culinary Collection*

2⅔	cups vanilla wafers, crushed	1½	tablespoons unflavored
½	cup butter, melted		gelatin
6	egg yolks	1	pint whipping cream
1	cup sugar	½	cup rum
½	cup cold water		

1. Mix the crushed cookies with the melted butter to form a crust. Press this into the bottom and sides of a 10-inch pie pan.
2. Beat the yolks until light. Add the sugar and continue beating until thick and the yolks are pale yellow.
3. In a saucepan combine the water with the gelatin and slowly bring to a boil. Add the egg mixture while beating.
4. Whip the cream stiff. Fold in the egg mixture, then the rum. Refrigerate until stiff peaks form and hold.
5. Fill the pie shell with this mixture and refrigerate 1 hour. Serve cold.

CHOCOLATE PIE

Chocolate Chiffon Pie

NEW YORK

Adapted from *A Library of Favorite Recipes from New York State*

Crumb pie shell:

1¼ cups fine shortbread cookie crumbs
¼ cup sugar

½ cup melted butter
¼ cup almonds, ground

Filling:

1 tablespoon unflavored gelatin
¼ cup cold water
½ cup boiling water
1–2 squares unsweetened chocolate

4 eggs, separated
1 cup sugar
½ teaspoon salt
1 teaspoon vanilla
1 cup whipped cream
salt

1. Mix the cookie crumbs, sugar, melted butter, and ground almonds together. Press into a 9-inch pie plate. Bake at 425° for 10 minutes.
2. Soften the gelatin in the cold water for 5 minutes.
3. Mix the boiling water and chocolate until smooth. Add the softened gelatin to the chocolate mixture and stir until dissolved.
4. Add the slightly beaten egg yolks, ½ cup of the sugar, the salt, and vanilla. Beat thoroughly. Cool until the mixture begins to thicken.
5. Beat the egg whites until foamy. Beat in the remaining sugar gradually and fold into the gelatin mixture. Pour into the pie shell and chill until firm. Top with whipped cream.

SPECIAL PIE

Amish Shoo Fly Pie

PENNSYLVANIA

Adapted from Lestz, *The Pennsylvania Dutch Cookbook*

1½ cups sifted flour
½ cup packed light brown sugar
¼ cup butter

¾ cup boiling water
¾ cup dark molasses
½ teaspoon baking soda
1 unbaked pie shell

1. Mix the flour, sugar, and butter until crumbly.
2. Combine the water, molasses, and baking soda and pour into an unbaked 9-inch pie shell, alternating with the crumb mixture.
3. Bake at 375° for 30 minutes, or until set.

Apple Roll

PENNSYLVANIA
Adapted from Lestz, *The Pennsylvania Dutch Cookbook*

2½	cups flour	½	cup sweet milk
½	teaspoon salt	5 – 6	tart apples
2	tablespoons sugar		cinnamon
4	teaspoons baking powder	2	cups granulated sugar
3	teaspoons lard	1	cup water
1	egg		

1. Combine the flour, salt, sugar, and baking powder. Cut in the lard, then add the egg and milk. Form into a dough.
2. Roll out the dough as for pie.
3. Peel, core, and cut the apples in thin slices and cover the dough.
4. Sprinkle the apples with cinnamon and roll up lengthwise, jelly-roll fashion. Cut the roll into pieces about 2-inches long.
5. Prepare a syrup by boiling the sugar in the water.
6. Place the slices in a greased 8-inch rectangular pan and pour the syrup over the slices.
7. Bake at 350° for 30 minutes.

Apple Jonathan

NEW YORK
Adapted from Wilson, *American Cooking: The Eastern Heartland*

1	cup flour	¼	cup milk
2	teaspoons baking powder	6	medium apples, peeled,
½	teaspoon salt		cored, and cut into ⅛"-
4	tablespoons butter		inch-thick slices
½	cup sugar	½	cup pure maple syrup
1	egg	1	cup heavy cream

1. Sift the flour, baking powder, and salt together.
2. Cream the butter and the sugar until light and fluffy. Beat in the egg. Add ½ cup of the flour mixture and mix until smooth.
3. Stir in the milk a tablespoon at a time, alternating with the remaining flour mixture, mixing until the batter is smooth.
4. Toss the apple slices with the maple syrup. Spread the apple slices across the bottom of a buttered 3-quart baking dish and pour in the batter.
5. Bake at 350° for 30 – 35 minutes, or until a toothpick inserted in the cake comes out clean. Provide cream in a pitcher at service.

Black Cherry Tarts

PENNSYLVANIA
Adapted from Reed, *The Philadelphia Cook Book of Town and Country*

Pastry:

½ pound butter, softened
¾ cup sugar
1 egg

1 teaspoon vanilla or almond extract
2 cups flour, sifted
1 egg white

Filling:

1 12-ounce can pitted black cherries

1 teaspoon potato flour
1 teaspoon vanilla

1. Cream the butter with the sugar until light. Beat in the egg until smooth. Add the vanilla and mix well.
2. Stir in the sifted flour to make a firm dough. Refrigerate the dough for several hours.
3. Roll the dough very thin, cut into circles, and wrap around conical forms.
4. Place the cornucopias on an ungreased baking sheet and brush them with beaten egg white. Bake at 325° for 15 minutes.
5. Drain the cherries and heat the liquid.
6. Mix the potato flour with a little water and stir it into the cherry liquid. Add the vanilla and cook until thickened. Stir in the cherries.
7. Allow the filling to cool. Fill the cornucopias with the filling just before serving.

Mango Pie

FLORIDA
Adapted from Nickerson, *Florida Cookbook*

1 cup sugar	1 tablespoon lemon juice
½ teaspoon cinnamon	1 tablespoon butter
¼ teaspoon nutmeg	1 unbaked 9-inch pie shell
2 tablespoons flour	1 top crust
3½ cups peeled, sliced, half-ripe mangoes	

1. Mix the sugar, cinnamon, nutmeg, and flour together.
2. Arrange a layer of mangoes in the pie shell. Sprinkle with some of the sugar mixture. Repeat, layering fruit and the sugar mixture until all of the ingredients are used. Sprinkle with lemon juice and dot with butter.
3. Cover the pie with a top crust. Slit the top.
4. Bake at 425° for 10 minutes. Reduce the heat to 350° and bake 30–40 minutes longer, or until the pie is bubbling in the center.

Oconee Apple Pie

SOUTH CAROLINA
Adapted from *A Taste of South Carolina*

6 apples	1–2 tablespoons flour (if apples are juicy)
½–⅔ cup sugar	pastry for a 2-crust pie
¼ teaspoon salt	2 tablespoons butter
½ teaspoon cinnamon	
¼ teaspoon nutmeg	

1. Pare, core, and slice the apples.
2. Sift the dry ingredients together and toss with the apples.
3. Line a 9-inch pie pan with pastry, fill with the apple mixture, dot with the butter, and cover with a top crust. Cut steam vents with a sharp knife.
4. Bake at 450° for 15 minutes, then reduce the heat to 350° and bake 45 minutes longer.

FRUIT AND BERRY PIES

Strawberry Pie

SOUTH CAROLINA
Adapted from *A Taste of South Carolina*

1	9-inch pie shell	1	cup cold water
1	3-ounce package straw-berry gelatin	1	pint strawberries, cleaned and cut in half
1	cup sugar	1	cup whipping cream
1	cup boiling water	¼	cup sugar
1	tablespoon cornstarch		

1. Bake the pie shell blind. Allow it to cool.
2. Dissolve the gelatin and 1 cup sugar in the boiling water in a saucepan.
3. Stir the cornstarch into the cold water to form a slurry and add it to the gelatin mixture. Boil to a clear glaze that begins to thicken. Allow to cool slightly.
4. Add the berries to the baked pie shell. Pour the glaze over and refrigerate several hours or overnight.
5. Whip the cream with the ¼ cup sugar until quite stiff. Pile on top of the pie.

Applesauce Pie

KENTUCKY
Adapted from *The Foxfire Book of Appalachian Cookery*

8	leftover biscuits	2	teaspoons cinnamon
2	cups applesauce	1½	cups light brown sugar

1. Slice the leftover biscuits in half and place half of them in the bottom of a buttered baking dish. Spread 1 cup of the applesauce over them. Sprinkle 1 teaspoon of cinnamon over.
2. Repeat with a second layer. Sprinkle the top layer with the brown sugar.
3. Bake at 300° until the brown sugar melts and forms a crust.

Tame Gooseberry Pie

WEST VIRGINIA

Adapted from *The Foxfire Book of Appalachian Cookery*

2	cups gooseberries	1	tablespoon butter
¾	cup sugar	1	recipe biscuit dough

1. Mash the berries with the sugar. Cook over medium heat. Stir in the butter and cook until thick. Pour the berry filling into a 9-inch pie plate.
2. Roll out the biscuit dough and cut it into ½-inch-wide strips. Place the strips of dough crosswise on the berries.
3. Bake at 450° until the crust is brown.

Egg Pie

TENNESSEE

Adapted from Dalsass, *Miss Mary's Down-Home Cooking*

1	stick (½ cup) butter or margarine	1	cup milk
½	cup sugar	2	eggs
2	tablespoons flour	1	teaspoon vanilla extract
		1	baked 9-inch pie shell

1. Melt the butter or margarine. Remove from the heat and stir in the sugar and flour.
2. Add the milk, eggs, and vanilla and beat well. Pour into the baked crust.
3. Bake the pie at 350° for 35–40 minutes, or until set and lightly browned along the edges.

Sour Cream Pumpkin Pie

SOUTH CAROLINA
Adapted from *A Taste of South Carolina*

12 ounces cream cheese
¾ cup sugar
1½ tablespoons flour
1 teaspoon grated orange peel
½ teaspoon grated lemon peel
2 eggs
2 egg yolks

1 cup cooked or canned pumpkin
⅛ teaspoon cinnamon
1 9-inch graham cracker crust, unbaked
2 cups sour cream, plus additional for finishing
3 tablespoons sugar
1 teaspoon vanilla

1. Blend the cream cheese, sugar, flour, and grated peels together. Add the eggs and egg yolks. Beat until smooth.
2. Mix in the pumpkin and cinnamon. Pour into the prepared crust.
3. Bake at 350° for 40 minutes, or until the custard is set.
4. Remove the pie from the oven and spread it with a mixture of the sour cream, sugar, and vanilla. Bake 10 minutes longer.
5. Remove from the oven. Cool and spread with a thin layer of cold sour cream.

Egg Custard Pie

SOUTH CAROLINA
Adapted from *The South Carolina Cook Book*

3 eggs
½ cup sugar
¼ teaspoon salt
1 teaspoon vanilla

3 cups milk, scalded
⅛ teaspoon grated nutmeg
1 unbaked 8-inch pie shell

1. Beat the eggs slightly. Add the sugar, salt, and vanilla.
2. Add the scalded milk and the nutmeg. Whisk briefly and pour this mixture into the pie shell.
3. Bake at 350° for about 30 minutes.

Cherry Cheese Pie

TENNESSEE

Adapted from Dalsass, *Miss Mary's Down-Home Cooking*

4 ounces cream cheese	1 can cherry pie filling
1 can condensed milk	1 graham cracker crust,
⅓ cup lemon juice	baked

1. Beat the cream cheese until light and fluffy. Add the milk and beat well.
2. Add the lemon juice and stir until the mixture is thick and creamy.
3. Pour the cream cheese mixture into the baked graham cracker crust. Spread the cherry pie filling over the top and chill.

Cushaw Pie

APPALACHIA

Adapted from *The Foxfire Book of Appalachian Cookery*

1 cup light brown sugar	3 eggs
¼ cup flour	3 tablespoons butter
¼ cup granulated sugar	2 cups cooked, mashed
1 teaspoon salt	cushaw
1 teaspoon cinnamon	1 teaspoon vanilla
½ teaspoon ginger	1 unbaked 9-inch deep-dish
½ teaspoon nutmeg	pie shell
1 cup milk	

1. Mix the dry ingredients together.
2. Add the milk, eggs, and butter and beat well.
3. Add the cooked squash and vanilla. Stir to form a smooth mixture. Pour the filling into the pie shell.
4. Bake at 425° for 15 minutes. Reduce the heat to 350° and bake for 25–30 minutes, or until set.

CUSTARD AND EGG PIES

Damson Pie

KENTUCKY

Adapted from *The Foxfire Book of Appalachian Cookery*

1	cup butter	1	teaspoon vanilla
1½	cups sugar	1	unbaked pie shell
6	eggs, beaten	1	top crust
1	cup damson plum preserves		

1. Cream the butter and sugar together. Add the beaten eggs and beat until smooth. Add the preserves and vanilla. Beat until smooth.
2. Pour the filling into the pie shell and cover with a top crust. Crimp the edges and cut a slit into the crust.
3. Bake at 350° until nicely browned.

Cheese Cake Pie

VIRGINIA

Adapted from *The Junior League Cook Book*

1¼	cup cottage cheese	1	pint milk
1	teaspoon butter	1	rind of lemon
1	cup sugar		
3	eggs	1	unbaked 9-inch pie shell
	pinch salt		cinnamon

1. Blend all filling ingredients together and pour the filling into the pie shell.
2. Sprinkle the top with cinnamon and bake at 325° for 45 minutes, or until set.

Sweet Potato Pie

VIRGINIA

Adapted from *The Junior League Cook Book*

2	egg yolks	3	medium sweet potatoes,
1	cup sugar		cooked and mashed
1	tablespoon butter,	½	teaspoon nutmeg
	softened	½	teaspoon vanilla
1½	cups milk	1	unbaked 9-inch pie shell

1. Beat the egg yolks with the sugar and butter until smooth.
2. Stir the milk into the cooked sweet potatoes. Add this to the egg mixture. Stir in the nutmeg and vanilla and beat until smooth.
3. Pour the filling into the pie shell.
4. Bake at 375° for 40 minutes, or until set in the center.

Brown Sugar Pie

KENTUCKY

Adapted from Patterson, *Kentucky Cooking*

5	tablespoons butter,	3	tablespoons flour
	softened	1½	cups heavy cream
2	cups light brown sugar	1	unbaked 9-inch pie shell
3	eggs		

1. Cream the butter and brown sugar together until light and fluffy.
2. Add the eggs, one at a time, beating well after each addition. Stir in the flour and cream.
3. Pour the filling into the pie shell.
4. Bake at 350° for 30 – 40 minutes, or until set.

CUSTARD AND EGG PIES

Stack Pie

KENTUCKY
Adapted from Patterson, *Kentucky Cooking*

Filling:

10	egg yolks	1½ cups melted butter
3	cups sugar	
1	cup heavy cream	5 unbaked 8-inch pie shells

Caramel icing:

½	cup butter, melted	¼ cup milk
1	cup light brown sugar	2 cups powdered sugar

1. Beat the egg yolks until light. Add the sugar and cream and beat until light. Stir in the melted butter.
2. Trim the pastry of 4 pie shells so that there are circular bottoms only. Leave 1 shell intact.
3. Pour the filling into all 5 pie shells. Bake at 350° until set, about 10 to 12 minutes.
4. Cool the pies. Remove all but the pie with the complete crust from their pans and stack them, one on top of another, onto the complete pie.
5. Prepare the caramel icing by cooking the melted butter with the brown sugar for 5 minutes over medium heat, stirring constantly.
6. Allow the mixture to cool slightly, then add the milk and beat until smooth.
7. Stir in the powdered sugar and spread the icing over the top and sides of the stacked pies.

Caramel Meringue Pie

TENNESSEE
Adapted from Dalsass, *Miss Mary's Down-Home Cooking*

Caramel filling:

1¼ cups sugar, divided	3 egg yolks
1½ cups milk	2 teaspoons vanilla extract
1 tablespoon butter	
¼ cup flour	1 baked 9-inch pie shell

Meringue:

3 egg whites, room temperature	½ teaspoon vanilla extract
	6 tablespoons sugar
⅛ teaspoon salt	

1. In a heavy saucepan, cook ½ cup of the sugar until it forms a golden brown syrup. Do not let it burn.
2. In the top of a double boiler, heat the milk and butter to scalding. Carefully add the caramel syrup to the milk. Heat until the syrup dissolves.
3. In a bowl, stir the remaining ¾ cup sugar with the flour.
4. Add about ½ cup of the hot milk mixture to the flour mixture to make a paste and then pour that paste back into a saucepan. Cook, stirring, until the mixture thickens and comes to a boil. Cook 2 minutes longer and remove from heat.
5. Beat the egg yolks in a bowl. Gradually beat in several tablespoons of the hot mixture.
6. Add the egg mixture to the saucepan and cook over very low heat 2 minutes. Remove from the heat and add the vanilla.
7. Allow the mixture to cool, stirring occasionally, and then pour it into the baked shell.
8. Whip the egg whites stiff with the salt, vanilla, and sugar.
9. Top the pie and bake at 400° until meringue is set and golden.

Pecan Chiffon Pie

NORTH CAROLINA
Adapted from *Pass the Plate*

1 cup dark or light brown sugar	1 cup pecans, toasted and coarsely chopped (reserve some for garnish)
1¾ cups water, divided	
4 tablespoons cornstarch	2 baked 8-inch pie shells
⅔ cup egg whites	½ pint whipping cream
¼ cup sugar	

1. Combine the brown sugar with 1½ cups of the water in a saucepan. Bring to a boil.
2. Mix the cornstarch and the remaining ¼ cup water together and stir. Whisk this into the boiling sugar. Stir constantly and cook until thick. Remove the mixture from the heat.
3. Whip the egg whites until soft peaks form. Slowly add ¼ cup sugar and beat until stiff peaks are formed.
4. Add the hot brown sugar mixture and the nuts to the whites and fold gently to incorporate.
5. Pour the filling into the baked pie shells. Chill thoroughly.
6. Whip the cream until stiff and spread on the pies. Sprinkle a few additional finely chopped pecans over the top for garnish.

"Best when served the same day."

Eggnog Pie

SOUTH CAROLINA
Adapted from *The South Carolina Cook Book*

½ cup sugar	⅛ teaspoon nutmeg
3 eggs, separated	½ teaspoon vanilla extract
2 cups light cream	
⅛ teaspoon salt	1 unbaked 9-inch pie shell

1. Beat the sugar, egg yolks, and cream until pale and smooth. Add the salt, nutmeg, and vanilla extract.
2. Beat the egg whites until stiff peaks form. Fold them into the egg yolk mixture. Pour the filling into the pie shell.
3. Bake at 450° for 10 minutes. Lower the heat to 325° and bake until set, about 25 minutes.

Brownie Pie

NORTH CAROLINA
Adapted from *Pass the Plate*

1 cup sugar	1 cup pecans, chopped
½ cup flour	1 cup chocolate chips
2 eggs, beaten slightly	1 teaspoon vanilla
½ cup butter, melted and cooled	1 unbaked 9-inch pie shell
	2 cups whipped cream

1. Mix the sugar and flour together. Add the eggs and the cooled, melted butter. Mix well.
2. Add the pecans, chocolate chips, and vanilla and pour into the pie shell.
3. Bake at 350° for 45 minutes. Allow to cool and top with whipped cream.

Oh-So-Good Pie

TENNESSEE
Adapted from Dalsass, *Miss Mary's Down-Home Cooking*

1 stick (½ cup) butter or margarine	½ teaspoon nutmeg
1 cup sugar	4 eggs
2½ teaspoons distilled white vinegar	1 cup finely diced dates
1 teaspoon cinnamon	½ cup coarsely chopped pecans
	1 baked 9-inch pie shell

1. Melt the butter or margarine. Remove from the heat and beat in the sugar, vinegar, cinnamon, and nutmeg. Add the eggs and mix thoroughly.
2. Stir in the dates and pecans. Pour the filling into the crust.
3. Bake at 350° until the pie is lightly browned and set, about 35–40 minutes. Serve with whipped cream.

SPECIAL PIES

Key Lime Pie

FLORIDA

Adapted from Nickerson, *Florida Cookbook*

3 eggs, separated
1 14-ounce can sweetened
   condensed milk
½ cup key lime juice

1 baked 8-inch pie shell
⅛ teaspoon cream or tartar
6 tablespoons sugar

1. Beat the egg yolks until pale and thick. Stir in the condensed milk. Add the lime juice slowly and blend until smooth. Pour the filling into the baked pie shell.
2. Whip the egg whites until foamy. Add the cream of tartar and beat until soft peaks form. Add the sugar and beat until soft, glossy peaks form. Top the pie with the meringue.
3. Bake at 350° for 15 minutes.

Florida Lime Pie

FLORIDA

Adapted from Nickerson, *Florida Cookbook*

5 egg yolks
1 can (14 ounces) sweetened
   condensed milk
⅔ cup fresh lime juice
½ teaspoon grated lime
   rind

3 egg whites, room
   temperature
1 baked 9-inch pie shell
1 cup heavy cream
2 tablespoons sugar
½ teaspoon vanilla

1. Beat the egg yolks until light and thick. Gradually beat in the milk and lime juice. Add the rind and mix to incorporate.
2. Beat the egg whites until they form soft peaks. Fold them into the lime juice mixture. Pour the filling into the pie shell.
3. Bake at 325° for 20 minutes, or until the filling is just set in the center. Allow to cool. Chill the pie thoroughly.
4. Whip the cream until thick. Add the sugar and vanilla and whip until stiff. Top the pie with the whipped cream.

"In the Hollow" Fresh Peach Cobbler

TENNESSEE
Adapted from Dalsass, *Miss Mary's Down-Home Cooking*

½ cup sugar	⅛ teaspoon salt
½ cup water	1 recipe 2-crust pastry
9 peaches, peeled and thickly sliced (about 7 cups)	

1. In a large, heavy saucepan, cook the sugar and water until the sugar dissolves. Add the peach slices and salt.
2. Cover the pan and simmer the peaches until tender, about 5 minutes.
3. Divide the pastry into two portions, one about twice as large as the other.
4. Roll out the larger ball to an 11-inch circle and fit it into a deep-dish 9-inch pie pan. Roll out the other piece of pastry big enough to cover the top of the pan.
5. Turn the peach slices and their cooking juices into the prepared pan. Cover with the top crust. Make a few slits in the crust and pinch the edges together.
6. Bake at 450° for 10 minutes. Lower the oven to 350° and bake 1 hour longer.

Sweet Potato Cobbler

WEST VIRGINIA
Adapted from *The Foxfire Book of Appalachian Cookery*

2 cups cooked and diced sweet potatoes	½ cup milk
⅔ cup molasses	½ teaspoon ginger
¼ cup butter	pinch salt
	1 recipe biscuit dough

1. Bring all of the ingredients, except the biscuit dough, to a boil.
2. Roll out the biscuit dough and cut half into cubes. Drop the pieces into the boiling mixture.
3. Pour the boiling mixture into a rectangular baking pan. Cut the remaining dough in thin strips and place on top, lattice fashion.
4. Bake at 400° degrees until the crust is brown.

Apricot Crescent Roll

TENNESSEE
Adapted from Dalsass, *Miss Mary's Down-Home Cooking*

Filling:

16 ounces dried apricots
⅓ cup sugar
1 cup water

2 tablespoons butter or
   margarine
2 tablespoons sugar

1 recipe for 2-crust pastry

Lemon sauce:

1 cup sugar
1 cup water
1 stick (½ cup) butter or
   margarine
6 tablespoons freshly
   squeezed lemon juice

2 tablespoons cornstarch dissolved in 2 tablespoons
   water
1 cup heavy cream, whipped
   stiff

1. Place the apricots, ⅓ cup sugar, and the water in a saucepan. Bring to a boil. Reduce the heat, cover, and simmer until the apricots are tender, about 30 minutes. Cool slightly and puree. Refrigerate several hours.
2. Roll out the pastry to an 18-by-14-inch rectangle and spread with the apricot puree to within ½ inch of the edges. Beginning with the long edge, roll up jelly-roll style.
3. Pinch the ends together, bending slightly to form a crescent shape, and place, seam side down, on a greased 9-by-13-inch pan. Dot with butter and sprinkle with 2 tablespoons sugar.
4. Bake the crescent at 350° until golden brown, about 1½ hours.
5. To prepare the lemon sauce, place the sugar, water, butter or marga-rine, and lemon juice in a saucepan. Bring the mixture to a boil.
6. Stir in the cornstarch mixture and cook until thickened.
7. Serve at room temperature with warm lemon sauce and top with whipped cream.

Georgia Peach Pie

GEORGIA

Adapted from the De Bolt, *Savannah Sampler Cookbook*

½ cup light brown sugar
½ cup sugar
⅛ teaspoon salt
3 tablespoons tapioca
5 cups sliced peaches (5–6 medium peaches)

⅛ teaspoon almond extract
    pastry for 2-crust 9-inch pie
2 tablespoons butter
    cold water
½ teaspoon sugar

1. Mix the sugars together and add the salt and tapioca. Pour over the sliced peaches and mix gently. Add the almond extract and toss gently.
2. Pour the peach mixture into an unbaked pie shell. Dot with butter and cover with a top crust. Seal the edges and prick the top with a fork.
3. Brush the top crust with cold water and sprinkle with sugar.
4. Bake at 450° for 10 minutes, then reduce the heat to 375° and continue to bake for 40 minutes, or until golden brown.

Cheese-Apple Pie

MISSISSIPPI

Adapted from *Tunica County Tasty Treats*

½ cup grated sharp cheese
1 unbaked 9-inch pie shell
5 cups (about 6) apples, pared, cored, and sliced thick

1 cup sugar
1 tablespoon butter

1. Place the cheese in the bottom of the pie shell. Add the apples. Sprinkle the top with the sugar and dot with the butter.
2. Bake the pie at 425° for 15 minutes. Reduce the heat to 350° and continue to bake for 30–35 minutes.

FRUIT PIES

Apple-Lemon Pie

MISSISSIPPI
Adapted from *Tunica County Tasty Treats*

¼ cup water
1 cup sugar
2 tablespoons butter
1 lemon, juice and rind
1 apple, grated
1 teaspoon vanilla

1 egg, well beaten
1 teaspoon flour
1 baked 9-inch pie shell
2 egg whites
1 tablespoon sugar

1. Add the water and sugar to the top of a double boiler and stir to dissolve the sugar. Over medium heat add the butter, lemon juice and rind, the grated apple, vanilla, egg, and flour. Cook until thickened.
2. Pour the filling into the baked pie shell.
3. Whip the egg whites with the sugar until stiff peaks form. Top the pie with the meringue and bake at 425° until the meringue browns.

CUSTARD AND EGG PIES

Southern Chess Pie

MISSISSIPPI
Adapted from *Tunica County Tasty Treats*

3 large eggs
1½ cups sugar
½ cup (1 stick) melted butter
1 tablespoon cornmeal

1 tablespoon vinegar
1 teaspoon vanilla
1 unbaked 9-inch pie shell

1. Mix all of the filling ingredients together until smooth and pour the filling into the unbaked pie shell.
2. Bake at 300° for approximately 40 minutes.

Molasses Pie

MISSISSIPPI

Adapted from *Tunica County Tasty Treats*

4 egg yolks	1½ teaspoons cinnamon
1 cup sugar	½ teaspoon cloves
1 cup molasses	1 unbaked 9-inch pie shell
1 rounded tablespoon butter	

1. Cook all of the filling ingredients together in the top of a double boiler until thick. Pour the filling into the unbaked pie shell.
2. Bake at 375° until set.

Old South Georgia Vinegar Pie

GEORGIA

Adapted from the De Bolt, *Savannah Sampler Cookbook*

¼ pound (1 stick) butter, room temperature	3 eggs
1½ cups sugar	2 tablespoons cider vinegar
	1 unbaked 8-inch pie crust

1. Cream the butter and sugar together until light and fluffy. Add the eggs one at a time, beating well after each. Stir in the vinegar. Pour into the pie shell.
2. Bake at 375° for about an hour, or until set.

Port Hudson Pie

MISSISSIPPI
Adapted from *Tunica County Tasty Treats*

6 eggs, separated	½ cup tart jelly
1 cup sugar	1 baked pastry shell
½ cup butter	2 tablespoons sugar
½ teaspoon vanilla	

1. Cook the egg yolks, sugar, and butter in the top of a double boiler until thick. Stir in the vanilla.
2. Pour the filling into the baked pie shell. Spread the surface with tart jelly.
3. Whip 3 of the egg whites until foamy. Add the 2 tablespoons sugar and beat until stiff. Top the pie with the meringue.
4. Bake at 400° until nicely browned.

Sweet Potato Custard Pie

MISSISSIPPI
Adapted from *Tunica County Tasty Treats*

1½ cups cooked sweet potatoes, mashed	1 teaspoon vanilla
½ cup sugar	¼ teaspoon salt
2 cups milk	3 eggs, separated
½ tablespoon cornstarch	½ teaspoon nutmeg
2 tablespoons butter	1 9-inch pie shell, partially baked

1. In a saucepan, mix the sweet potatoes with the sugar until the sugar dissolves.
2. Mix the milk with the cornstarch and add it to the potato mixture. Stir in the butter, vanilla, and salt. Bring the mixture to a boil over medium heat, stirring frequently.
3. Mix some of the hot mixture with the egg yolks and stir them back into the potato mixture. Cook for 2 minutes.
4. Stir in the nutmeg and pour the filling into the partially baked pie shell.
5. Bake at 350° for 15 minutes.
6. Whip the egg whites until stiff and top the pie with them. Bake an additional 10–12 minutes, or until the pie is golden brown.

Georgia Sweet-Potato Pie

GEORGIA

Adapted from the De Bolt, *Savannah Sampler Cookbook*

2 cups milk or cream	½ teaspoon ground cloves
3 eggs	2 cups mashed, cooked sweet
1 cup sugar	potatoes
1 teaspoon cinnamon	1 unbaked pie shell

1. Stir the milk or cream into the eggs. Stir in the sugar.
2. Mix the spices with the sweet potatoes and stir in the egg mixture until smooth. Pour into the pie shell.
3. Bake at 400° for 35 minutes, or until set in the center.

Cream Pie

MISSISSIPPI

Adapted from *Tunica County Tasty Treats*

⅓ cup flour	2 tablespoons butter
⅔ cup sugar	½ teaspoon vanilla
¼ teaspoon salt	1 baked 9-inch pie shell
2 cups scalded milk	6 tablespoons sugar
3 eggs, separated	

1. Mix the flour, ⅔ cup sugar, salt, and milk together and cook in the top of a double boiler until thick.
2. Add a small amount of the hot mixture to the egg yolks, then stir them into the milk mixture. Cook for 2 minutes over medium heat.
3. Stir in the butter and vanilla and pour the filling into the baked pie shell.
4. Beat the egg whites stiff with the 6 tablespoons sugar and top the pie with the meringue.
5. Bake at 425° for 6 minutes, or until the meringue is browned.

Spicy Apple Cream Pie

GEORGIA

Adapted from the De Bolt, *Savannah Sampler Cookbook*

¾ cup sugar
2 tablespoons flour
¾ teaspoon allspice
½ teaspoon salt
1 unbaked 8-inch pie shell

4 (1½ pounds) crisp, tart
   apples pared, cored, and
   sliced
½ cup heavy cream

1. Mix the first 4 ingredients together well.
2. Sprinkle half of the mixture evenly over the bottom of the pie shell.
   Add the prepared apples evenly over this mixture.
3. Sprinkle the remaining sugar mixture over the apples. Pour the
   cream evenly over the top.
4. Bake at 450° for 15 minutes, then reduce the heat to 350° and bake
   about 45 minutes longer.

Lemon and Potato Pie

ALABAMA

Adapted from *Gulf City Cook Book*

3 medium sweet potatoes,
   cooked and riced
2 cups half-and-half
4 ounces butter, softened
2 cups sugar

   juice of 3 lemons
   rind of 1 lemon, grated
6 eggs, separated
1 unbaked 9-inch pie shell

1. Put the sweet potatoes through a ricer and mix with the half-and-
   half.
2. Beat in the butter and sugar to form a smooth mixture. Add the
   lemon juice, lemon rind, and the egg yolks. Mix well. Pour the filling into the pie shell.
3. Bake at 400° until set.
4. Whip the egg whites stiff and top the pie with the meringue.
   Return the pie to the oven to brown the meringue.

Lemon Chiffon Pie

MISSISSIPPI

Adapted from *Tunica County Tasty Treats*

½ tablespoon gelatin
⅓ cup cold water
4 eggs, separated
1 cup sugar
   juice and grated rind of
   2 lemons

1 baked 9-inch pie shell
1 cup sweetened whipped
   cream

1. Soften the gelatin in the water.
2. Beat the egg yolks with ½ cup of the sugar, the lemon juice, and the lemon rind. Cook in the top of a double boiler until thick. Stir in the gelatin while hot.
3. Beat the egg whites until foamy. Add the remaining sugar and beat stiff. Fold this into the lemon mixture.
4. Pour the filling into the baked pie shell and refrigerate until set. Top with the whipped cream.

Dolly Madison Pie

MISSISSIPPI

Adapted from *Tunica County Tasty Treats*

4 eggs, separated
2 cups sugar
3 teaspoons vinegar
1 teaspoon cinnamon
1 teaspoon cloves

1 tablespoon melted butter
1 cup chopped raisins
1 cup chopped nuts
1 unbaked 9-inch pie shell

1. Beat the egg yolks with the sugar until pale. Stir in the vinegar, spices, and butter.
2. Whip the egg whites until stiff and fold them in.
3. Add the raisins and nuts and pour the filling into the unbaked pie shell.
4. Bake at 375° until set.

NUT AND CHOCOLATE PIES

Chocolate Pie

MISSISSIPPI

Adapted from *Tunica County Tasty Treats*

4 ounces grated semisweet chocolate	1 cup sugar
1¼ cups milk	3 eggs, separated
1 lump of butter the size of an egg	1 teaspoon vanilla
	1 baked 9-inch pie shell
	3 tablespoons sugar

1. Add the chocolate, milk, butter, sugar, egg yolks, and vanilla to the top of a double boiler and cook until thick, stirring constantly. Pour the filling into the baked pie crust.
2. Whip the egg whites and sugar to form stiff peaks. Top the pie with the meringue and brown at 350°.

Peanut Butter Pie

GEORGIA

Adapted from the De Bolt, *Savannah Sampler Cookbook*

3 eggs	½ teaspoon vanilla
1 cup dark corn syrup	1 cup shelled, roasted peanuts
½ cup sugar	1 unbaked pie shell
½ cup smooth peanut butter	

1. Beat the eggs in a large bowl. Beat in the corn syrup, sugar, peanut butter, and vanilla. Stir in the peanuts. Pour the filling into the pie shell.
2. Bake at 400° for 15 minutes. Lower the heat to 350° and continue to bake for 30–35 minutes.

Nut-Butterscotch Pie

GEORGIA

Adapted from the De Bolt, *Savannah Sampler Cookbook*

Filling:

1¼ cups dark brown sugar	1 teaspoon vanilla extract
⅓ cup flour	1 tablespoon butter
¼ teaspoon salt	½ cup pecans
3 egg yolks	
2 cups milk	1 baked 9-inch pie shell

Basic meringue:

3 egg whites	6 tablespoons sugar
¼ teaspoon cream of tartar	

1. Mix the sugar, flour, and salt together. Add the egg yolks and milk. Mix until smooth. Cook in the top of a double boiler over hot water until thick and creamy.
2. When the filling thickens, add the vanilla, butter, and pecans. Mix and pour into the baked pie shell.
3. Prepare the meringue by beating the egg whites until frothy. Add the cream of tartar and continue to beat until stiff and glossy. Do not overbeat. Add the sugar, a little at a time, and beat until the mixture holds stiff peaks. Spread the meringue evenly over the pie.
4. Bake at 400° for 8–10 minutes.

Graham Nut Pie

GEORGIA

Adapted from the De Bolt, *Savannah Sampler Cookbook*

3 eggs, separated	1 cup graham cracker crumbs
1 cup sugar	1 cup coarsely chopped
1 tablespoon maple syrup	pecans

1. Beat the egg whites until stiff. Add ½ cup of the sugar and fold in gradually.
2. Beat the egg yolks until pale. Add the remaining sugar and the maple syrup. Fold in the graham cracker crumbs and pecans.
3. Fold this mixture into the egg whites and pour into a well-buttered 9-inch pie plate.
4. Bake at 400° for 30 minutes.

NUT AND CHOCOLATE PIES

Special Pecan Pie

GEORGIA
Adapted from the De Bolt, *Savannah Sampler Cookbook*

3 eggs	1 cup sugar
½ cup heavy cream	⅛ teaspoon salt
½ cup dark corn syrup	2 tablespoons melted butter
1 teaspoon vanilla extract	2 cups thinly sliced pecans
3 tablespoons bourbon or rum	1 unbaked 9-inch pie shell

1. Beat the eggs well. Stir in the remaining ingredients and pour into the unbaked pie shell.
2. Bake at 400° for 35 minutes, or until the crust is browned and the filling is slightly puffy.

COBBLERS, CRISPS, AND TARTS

Apple Crisp

MISSISSIPPI
Adapted from *Tunica County Tasty Treats*

3–4 medium apples, pared, cored, and sliced thin	½ cup flour
¾ cup quick-cooking oats	1 teaspoon cinnamon
¾ cup light brown sugar	½ cup butter

1. Arrange the apple slices across the bottom of a greased 8-inch round cake pan.
2. Mix the oats, sugar, flour, and cinnamon together and cut in the butter. Sprinkle this mixture over the apples.
3. Bake at 350° for 35 minutes.

Tourtes Douces (Blackberry Turnovers)

LOUISIANA

Adapted from Feibleman, *American Cooking: Creole and Acadian*

5 cups unsifted flour	8 tablespoons vegetable
2 teaspoons baking powder	shortening, softened
1 teaspoon salt	1½ cups granulated sugar
1 teaspoon vanilla extract	2 eggs
¾ cup milk	5 cups blackberry jam
8 tablespoons butter,	powdered sugar
softened	

1. Sift the flour, baking powder, and salt together.
2. Add the vanilla extract to the milk.
3. Cream the softened butter, vegetable shortening, and granulated sugar together until the mixture is light and fluffy. Beat in the eggs, one at a time.
4. Add the flour mixture to the creamed mixture in portions, alternating with the milk mixture. Mix to form a smooth dough.
5. Divide the dough into 24 pieces and shape each portion into a ball. Refrigerate for 1 hour.
6. Warm the blackberry jam and sieve it to remove any seeds.
7. Roll each dough piece into an 8-inch circle. Spoon about three tablespoons of the blackberry jam onto the center of each circle and spread it evenly, leaving a ½-inch border of the dough exposed.
8. Moisten the edges with water and fold to make a half circle. Crimp the edges with a fork. Place them on a buttered baking sheet.
9. Bake at 375° for 20 minutes, or until turnovers are lightly browned. When cool, sprinkle the turnovers lightly with powdered sugar.

Brown Betty

MISSISSIPPI

Adapted from *Tunica County Tasty Treats*

4–5 apples, pared, cored, and sliced thick	¼ pound butter
½ cup sugar	½ cup light brown sugar
1 teaspoon cinnamon	¾ cup flour

1. Toss the apples with the sugar and cinnamon and place in an 8-inch square baking pan.
2. Cream the butter, brown sugar, and flour until soft and smooth. Pat the dough out and spread it over the apples.
3. Bake at 350° until bubbly and browned.

Imitation Apple Pie

ILLINOIS
Adapted from Linsenmeyer, *Cooking Plain*

4 cups raw green pumpkin, peeled and sliced thin	3 tablespoons flour
¾ cup sugar	¼ cup water
½ teaspoon salt	⅛ teaspoon nutmeg
¼ cup vinegar	2 unbaked 9-inch pie shells

1. Mix the pumpkin with the sugar and set aside.
2. Dissolve the salt in the vinegar.
3. Mix the flour and water until smooth and combine with the vinegar. Pour over the pumpkin, add the nutmeg, and set aside while mixing pie dough.
4. Line a pie pan with pastry. Turn the pumpkin into the pie shell and cover with the top crust, which has been slit in a leaf pattern to permit steam to escape while baking.
5. Bake at 400° for 15 minutes. Lower the heat to 350° and bake for 45 minutes longer, or until well browned.

Mulberry Pie

ILLINOIS
Adapted from Linsenmeyer, *Cooking Plain*

4 cups ripe mulberries	1 tablespoon butter
⅔ cup sugar	1 teaspoon cinnamon
1 tablespoon lemon juice	2 unbaked 9-inch pie shells
1 tablespoon grated lemon rind	

1. Wash the mulberries, discarding imperfect ones.
2. Turn the fruit into a prepared pie shell, mounding slightly in the center, and sprinkle with sugar.
3. Sprinkle the lemon juice and grated lemon rind over the berries and dot with butter. Sprinkle the cinnamon over.
4. Cover with the top crust and slit in a leaf pattern to permit steam to escape while baking.
5. Bake at 425° for 10 minutes, reduce heat to 350°, and bake 25–35 minutes longer, until crust is nicely browned.

"The flavor will be improved if a few red but not quite ripe [mulberries] are included."

Gooseberry Pie

ILLINOIS

Adapted from Linsenmeyer, *Cooking Plain*

4 cups gooseberries	1 tablespoon butter
1 cup sugar	2 unbaked 9-inch pie crusts
2 tablespoons flour	

1. Toss the berries with the sugar and flour. Place in the bottom crust of an 8-inch pie pan.
2. Dot with butter and place the top crust over. Cut steam vents in the top crust.
3. Bake at 350° for 25–30 minutes, or until the filling is bubbling from the steam vents.

Apple Mince Pie with Cheese Crust

INDIANA

Adapted from *The Hoosier Cookbook*

Crust:

2 cups sifted flour	½ cup shredded "nippy"
½ teaspoon salt	cheese
⅔ cup shortening	5–6 tablespoons cold water

Filling:

1 cup mincemeat	¾ cup sugar
2 tablespoons flour	4 cups apples, sliced
¼ teaspoon salt	2 tablespoons butter
1 teaspoon cinnamon	

1. Sift the flour with the salt. Cut in the shortening and cheese until the mixture resembles coarse meal. Add the water, stirring with a fork until a dough forms.
2. Roll out half of the dough to fill a 9-inch pie tin. Spread the mincemeat over the bottom.
3. Combine the flour, salt, cinnamon, and sugar and toss the apples with this mixture.
4. Fit the apple slices into the pie shell on top of the mincemeat. Dot with butter and moisten the edge of the crust with cold water.
5. Roll out the other half of the dough and place it over the top of the apples. Crimp the edges together. Make several steam vents.
6. Bake at 475° for 10 minutes. Reduce heat to 350° and bake an additional 45 minutes, or until the apples are bubbling.

Caramel Crunch Apple Pie

INDIANA
Adapted from *The Hoosier Cookbook*

28	caramels	¾	cup flour
2	tablespoons water	⅓	cup sugar
4	cups apples, peeled and sliced	½	teaspoon cinnamon
		½	cup chopped walnuts
1	unbaked 9-inch pie shell	⅓	cup butter

1. Melt the caramels with the water in a saucepan over low heat, stirring occasionally until the sauce is smooth.
2. Layer the apples and caramel sauce into the pie shell.
3. Combine the flour, sugar, cinnamon, and nuts. Cut in the butter until the mixture resembles coarse crumbs. Sprinkle over the apples.
4. Bake at 375° for 40 – 45 minutes.

Amber Pie

INDIANA
Adapted from *The Hoosier Cookbook*

½	cup soft butter	½	cup tart plum jelly
1	cup sugar	1	unbaked 9-inch pie shell
3	eggs, separated	6	tablespoons sugar
1	whole egg	¼	teaspoon cream of tartar
2	tablespoons flour	1	teaspoon lemon juice
½	cup sour cream		

1. Cream the butter and 1 cup sugar until well blended. Add the three egg yolks and 1 whole egg, beating well.
2. Add the flour, sour cream, and jelly. Mix well.
3. Place the filling into an unbaked 9-inch pie shell. Bake at 375° for 10 minutes. Reduce the heat to 325° and continue baking until a silver knife inserted near the center comes out clean.
4. Beat the egg whites with the 6 tablespoons sugar, cream of tartar, and lemon juice until glossy peaks form. Spread over the pie.
5. Bake at 350° until brown.

Golden Treasure Pie

INDIANA

Adapted from *The Hoosier Cookbook*

17 ounces undrained crushed pineapple	¼ cup sifted flour
½ cup sugar	1 cup cottage cheese
2 tablespoons cornstarch	1 teaspoon vanilla
2 tablespoons water	½ teaspoon salt
⅔ cup sugar	2 eggs, slightly beaten
1 tablespoon butter, softened	1¼ cups milk
	1 unbaked 10-inch pie shell

1. Combine the pineapple, ½ cup sugar, cornstarch, and water in a small saucepan. Bring to a boil. Cook 1 minute, stirring occasionally. Cool.
2. Blend the ⅔ cup sugar and the butter. Add the flour, cottage cheese, vanilla, and salt. Beat until smooth.
3. Slowly add the eggs, followed by the milk, beating constantly.
4. Pour the pineapple into the crust, spreading evenly. Gently pour the filling onto the pineapple layer.
5. Bake at 450° for 15 minutes, then reduce the heat to 325° and bake 45 minutes longer.

Shaker Lemon Pie

OHIO

Adapted from Macmillan, *In a Shaker Kitchen*

Filling:

2–3 medium sized juicy lemons	4 eggs
2 cups sugar	

Pie crust:

2 cups flour	1 egg yolk, lightly beaten
½ teaspoon salt	with 3 tablespoons cold
¼ cup vegetable shortening	water
6–8 tablespoons cold butter, cut in pieces	soft butter

1. Cut the lemons into paper-thin slices, then quarter the slices. Remove any seeds and discard the end slices.
2. Layer the lemon slices in a bowl, sprinkling with the sugar. Cover the bowl and let stand several hours, or overnight if more convenient.
3. To make the pie crust dough, put the flour and salt in the food processor and turn the machine on briefly to blend. Add the shortening and butter and process until the mixture resembles coarse crumbs, turning the machine on and off several times.
4. Add the egg yolk mixture to bind the ingredients.
5. Turn the dough onto a work surface and mix briefly with your hands to make a smooth dough. Gather into a ball, wrap, and refrigerate 20 minutes.
6. Divide the dough into two portions, one slightly larger than the other.
7. Roll out the larger portion and use to line a 9-inch pie plate. Brush the bottom of the pie crust with a film of soft butter.
8. Lift the lemon slices out of the bowl and layer them in the pie crust. Sprinkle with a little more sugar if desired.
9. Add the 4 eggs to the sugary lemon juice in the bowl and beat until well blended. Pour over the lemon slices
10. Roll out the remaining dough for the top crust and crease the edges to seal. Cut a few slits in the top crust as steam vent holes.
11. Bake the pie at 375° until the pastry is golden brown, about 45 minutes.

Black Bottom Lemon Pie

INDIANA
Adapted from *The Hoosier Cookbook*

2 ounces semisweet chocolate
1 baked 9-inch pie shell, cooled
4 eggs, separated

¼ cup lemon juice
3 tablespoons water
1 teaspoon lemon peel
1 cup sugar, divided

1. Melt the chocolate. Spread it evenly over the bottom of the cooled pie shell.
2. In the top of a double boiler, beat the egg yolks until thick and lemon colored. Add the lemon juice and water, mixing well. Stir in the lemon peel and ½ cup of the sugar.
3. Cook over hot (not boiling) water, stirring constantly, until thick (about 12 minutes). Remove from the hot water.
4. Beat the egg whites until frothy. Add the remaining ½ cup sugar gradually, beating until stiff, glossy peaks form.
5. Fold half of the egg whites into the egg yolk mixture. Pour over the chocolate in the pie shell.
6. Spoon the remaining egg white mixture into a pastry tube. Pipe a lattice design on top of the filling.
7. Bake at 350° for 10–15 minutes, or until lightly browned.

Angel Food Pie

INDIANA
Adapted from *The Hoosier Cookbook*

1 cup crushed pineapple and liquid
1 cup sugar
1 cup water
pinch salt
3 heaping tablespoons cornstarch

3 egg whites, stiffly beaten
1 cup whipping cream
1 small jar maraschino cherries, chopped
1 baked 9-inch pie shell

1. Bring the first 4 ingredients to a boil.
2. Dissolve the cornstarch in a small amount of water, then stir it into the rapidly boiling mixture.
3. Cook about 1 minute, until the cornstarch mixture is clear. Cool.
4. Fold in the stiffly beaten egg whites.
5. Whip the cream and fold it into the filling. Add the maraschino cherries.
6. Pour into a 9-inch baked pie crust.

Sugar Cream Pie

INDIANA

Adapted from *The Hoosier Cookbook*

1½ cups sugar
⅓ cup flour
½ teaspoon salt
2½ cups cream

2 teaspoons vanilla
1 tablespoon butter, melted
1 unbaked 9-inch pie shell

1. Blend the sugar, flour, and salt together. Stir in the cream, vanilla, and butter. Beat well.
2. Pour this mixture into the unbaked pie shell.
3. Bake at 450° for 10 minutes. Reduce heat to 325° and bake for an additional 35 minutes.

Cream Sherry Pie

OHIO

Adapted from DuSablon, *Cincinnati Recipe Treasury*

1½ cups graham cracker crumbs
⅓ cup butter, melted
½ cup cold water
1 envelope unflavored gelatin
⅔ cup sugar, divided

⅛ teaspoon salt
3 eggs, separated
½ cup cream sherry
1 cup heavy cream
red food coloring (optional)

1. Combine the graham cracker crumbs with the butter.
2. Press in a 9-inch pie pan and bake at 350° for 10 minutes.
3. Pour the water into a saucepan and sprinkle the gelatin over it. Allow it to soften.
4. Add ⅓ cup of the sugar, the salt, and the egg yolks to the gelatin. Stir to blend. Place over a low heat and stir until the gelatin dissolves and the mixture thickens. Do not boil.
5. Remove from heat and stir in the cream sherry. Chill until the mixture starts to mound slightly.
6. Beat the egg whites. Add the remaining sugar and beat until stiff peaks are formed. Fold the meringue into the thickened gelatin mixture.
7. Whip the cream. Fold it into the mixture. Add food coloring if desired.
8. Turn the mixture into the crust and chill several hours or overnight.

Hershey Bar Pie

OHIO

Adapted from DuSablon, *Cincinnati Recipe Treasury*

1	9-inch pie crust	4	Hershey chocolate bars
20	marshmallows	1	cup cream
½	cup milk		

1. Bake the pie crust blind. Allow it to cool.
2. Combine the marshmallows, milk, and chocolate bars in the top of a double boiler. Cook gently until all ingredients are melted. Allow to cool.
3. Whip the cream and fold it into the candy mixture. Pour it into the pie crust and refrigerate several hours.

"A graham cracker crust may be used."

Pumpkin Pecan Pie

INDIANA

Adapted from *The Hoosier Cookbook*

3	eggs, slightly beaten	½	teaspoon cinnamon
1	cup cooked pumpkin	¼	teaspoon salt
1	cup sugar	1	unbaked 9-inch pie shell
½	cup dark corn syrup	1	cup chopped pecans
1	teaspoon vanilla		whipped cream

1. Combine the eggs, pumpkin, sugar, corn syrup, vanilla, cinnamon, and salt. Mix well. Pour into an unbaked pie shell. Top with the chopped pecans.
2. Bake at 350° for about 40 minutes.
3. Chill. Serve topped with whipped cream.

Sorrel Pie

ILLINOIS

Adapted from Linsenmeyer, *Cooking Plain*

16 cups sheep sorrel (or garden French sorrel)	⅛ teaspoon nutmeg
	1 tablespoon lemon juice
¾ cup, or to taste, sugar	2 unbaked 9-inch pie crusts
⅛ teaspoon salt	

1. Wash the sorrel well and pinch off the heavier stems. Drain thoroughly and pat dry. Cut or tear each cluster into smaller pieces.
2. Blend the sugar, salt, and nutmeg. Pour this over the sorrel and toss lightly with a fork.
3. Turn into the pie shell. Sprinkle the lemon juice over the top.
4. Cut the top crust into strips and weave a lattice over the pie.
5. Bake at 425° for 15 minutes. Reduce heat to 350° and bake 30 minutes longer.

Soda Cracker Pie

ILLINOIS

Adapted from Linsenmeyer, *Cooking Plain*

¼ cup boiling water	juice and grated rind of
8 crackers, pounded fine	1 lemon
8 tablespoons vinegar	1 unbaked 8-inch pie shell
8 tablespoons sugar	

1. Pour the boiling water over the crackers to soften. Stir in the vinegar, sugar, and lemon juice and rind. If the mixture is too stiff, add a little more water.
2. Beat until the crackers are well dissolved. Turn into an unbaked pie shell.
3. Bake at 350° until set and lightly browned, about 35–40 minutes. Best served hot.

Grandma Smith's Raspberry Pie

WISCONSIN
Adapted from *St. Paul's Centennial Cookbook*

⅓ cup butter, softened
1   egg
2   tablespoons flour

1   cup sugar
2   cups fresh raspberries
1   9-inch pie shell, unbaked

1. Cream the butter. Add the egg and beat it in. Scrape down the bowl and add the flour and sugar.
2. Place the berries in the pie shell and top with the creamed mixture.
3. Bake at 350° for 45 minutes or until browned and set.

Orange Pie

WISCONSIN
Adapted from *"The Four Hundred" Cook Book*

1   cup sugar
    grated rind of 1 orange
½ cup water

½ cup rolled cracker crumbs
12 oranges
1   unbaked 9-inch pie shell

1. Mix the sugar, orange rind, water, and cracker crumbs together.
2. Peel the oranges and cut the pulp into chunks. Toss into the above mixture and place in the pie shell.
3. Bake at 375° for 15 minutes.

CUSTARD AND EGG PIES

Quad Cities Baked Apple and Pumpkin Pie

IOWA

Adapted from Schultz, *As American as Apple Pie*

Pastry:

1½	cups all-purpose flour	1	large egg yolk, lightly beaten
1	teaspoon sugar		
½	teaspoon salt	1	teaspoon red wine vinegar
6	tablespoons lard, chilled	2–3	tablespoons cold water

Filling:

1	pound cooked pumpkin	⅛	teaspoon freshly grated nutmeg
1½	cups pureed baked apples		
3	tablespoons unsalted butter, melted	¼	teaspoon ground cloves
		3	medium eggs, separated
½	cup sugar	½	cup milk
¼	cup maple syrup	¼	cup heavy cream
1	teaspoon ground cinnamon		sweetened whipped cream

1. Mix the flour, sugar, and salt together. Cut in the lard with a pastry knife. Blend to form coarse crumbs.
2. Add the beaten egg yolk, vinegar, and water and blend to form a very soft dough. Refrigerate until needed.
3. Mix the pumpkin with the pureed apples. Beat in the butter, sugar, maple syrup, spices, 3 egg yolks, milk, and cream. Blend until smooth.
4. Beat the egg whites until stiff. Fold them into the filling.
5. Roll out the pastry and line a 10-inch deep pie pan. Pour in the filling.
6. Bake at 325° for 1 hour, or until firm in the center.

Butternut Squash Pie

SOUTH DAKOTA

Adapted from Hawkins and Hawkins, *The American Regional Cookbook*

1 cup cooked butternut squash, mashed	1 teaspoon nutmeg
	1 teaspoon cinnamon
1 cup heavy cream	¾ teaspoon ginger
1 cup sugar	¼ teaspoon mace
3 eggs, slightly beaten	½ teaspoon salt
¼ cup brandy	1 unbaked 9-inch pie shell

1. Mix the squash, cream, sugar, eggs, brandy, spices, and salt together. Pour the filling into the pie shell.
2. Bake at 400° for 5 minutes. Reduce the heat to 300° and bake for 40–50 minutes, or until a knife blade comes out clean when inserted in the center of the pie.

Caramel Pie

KANSAS

Adapted from *The Centennial Treasury of Recipes*

28 caramels	1 cup sweet cream
1 cup milk	⅔ cup pecans
1 envelope gelatin	1 baked 9-inch pie shell
¼ cup cold water	

1. Melt the caramels and milk in the top of a double boiler.
2. Soften the gelatin in the cold water. Stir this into the caramel mixture to dissolve.
3. Whip the cream and fold it into the filling. Stir in the pecans.
4. Pour the filling into the baked pie shell and allow to chill overnight.

CHIFFON AND CREAM PIES

Heavenly Pie

OKLAHOMA

Adapted from Wilhelm, *Smidgen of Honey*

2 unbeaten egg whites	2 ripe bananas, mashed
1 cup sugar	1 baked 9-inch pie shell
⅛ teaspoon salt	½ pint whipping cream
⅛ teaspoon almond extract	¼ cup chopped nuts

1. Beat the egg whites, sugar, salt, and extract until stiff peaks form. Fold in the bananas. Pour the filling into the baked pie crust.
2. Bake at 350° for 20–25 minutes. Allow to cool thoroughly.
3. Whip the cream and spread it over the top and garnish with chopped nuts.

CHOCOLATE PIE

Hershey Bar Torte

WISCONSIN

Adapted from DeMasters, *Dining In—Milwaukee*

1½ cups finely crushed vanilla wafer crumbs	6 4-ounce Hershey's chocolate bars, broken into pieces
2 tablespoons melted butter	
2 teaspoons unflavored gelatin	2 cups miniature marshmallows
¼ cup milk	3 cups stiff whipped cream chocolate shavings

1. Mix the wafer crumbs with the melted butter. Press them into the bottom of a greased 9-by-13-inch pan. Bake at 300° for 10 minutes. Allow to cool.
2. Soften the gelatin in the milk, then stir to dissolve the gelatin.
3. Heat the gelatin mixture in the top of a double boiler. Add the candy bar pieces and marshmallows. Cook over a low heat until the candy and marshmallows have melted. Allow the mixture to cool for 15 minutes.
4. Fold three fourths of the whipped cream into the chocolate mixture. Pour the filling into the cooled crust.
5. Spread the remaining whipped cream over the filling and decorate with chocolate curls. Refrigerate until served.

Delmonico's Pie

WISCONSIN

Adapted from *"The Four Hundred" Cook Book*

6   tart apples, peeled, cored,   1   cup sugar
    and cut into wedges   1   cup heavy cream
1   unbaked 9-inch pie shell   1   teaspoon cinnamon

1. Place the apples in the pie shell. Sprinkle with sugar.
2. Pour in the cream and bake at 375° for 30 – 40 minutes, or until
    bubbling in the center. Sprinkle with cinnamon.

Butter Roll Pie

OKLAHOMA

Adapted from Wilhelm, *Smidgen of Honey*

1   recipe 2-crust pie dough   1   teaspoon cinnamon
4   ounces butter   ½   cup light cream
⅓   cup sugar

1. Roll the pie doughs out to approximately 10 inches in diameter.
    Dot each with half the butter.
2. Mix the sugar and cinnamon together. Sprinkle over the butter.
    Roll each dough into a cylinder. Slash tops crosswise in several
    places. Arrange around a baking dish used for cobblers. Pour the
    cream over.
3. Bake at 375° until crusts are brown.

BERRY PIE

Elderberry Pie

ARIZONA

Adapted from Weiner, *Arizona Territorial Cookbook*

4–6	cups elderberries	1	unbaked 9-inch pie shell
1	cup sugar	1	top crust
1	tablespoon good vinegar	2	tablespoons milk

1. Sprinkle the fresh elderberries with the sugar and vinegar.
2. Fill the pie shell with the fruit mixture. Cover with a top crust and wash it over with a little milk.
3. Bake at 325° for 1 hour, or until crust is golden.

CUSTARD PIES

Banana Yucca Pie

ARIZONA

Adapted from Weiner, *Arizona Territorial Cookbook*

3–4	tablespoons butter	½	teaspoon salt
2	egg yolks	½	cup thick cream
½	teaspoon vanilla extract	4–6	cups diced banana yucca fruit
⅓–¾	cup sugar, depending on the sweetness of the fruit	1	unbaked pie shell
½	teaspoon cinnamon	1	top crust
½	teaspoon nutmeg		melted butter or egg white
2	teaspoons cornstarch		

1. Cream the butter with the egg yolks and vanilla.
2. Mix the dry ingredients and add to the creamed mixture.
3. Add the cream to the dry ingredients slowly, stirring constantly to avoid lumps. Fold in the fruit.
4. Spoon this mixture into the pie shell. Top with the second crust and slit the top in several places. Brush with butter or egg white.
5. Bake at 350° for 45 minutes, or until golden brown.

Christina's Always-Perfect Flan*

NEW MEXICO
Adapted from Cameron, *The Best from New Mexico Kitchens*

½ cup sugar
8 egg yolks
2 egg whites
1 14-ounce can sweetened condensed milk

1 13-ounce can evaporated milk
2 cups whole milk or water
1 teaspoon vanilla

1. In a heavy skillet, melt the sugar, stirring constantly. When it is light brown, pour it into a 2-quart mold. Tip the mold quickly in all directions so that the caramel coats the inside.
2. Beat the egg yolks and whites together until thick. Beat in the condensed milk, evaporated milk, milk (or water), and vanilla. Pour into the prepared mold.
3. Bake in a pan of warm water at 350° for 20–30 minutes, or until set in the center.

Think of this as a "crustless" pie.

Cracker Pie

TEXAS
Adapted from the *Capitol Cook Book*

⅛ teaspoon salt
3 egg whites
1 teaspoon vanilla
1 cup sugar

¾ cup chopped nuts
¾ cup saltine cracker crumbs
1 teaspoon baking powder
¾ cup whipping cream

1. Add the salt to the egg whites and beat until stiff, but not dry. Stir in the vanilla and sugar and beat until stiff and shiny.
2. Fold in the nuts and the cracker crumbs, which have been mixed with the baking powder. Fill a buttered 8-inch pie pan.
3. Bake at 350° for 30–40 minutes.
4. Whip the cream and spread over the cooled pie. Refrigerate before serving.

Black Bottom Pie

TEXAS
Adapted from Ross, *Nanny's Texas Table*

4 ounces gingersnaps, crushed fine	1 envelope unflavored gelatin softened in ¼ cup water
4 tablespoons butter, melted	1 teaspoon vanilla
2 cups milk	½ teaspoon cream of tartar
4 eggs, separated	1 teaspoon rum
1 cup sugar, divided	1 cup whipping cream
1 tablespoon cornstarch	2 tablespoons powdered sugar
1½ ounces unsweetened chocolate, melted	½ ounce shaved chocolate

1. Mix the gingersnaps with the melted butter and pat evenly into a 9-inch deep pie pan.
2. Scald the milk in a nonreactive saucepan. Beat the egg yolks with ½ cup sugar and the cornstarch. Add the scalded milk while whisking. Return the mixture to the saucepan and cook over low heat until thickened.
3. Remove 1 cup of the custard, add the melted chocolate, and stir until uniform. Cover and chill.
4. To the remaining hot custard, add the softened gelatin. Allow to cool. Stir in the vanilla.
5. Beat the egg whites until frothy. Add the cream of tartar and rum and beat stiff. Fold into the cooled gelatin custard.
6. Whip the cream with the powdered sugar until stiff.
7. Assemble the pie by first adding the chocolate custard to the crust. Smooth over and add the rum-flavored custard mousse. Top with whipped cream and shaved chocolate. Refrigerate at least 3 hours.

Piñon Pie

NEW MEXICO

Adapted from Cameron, *The Best from New Mexico Kitchens*

¼ cup butter	1 cup piñon nuts (pine nuts)
¾ cup light brown sugar	¼ teaspoon salt
4 eggs	1 teaspoon lemon juice
1 cup light corn syrup	1 baked 8-inch pie shell

1. Cream the butter and brown sugar together. Beat in the eggs, one at a time, until the mixture is light and fluffy.
2. Beat in the corn syrup. Stir in the nuts, salt, and lemon juice. Pour into the baked pie shell.
3. Bake at 375° for 30 – 40 minutes. Serve plain or with whipped cream or ice cream.

Chocolate Pecan Pie

TEXAS

Adapted from the *Capitol Cook Book*

2 tablespoons melted butter	1 cup dark corn syrup
1-ounce square unsweetened chocolate	1 teaspoon vanilla
	pinch salt
3 eggs, beaten	1 cup broken pecans
1 cup sugar	1 unbaked 8-inch pie shell

1. Melt the butter and chocolate in a microwave or in the top of a double boiler.
2. Beat the eggs with the sugar, corn syrup, vanilla, and salt. Add the melted chocolate mixture and the pecans. Mix thoroughly. Pour into the unbaked pie shell.
3. Bake at 300° for 1 hour.

Empanaditas with Peach Butter and Piñons

NEW MEXICO
Adapted from Dent, *The Feast of Santa Fe*

Pastry dough:

2	cups flour	2	teaspoons sugar
½	teaspoon baking powder	6	tablespoons lard, cut into
½	teaspoon salt		12 pieces
¼	teaspoon cloves	6	tablespoons cold water
½	teaspoon cinnamon		

Filling:

½	cup shelled piñons (pine nuts)		grated peel of ½ lemon
¼	cup peach butter	¼	cup dark brown sugar
			powdered sugar

1. Place all of the pastry ingredients except the water in a food processor and blend to a coarse meal. Add the water and process a few seconds more to incorporate it. Form the dough into a ball. Refrigerate while the filling is prepared.
2. Place all of the ingredients for the filling (except the powdered sugar) in a food processor and blend until mixed, about 5 seconds. The piñons should not be completely ground.
3. Divide the dough into quarters and divide each piece into fourths. Roll each of the 16 pieces into a 3-inch circle.
4. Place a heaping teaspoon of the filling in the middle of each circle. Moisten the edges with water and fold the circle in half. Crimp the edges with a fork. Place the pies on ungreased cookie sheets.
5. Bake at 400° for 10–12 minutes, or until golden brown. When cool, top each pie with powdered sugar.

Willie's Peach Dumpling

TEXAS

Adapted from Coleman and Coleman, *The Texas Cookbook*

Dumplings:

1	recipe pie dough	1	tablespoon butter
4 – 6	Hill Country peaches	1	teaspoon allspice
⅓	cup sugar		

Sauce:

1	tablespoon flour	1	cup boiling water
⅓	cup butter	1	cup sugar

1. Roll out the dough fairly thick.
2. Peel and stone the peaches. Toss them with the sugar. Add them to the pie dough.
3. Dot with butter and sprinkle with the allspice. Fold into an oblong shape. Seal the edges of the dough firmly together.
4. Place the dumpling in a buttered baking dish and slash with a knife at 2-inch intervals.
5. Prepare the sauce by cutting together the flour and the butter. Add the boiling water and stir until smooth. Add the sugar and cook until smooth. Pour this sauce over the dumpling.
6. Bake at 350° until golden.

CUSTARD PIE

Rum Pie

WYOMING

Adapted from *Cooking in Wyoming*

4	eggs, separated	¼	cup cold water
1	cup sugar, divided	¼	cup rum
½	teaspoon salt	1	teaspoon nutmeg
½	cup hot water	1	baked 9-inch pie shell
1	envelope gelatin		

1. Beat the egg yolks with ½ cup of the sugar and the salt. Add the hot water gradually and cook, stirring constantly, in the top of a double boiler until it's the consistency of custard.
2. Soften the gelatin in the cold water, add it to the hot custard, and stir until the gelatin is dissolved. Cool.
3. Add the rum and nutmeg to the custard mixture.
4. Beat egg whites until stiff and dry. Fold in other ½ cup of sugar.
5. When the custard mixture begins to thicken, fold in the egg whites.
6. Fill the baked pie shell and put in the refrigerator to chill.
7. When ready to serve, garnish with a sprinkle of nutmeg.

CREAM PIE

Grasshopper Pie

NEVADA

Adapted from Hemingway and Armstrong, *Dining In—Sun Valley*

Chocolate pie crust:

¾	cup finely crushed chocolate wafers	¼	cup finely crushed graham crackers
		4–5	tablespoons melted butter

Filling:

1	7-ounce jar marshmallow creme	1½	cups whipping cream
¼	cup crème de menthe	1	4-ounce bar semisweet chocolate

1. Mix the chocolate cookie crumbs with the graham cracker crumbs and the melted butter. Press the mixture into the bottom and up the sides of a 9-inch pie pan.
2. Bake at 300° for 15 minutes. Allow to cool before filling.
3. Beat marshmallow creme and crème de menthe together until smooth.
4. Whip the cream stiff and fold into the marshmallow creme mixture. Pour the filling into the crust and shave the semisweet chocolate on top. Refrigerate 2 hours before serving.

Chocolate Chip Pie

COLORADO

Adapted from *Nuggets: Recipes Good as Gold*

3 eggs	1½ cups chopped pecans
1½ cups sugar	1 unbaked 9-inch pie shell
6 tablespoons butter, melted and cooled	vanilla ice cream
	semisweet chocolate
2 teaspoons vanilla	shavings
¾ cup flour	
1½ cups semisweet chocolate minichips	

1. Combine the eggs, sugar, butter, and vanilla, beating until blended.
2. Stir in the flour, chocolate chips, and pecans. Mix well. Pour the filling into the pie shell.
3. Bake at 350° for 1 hour, or until a knife inserted in the center comes out clean. Refrigerate for 4 hours or overnight.
4. The pie may be served warm with vanilla ice cream sprinkled with chocolate shavings.

Osgood Pie I

WYOMING

Adapted from *Cooking in Wyoming*

1 cup pecans	½ teaspoon cloves
1 cup raisins	½ teaspoon cinnamon
1½ cups sugar	½ teaspoon allspice
½ cup grape juice	1 unbaked 9-inch pie shell
5 eggs, beaten slightly	

1. Mix all the ingredients together in a bowl. Pour into the unbaked pie shell.
2. Bake at 400° for 10 minutes. Lower heat to 350° and continue to bake until just firm. Do not overbake.

"A little red food coloring makes the pie prettier."

NUT AND CHOCOLATE PIES

Osgood Pie II

IDAHO
Adapted from *American Cooking: The Great West*

1	unbaked 9-inch pie shell	3	tablespoons distilled white vinegar
4	eggs, separated		
1	cup sugar	2	tablespoons bourbon or dry sherry
1	tablespoon flour		
1	teaspoon ground cinnamon	1	tablespoon butter, melted and cooled
½	teaspoon ground cloves	1	cup finely chopped pecans
½	teaspoon ground nutmeg	1	cup seedless raisins

1. Bake the pie shell at 350° for 8 minutes, until partially baked.
2. Whip the egg whites until they form stiff peaks.
3. Beat the egg yolks with the sugar, flour, cinnamon, cloves, and nutmeg. Beat in the vinegar, bourbon or sherry, and melted butter until smooth. Stir in the pecans and the raisins.
4. Fold in the egg whites, gently blending until uniform. Pour the filling into the pie shell.
5. Bake at 350° for 25–30 minutes, or until the filling is set.

SPECIAL PIE

Cottage Cheese Pie

COLORADO
Adapted from *Pioneer Potluck*

4	egg yolks		juice and grated rind of ½ lemon
1½	cups sugar		
2	cups cottage cheese, sieved	⅛	teaspoon salt
1	cup thin cream	2	egg whites, beaten stiff
½	cup seedless raisins	1	unbaked pie shell

1. Beat the egg yolks slightly. Add the sugar, cottage cheese, cream, raisins, lemon juice and rind, and salt and stir well. Fold in the egg whites.
2. Pour this into a pie plate lined with pastry.
3. Bake at 450° for 10 minutes. Reduce the heat to 325° and bake for 20 minutes.

Apple Tart in Ginger Pastry

OREGON

Adapted from Brooks, *Oregon's Cuisine of the Rain*

Crust:

¾ teaspoon finely chopped, peeled fresh ginger

1¼ cups unbleached white flour

¼ pound unsalted butter, chilled and cut into ½-inch pieces

3 tablespoons water

Apple filling:

2 tablespoons unsalted butter

5 tart green apples, peeled, cored, and thinly sliced

3 tablespoons light brown sugar

pinch ground cinnamon

1 tablespoon slivered crystal-lized ginger

Glaze:

⅓ cup apricot preserves

1–2 tablespoons apple brandy or Calvados

1. To make the crust, toss the ginger with the flour. Cut in the cold butter with a pastry knife to form coarse meal. Add the water, a little at a time, to form a dough.
2. Roll the dough out and line a 9-inch tart pan with a removable bottom.
3. To fill the tart, dot the pastry with the butter and arrange the apples decoratively, in a pinwheel fashion.
4. Mix the brown sugar, cinnamon, and crystallized ginger together and cover the apples with this topping.
5. Bake at 375° until bubbling in the center. Allow to cool.
6. To make the glaze, heat the preserves with the brandy and brush on the tart.

Sandy River Raspberry Rhubarb Pie

OREGON
Adapted from Brooks, *Oregon's Cuisine of the Rain*

4	cups diced rhubarb		zest and juice of 1 orange
2	pints raspberries	1	tablespoon lemon juice,
1¾	cups sugar		freshly squeezed
¼	cup quick-cooking tapioca	2	9-inch pie crusts

1. Mix all ingredients (except pie shells) together and allow to stand 15 minutes.
2. Roll out the bottom crust and fit it in a 9-inch deep pie pan. Add the filling.
3. Roll out the top crust and place it over the filling. Crimp edges to seal and decorate. Slash several steam holes,
4. Bake in a preheated 450° oven for 20 minutes. Lower heat to 350°, cover with foil, and continue to bake for 40 minutes.

Mountain Bartlett Pear Pie

CALIFORNIA

Adapted from Berger and Custis, *Sumptuous Dining in Gaslight San Francisco 1875–1915*

1 unbaked 9-inch pie shell	1 teaspoon vanilla
4 cups Bartlett pears, peeled, cored, and thinly sliced	4 tablespoons sifted flour
½ cup butter	½ teaspoon salt
1 cup sugar	¼ teaspoon nutmeg
2 eggs, beaten	¼ teaspoon cinnamon
	¼ teaspoon allspice

1. Fill the pie shell to the top with the Bartlett pear slices.
2. Cream the butter and sugar together until light and fluffy. Beat in the eggs and vanilla.
3. Stir in the flour, salt, nutmeg, cinnamon, and allspice. Beat until smooth. Pour this mixture over the pears.
4. Bake at 400° for 15 minutes. Reduce the heat to 350° and bake until the crust is brown and the pears are tender.

Sour-Cherry Pie

WASHINGTON

Adapted from Brown, *American Cooking: The Northwest*

6 cups pitted sour cherries (from about 3¾ pounds)	¼ teaspoon almond extract
¼ cup quick-cooking tapioca	1 unbaked 9-inch pie shell
1 cup sugar	2 tablespoons unsalted butter, cut into ¼-inch bits
1½ tablespoons strained fresh lemon juice	1 top crust

1. Mix the sour cherries, tapioca, sugar, lemon juice, and almond extract together, stirring gently. Allow the mixture to stand for 10 minutes.
2. Pour the filling into the pie shell and dot the top with the butter bits. Add the top crust, sealing the edge with water. Cut a 1-inch hole in the center of the pie crust.
3. Bake at 450° for 10 minutes. Lower the heat to 350° and bake an additional 40–45 minutes, or until the top is golden brown and the filling bubbles from the center hole.

Fresh Strawberry Pie

OREGON

Adapted from Brown, *American Cooking: The Northwest*

6   cups (1½ quarts) firm, ripe strawberries, preferably wild
1   baked 9-inch pie shell, cooled
½   cup sugar

3   tablespoons cornstarch
2   tablespoons cold water
1   tablespoon strained fresh lemon juice
1   cup heavy cream, chilled

1. Place half of the strawberries in the cooled baked pie shell.
2. Chop the remaining berries fine and mix them with the sugar. Cook them over low heat in a nonreactive saucepan to simmering.
3. Mix the cornstarch, cold water, and lemon juice together to make a smooth paste. Pour the paste into the berry mixture and continue to cook, stirring constantly, for 2–3 minutes, until the mixture thickens. Sieve this mixture.
4. Pour the puree over the berries in the pie shell. Cover and refrigerate for 2 hours.
5. Whip the cream stiff and top the pie in a decorative manner.

Wild Blackberry Pie

WASHINGTON

Adapted from Hawkins and Hawkins, *The American Regional Cookbook*

6   cups fresh, ripe wild blackberries, picked over and washed
1   unbaked 9-inch pie shell
1   cup sugar, white or brown

¼   teaspoon cinnamon, nutmeg, or ginger
1   tablespoon flour
¼   cup butter
1   top crust

1. Add the berries to the pie shell.
2. Mix the sugar with spice and flour and sprinkle this over the berries. Dot the surface with butter.
3. Place the top crust over the pie, crimp the edges, and cut steam vents.
4. Bake at 425° for 15 minutes. Reduce the heat to 350° and bake 20–30 minutes longer, or until the filling is bubbling through the steam vents.

Autumn Pear and Goat Cheese Tart

OREGON

Adapted from Brooks, *Oregon's Cuisine of the Rain*

1   9-inch unbaked pie shell

Fruit:

1   vanilla bean
2   cups water
1   cup dry white wine
1½ cups sugar

juice of 1 lemon
1   cinnamon stick
4   ripe pears, peeled, halved
    lengthwise, and cored

Custard:

¼   pound mild goat cheese,
    room temperature
1   tablespoon unbleached all-
    purpose flour

2   large eggs
¼   cup half-and-half
1   vanilla bean

1. Bake the pie shell partially, about 8 minutes.
2. Cut the vanilla bean in half lengthwise and scrape out the seeds into a nonreactive saucepan. Add the water, wine, sugar, lemon juice, and cinnamon stick. Bring the mixture to a boil.
3. Lower the heat and add the pears, cut sides up. Simmer until the pears are tender but firm to a knife point. Remove the pears from the liquid and allow to cool.
4. To prepare the custard, beat the goat cheese until smooth. Add the flour and the beaten eggs, one at a time, beating well after each addition. Add the half-and-half and the seeds of a vanilla bean. Beat until well blended.
5. Arrange the cooled pears in the pie shell, cut side down. Spoon the custard over the pears, covering completely.
6. Bake the tart at 350° until the custard sets, about 20 minutes.

Margarita Pie

CALIFORNIA
Adapted from *The Los Angeles Times California Cookbook*

1	envelope unflavored gelatin	1	teaspoon grated lime peel
¼	cup cool water	⅓	cup tequila
1	cup sugar	3	tablespoons Cointreau or
¼	teaspoon salt		Triple Sec
4	eggs, separated	1	baked 9-inch pie shell
½	cup lime juice		

1. Soak the gelatin in ¼ cup water for 2 minutes. Add ½ cup of the sugar and the salt.
2. Beat the egg yolks and lime juice together and add to the gelatin mixture. Cook over low heat until the gelatin is dissolved. Remove from the heat and stir in the lime peel, tequila, and liqueur. Refrigerate until the mixture mounds slightly when dropped from a spoon.
3. Beat the egg whites and remaining ½ cup sugar until stiff and glossy. Fold the whites into the gelatin mixture.
4. Pour the filling into the pastry shell and chill until firm.

Fresh Coconut Cream Pie

HAWAII
Adapted from Toupin, *Hawaii Cookbook & Backyard Luau*

2	cups milk	½	cup grated fresh coconut
½	cup sugar	1	tablespoon butter
	pinch salt	½	teaspoon vanilla
3	tablespoons cornstarch	1	baked 9-inch pie shell
4	egg yolks		sweetened whipped cream
1	teaspoon water		

1. Combine the milk, sugar, and salt and heat to a simmer.
2. Mix the cornstarch, egg yolks, and water together and stir into the milk mixture. Add the grated coconut and cook until thick. Stir in the butter and vanilla and allow the filling to cool.
3. Pour the filling into the baked pie shell and allow to cool.
4. Top the pie with whipped cream.

Passion Fruit Chiffon Pie

HAWAII

Adapted from Toupin, *Hawaii Cookbook & Backyard Luau*

1 tablespoon gelatin	½ cup passion fruit juice
¼ cup water	1 baked 9-inch pie shell
¾ cup sugar	1 cup heavy cream, whipped
4 eggs, separated	

1. Soften the gelatin in the water.
2. Beat ¼ cup of the sugar and the egg yolks together until pale and light. Cook in the top of a double boiler, stirring constantly, until the mixture is thick. Remove from the heat and stir in the gelatin. Allow the filling to cool.
3. Stir in the passion fruit juice and chill until slightly thickened.
4. Beat the egg whites until soft peaks form. Gradually add the remaining sugar and beat until stiff peaks form. Fold the passion fruit mixture into the beaten egg whites.
5. Pour the filling into the baked pie shell and chill until firm.
6. Top with whipped cream.

Guava Chiffon Pie

CALIFORNIA

Adapted from *The Los Angeles Times California Cookbook*

1 envelope unflavored gelatin	several drops red food color
1 tablespoon lemon juice	⅛ teaspoon cream of tartar
4 eggs, separated	1 baked 9-inch pie shell
1 cup guava juice	sweetened whipped cream
¾ cup sugar, divided	guava slices

1. Soften the gelatin in the lemon juice, allowing it to stand for 2 minutes.
2. Combine the egg yolks, guava juice, and ½ cup of the sugar. Add a few drops of red food color and cook over medium heat until mixture thickens.
3. Add the gelatin mixture and stir until dissolved. Cool the mixture until it thickens and forms ribbons.
4. Beat the egg whites and cream of tartar together until soft peaks form. Gradually add the remaining ¼ cup sugar and beat to form stiff peaks. Fold into the gelatin mixture and pour into the baked pie shell. Chill thoroughly.
5. Top with sweetened whipped cream and garnish with guava slices.

CHIFFON AND CREAM PIES

Gooseberry Chiffon Pie

OREGON
Adapted from Hawkins and Hawkins, *The American Regional Cookbook*

1½ cups ripe gooseberries,
    picked over and rinsed
1½ cups water
1 cup sugar
1 envelope unflavored gelatin

¼ cup water
2 eggs, separated
1 baked 9-inch pie shell
1 cup sweetened whipped
    cream

1. Cook the gooseberries in the water until soft. Sieve to remove the skins and seeds. Add the sugar and bring to a boil.
2. Soften the gelatin in the water and add it to the hot mixture.
3. Beat the egg yolks and add them carefully to the berry mixture, stirring constantly.
4. Beat the egg whites stiff and fold them into the berry mixture. Pour the filling into the baked pie shell and refrigerate until set.
5. Top the pie with the whipped cream and serve.

NUT AND CHOCOLATE PIES

Macadamia Nut Cream Pie

CALIFORNIA
Adapted from *The Los Angeles Times California Cookbook*

1⅓ cups milk, divided
¾ cup sugar, divided
½ cup chopped, toasted
    macadamia nuts, divided
⅛ teaspoon salt

1 teaspoon vanilla
3 eggs, separated
1 tablespoon cornstarch
1 baked 8-inch pastry shell
2 cups whipped cream

1. Combine 1 cup of the milk, ¼ cup of the sugar, ¼ cup of the nuts, the salt, and vanilla in the top of a double boiler. Cook to scald the milk.
2. Combine the remaining milk with the egg yolks and cornstarch. Add this to the hot milk mixture. Cook, stirring until thickened. Cool slightly.
3. Beat the egg whites with the remaining ½ cup sugar until stiff and glossy. Fold them gently into the custard and pour this filling into the baked pie shell.
4. When cool, top with whipped cream and sprinkle with the remaining chopped nuts.

Macadamia Nut Pie

HAWAII

Adapted from Toupin, *Hawaii Cookbook & Backyard Luau*

Pastry:

1 cup flour	⅓ cup butter
⅛ teaspoon salt	2 tablespoons ice water
1 tablespoon sugar	

Filling:

¼ pound butter	¼ teaspoon salt
¾ cup sugar	1 teaspoon vanilla
3 eggs, slightly beaten	1 cup unsalted macadamia
¾ cup dark corn syrup	nuts, chopped

1. Sift the flour, salt, and sugar together. Cut in the butter with a pastry knife. Add the ice water and mix lightly. Roll the dough out and line a 9-inch pie plate, fluting the edges.
2. Prepare the filling by creaming the butter with the sugar until smooth. Beat in the eggs, corn syrup, salt, and vanilla. Stir in the nuts. Pour the filling into the prepared pie shell.
3. Bake at 350° for 35–40 minutes.

Banana Paradise Pie

HAWAII

Adapted from Toupin, *Hawaii Cookbook & Backyard Luau*

Filling:

4	cups sliced firm ripe bananas	¼	cup sugar
¼	cup pineapple juice	½	teaspoon cinnamon
2	tablespoons lemon juice	1	unbaked 8-inch pie shell
1½	teaspoons grated lemon rind	1	teaspoon cornstarch

Topping:

⅓	cup chopped macadamia nuts	¾	cup light brown sugar
¾	cup flour	¾	teaspoon cinnamon
		6	tablespoons butter

1. Marinate the bananas in the pineapple and lemon juices for 20 minutes. Drain, saving the juices. Toss the bananas with the grated lemon rind, sugar, and cinnamon. Fill the pie shell with this mixture.
2. Cook the reserved juices with the cornstarch until thick and add this to the pie.
3. Prepare the topping by mixing all of the ingredients except the butter together. Cut in the butter with a pastry knife until a crumbly mixture forms. Top the pie with this mixture.
4. Bake at 400° degree oven for 20 minutes, or until the crust is brown.

Coconut Turnovers

HAWAII
Adapted from Toupin, *Hawaii Cookbook & Backyard Luau*

Pastry:

2 cups sifted flour	⅓ cup lard
1 teaspoon salt	⅓ cup butter
1½ tablespoons sugar	⅓ cup cold water

Filling:

¼ cup butter	3 cups grated fresh coconut
1 cup powdered sugar, divided	2 egg whites

1. Sift the flour, salt, and sugar together. Cut in the lard and butter with a pastry blender. Sprinkle with the cold water and gather the dough into a ball. Refrigerate until needed.
2. For the filling, cream the butter with half of the powdered sugar. Add the coconut and blend.
3. Beat the egg whites to form soft peaks. Gradually add the remaining powdered sugar and beat to form stiff peaks. Fold this into the coconut mixture.
4. Roll out the pastry dough and cut it into 4-inch squares.
5. Place 2 tablespoons of the coconut mixture in the lower half of each square. Fold over to form a rectangle. Crimp the edges and prick the top with a fork. Place the turnovers onto an ungreased cookie sheet.
6. Bake at 425° for 15 minutes, or until golden brown.

Cakes

Cakes

Wine Cake

VERMONT

Adapted from Pixley, *Vermont Country Cooking*

½	cup butter	¼	teaspoon baking soda
2	cups powdered sugar	4	egg whites, beaten
4	egg yolks	3½	cups sifted flour
4	ounces sherry or Madeira	½	teaspoon nutmeg
½	cup cream		

1. Cream the butter and powdered sugar until fluffy. Add the egg yolks and sherry or Madeira and beat until smooth and light.
2. Add the cream and baking soda and beat for 2 minutes.
3. Fold the beaten egg whites into the creamed mixture, followed by the sifted flour and nutmeg. Pour into a greased 9-inch loaf pan.
4. Bake at 350° for 30 minutes, or until done.

Seed Cake

VERMONT

Adapted from Pixley, *Vermont Country Cooking*

2	tablespoons butter	½	pound flour
2	tablespoons sugar	1	teaspoon caraway seeds
3	eggs	½	teaspoon salt

1. Cream the butter and sugar until light and fluffy. Add the eggs, one at a time, beating well after each addition.
2. Stir in the flour and caraway seeds, along with the salt.
3. Bake in an 8- or 9-inch loaf or round pan at 350° for forty minutes.

Mother's White Moon Cake

NEW HAMPSHIRE
Adapted from Berquist, *The High Maples Farm Cookbook*

3 cups cake flour	2 teaspoons vanilla
3 teaspoons baking powder	5 egg whites, beaten very stiff
½ teaspoon salt	and glossy
2 cups sifted sugar	3 cups powdered sugar
⅔ cup vegetable shortening	1 teaspoon kirsch
1 cup milk	

1. Sift the flour, baking powder, and salt together.
2. Cream the sugar and shortening until light and fluffy.
3. Add the milk mixed with the vanilla, alternating with the flour mixture. Beat well after each addition. Lightly fold in the egg whites.
4. Bake in 2 greased 9-inch cake pans at 350° for 30 minutes. Cool slightly.
5. Frost while cakes are still warm with a thin icing made from the powdered sugar, kirsch, and sufficient water to make a thin icing.

"Let the top frosting run down over the sides of the cake in droplets, thus adding a silvery appearance."

Esther's Sour Cream Cake

NEW HAMPSHIRE
Adapted from Berquist, *The High Maples Farm Cookbook*

1¾ cups pastry flour	1 cup well-soured heavy
1 teaspoon cream of	cream
tartar	1 cup sugar
½ teaspoon baking soda	1 teaspoon vanilla
¼ teaspoon salt	2 eggs, lightly beaten

1. Sift the flour, cream of tartar, baking soda, and salt together twice.
2. Beat the soured cream, sugar, and vanilla together until smooth. Stir in the eggs.
3. Fold in the flour mixture and beat to form a smooth batter. Pour the batter into a greased 9-inch square baking pan.
4. Bake at 350° for 30 minutes, or until the cake is set in the center.

Lazy Cake

CONNECTICUT

Adapted from *The Neighborhood Cook Book*

1	cup flour	⅓	cup melted butter
1	cup sugar	2	eggs
1	teaspoon baking powder	½	cup milk

1. Mix the flour, sugar, and baking powder together.
2. Add the melted butter, eggs, and milk. Stir for 5 minutes.
3. Grease the bottom of a 9-inch round cake pan and pour in the batter.
4. Bake at 350° for 15–20 minutes.

"Can be made while your guests are coming up the front walk."

Dundee Cake

CONNECTICUT

Adapted from *The Neighborhood Cook Book*

1	cup butter	¾	cup sultana raisins
¾	cup sugar	½	cup currants
4	eggs	½	teaspoon nutmeg
1½	cups flour	½	teaspoon cloves
⅛	teaspoon salt	½	teaspoon vanilla
½	teaspoon baking powder	¼	cup cream or milk
¼	lemon peel, cut in thin, small strips	½	cup almonds, blanched and slivered

1. Cream the butter with the sugar. Add the eggs, one at a time, beating thoroughly between additions.
2. Add the flour sifted with the salt and the baking powder. Stir in the lemon peel, raisins, currants, spices, and vanilla to form a smooth batter.
3. Stir in the cream and half of the almonds. Pour in a greased loaf tin and sprinkle the remaining almonds over the top.
4. Bake at 350° for 1 hour.

One, Two, Three, Four Cake

MASSACHUSETTS

Adapted from Hawkins, Havemeyer, and Havemeyer, *Nantucket and Other New England Cooking*

Cake:

1 cup butter, softened	3 cups flour
2 cups sugar	1 cup milk
4 eggs	1 teaspoon vanilla extract

Chocolate filling:

½ cup grated unsweetened chocolate	1 egg yolk
½ cup milk	1 cup sugar
	1 teaspoon vanilla extract

Frosting for cake:

1 egg white	1½ cups powdered sugar

1. Cream the butter and sugar. Beat until fluffy. Add the eggs, beating well.
2. Add the flour alternately with the milk. Add the vanilla.
3. Spoon into 3 parchment-lined layer-cake pans.
4. Bake at 350° for 35–40 minutes, or until cake springs back when touched.
5. To prepare the filling, cook all the ingredients together over low heat until the mixture is firm. Cool, then spread between the cake layers.
6. To prepare the frosting, beat the egg white to soft peaks. Add the sugar and beat to stiff peaks. Frost the cake.

Three-Egg Cake

MASSACHUSETTS

Adapted from *Boston Chapter, No. 28 Order of Eastern Star Cook Book*

2 cups sugar	⅛ teaspoon salt
1 cup butter	1 cup milk
3 eggs, separated	½ teaspoon lemon extract
3 cups flour	½ teaspoon vanilla extract
2½ teaspoons baking powder	

1. Cream the sugar and butter together until fluffy. Add the egg yolks and beat until smooth.
2. Whip the egg whites stiff but not dry.
3. Sift the flour with the baking powder and salt. Add this to the creamed butter mixture, alternating with the milk.
4. Fold in the egg whites. Stir in the lemon and vanilla extracts. Pour the batter into a greased 9-inch cake pan.
5. Bake at 350° for 20 minutes, or until done in the center.

Old-Time Cider Cake

VERMONT

Adapted from Pixley, *Vermont Country Cooking*

1½ cups sugar	8 ounces cider
½ pound butter	8 cups flour
2 teaspoons baking soda	1 teaspoon grated nutmeg
½ cup water	

1. Cream the sugar and butter until light. Add the baking soda, water, and cider. Stir in the flour and the nutmeg.
2. Bake in a greased 10-inch round cake pan at 350° for 30 minutes.

Ribbon Cake

MASSACHUSETTS
Adapted from *Boston Chapter, No. 28 Order of Eastern Star Cook Book*

Light batter:

½ cup butter	1 cup sifted flour
1¼ cups sugar	1 teaspoon cream of tartar
3 egg whites	¼ cup sugar
¼ cup sweet milk	½ teaspoon baking soda

Dark batter:

3 egg yolks	½ teaspoon baking soda, dissolved in 2 tablespoons hot water
¼ cup butter	
¼ cup sugar	1 cup chopped raisins
½ cup molasses	1 teaspoon nutmeg

Frosting:

1 cup light brown sugar	1 egg white
2 tablespoons water	

1. Prepare the light batter by creaming the butter with the sugar. Add the egg whites and beat 1 minute.
2. Add the milk, alternating with the flour, which has been sifted with the cream of tartar, sugar, and baking soda.
3. Prepare the dark batter by creaming the egg yolks with the butter. Add the sugar, molasses, and the baking soda dissolved in the hot water. Stir in the raisins and nutmeg.
4. Pour the light batter into 2 greased 8-inch cake pans. Drizzle the dark batter on the light, creating ribbons through the light batter.
5. Bake at 350° for 20 minutes, or until done.
6. Prepare the frosting by boiling the brown sugar, water, and egg white, which have been properly mixed, until soft threads form. Ice the cooled cake with this cooled mixture.

Hungry Cake

MASSACHUSETTS
Adapted from *Boston Chapter, No. 28 Order of Eastern Star Cook Book*

½ cup butter
2 cups light brown sugar
2 egg yolks
1 cup sour milk
1 teaspoon baking soda

½ teaspoon cloves
½ teaspoon nutmeg
2 cups flour
¼ teaspoon salt

1. Cream the butter and brown sugar. Add the egg yolks and sour milk. Beat 1–2 minutes.
2. Sift the baking soda and spices with the flour and salt and stir into the creamed mixture to form a smooth batter.
3. Bake in a greased 7-inch loaf pan at 350° for 20 minutes, or until firm at center.

Blueberry Cake

VERMONT
Adapted from *Out of Vermont Kitchens*

3 tablespoons shortening
1 cup sugar
1 egg
¾ cup milk

1¾ cups flour
2 teaspoons baking powder
1½ cups blueberries

1. Cream the shortening and add the sugar. Continue to beat 2 minutes. Beat in the egg and milk.
2. Sift the flour and baking powder together and add to the creamed mixture. Stir in the blueberries gently.
3. Bake in a shallow greased 8-inch square pan at 350° for 35–40 minutes.

"Serve while hot with butter."

Pineapple Upside-Down Cake

NEW HAMPSHIRE

Adapted from Berquist, *The High Maples Farm Cookbook*

3 tablespoons butter	½ teaspoon salt
½ cup light brown sugar	½ cup butter
8 canned pineapple slices, drained (reserve the juice)	½ cup sugar
	1 large egg
8 maraschino cherries	1 teaspoon vanilla
1½ cups all-purpose flour	½ cup reserved pineapple
2 teaspoons baking powder	juice

1. Melt the butter and brown sugar together in a skillet and sauté the pineapple rings for 2 minutes.
2. Remove the pineapple and spread the hot butter-sugar mixture in a greased 11-by-7-inch baking pan. Arrange the pineapple slices in a single layer. Place a cherry in the center of each pineapple ring.
3. Sift the flour, baking powder, and salt together.
4. Cream the butter and sugar until light and fluffy. Beat in the egg and vanilla. Add the flour mixture alternately with the reserved pineapple juice. Mix to form a smooth batter. Spread this batter over the pineapples.
5. Bake at 350° for 30 – 40 minutes.
6. To serve, invert over a serving plate while still warm.

Frances' Devil's Fun Cake

NEW HAMPSHIRE
Adapted from Berquist, *The High Maples Farm Cookbook*

1¾ cups cake flour
¾ teaspoon baking soda
½ teaspoon salt
6 ounces baking chocolate,
    cut into small pieces
¾ cup boiling water
½ cup softened butter
1 teaspoon vanilla

1¾ cups sifted sugar
5 large eggs
¾ cup buttermilk
1 tablespoon hot water
¼ cup softened butter
2 teaspoons vanilla
1 pound powdered sugar

1. Sift the flour, baking soda, and salt together.
2. To 4 ounces of the chocolate add the boiling water and stir until the chocolate is dissolved. Cool to lukewarm and beat in the butter, vanilla, and sugar until smooth. Add 3 of the eggs, one at a time, beating after each addition.
3. Add the dry ingredients alternately with the buttermilk, mixing only enough to make a smooth batter.
4. Bake in 2 greased 9-inch layer cake pans at 350° for 35 minutes, or until done in the center. Allow the cakes to cool before frosting.
5. To prepare the frosting, combine the remaining chocolate and the tablespoon of hot water in the top of a double boiler. Stir in the 2 remaining eggs. Cook for 2 minutes stirring constantly. Remove from heat and beat in the ¼ cup butter, 2 teaspoons vanilla, and enough powdered sugar to have spreading consistency. Fill and frost the cake.

CHOCOLATE CAKES

Chocolate Nougat Cake

MASSACHUSETTS
Adapted from *Boston Chapter, No. 28 Order of Eastern Star Cook Book*

¼	cup butter	½	teaspoon vanilla
1½	cups powdered sugar	2	squares unsweetened
1	egg		chocolate, melted
1	cup milk, divided	⅓	cup powdered sugar
2	cups bread flour	⅔	cup almonds, blanched
3	teaspoons baking powder		and chopped

1. Cream the butter until light and gradually add the 1½ cups powdered sugar. Add the egg (unbeaten). Mix well.
2. Add ⅔ cup of the milk, then the flour sifted with the baking powder. Add the vanilla.
3. To the melted chocolate add the ⅓ cup powdered sugar. Add the remaining milk and cook over a low flame until smooth. Cool slightly and add to cake mixture.
4. Bake in a greased 9-inch cake pan at 350° for 15–20 minutes.

Sour Milk Chocolate Cake

MASSACHUSETTS
Adapted from *Boston Chapter, No. 28 Order of Eastern Star Cook Book*

¼	cup butter	1	teaspoon baking soda
1	cup sugar	1	cup sour milk
2	tablespoons cocoa	1½	cups pastry flour
1	teaspoon salt	1	egg, unbeaten
1	teaspoon vanilla		

1. Cream the butter and sugar together until light and fluffy. Add the cocoa, salt, and vanilla.
2. Dissolve the baking soda in the sour milk and add to the creamed ingredients. Stir in the pastry flour and egg to form a smooth batter.
3. Bake in a greased 9-inch loaf pan at 350° for 20–30 minutes.

Butternut Cake

VERMONT
Adapted from Pixley, *Vermont Country Cooking*

½	cup butter	2	teaspoons baking powder
½	cup sugar	1	teaspoon baking soda
1	cup maple syrup	½	teaspoon ginger
2	eggs, beaten	½	cup hot water
2½	cups flour	½	cup butternut meats

Frosting:

2	cups maple sugar	½	cup butternut meats
1	cup cream		

1. Cream the butter and sugar. Add the syrup and stir in the eggs.
2. Sift the flour, baking powder, baking soda, and ginger together.
3. Add the hot water and stir to form a smooth batter. Fold in the ½ cup butternut meats.
4. Bake in a greased 9-inch loaf pan at 350° for 20–30 minutes.
5. Prepare the frosting by boiling the sugar and cream together to the soft ball stage. Add the butternut meats and stir to thicken. Frost the cooled cake.

Ellen's Applesauce Cake

NEW HAMPSHIRE
Adapted from Berquist, *The High Maples Farm Cookbook*

2	cups all-purpose flour	¾	cup sugar
1	teaspoon baking powder	½	cup softened butter
½	teaspoon salt	¾	cup applesauce
½	teaspoon cinnamon	¼	cup molasses
½	teaspoon cloves	1	teaspoon baking soda
½	teaspoon nutmeg	½	cup broken walnut meats
⅛	teaspoon ginger	½	cup raisins

1. Sift the flour, baking powder, salt, and spices together twice.
2. Cream the sugar and butter together until light and fluffy.
3. Mix the applesauce, molasses, and baking soda together.
4. Stir the applesauce mixture into the butter mixture. Mix in the flour mixture. Stir to blend. Fold in the nut meats and raisins.
5. Bake in a greased 9-inch loaf pan at 350° degrees for 1 hour, or until cake is set in the center.

SPICE, NUT, AND FRUIT CAKES

Inexpensive Never-Fail Fruit Cake

VERMONT

Adapted from *Out of Vermont Kitchens*

2½ cups cold water
½ pound currants
2 cups sugar
1 teaspoon salt
1 teaspoon allspice
2 apples, cut up
2 pounds seedless raisins
1 pound dates
1 teaspoon cloves
1 teaspoon cinnamon

1 small can crushed
   pineapple
4 cups flour
2 teaspoons baking soda
¼ pound chopped nuts
1 cup candied lemon
1 cup candied orange peel
1 cup citron
1 cup candied cherries

1. Mix the first 11 ingredients together and boil for 5 minutes. Set aside to cool.
2. Sift the flour and baking soda together. Stir this into the cooled mixture.
3. Add the nuts and fruits and stir to incorporate.
4. Bake at 250° for 3 hours.

Auntie's Boiled Cake

NEW HAMPSHIRE

Adapted from Berquist, *The High Maples Farm Cookbook*

1¼ cups cold water
1 cup sugar
¼ cup butter
⅓ cup raisins
⅓ cup mixed candied fruits
   and peels
1 teaspoon cinnamon

½ teaspoon allspice
½ teaspoon nutmeg
2¼ cups all-purpose flour
1 teaspoon baking soda
1 teaspoon baking powder
1 large egg, beaten until light
⅓ cup broken walnut meats

1. Put the cold water, sugar, butter, raisins, candied fruits and peels, cinnamon, allspice, and nutmeg in a saucepan and bring to a boil. Remove from the heat and cool to lukewarm.
2. Sift the flour, baking soda, and baking powder together.
3. Add the egg to the cooled spice mixture. Stir in the flour mixture. Fold in the nut meats.
4. Bake in a greased 9-inch loaf pan at 350° for 40 minutes, or until cake is done.

"The top should be glazed and slightly 'crackled.'"

Hoover Cake

MASSACHUSETTS
Adapted from *Boston Chapter, No. 28 Order of Eastern Star Cook Book*

1 cup light brown sugar	1 cup water
⅓ cup lard	1 teaspoon baking soda
2 cups raisins	¼ cup warm water
1 teaspoon cinnamon, ground	2 cups flour
	1 teaspoon baking powder
¼ teaspoon nutmeg, ground	½ cup shelled nuts
1 teaspoon cloves, ground	

1. Boil the first 7 ingredients together for 3 minutes.
2. When cool, add the baking soda dissolved in the warm water, followed by the remaining ingredients. Mix to form a smooth batter.
3. Bake at 350° for 20 minutes in a greased 9-inch cake pan. Frost as desired.

Mother's Yum Yum Cake

VERMONT
Adapted from *Out of Vermont Kitchens*

½ cup raisins	1 teaspoon cinnamon
1 cup sugar	½ teaspoon cloves
¼ cup shortening	½ teaspoon salt
1 cup water	½ teaspoon baking soda
1½ cups flour	

1. Place the raisins, sugar, shortening, and water in a saucepan and bring to a boil. Allow to cool.
2. Sift the remaining ingredients together and add to the cooled mixture. Stir to form a smooth batter. Pour the batter into a greased 8-inch deep cake pan.
3. Bake at 350° for 20 minutes.

Maple Nut Cake

VERMONT
Adapted from *Out of Vermont Kitchens*

Cake:

⅓	cup butter	¼	teaspoon salt
1	cup light brown sugar	2	teaspoons baking powder
2	eggs, separated	1	cup chopped nuts
½	cup milk	1	teaspoon vanilla
1½	cups flour		

Maple icing:

1	cup light brown sugar	1	teaspoon maple flavoring
⅓	cup butter		powdered sugar
¼	cup milk		

1. Cream the butter and brown sugar together. Add the egg yolks and milk. Beat until smooth.
2. Sift the flour, salt, and baking powder together and add to the creamed mixture. Add the nuts and vanilla.
3. Beat the egg whites stiff and fold into the batter. Pour into 2 greased 8-inch cake pans.
4. Bake at 350° for 35–45 minutes.
5. To prepare the icing, combine the first 3 ingredients and cook for 3 minutes. Cool, then add the flavoring and enough sifted powdered sugar to be at spreading consistency.

New England Raised Cake

RHODE ISLAND
Adapted from Dyer, *The Newport Cookbook*

1 cup milk	1 teaspoon salt
1 tablespoon dry yeast	¾ cup seedless raisins
2 cups sugar, divided	1 cup chopped citron
3 cups flour, divided	½ cup chopped maraschino
½ pound butter	cherries
1 egg, lightly beaten	

1. Scald the milk. Cool to lukewarm and add the yeast. Stir to blend. Add ¼ cup of the sugar and 1 cup of the flour. Allow to rise in a warm place until foamy, about 1 hour.
2. Cream the butter with the remaining sugar and add this to the yeast mixture, alternating with the remaining flour. Add the egg and beat to form a smooth dough.
3. Fold in the remaining ingredients. Pour the batter into 2 well-buttered loaf pans. Allow to stand at room temperature for 2 hours.
4. Bake at 350° for 15 minutes. Lower the heat to 300° and continue to bake for 1 hour, or until the cakes are firm and golden.

Mary's Apple-Flopped Cake

NEW HAMPSHIRE
Adapted from Berquist, *The High Maples Farm Cookbook*

6 apples, peeled, cored, and sliced thin	¼ cup softened butter
	½ cup sugar
2 drops red food coloring	1 large egg
1 cup all-purpose flour	½ teaspoon vanilla
1½ teaspoons baking powder	1 cup milk
¼ teaspoon salt	

1. Put the apples, food coloring, and enough water to cover in a saucepan. Bring to a boil, then drain. Arrange the apple slices in a buttered 9-inch square baking pan.
2. Sift the flour, baking powder, and salt together.
3. Cream the butter with the sugar until light and fluffy. Beat in the egg and vanilla.
4. Add the flour mixture alternately with the milk, beating well after each addition. Spread the batter over the apple slices.
5. Bake at 350° for 30–40 minutes.
6. To serve, invert the cake onto a platter while warm.

CUPCAKES

Molasses Spice Cupcakes

NEW HAMPSHIRE
Adapted from Berquist, *The High Maples Farm Cookbook*

2 cups all-purpose flour	¼ teaspoon allspice
½ teaspoon baking soda	½ cup sugar
1 teaspoon cream of tartar	1 cup thick sour cream
1 teaspoon ginger	2 large eggs
¼ teaspoon ground cloves	⅓ cup light molasses

Lemon frosting:

⅓ cup soft butter	¼–⅓ cup fresh lemon juice
2½ cups powdered sugar	4 drops yellow food coloring

1. Sift the flour, baking soda, cream of tartar, ginger, cloves, and allspice together.
2. Cream the sugar and sour cream together until the sugar is dissolved. Add the eggs and mix well. Stir in the molasses.
3. Add the flour mixture and beat until smooth. Do not overbeat. Spoon the batter into a paper-lined cupcake pan.
4. Bake at 350° for 30 minutes, or until cupcakes are done. Allow to cool before frosting.
5. Prepare the frosting by beating all the ingredients together until smooth and fluffy. Top each cupcake with this mixture.

ROLL CAKE

Chocolate Roll

CONNECTICUT
Adapted from *The Neighborhood Cook Book*

4 eggs	½ cup sugar
1½ tablespoons cocoa	2 cups heavy cream

1. Separate the eggs and whip the whites to soft peaks.
2. Beat the yolks until pale and light. Stir in the cocoa and 1½ tablespoons of the sugar.
3. Fold in the beaten egg whites and spread this mixture on a parchment-lined jelly-roll pan. Bake at 275° until done, about 20 minutes.
4. In the meantime, whip the cream with the remaining sugar. Spread ⅔ of this over the cooled cake and roll up, jelly-roll fashion. Decorate with remaining whipped cream.

Lady Cake

PENNSYLVANIA

Adapted from Reed, *The Philadelphia Cook Book of Town and Country*

¾ pound sweet butter	¼ cup cornstarch
2 cups sugar	½ teaspoon baking powder
16 egg whites, divided	1 teaspoon almond extract
4 cups flour	

1. Cream the butter and sugar together until smooth. Add 8 egg whites and beat until light.
2. Sift the flour, cornstarch, and baking powder together and add this to the creamed mixture.
3. Beat the remaining egg whites until very stiff and fold them into the batter gently. Stir in the almond extract, mixing lightly. Pour the batter into 2 greased and parchment-lined 9-inch cake pans.
4. Bake at 300° for about 1½ hours.

Eliza Cake

MARYLAND

Adapted from *Tested Maryland Recipes*

8 ounces raisins	1 cup milk
2 ounces brandy	½ teaspoon baking soda
1⅓ cups butter	3⅓ cups flour
2 cups sugar	½ teaspoon cream of tartar
3 eggs, separated	

1. Plump the raisins by soaking in the brandy.
2. Cream the butter with the sugar until light and fluffy. Add the egg yolks and beat until smooth.
3. Mix the milk and baking soda together and add this to the creamed mixture.
4. Beat the egg whites with the cream of tartar to form soft peaks.
5. Sift the flour and cream of tartar together and add it to the creamed mixture. Stir in the egg whites to form a smooth batter.
6. Drain the raisins, toss them with a little flour, and stir them in. Mix in any remaining brandy.
7. Bake in 2 greased 8-inch cake pans at 350° for 20 minutes, or until a tester comes out clean.

Crumb Cake

NEW JERSEY

Adapted from *Chicken Foot Soup and Other Recipes from the Pine Barrens*

Cake:

½ cup butter or margarine
1 cup sugar
2 eggs
¾ cup milk

2 cups flour
2 teaspoons baking powder
1 teaspoon vanilla

Crumb topping:

½ cup butter or margarine
1 cup sugar

2 cups prepared biscuit mix
2 teaspoons cinnamon

Garnish:

powdered sugar

1. Cream the butter and sugar together until light and fluffy.
2. Beat the eggs and the milk together.
3. Sift the flour with the baking powder. Add these dry ingredients in thirds, alternating with the milk mixture, to the creamed mixture. Stir in the vanilla extract.
4. To prepare the crumb topping, cut the butter into the dry ingredients with a pastry knife.
5. Pour the cake batter into a greased 9-by-12-inch pan. Spread the crumb topping over the batter.
6. Bake at 350° for about 30 minutes. Sprinkle with powdered sugar before serving.

Sour Cream Pound Cake

DELAWARE
Adapted from *Winterthur's Culinary Collection*

1	teaspoon baking soda	6 eggs, separated
1	cup sour cream	3 cups flour, sifted
½	pound butter, softened	1 teaspoon vanilla
3	cups sugar	

1. Grease and lightly flour a tube pan.
2. Add the baking soda to the sour cream and set aside.
3. Cream the butter and sugar. Add the egg yolks, one at a time.
4. Alternately mix in the sour cream and flour. Mix well. Add the vanilla.
5. Beat the egg whites stiff and fold them into the batter. Pour into the prepared pan.
6. Bake at 300° for 1½ hours. Cool before serving.

WHITE CAKES

Pear Upside-down Cake

PENNSYLVANIA
Adapted from Wilson, *American Cooking: The Eastern Heartland*

1	pound butter, melted	¼	teaspoon ground cloves
1	cup light brown sugar	1	teaspoon salt
3	medium-sized pears, peeled, halved, and cored	½	cup dark molasses
2½	cups unsifted flour	½	cup honey
1½	teaspoons baking soda	¾	cup hot water
1	teaspoon ground cinnamon	1	egg
1	teaspoon ground ginger	½	cup sugar

1. Coat a 9-inch springform pan with a little of the melted butter.
2. Mix 6 tablespoons of the melted butter with the brown sugar and pat the mixture smoothly over the bottom of the pan.
3. Poach the pear halves in enough water to cover until just tender to a knife point. Remove them and allow them to drain for a minute. Save one pear and dice it. Arrange the remaining 2 pears neatly on the brown sugar mixture in the pan.
4. Sift the flour, baking soda, cinnamon, ginger, cloves, and salt together.
5. Combine the molasses, honey, and hot water and mix together thoroughly. Beat in the egg and sugar until light and smooth. Stir in the remaining melted butter.
6. Add the flour mixture to the molasses mixture in parts. Mix to form a smooth batter. Gently stir in the reserved chopped pears and pour the batter slowly into the pear-lined pan.
7. Bake at 350° for about 1 hour, or until set in the center. Allow to cool in the pan for about 5 minutes.
8. To serve, invert on a serving plate.

Lightening Layer Cake

PENNSYLVANIA
Adapted from *Choice Recipes*

3⅓ cups cake flour
2 teaspoons baking powder
1 teaspoon salt
2 eggs

½ cup shortening
1 cup milk
2 cups sugar
1 teaspoon vanilla

1. Sift the dry ingredients together. Add the eggs and shortening.
2. Add the milk, sugar, and vanilla. Beat 2 minutes.
3. Pour batter into a greased 8-inch loaf pan.
4. Bake at 375° for 25 minutes.

Royal Mystery Cake

PENNSYLVANIA
Adapted from *Choice Recipes*

½ cup butter
½ cup sugar
grated rind of ½ orange
1 egg, separated
1 egg yolk
2½ cups cake flour

4 teaspoons baking powder
¼ teaspoon salt
1 cup milk
1½ squares unsweetened chocolate, melted

1. Cream the butter and sugar with the grated orange rind. Add the two egg yolks.
2. Sift the flour, baking powder, and salt together and add to the creamed mixture alternately with the milk.
3. Beat the egg white and fold it in.
4. Divide the batter in 2 parts and stir the melted chocolate into one portion. Drop both batters by spoonfuls into 3 greased layer-cake pans.
5. Bake at 350° for 20 minutes.

Cherry Cake

NEW JERSEY

Adapted from *Chicken Foot Soup and Other Recipes from the Pine Barrens*

Cake:

1	stick butter or margarine	1	cup milk
1½	cups sugar	1	teaspoon almond extract
2	large eggs	½	cup finely chopped walnuts
4	cups flour	½	cup finely chopped mara-
3	teaspoons baking powder		schino cherries

Frosting:

2	ounces softened butter	½	teaspoon almond extract
3	ounces softened cream cheese	1	pound powdered sugar milk

1. Beat the butter and sugar together until light and fluffy. Beat in the eggs.
2. Sift the flour with the baking powder and add it to the creamed mixture in thirds, alternating with the milk. Stir well after each addition.
3. Add the almond extract and fold in the walnuts and cherries. Pour the batter into two 9-inch layer pans.
4. Bake at 350° for 30–40 minutes.
5. To prepare the frosting, cream the butter and cream cheese together until smooth. Beat in the almond extract followed by the powdered sugar. Add enough milk to form a spreadable mixture. Ice the cake when cool.

Mimere's Dark Chocolate Cake

NEW YORK

Adapted from *A Library of Favorite Recipes from New York State*

1	cup sugar	1	teaspoon baking soda
¼	teaspoon salt	2	heaping tablespoons cocoa
1	egg	½	cup boiling water
½	cup sour cream	2	teaspoons vanilla
1½	cups flour		

1. Mix the sugar, salt, egg, and sour cream together until blended. Sift the flour with the baking soda and cocoa and stir in to form a smooth batter.
2. Add the boiling water. Stir until smooth. Pour into a greased 8-inch loaf pan.
3. Bake at 350° for 30 – 40 minutes.

Black Joe Cake

PENNSYLVANIA

Adapted from Lestz, *The Pennsylvania Dutch Cookbook*

1	cup light brown sugar	1	cup boiling water
1	cup granulated sugar	1	teaspoon baking soda
½	cup lard	1	teaspoon vanilla
1	cup buttermilk	3½	cups sifted flour
½	cup cocoa	⅛	teaspoon salt

1. Mix the sugars with the lard. Add the buttermilk.
2. Mix the cocoa with the boiling water and add the baking soda and vanilla. Add this to the sugar mixture.
3. Add the flour and salt. Stir to a smooth batter.
4. Bake in 2 greased 9-inch cake pans at 350° for 20 minutes, or until tester comes out clean from the center.

CHOCOLATE CAKES

Mama's Fudge Cake

PENNSYLVANIA
Adapted from Lestz, *The Pennsylvania Dutch Cookbook*

Cake:

2	cups light brown sugar	1	teaspoon baking soda
½	cup butter	2	tablespoons cocoa
2	eggs	½	cup hot water
2	cups flour		

Filling:

⅔	cup light brown sugar	½	cup cold water
1	tablespoon cocoa	1	tablespoon butter
1	cup boiling water	1	teaspoon vanilla
2	tablespoons cornstarch		

1. Cream the sugar with the butter for 2 minutes. Add the eggs, one at a time.
2. Mix the flour, baking soda, and cocoa together. Add alternately with the hot water. Mix until a smooth batter is formed.
3. Bake in two 9-inch parchment-lined cake pans at 350° for 25 minutes.
4. Mix and boil the first 5 filling ingredients. Stir in the butter.
5. Let the filling stand a few minutes. Add the vanilla then spread it on the cake layers.

The filling will "enhance the cake immeasurably."

Never Fail Chocolate Cake

NEW JERSEY

Adapted from *Chicken Foot Soup and Other Recipes from the Pine Barrens*

3 ounces baking chocolate
½ cup butter or lard
1¾ cups sugar
1 cup boiling water
2¼ cups flour, sifted
1 teaspoon vanilla

½ cup sour milk (add 1 tea-
    spoon vinegar to ½ cup
    milk)
1½ teaspoons baking soda
2 eggs, beaten

1. Melt the chocolate and lard in a saucepan. Stir in the sugar. Add the boiling water, flour, and vanilla.
2. Mix the sour milk and baking soda together and add it to the chocolate mixture. Beat in the eggs. Stir to form a smooth batter. Pour the batter into a greased 9-inch loaf pan.
3. Bake at 350° for 30 minutes.

Black Cocoa Cake

DELAWARE

Adapted from *Winterthur's Culinary Collection*

2 cups all-purpose flour
2 cups sugar
1 cup cocoa
1 teaspoon baking powder
2 teaspoons baking soda

½ cup butter, melted
1 cup milk
1 cup brewed coffee, hot
2 eggs, beaten
1 teaspoon vanilla

1. Sift all the dry ingredients together in a large bowl.
2. Add the remaining ingredients and mix well.
3. Bake in a greased and floured tube pan at 350° for 30 – 40 minutes.

SPICE, NUT, AND FRUIT CAKES

14 Carat Cake

NEW JERSEY
Adapted from *Chicken Foot Soup and Other Recipes from the Pine Barrens*

Cake:

2 cups sugar	1½ teaspoons salt
1½ cups vegetable oil	2 teaspoons cinnamon
4 eggs	2 cups finely grated carrots
2 cups flour	½ cup chopped nuts
2 teaspoons baking powder	1 8½-ounce can crushed
1½ teaspoons baking soda	pineapple, well drained

Cream cheese frosting:

½ cup butter or margarine	1 teaspoon vanilla
8 ounces cream cheese	1 pound powdered sugar

1. Whisk the sugar, oil, and eggs together. Stir in the flour, baking powder, baking soda, salt, and cinnamon. Mix well to form a smooth batter.
2. Add the carrots, nuts, and drained pineapple, blending thoroughly. Pour the batter into 2 greased and floured 9-inch cake pans.
3. Bake at 350° for 35–40 minutes. Allow the cake to cool while preparing the frosting.
4. Cream the butter with the cream cheese until smooth. Stir in the vanilla.
5. Add the powdered sugar gradually, beating well. Fill and frost the cake with this mixture.

War Cake

NEW JERSEY
Adapted from *Chicken Foot Soup and Other Recipes from the Pine Barrens*

2 cups cold water	1 teaspoon ginger
2 cups sugar	1 teaspoon cinnamon
1 pound seedless raisins	1 teaspoon allspice
2 tablespoons lard	1 teaspoon baking soda
3 cups flour	2 tablespoons warm water

1. Heat the water with the sugar, raisins, and lard to boiling. Allow to cool.
2. Sift the flour and spices together.
3. Dissolve baking soda in the 2 tablespoons warm water. Add this to the other liquids and stir in flour mixture to form a smooth batter.
4. Bake in a greased loaf pan at 325° for 1 hour.

Old German Spice Cake

PENNSYLVANIA

Adapted from Lestz, *The Pennsylvania Dutch Cookbook*

2 cups light brown sugar	1½ teaspoons allspice
¾ cup lard	2 cups sifted flour
3 eggs, separated	1 cup cold water
1½ teaspoons ground cloves	raisins or nuts (optional)
1 teaspoon baking soda	

1. Mix the sugar and lard. Beat 2 minutes to cream the ingredients. Add the egg yolks, one at a time.
2. Mix the cloves, baking soda, allspice, and flour together. Add alternately with the water.
3. Beat the egg whites to form stiff peaks. Fold them in to the batter. Add raisins or nuts, if desired.
4. Bake in two greased 9-inch cake pans at 350° for 20 minutes, or until done in the center.

Black Walnut Cake

PENNSYLVANIA

Adapted from Lestz, *The Pennsylvania Dutch Cookbook*

½ cup butter	¾ cup cold water
1½ cups sugar	4 egg whites
1 teaspoon baking powder	1 cup chopped black walnuts
2 cups flour	

1. Cream the butter and gradually add the sugar, creaming until light and fluffy, about 2 minutes.
2. Sift the baking powder and flour together, adding it alternately with the water to the creamed mixture.
3. Beat the egg whites to form soft peaks.
4. Carefully fold the nuts into the creamed mixture and then the beaten egg whites.
5. Bake in two greased 8-inch layer cake pans at 350° for 30–35 minutes.
6. Frost with a walnut frosting.

SPICE, NUT, AND FRUIT CAKES

Sour Applesauce Cake

PENNSYLVANIA
Adapted from *Choice Recipes*

1 cup light brown sugar	1 teaspoon baking soda
½ cup butter and lard, mixed	3 tablespoons hot water
1 teaspoon cloves	1 cup sour applesauce
1 teaspoon cinnamon	1 cup chopped raisins
pinch salt	2 cups flour

1. Add ingredients in order to a mixing bowl. Beat until smooth.
2. Bake in a greased 9-inch loaf pan for 45 minutes.

Grandma's Cinnamon Flop

PENNSYLVANIA
Adapted from Lestz, *The Pennsylvania Dutch Cookbook*

4 ounces butter	2 teaspoons baking powder
1 cup granulated sugar	1 cup light brown sugar
1 cup milk	1 tablespoon butter
2 cups flour	2 teaspoons cinnamon
¼ teaspoon salt	1 teaspoon nutmeg

1. Cream the 4 ounces butter. Add the sugar and continue to beat 2 minutes. Add the milk.
2. Mix the flour, salt, and baking powder together and add to the creamed mixture to form a batter. Pour into a greased 8-inch square pan.
3. Mix the remaining ingredients to form crumbs. Spread evenly over batter.
4. Bake at 425° for 20 minutes.

Applesauce Cake

NEW YORK

Adapted from *A Library of Favorite Recipes from New York State*

2 cups sugar	2 teaspoons baking soda
3 cups flour	2 tablespoons apple juice
1 teaspoon cloves	2 cups unsweetened
2 teaspoons cinnamon	applesauce
2 teaspoons cocoa	½–1 cup nuts
1 teaspoon salt (optional)	½–1 cup raisins
3 tablespoons cooking oil	

1. Place the sugar, flour, cloves, cinnamon, cocoa, and salt in a large mixing bowl.
2. Form a well in the dry ingredients. Add the oil and baking soda dissolved in the apple juice. Stir to form a smooth batter.
3. Stir in the nuts and raisins. Pour the batter into a greased 8-inch loaf pan.
4. Bake at 350° for 30 minutes, or until done in the center.

Angel Cake

PENNSYLVANIA

Adapted from Reed, *The Philadelphia Cook Book of Town and Country*

1 cup (8–10) egg whites	¾ teaspoon vanilla extract
¼ teaspoon salt	¼ teaspoon almond extract
1 teaspoon cream of tartar	1 cup sifted cake flour
1¼ cups sifted sugar	

1. Whip the egg whites until frothy. Add the salt and cream of tartar and whip the egg whites until stiff peaks form, but they are not dry. Gradually fold in the sugar and the flavorings.
2. Sift the flour twice after measuring. Fold the flour into the egg white mixture, sifting about ¼ cup at a time over the surface.
3. Bake in an ungreased tube pan at 325° for 1 hour. Invert the pan to cool.

Strawberry Spongecake

NEW YORK

Adapted from Wilson, *American Cooking: The Eastern Heartland*

1 quart firm ripe strawberries, cleaned and rinsed	2 teaspoons vanilla extract, divided
1 cup sugar, divided	2 tablespoons butter, softened
1 cup unsifted flour	2 cups heavy cream, chilled
pinch salt	2 tablespoons powdered sugar
6 eggs, separated	

1. Select 2 cups of the most attractive berries and set them aside.
2. To the remaining berries add ½ cup of the sugar and mash the berries to a thick puree.
3. Sift the flour and the salt together.
4. Beat the egg whites to form soft peaks. Beat the egg yolks, ½ cup sugar, and 1 teaspoon of the vanilla together until they are thick and lemon-colored.
5. Add the flour mixture to the egg whites, pour the egg yolk mixture over them, and fold together lightly. Pour the batter into two 9-inch cake pans that have been greased with the softened butter and floured.
6. Bake at 350° for about 20 minutes, or until the cakes begin to shrink away from the sides of the pans.
7. Whip the cream until frothy. Add the powdered sugar and the remaining vanilla. Continue to beat until the cream is stiff.
8. To assemble, slice each cake in half horizontally to make 4 thin layers. Place one of the layers, cut side up, on a serving plate and spread it with about ½ cup of the pureed strawberries. Repeat 2 more times. Carefully put the fourth layer on the top, cut side down.
9. Spread the whipped cream smoothly over the top and sides of the cake. Cut a dozen or so of the reserved strawberries in half lengthwise and set them on the plate, cut side up, in a ring around the cake. Arrange the remaining whole strawberries on the top of the cake and serve at once.

Hurry Up Cake

NEW JERSEY

Adapted from *Chicken Foot Soup and Other Recipes from the Pine Barrens*

Cake:

1½ cups flour	2 eggs
1 cup sugar	¾ cup cream
2 teaspoons baking powder	2 teaspoons vanilla
½ teaspoon salt	

Topping:

5 tablespoons light brown sugar	3 tablespoons butter
3 tablespoons cream	½ cup coconut

1. Sift the dry ingredients together.
2. Mix the eggs with the cream. Stir in the vanilla. Add the liquids to the dry ingredients. Mix to form a smooth batter. Pour the batter into a greased 8-inch square baking pan.
3. Bake at 375° for 30 minutes.
4. Prepare the topping by mixing all of the ingredients together. Spread them over the hot cake and place under a broiler until the topping melts and browns slightly.

Moravian Sugar Cake

PENNSYLVANIA
Adapted from Wilson, *American Cooking: The Eastern Heartland*

2 cups water	1 teaspoon salt
2 medium-sized potatoes, peeled and quartered	2 eggs
	2 tablespoons butter, softened
1 pound butter, cut into ½-inch bits	2¼ cups (1 pound) light brown sugar
1 package active dry yeast	
1 cup granulated sugar	2 teaspoons ground cinnamon
6–6½ cups unsifted flour	

1. Bring the water to a boil in a heavy saucepan. Add the potatoes and cook until they can be easily mashed. Drain and reserve 1 cup of the potato water.

2. Sieve the potatoes and allow to air dry for 2 minutes. Puree the potatoes. Beat in 8 tablespoons of the butter bits and cover.

3. When the reserved potato water is cooled, use ¼ cup to dissolve the yeast. Add 1 teaspoon of the granulated sugar and allow the mixture to stand for 2–3 minutes. Stir well.

4. Combine 6 cups of the flour, the remaining sugar, and the salt. Add the potato puree, the yeast mixture, the eggs, and the remaining ¾ cup of potato water. Stir until the dough is smooth and elastic.

5. Knead for 10 minutes and gather into a ball. Allow to rise for about 1½ hours, or until doubled in bulk.

6. Brush the softened butter over two 16-by-11-inch jelly-roll pans. Punch the dough down and divide it in half. Roll each half into a 16-by-11-inch rectangle about ½-inch thick. Place the dough in the buttered pans and set them aside to rise again for 45 minutes.

7. Stir 2 cups of the brown sugar and cinnamon together. Make parallel rows of small indentations in the top of each cake with your fingertips. Drop the remaining 8 tablespoons of butter bits into the indentations and fill the holes with the brown sugar mixture. Scatter the rest of the brown sugar over the surface of the cakes.

8. Bake at 350° for 25–30 minutes, or until the topping is brown and crusty.

Feather Cake

MARYLAND
Adapted from *Tested Maryland Recipes*

Cake:

½ cup butter
2 cups sugar
⅔ cup milk

3 eggs
3 cups flour
3 teaspoons yeast powder

Icing:

½ cup boiling water
1 cup sugar

2 egg whites, well beaten

1. Cream the butter with the sugar until light and fluffy. Stir in the milk and eggs. Beat until smooth.
2. Add the flour, which has been mixed with the yeast. Mix to form a smooth batter. Pour the batter into 3 greased 8-inch cake pans and allow to rise for 1 hour.
3. Bake at 350° for 20 minutes, or until a tester comes out clean. Allow to cool while preparing the frosting.
4. Boil the water and sugar together to form a thick, lightly colored syrup.
5. Beat the egg whites to soft peaks. Continue to beat while slowly pouring the syrup in. Continue to beat until firm. Spread this frosting on the layers and ice the cake.

Krummel Kuchen

PENNSYLVANIA
Adapted from Lestz, *The Pennsylvania Dutch Cookbook*

2 cups flour
1½ cups granulated sugar
2 tablespoons baking powder
¼ teaspoon salt
½ cup butter

2 eggs, well beaten
⅛ teaspoon vanilla
½ cup milk
cinnamon (optional)

1. Sift the first 4 dry ingredients together. Work in the butter with a wooden spoon. Reserve ½ cup of this mixture.
2. Add the eggs and vanilla to the milk and stir. Add this to the flour mixture and beat well.
3. Pour the batter into a buttered and floured 9-inch cake pan and top with the reserved dry mixture. Sprinkle with cinnamon if desired.
4. Bake at 350° for 50 minutes.

Holiday Hazelnut Torte

NEW YORK

Adapted from *A Library of Favorite Recipes from New York State*

8 eggs, separated
1 cup granulated sugar
1 teaspoon vanilla
1 tablespoon flour
¼ teaspoon baking powder

6 ounces hazelnuts, ground fine
¼ teaspoon salt
2 cups sweetened whipped cream

1. Beat the egg yolks, sugar, vanilla, flour, baking powder, and nuts. Add the salt and mix well.
2. Beat the egg whites very stiff and fold into the nut mixture. Pour into a lightly greased 10-inch springform pan.
3. Bake at 350° for 1 hour.
4. Allow to cool and split into 2 layers. Fill and top with the whipped cream.

Italian Cheesecake

NEW YORK

Adapted from *A Library of Favorite Recipes from New York State*

1 pound ricotta
1 pound cream cheese
4 eggs
1½ cups sugar
3 tablespoons lemon juice
½ pound melted butter

3 tablespoons sifted flour
3 tablespoons cornstarch
2 teaspoons vanilla
1 pint sour cream, room temperature

1. Beat the ricotta and cream cheese together.
2. Beat the eggs, sugar, and lemon juice together until fluffy. Pour this into the cheese mixture followed by the melted butter. Beat until smooth.
3. Add the flour, cornstarch, and vanilla, beating well. Stir in the sour cream. Pour into a 9-inch springform pan.
4. Bake at 375° for 45 minutes. Shut off the oven and bake 20 minutes more.

Old Fashioned Blackberry Jam Cake

TENNESSEE
Adapted from Dalsass, *Miss Mary's Down-Home Cooking*

¾ cup butter	1 teaspoon cinnamon
1 cup sugar	½ teaspoon nutmeg
3 eggs	½ teaspoon cloves
1 heaping teaspoon baking soda	½ teaspoon allspice
1 cup buttermilk	1 teaspoon baking powder
2 cups flour	1 teaspoon vanilla
	¾ cup blackberry jam

1. Cream the butter and sugar. Add the eggs and continue to beat.
2. Add the baking soda to the buttermilk.
3. Sift the dry ingredients together. Alternately add the dry ingredients with the buttermilk to the butter mixture.
4. Add the vanilla. Fold in the blackberry jam. Pour into a greased and floured 16-by-8-by-1½-inch pan.
5. Bake at 350° for 35–40 minutes. Frost as desired when cool.

Hot Milk Cake

SOUTH CAROLINA
Adapted from *A Taste of South Carolina*

4 eggs	⅛ teaspoon salt
2 cups sugar	1 teaspoon vanilla
2 cups flour	1 cup milk
1 tablespoon baking powder	¼ pound butter or margarine

1. Beat the eggs until light. Add the sugar and beat well.
2. Mix the flour, baking powder, and salt together. Add this to the sugar mixture and beat well. Add the vanilla.
3. Heat the milk and butter until hot, but not boiling. Add the milk to the cake batter. Pour into a greased 13-by-9-by-2-inch pan.
4. Bake at 375° for 15–20 minutes.

"Makes an excellent shortcake."

WHITE CAKES

Pink Party Cake

SOUTH CAROLINA
Adapted from *The South Carolina Cook Book*

Cake:

2½	cups sifted cake flour	1	teaspoon vanilla
1½	cups sugar	2	teaspoons almond extract
3½	teaspoons baking powder	4	egg whites, unbeaten
1	teaspoon salt	18	canned cherries, well
½	cup shortening or butter		drained and finely chopped
¾	cup milk	½	cup walnut meats, finely
¼	cup cherry juice		chopped

Frosting:

2	tablespoons shortening	4	cups sifted powdered sugar
1	teaspoon vanilla	½	cup scalded cream
½	teaspoon almond extract		several drops red food
1	teaspoon salt		coloring

1. Sift the flour, sugar, baking powder, and salt together. Drop in the shortening or butter. Do not cream.
2. Combine the milk and cherry juice. Add ¾ cup of this liquid to the flour mixture (discard the remaining liquid). Add the vanilla and almond extracts. Beat 2 minutes.
3. Beat the egg whites to soft peaks and fold into the batter. Fold in the cherries and nuts.
4. Bake in a greased tube pan at 375° until done, about 30 minutes. Allow the cake to cool before frosting.
5. Prepare the frosting by combining the shortening, vanilla, almond extract, and salt. Beat 1 minute. Beat in ½ cup powdered sugar.
6. Add the hot cream, alternating with the remaining powdered sugar. Beat well after each addition. Add a few drops of red food coloring to tint the frosting a delicate pink. Frost the cake with this icing.

Million-Dollar Pound Cake

KENTUCKY

Adapted from *The Foxfire Book of Appalachian Cookery*

1 pound butter, softened	¾ cup milk
3 cups sugar	1 teaspoon almond extract
6 eggs	1 teaspoon vanilla
4 cups flour	

1. Cream the butter with the sugar until light and fluffy. Add the eggs, one at a time, beating well after each addition.
2. Add the flour to the creamed mixture in thirds, alternating with the milk. Stir in the extracts. Mix to form a smooth batter. Pour the batter into a well-greased and floured tube pan.
3. Bake at 300° for 1½ hours.

Plantation Cake

FLORIDA

Adapted from *Palm Beach Entertains Then and Now*

1 cup butter	2 cups flour
2⅛ cups sugar	1 teaspoon baking powder
2 eggs	¼ teaspoon salt
1 cup sour cream	1 cup chopped pecans
½ teaspoon vanilla	1 teaspoon cinnamon

1. Cream the butter with 2 cups of the sugar until light and fluffy. Beat in the eggs, one at a time. Stir in the sour cream and vanilla.
2. Sift the flour with the baking powder and salt and fold this into the creamed mixture.
3. Mix the remaining sugar, the pecans, and the cinnamon together.
4. Pour ⅓ of the batter in a well-greased 9-inch tube pan. Sprinkle with ¾ of the pecan mixture. Spoon in the remaining batter and top with the remaining pecan mixture.
5. Bake at 350° for 1 hour, or until done.

WHITE CAKES

Fresh Coconut Layer Cake with Lemon Frosting

FLORIDA
Adapted from Nickerson, *Florida Cookbook*

Cake:

1	cup shredded fresh coconut, reserved	½	teaspoon salt
1	cup milk	⅔	cup butter, softened
	liquid drained from a fresh coconut	¼	cup cream
		1	cup sugar
2	cups sifted cake flour	3	eggs, room temperature
2½	teaspoons baking powder	1	teaspoon vanilla

Lemon frosting:

3	egg whites, room temperature	1½	tablespoons fresh lemon juice
6	tablespoons powdered sugar	¾	teaspoon grated lemon rind
1	cup plus 1 tablespoon white corn syrup	1	cup shredded fresh coconut

1. For the cake, cover the shredded coconut with the milk. Refrigerate overnight. Sieve the coconut, pressing out and reserving the milk.
2. To the coconut liquid add enough of the drained milk to make ⅔ cup.
3. Sift the flour, baking powder, and salt together.
4. Cream the butter with the sugar for 2 minutes. Add the cream and beat until light and fluffy. Beat in the eggs, one at a time, beating thoroughly. Stir in the vanilla and shredded coconut.
5. To the creamed mixture add the flour mixture in thirds, alternating with the coconut liquid mixture. Stir to form a smooth batter. Do not overmix. Pour into two greased 8-inch cake pans.
6. Bake at 350° for 20–25 minutes, or until firm to the touch in the center. Allow to cool before frosting.
7. Prepare the frosting by beating the egg whites until soft peaks form. Add the powdered sugar, 1 tablespoon at a time, and continue to beat to form stiff peaks.
8. Bring the corn syrup to a boil in a small saucepan. Allow to boil to the soft ball stage.
9. Pour the syrup over the egg whites in a slow, thin stream, beating constantly. Beat until the frosting is cool. Stir in the lemon juice and rind.
10. Cut the cakes laterally, forming 4 thin layers. Fill and frost the cake. Sprinkle with 1 cup shredded coconut.

Bourbon Pound Cake

KENTUCKY

Adapted from Patterson, *Kentucky Cooking*

1½ cups butter, softened	¼ teaspoon salt
2 cups sugar	1 teaspoon ground mace
2 cups light brown sugar	1½ cups bourbon whiskey
8 eggs	2 cups pecan pieces
5 cups flour	

1. Cream the butter with both sugars until smooth and light. Add the eggs, one at a time, beating well after each addition.
2. Sift the flour, salt, and mace together. Add this in thirds, alternating with the bourbon, to the creamed mixture. Mix until a smooth batter forms. Stir in the pecans. Pour the batter into a greased 10-inch tube pan.
3. Bake at 300° for about 1½ hours, or until firm to the touch in the center.

Devil's Food

VIRGINIA

Adapted from *The Junior League Cook Book*

½ cup butter	4 eggs, well beaten
2 cups sugar	2½ cups flour
2 teaspoons soda	6 tablespoons cocoa
2 cups buttermilk	

1. Melt the butter and beat in the sugar.
2. Dissolve the baking soda in the buttermilk and add it to the butter mixture. Beat well. Add the eggs and beat until smooth.
3. Sift the flour and cocoa together and beat this into the liquids. Pour the batter into a greased 9-inch cake pan.
4. Bake at 375° for 30 minutes, or until firm to the touch in the center.

Dr. Pepper Chocolate Cake

SOUTH CAROLINA
Adapted from *A Taste of South Carolina*

Cake:

4 cups plain flour	1 pound butter
8 tablespoons cocoa	2 cups Dr. Pepper
3 teaspoons cinnamon	4 eggs
1 teaspoon salt	4 teaspoons vanilla
2 teaspoons soda	1 cup buttermilk
4 cups sugar	

Dr. Pepper icing:

½ cup butter	1 cup chopped pecans
½ cup Dr. Pepper	2 teaspoons vanilla
6 tablespoons cocoa	1 pound powdered sugar

1. To make the cake, sift all the dry ingredients together.
2. Heat the butter and Dr. Pepper until the butter melts. Add the eggs, vanilla, and buttermilk and mix well.
3. Add the liquids gradually to the dry ingredients and beat until smooth. Pour the batter into 2 greased and floured 11-by-17-inch tube pans.
4. Bake at 350° for 30 minutes.
5. To prepare the Dr. Pepper icing, heat the butter and Dr. Pepper together without boiling. Add the next 4 ingredients and mix well.
6. Ice the cake while warm.

Chocolate Syrup Cake

TENNESSEE
Adapted from Dalsass, *Miss Mary's Down-Home Cooking*

Cake:

1	stick butter, softened	2	cups chocolate syrup
⅔	cup sugar	2	cups flour
4	eggs	1	teaspoon baking powder

Icing:

2	ounces unsweetened chocolate	1	teaspoon vanilla extract
		¼	cup milk
3	tablespoons butter	2	cups powdered sugar

1. Cream the butter with the sugar. Beat in the eggs and the chocolate syrup.
2. In a bowl, stir the flour and the baking powder together. Beat into the chocolate mixture until just combined. Pour the batter into a greased and floured 9-by-13-inch baking pan.
3. Bake at 350° for 35–40 minutes, or until a toothpick inserted in the center comes out clean. When the cake has cooled completely, make the icing.
4. Melt the chocolate and butter in a saucepan. Beat in the vanilla and half of the milk. Beat in the powdered sugar and enough milk to make an icing of good consistency.
5. Spread over the cake and let the icing set at least 10 minutes before cutting.

Brown Stone Front Cake

VIRGINIA

Adapted from *The Junior League Cook Book*

Cake:

1 cup cocoa	2¾ cups sugar
1 cup boiling water	4 eggs, separated
2 teaspoons baking soda	4 cups flour
1 cup buttermilk	1 teaspoon baking powder
1 cup butter	1 teaspoon vanilla

Filling:

3 cups light brown sugar	1 tablespoon butter
¾ cup half-and-half cream	

1. Dissolve the cocoa in the boiling water and allow it to cool.
2. Dissolve the baking soda in the buttermilk.
3. Cream the butter with the sugar. Add the egg yolks and beat until smooth.
4. Sift the flour with the baking powder and add this in thirds to the creamed mixture, alternating with the buttermilk mixture. Beat in the cocoa mixture until smooth.
5. Beat the egg whites stiff and fold them into the batter. Stir in the vanilla. Pour the batter into a greased 9-inch cake pan.
6. Bake at 350° for 30 minutes, or until a tester comes out clean from the center.
7. Prepare the filling by boiling the ingredients together until it is at the soft ball stage.
8. Cut the cake into 2 layers and fill with this mixture.

Chocolate Marble Layer Cake

SOUTH CAROLINA
Adapted from *The South Carolina Cook Book*

Cake:

1	square unsweetened chocolate	½	cup vegetable shortening
2¼	cups sifted cake flour	1	cup milk
1	tablespoon baking powder	2	eggs
		1	teaspoon vanilla

Chocolate icing:

3	ounces unsweetened chocolate	1	tablespoon shortening
½	cup water	1	teaspoon vanilla
2	tablespoons butter	3¾	cups powdered sugar

1. Melt the chocolate over hot water or in a microwave oven.
2. Sift the dry ingredients together. Add the vegetable shortening and milk. Mix briefly.
3. Add the eggs and vanilla. Mix to form a smooth batter.
4. Remove half of the batter to another bowl and stir in the melted chocolate.
5. Add white and chocolate batters alternately to 2 greased 8-inch cake pans.
6. Bake at 375° for 25 minutes. Allow to cool before icing.
7. Prepare the icing by melting the chocolate over hot water or in a microwave oven.
8. Heat the water, butter, and shortening together. Add the melted chocolate. Cool, then add the vanilla and powdered sugar.
9. Beat until creamy and smooth. Frost the cake with this icing.

SPICE, NUT, AND FRUIT CAKES

Prince of Wales Cake

VIRGINIA
Adapted from *The Junior League Cook Book*

Cake:

½ cup butter
½ cup sour milk
3 eggs, separated
2 cups flour
½ teaspoon baking soda
1 cup light brown sugar

2 tablespoons molasses
1½ teaspoons cinnamon
½ teaspoon cloves
2 level teaspoons baking
  powder
1 teaspoon nutmeg

Filling:

1 tablespoon butter
2 cups powdered sugar
6 tablespoons cream

½ cup chopped raisins
1 teaspoon vanilla

1. Beat the butter with the milk and egg yolks until smooth. Add the flour and baking soda and blend. Stir in the brown sugar and molasses. Beat until smooth.
2. Stir in the remaining ingredients to form a smooth batter.
3. Bake in two greased 8-inch cake pans at 350° for 20 minutes, or until done.
4. Prepare the filling by beating all of the ingredients together.
5. Fill when the cake layers are cool.

Belle's Prune Cake

WEST VIRGINIA

Adapted from *The Foxfire Book of Appalachian Cookery*

Cake:

2 cups flour	3 eggs
1 teaspoon baking soda	1 teaspoon vanilla
¼ teaspoon salt	1 cup buttermilk
1 tablespoon cinnamon	1½ cups pitted prunes, coarsely
1 tablespoon nutmeg	cut, cooked, and drained
1 tablespoon allspice	1 cup walnuts or pecans,
1 cup corn oil	chopped
1½ cups sugar	

Glaze:

1 cup sugar	¼ cup light corn syrup
½ cup buttermilk	½ teaspoon baking soda
¼ cup butter	½ teaspoon vanilla

1. Sift the dry ingredients together.
2. Beat the corn oil and sugar together. Add the eggs, one at a time, beating well after each addition. Stir in the vanilla.
3. Add the dry ingredients in thirds to the creamed mixture, alternating with the buttermilk. Blend well after each addition. Stir in the prunes and nuts. Pour the batter into an ungreased tube pan.
4. Bake at 350° for 1 hour.
5. Prepare the glaze by boiling all of the ingredients together in a nonreactive saucepan for 10 minutes.
6. Pour the glaze over the warm cake.

Jack Nicklaus's Favorite Cake

FLORIDA
Adapted from *Palm Beach Entertains Then and Now*

Cake:

2 cups flour	½ cup buttermilk
1½ cups sugar	3 eggs
1 teaspoon baking soda	1 cup stewed pitted prunes, chopped
1 teaspoon salt	
1 teaspoon cinnamon	1 cup chopped pecans
1 teaspoon nutmeg	1 teaspoon vanilla
1 cup vegetable oil	

Sauce:

1 cup sugar	½ cup buttermilk
½ cup butter	1 teaspoon baking soda

1. Sift the flour, sugar, baking soda, salt, cinnamon, and nutmeg together. Add the oil, buttermilk, and eggs and mix to form a smooth batter.
2. Stir in the prunes, nuts, and vanilla. Pour the mixture into a greased and floured 13-by-9-inch baking dish.
3. Bake at 350° for 35–40 minutes.
4. To prepare the sauce, combine all of the ingredients in a nonreactive saucepan and bring to a boil, stirring constantly.
5. While the cake is warm, prick the top in several places with a fork or skewer. Pour the warm sauce over the warm cake.

Sunshine Cake

VIRGINIA
Adapted from the *Marion Cook Book*

6 eggs, separated	½ teaspoon salt
2 teaspoons lemon juice	1 teaspoon vanilla extract
1¼ cups sugar	1 cup pastry flour

1. Whip the egg whites stiff. Add the lemon juice and continue to mix.
2. Stir in the sugar and continue to mix until dissolved.
3. Beat the yolks hard with the salt. Add to the whites. Add the vanilla.
4. Sift the flour several times and fold gently into the whites to form a smooth batter.
5. Bake at 375° for 30 – 40 minutes in a loaf pan lined with parchment.

Festival Orange Cheesecake

FLORIDA
Adapted from Nickerson, *Florida Cookbook*

Crust:

1 cup unsifted flour	½ cup butter, room
¼ cup sugar	temperature
1 tablespoon grated orange	1 egg yolk
rind	½ teaspoon vanilla

Filling:

2½ pounds cream cheese, room	¼ teaspoon vanilla
temperature	¼ teaspoon salt
1⅔ cups sugar	5 eggs
3 tablespoons flour	2 egg yolks
2 teaspoons grated orange	¼ cup orange juice
rind	fresh orange sections

1. Mix the flour, sugar, and orange rind together.
2. Cut in the butter with a pastry knife until smooth. Add the egg yolk and vanilla. Blend to form a smooth dough. Refrigerate until needed.
3. Press ⅓ of the dough over the bottom of a 9-inch springform pan. Bake at 400° for 7 minutes, or until the dough is golden brown.
4. When the pan cools, pat the remaining chilled dough around the sides of the pan to within ½ inch of the top edge.
5. To prepare the filling, beat the cream cheese until soft and smooth. Beat in the sugar, flour, orange rind, vanilla, and salt.
6. Mix in the eggs and the yolks, one at a time, then the orange juice. Pour the filling into the prepared pan.
7. Bake at 400° for 10 minutes. Reduce heat to 225° and bake 1½ hours.
8. Turn off the heat, open the oven door, and let the cake cool in the oven for an hour. When cool, refrigerate overnight.
9. Arrange orange sections on cake before serving.

Granny's Chocolate Cup Cakes

TENNESSEE
Adapted from Dalsass, *Miss Mary's Down-Home Cooking*

Cupcakes:

½	cup shortening	½	teaspoon baking soda
1	cup sugar	½	cup cocoa
1	egg	½	cup milk
1⅓	cups flour	1	teaspoon vanilla
¼	teaspoon salt	½	cup strong hot coffee
1	teaspoon baking powder		

Mocha frosting:

4	ounces butter	1	teaspoon vanilla
¼	cup cocoa	5–6	tablespoons hot coffee
1	pound powdered sugar		

1. Cream the shortening. Add the sugar gradually, then add the egg, beating well.
2. Alternating with the milk, add the flour sifted with the salt, baking powder, baking soda, and cocoa. Add the vanilla.
3. Add the coffee and beat well. Fill a greased cupcake pan two-thirds full.
4. Bake at 375° for 20 minutes.
5. Ice with a frosting made by melting the butter in a 2-quart saucepan. Add the cocoa, sugar, and vanilla, mixing well.
6. Add the coffee 1 tablespoon at a time until the frosting is the right consistency to spread.

ROLL CAKE

Jelly Roll

SOUTH CAROLINA

Adapted from *The South Carolina Cook Book*

4 eggs, separated	¾ teaspoon baking powder
¾ cup sugar	¼ teaspoon salt
1 teaspoon vanilla	½ cup strawberry preserves
¾ cup flour	powdered sugar

1. Beat the egg yolks until pale and light. Add the sugar gradually, then the vanilla.
2. Add the flour, which has been sifted with the baking powder and salt.
3. Beat the egg whites stiff, but not dry. Fold them into the batter.
4. Line a 15-by-10-inch pan with parchment paper. Pour in the batter.
5. Bake at 375° for about 8 minutes.
6. While the cake is hot, trim the edges and roll up in a towel to cool.
7. Unroll and spread the cake with the preserves. Sprinkle with powdered sugar.

Deep South

WHITE CAKES

Feather Cake

MISSISSIPPI

Adapted from *Tunica County Tasty Treats*

1 scant cup butter	1 cup milk
2 cups sugar	6 egg whites, beaten stiff
3 cups flour	1 teaspoon vanilla
2 teaspoons baking powder	

1. Cream the butter and sugar together until light and fluffy.
2. Sift the flour with the baking powder and add it to the creamed mixture in portions, beating well after each addition. Add the milk and mix well.
3. Fold in the beaten egg whites and stir in the vanilla. Pour the batter into a greased 10-inch springform pan.
4. Bake at 350° for 30 minutes, or until firm to the touch in the center.

Light'ning Cake

MISSISSIPPI

Adapted from *Tunica County Tasty Treats*

1	cup sugar	1	stick butter, melted
2	eggs	½	teaspoon vanilla
1	cup flour	1	cup pecans, chopped fine
1	teaspoon baking powder		

1. Beat the sugar and eggs together until pale and light.
2. Sift the flour and baking powder together and add to the egg mixture.
3. Stir in the melted butter and vanilla to form a smooth batter.
4. Pour the batter into a greased 9-inch square pan and top with the pecans.
5. Bake at 400° for about 20 minutes.

Harvest Moon Glow Cake

MISSISSIPPI

Adapted from *Tunica County Tasty Treats*

2	sticks butter	6	eggs
2	cups sugar	1	teaspoon vanilla
2	cups flour		

1. Cream the butter and sugar with 2 tablespoons of the flour. Beat in the eggs, 1 at a time.
2. Add the remaining flour and stir in the vanilla.
3. Bake in a greased 9-inch loaf pan at 350° for 1 hour.

WHITE CAKES

Corn Starch Cake

ALABAMA
Adapted from *Gulf City Cook Book*

¾ **pound butter**
1½ **cups sugar**
6 **eggs**

4 **cups cornstarch**
1 **cup flour**

1. Cream the butter with the sugar until light and fluffy. Add the eggs, 1 at a time, beating well after each addition.
2. Sift the cornstarch with the flour and gently beat it into the creamed mixture. Pour the batter into a greased 9-inch round cake pan.
3. Bake at 350° for 40 minutes, or until firm to the touch in the center.

Measure Cake

ALABAMA
Adapted from *Gulf City Cook Book*

1½ **cups butter**
3 **cups sugar**
6 **eggs**
6 **cups flour**

3 **teaspoons cream of tartar**
1½ **teaspoons baking soda**
1½ **cups milk**

1. Cream the butter with the sugar until light and fluffy. Add the eggs, one at a time, beating well after each addition.
2. Sift the dry ingredients together and add them in thirds to the creamed mixture alternately with the milk. Pour the batter into a greased 9-inch loaf pan.
3. Bake at 350° for 40 minutes, or until a tester comes out clean.

Lane Cake

GEORGIA
Adapted from DeBolt, *Savannah Sampler Cookbook*

Cake:

3¼ cups sifted cake flour	2 teaspoons vanilla
2 teaspoons baking powder	8 egg whites
8 ounces butter, softened	1 cup milk
2 cups sugar	

Filling:

8 egg yolks	½ cup bourbon
1 cup sugar	1 teaspoon vanilla
4 ounces butter, softened	
1 cup raisins, chopped	1 recipe boiled white icing

1. For the cake, sift the flour and baking powder together.
2. Cream the butter, the sugar, and the vanilla. Add the egg whites, 2 at a time, and beat to incorporate between additions.
3. Fold the dry ingredients into the batter, alternating with the milk. Stir to form a smooth batter.
4. Bake in four greased 9-inch cake pans at 375° for about 20 minutes. Allow to cool.
5. Prepare the filling by beating the egg yolks with the sugar in a non-reactive saucepan.
6. Add the butter. Cook over moderate heat until quite thick. Remove from heat.
7. Stir in the raisins, bourbon, and vanilla. Cool slightly.
8. Put the cake layers together with the filling. Ice with boiled white icing.

WHITE CAKES

Italian Cream Cake

GEORGIA
Adapted from DeBolt, *Savannah Sampler Cookbook*

4 ounces butter or margarine	1 teaspoon baking soda
½ cup vegetable shortening	1 cup buttermilk
2 cups sugar	1 teaspoon vanilla extract
5 eggs, separated	3½ ounces grated coconut
2 cups sifted flour	1 cup chopped pecans

1. Cream the butter or margarine and shortening until fluffy. Add the sugar and beat until smooth. Add the egg yolks and beat well.
2. Combine the flour and baking soda and add this to the creamed mixture alternately with the buttermilk. Stir in the vanilla.
3. Fold in the coconut and chopped nuts.
4. Beat the egg whites stiff and fold them in. Pour the batter into 3 greased and floured 8-inch cake pans.
5. Bake at 350° for 20 minutes, or until firm in the center.
6. Allow to cool and frost with your favorite cream cheese frosting.

CHOCOLATE CAKES

Mother's Self-Ice Cake

GEORGIA
Adapted from DeBolt, *Savannah Sampler Cookbook*

1 cup chopped dates	2 eggs
1 cup boiling water	1¾ cups flour
1 teaspoon baking soda	½ teaspoon salt
½ cup vegetable shortening	½ teaspoon cream of tartar
1 cup sugar	6 ounces chocolate chips
2 teaspoons cocoa	¾ cup chopped nuts
1 teaspoon vanilla extract	

1. Combine the dates with the boiling water and baking soda. Allow to cool.
2. Cream the shortening and sugar until fluffy. Add the eggs and beat well. Stir in the cocoa and vanilla.
3. Sift together the flour, salt, and cream of tartar and add gradually. Stir until well blended. Add the date mixture and mix to form a smooth batter.
4. Pour into a greased 13-by-9-by-2-inch pan. Sprinkle the chocolate chips and nuts over the batter.
5. Bake at 350° for 30 minutes.

"This is especially nice for picnics."

Milky Way Cake

ARKANSAS
Adapted from Marshall, *Cooking Across the South*

Cake:

8	1⅞-ounce Milky Way candy bars	1	teaspoon vanilla extract
½	cup melted butter	½	teaspoon baking soda
2	cups sugar	1¼	cups buttermilk
½	cup margarine, softened	3	cups all-purpose flour
4	eggs	1	cup chopped pecans

Milk chocolate frosting:

2½	cups sugar	6	ounces semisweet chocolate chips
1	cup evaporated milk		
½	cup melted butter	1	cup marshmallow cream

1. Heat the candy bars and the melted butter together until the candy bars are melted. Stir constantly. Allow the mixture to cool.
2. Cream the sugar and softened margarine until light and fluffy. Add the eggs, one at a time, beating well after each addition. Stir in the vanilla.
3. Dissolve the baking soda in the buttermilk. Add this to the creamed mixture in thirds, alternating with the flour. Beat well after each addition.
4. Stir in the candy bar mixture and pecans. Pour the batter into a greased and floured 10-inch tube pan.
5. Bake at 325° for 1½ hours, or until firm to the touch in the center. Allow the cake to cool before icing.
6. To prepare the frosting, cook the sugar, evaporated milk, and butter to the soft ball stage.
7. Remove the pan from the heat and stir in the chocolate pieces and marshmallow cream. Beat well. Frost the cake with this mixture.

Mississippi Mud Cake

GEORGIA
Adapted from DeBolt, *Savannah Sampler Cookbook*

Cake:

2 cups sugar	1½ cups chopped pecans
½ pound butter	⅛ teaspoon salt
4 eggs	1 teaspoon vanilla extract
1½ cups flour	miniature marshmallows to
½ cup cocoa	cover cake

Mud icing:

1 pound powdered sugar	½ teaspoon vanilla extract
⅓ cup cocoa	6 tablespoons milk

1. Cream the sugar and butter together until fluffy. Add eggs, one at a time, and blend well.
2. Add the remaining ingredients, except the miniature marshmallows, and mix to form a smooth batter. Pour into a greased and floured 13-by-9-inch pan.
3. Bake at 350° for 35 minutes. When the cake is done, immediately cover the top with miniature marshmallows. Do not remove the cake from the pan.
4. Prepare the mud icing by sifting the powdered sugar with the cocoa. Add the vanilla and milk and beat until smooth and of spreading consistency. Spread over marshmallows after the cake has completely cooled.

Hundred Dollar Cake

MISSISSIPPI
Adapted from *Tunica County Tasty Treats*

1 cup sugar	1 cup salad dressing [Miracle
2 cups flour	Whip]
4 tablespoons cocoa	1 cup cold water
1½ teaspoons baking soda	2 teaspoons vanilla
1½ teaspoons baking powder	

1. Sift the dry ingredients together.
2. Stir in the salad dressing, water, and vanilla. Mix to form a smooth batter. Pour the batter into a greased 9-inch round cake pan.
3. Bake at 350° for 20 minutes, or until firm to the touch in the center.

Spice Cake with Raisin Cream

MISSISSIPPI
Adapted from *Tunica County Tasty Treats*

Cake:

½ cup shortening	3 teaspoons baking powder
1½ cups light brown sugar	½ teaspoon salt
2 eggs	1 teaspoon cinnamon
1 teaspoon vanilla	½ teaspoon cloves
½ teaspoon baking soda	¼ teaspoon nutmeg
1 cup buttermilk	¼ teaspoon allspice
2 cups cake flour	

Raisin cream filling:

1 cup sugar	1 cup ground raisins
2 tablespoons cornstarch	2 tablespoons butter
1 cup cream	½ teaspoon vanilla
4 egg yolks	⅛ teaspoon salt

1. Cream the shortening and brown sugar together until smooth and light. Add the eggs and vanilla. Beat until smooth.
2. Dissolve the baking soda in the buttermilk. Add this to the creamed mixture.
3. Sift the remaining dry ingredients together and stir them in. Beat gently until smooth. Pour the batter into 2 greased 8-inch round cake pans.
4. Bake at 350° for 25 minutes. Allow the cakes to cool while preparing the filling.
5. Mix the sugar, cornstarch, cream, egg yolks, raisins, and butter together in the top of a double boiler. Cook until thickened. Stir in the vanilla and salt.
6. Allow this mixture to cool before filling and icing the cake.

SPICE, NUT, AND FRUIT CAKES

Applesauce Cake

MISSISSIPPI
Adapted from *Tunica County Tasty Treats*

½ cup butter
1 cup sugar
1 egg
1 cup hot applesauce
½ teaspoon baking soda
½ cup nuts

½ cup raisins
1¾ cups flour
1 teaspoon vanilla
¼ teaspoon salt
½ teaspoon cinnamon
½ teaspoon cloves

1. Cream the butter and sugar together until light and fluffy. Beat in the egg.
2. Stir the applesauce and baking soda together and add to the creamed mixture.
3. Toss the nuts and raisins with a bit of the flour and add them to the creamed mixture. Beat in the remaining flour to form a smooth batter.
4. Stir in the vanilla, salt, and spices and pour the batter into a greased, deep 9-inch cake pan.
5. Bake at 350° for 1 hour.

Kentucky Blackberry Cake

GEORGIA

Adapted from DeBolt, *Savannah Sampler Cookbook*

Cake:

4	cups flour	2	cups sugar
2	teaspoons ground allspice	6	eggs
2	teaspoons ground cloves	2	cups blackberry jam
2	teaspoons ground cinnamon	1½	cups buttermilk
¾	pound butter, room temperature	2	teaspoons baking soda

Walnut frosting:

2	cups sugar	2	egg yolks
2	cups firmly packed light brown sugar	1	cup coarsely chopped walnuts
1½	cups light cream	½	teaspoon vanilla extract
¼	pound butter		

1. Sift the flour and spices together.
2. Cream the butter and sugar until fluffy. Beat the eggs lightly and blend them, along with the jam, into the butter mixture.
3. Add the flour mixture, alternating with the buttermilk in which the soda is dissolved.
4. Pour the batter into 3 buttered and floured 9-inch round cake tins.
5. Bake at 350° for 35 minutes, or until a cake tester inserted in the center comes out clean.
6. Prepare the frosting by combining the sugars and light cream, butter, and egg yolks in a nonreactive saucepan. Cover and bring the mixture to a boil over moderate heat. Remove the cover and stir until the mixture is thickened, about 10 minutes.
7. Remove the pan from the heat and stir in the walnuts and vanilla.
8. Allow the frosting to cool to spreading consistency. Spread frosting on the cooled cake.

King's Cake

LOUISIANA
Adapted from Feibleman, *American Cooking: Creole and Acadian*

Cake:

2	packages dry yeast
½	cup lukewarm water
½	cup granulated sugar
3½– 4½	cups unsifted flour
1	teaspoon nutmeg
2	teaspoons salt
1	teaspoon fresh lemon peel
½	cup lukewarm milk
5	egg yolks
8	tablespoons butter, cut into ½-inch bits and softened

2	tablespoons butter, softened
½	cup finely chopped candied citron
1	shelled pecan half, un-cooked dried bean, or plastic doll
1	egg
1	tablespoon milk

Sugars:

green, purple, and yellow food coloring pastes	12 tablespoons granulated sugar

Icing:

3	cups powdered sugar
¼	cup strained fresh lemon juice

3 – 6	tablespoons water
2	candied cherries, cut lengthwise into halves

1. Dissolve the yeast in the warm water with 2 teaspoons of the sugar. Allow to stand for 10 minutes.
2. Sift 3½ cups of the flour, the remaining sugar, the nutmeg, and the salt together. Stir in the lemon peel and add the yeast mixture and the milk. Stir to blend well. Add the egg yolks. Beat until smooth.
3. Beat in the 8 tablespoons of butter bits, 1 tablespoon at a time. Beat 2 minutes.
4. Knead, incorporating up to 1 cup more flour, until the dough is not sticky. Knead 10 minutes longer, until the dough is smooth and elastic. Allow to rise for 1½ hours, or until the dough doubles in volume.
5. Punch the dough down and place it on a lightly floured surface. Scatter the citron over the top, kneading the dough until the citron is well distributed.
6. Shape the dough into a cylinder about 14 inches long. Loop the cyl-inder together to form a ring, pinching the ends, on a baking sheet that has been greased with the 2 tablespoons softened butter. Insert the pecan half, dried bean, or baby into the ring so that it is hidden by the dough.

7. Allow the dough to rise, covered, until doubled in bulk.
8. Whisk the egg in the milk and brush the top and sides of the ring with it.
9. Bake the cake at 375° for about 25–30 minutes, or until it is golden brown.
10. Prepare the 3 colored sugars by rubbing 4 tablespoons of sugar with each of the three food coloring pastes. Use enough coloring to make the sugars bright and colorful.
11. To make the icing, beat the powdered sugar, lemon juice, and 3 tablespoons of the water until the icing mixture is smooth. Add more water, 1 teaspoon at a time, if the icing is too stiff.
12. Spread the icing over the top of the cake, allowing it to drip down the sides. Sprinkle the colored sugars over the icing immediately, forming a row of purple, yellow, and green stripes, each about 2 inches wide, on both sides of the ring. Arrange two cherry halves at each end of the cake, pressing them gently into the icing.

No-Crust Cheese Cake

GEORGIA
Adapted from *Savannah Sampler Cookbook*

1 pound cream cheese, at room temperature	⅔ cup sugar
	⅛ teaspoon almond extract
3 eggs	

Topping:

1 cup sour cream	1 teaspoon vanilla
3 tablespoons sugar	

1. Beat the cream cheese until fluffy. Beat in the eggs one at a time, allowing each to be incorporated before adding the next one. Add the ⅔ cup sugar and the almond extract.
2. Pour this mixture into a 9-inch pie pan and bake at 325° for 50 minutes. Allow to cool for 20 minutes before adding the topping.
3. Stir the sour cream, sugar, and vanilla together. Spread over the cheese cake and return it to the oven for 15 minutes. Allow the cheese cake to cool and refrigerate before serving.

Banana Cup Cakes

MISSISSIPPI
Adapted from *Tunica County Tasty Treats*

1 cup sugar	1 cup mashed bananas
½ cup butter	1 teaspoon vanilla
2 eggs	1 cup nuts
1½ cups flour	
1½ teaspoons baking soda dissolved in 3 tablespoons water	

1. Cream the sugar with the butter until light and fluffy. Beat in the eggs until blended.
2. Stir in the flour and add the dissolved baking soda. Beat until smooth. Stir in the bananas, vanilla, and nuts.
3. Pour the batter into paper-lined muffin tins and bake at 350° for 25 to 30 minutes or until done.

Mother Ann's Birthday Cake

OHIO

Adapted from Macmillan, *In a Shaker Kitchen*

6 egg whites	2½ cups cake flour
⅛ teaspoon cream of tartar	1 tablespoon baking powder
1½ cups sugar	¾ cup milk
1 cup soft butter	¾ cup peach preserves
1 teaspoon pure vanilla extract	

Frosting:

3 cups powdered sugar, sifted	2 tablespoons half-and-half
9 tablespoons soft butter	or milk
½ tablespoon pure vanilla extract	

1. Beat the egg whites until frothy. Add the cream of tartar and continue beating until soft peaks form. Gradually sprinkle ¼ cup of the sugar over the whites and beat until glossy and stiff peaks form.
2. In a bowl beat the butter with the remaining sugar and the vanilla until pale and very fluffy.
3. Sift the flour and baking powder together. Gradually add to the butter mixture alternately with the milk.
4. Add a large spoonful of the egg whites to the batter. Fold in the remaining whites with a rubber spatula.
5. Line the bottom of two 9-inch round cake pans with a disk of waxed paper and divide the batter equally among them.
6. Bake at 350° for 30 minutes, or until golden brown and skewer in the center comes out clean.
7. When the cake layers are cool, spread one with the peach preserves and set the second layer on top.
8. To make the frosting, gradually beat the powdered sugar into the soft butter to make a pale, fluffy mixture. Beat in the vanilla and enough milk to make a frosting with a spreadable consistency.
9. Spread the frosting over the top and the sides of the cake.

Buttermilk Cake

ILLINOIS
Adapted from Linsenmeyer, *Cooking Plain*

1	cup butter	1	teaspoon cream of tartar
2	cups sugar	1	cup buttermilk
3	cups cake flour	6	egg whites
½	teaspoon salt	1	teaspoon vanilla
1	teaspoon baking soda	1	teaspoon lemon extract

1. Cream the butter and sugar until fluffy.
2. Sift the flour, salt, baking soda, and cream of tartar together and add to the creamed mixture in thirds alternately with the buttermilk.
3. Beat the egg whites until stiff. Add the vanilla and lemon extract. Fold into the batter. Turn into an ungreased 10-inch tube pan.
4. Bake at 350° for 45 minutes.

Fluffy Banana Cake

INDIANA
Adapted from *The Hoosier Cookbook*

2¼	cups unsifted cake flour	3	large eggs
1¼	teaspoons baking powder	1	cup mashed banana
1¼	teaspoons baking soda		(2 medium), divided
½	teaspoon salt	1	teaspoon vanilla
⅔	cup shortening	1¼	cups milk
1⅔	cups sugar	1	package white frosting mix

1. Sift the flour, baking powder, and salt together.
2. Beat the shortening, sugar, and eggs until light and fluffy.
3. Gradually add ¾ cup mashed banana and the vanilla to the shortening mixture. Add the flour mixture and milk, beginning and ending with the flour.
4. Bake at 350° for 35–40 minutes in 2 greased 8-inch cake pans. Cool completely.
5. To prepare a frosting, use 1 package creamy vanilla white frosting made according the directions on the package, except add the remaining ¼ cup bananas. Beat until smooth and creamy.

Pie Filling Cake

INDIANA
Adapted from *The Hoosier Cookbook*

Cake:

2 cups flour	⅔ cup cooking oil
1 cup sugar	1 cup raisins
1½ teaspoons baking soda	1 cup nuts
1 teaspoon salt	1 can apple or pineapple pie
1 teaspoon vanilla	filling
2 eggs, beaten	

Icing:

1 3-ounce package cream cheese	1 teaspoon vanilla
	½ stick margarine
1 cup powdered sugar	

1. With a spoon, stir all of the cake ingredients together in the order given. Do not beat. Pour into an ungreased 13-by-9-by-2-inch pan.
2. Bake at 350° for 40–50 minutes.
3. To make the icing, beat the ingredients together and spread over the cooled cake.

Dump Cake

OHIO
Adapted from DuSablon, *Cincinnati Recipe Treasury*

1 21-ounce can cherry pie filling	⅔ cup shredded coconut
	2 cups yellow cake mix
1 13-ounce can pineapple tidbits	4 tablespoons margarine

1. Pour the cherries into an ungreased 8-inch cake pan. Pour the pineapple evenly over the cherries. Cover with the coconut.
2. Sprinkle on the cake mix. Top this with pats of margarine.
3. Bake for 50–60 minutes, or until the top is golden brown.

Biscuit Dough Shortcake

ILLINOIS
Adapted from Linsenmeyer, *Cooking Plain*

2 cups all-purpose flour	¼–⅓ cup sweet milk
½ teaspoon salt	melted butter
3 teaspoons baking powder	2 quarts strawberries
2 tablespoons sugar	2 cups sugar
3 tablespoons butter	2 cups whipped cream

1. Sift the dry ingredients into a large bowl. Cut in the butter.
2. Add the milk until a soft dough is formed. Roll out or pat on a well-floured board to ¼-inch thickness.
3. Cut rounds with a large biscuit cutter. Brush half the rounds lightly with melted butter. Top with a second round of dough.
4. Bake on a lightly greased pan at 425° for 12–15 minutes, or until golden brown.
5. Hull the berries and wash quickly. Slice or crush with a masher. Add the sugar and allow to stand until sugar is dissolved.
6. To serve, remove the top biscuit, heap the berries on the bottom biscuit, lay the second biscuit on top, crust side down. Heap on another good stack of berries.
7. Top with whipped cream.

Piecrust Shortcake

ILLINOIS
Adapted from Linsenmeyer, *Cooking Plain*

2 cups sifted flour	2 quarts strawberries
1 teaspoon salt	2 cups sugar
¼ cup ice water	2 cups whipped cream
⅔ cup butter	

1. Resift the flour with the salt.
2. Measure ⅓ cup of this mixture and stir it into the ice water to form a smooth paste.
3. Cut the butter into the remainder of the flour until it is the size of peas. Stir the flour paste into the dough and work it quickly into a ball. Chill for at least ½ hour, wrapped in wax paper.
4. Roll out on a floured board to ⅛-inch thickness. Cut three 10-inch discs. Prick lightly with fork tines and place on ungreased cookie sheets.
5. Bake 10–12 minutes, at 425°, or until pale golden colored.
6. Hull berries and wash quickly. Slice or crush with a masher. Add the sugar and allow to stand until sugar is dissolved.
7. Place a crust in a large shallow bowl and add ⅓ of the crushed strawberries. Repeat until crust is used up, making sure you heap strawberries on top.
8. Spoon into individual dessert dishes and top with whipped cream.

Poppy Seed Cake

ILLINOIS
Adapted from Linsenmeyer, *Cooking Plain*

Cake:

⅔	cup poppy seeds	3	teaspoons baking powder
1	cup milk	½	teaspoon salt
1	cup butter	1	grated lemon rind
2	cups sugar	½	cup milk
5	egg yolks	1	teaspoon vanilla
2½	cups sifted cake flour	5	egg whites, beaten

Custard topping:

1	cup sugar	4	egg yolks, beaten
3	tablespoons cornstarch	2	cups milk
¼	teaspoon salt	1	teaspoon vanilla

1. Soak the poppy seeds in the 1 cup milk for an hour.
2. Cream the butter until lemon colored and fluffy. Add the sugar ¼ cup at a time and beat until the mixture resembles whipped cream. Beat in the egg yolks, one at a time.
3. Sift the flour with the baking powder and salt and add to the batter in thirds, alternating with the ½ cup milk. Stir in the poppy seeds, lemon rind, and vanilla and blend thoroughly.
4. Beat the egg whites until stiff but not dry and fold into the batter. Turn into a 10-by-4-inch loaf pan or 10-inch round pan that has been lightly greased and dusted with flour.
5. Bake at 350° for 45 minutes, or until the cake springs back when touched lightly with a fingertip.
6. To prepare the custard topping, combine the sugar, cornstarch, and salt in the top of a double boiler, add the egg yolks, and beat until smooth.
7. Add the milk gradually and continue mixing until smooth.
8. Cook over medium heat until thick, stirring constantly.
9. Stir in the vanilla. Cool and pour over slices of poppy seed cake as served.

Red Beet Cake

INDIANA
Adapted from *The Hoosier Cookbook*

1½ cups canned red beets	1½ cups sugar
1 cup oil	1¾ cups flour
2 squares unsweetened chocolate, melted	1½ teaspoons baking soda
	½ teaspoon salt
3 eggs	1 teaspoon vanilla

1. Blend the red beets, oil, and melted chocolate in a blender until smooth. Set aside.
2. Beat the eggs and sugar. Add the blender mixture and other ingredients.
3. Mix well and pour into 2 greased 8-inch cake pans.
4. Bake at 350° for 25–35 minutes, or until done.

Chocolate Kraut Cake

INDIANA
Adapted from *The Hoosier Cookbook*

2¼ cups sifted all-purpose flour	1½ cups sugar
1 teaspoon baking powder	3 eggs
1 teaspoon baking soda	1¼ teaspoons vanilla
¼ teaspoon salt	1 cup water
½ cup cocoa	½ cup sauerkraut, well drained
⅔ cup shortening	

1. Sift the flour, baking powder, baking soda, salt, and cocoa together.
2. Cream the shortening with the sugar and beat well. Add the eggs, one at a time, beating well after each addition. Add the vanilla.
3. Add the dry ingredients alternately with the water. Blend until smooth.
4. Fold in the sauerkraut. Spoon into a greased 13-by-9-inch pan.
5. Bake at 375° for 35–40 minutes, or until done.

Aunt Caroline's Coca-Cola Cake

OHIO

Adapted from DuSablon, *Cincinnati Recipe Treasury*

Cake:

2	cups sugar	1	teaspoon baking soda
2	cups flour	1	teaspoon vanilla extract
½	cup salad oil	2	eggs
3	tablespoons cocoa powder	1½	cups miniature
½	cup buttermilk		marshmallows
1	cup Coca-Cola		

Icing:

4	tablespoons butter	8	ounces powdered sugar
4	teaspoons cocoa powder	½	teaspoon vanilla extract
3	tablespoons Coca-Cola	½	cup chopped nuts

1. Sift the sugar and flour together.
2. Place the oil, cocoa, buttermilk, and Coca-Cola in a saucepan. Stir and bring to a boil.
3. Pour the boiling mixture over the flour and sugar and beat well.
4. Add the remaining cake ingredients and mix well (the marshmallows do not liquefy, and the batter will be thin). Pour into a greased and floured 9-by-13-inch pan.
5. Bake at 350° for 45 minutes.
6. For the icing, place the butter, cocoa, and Coca-Cola in a saucepan and bring to a boil.
7. Remove from the heat and add the powdered sugar, vanilla, and nuts. Mix well. Spread on the cake while the icing is still warm.

Chocolate "Wacky" Cake

INDIANA
Adapted from *The Hoosier Cookbook*

1½ cups flour	1 teaspoon vanilla
3 tablespoons cocoa	1 tablespoon vinegar
1 cup sugar	5 tablespoons melted short-ening or oil
1 teaspoon baking soda	
¼ teaspoon salt	1 cup warm water

1. Sift the flour, cocoa, sugar, baking soda, and salt directly into a 10-by-7-by-1½-inch oblong pan that the cake will be baked in. Make a well in one corner and add the vanilla and vinegar.
2. Draw a line through the middle and add the melted shortening.
3. Pour the warm water over all and mix together.
4. Bake at 350° for 30–35 minutes.

Old-Fashioned Layer Cake with Fudge Frosting

ILLINOIS
Adapted from Schultz, *As American as Apple Pie*

Cake:

- 4 ounces semisweet chocolate, chopped
- 1 cup milk, divided
- 1 cup light brown sugar
- 3 large egg yolks
- 2 cups sifted cake flour
- 1 teaspoon baking soda
- ½ teaspoon salt
- 4 ounces unsalted butter, softened
- 1 cup sugar
- ¼ cup water
- 1 teaspoon vanilla
- 2 large egg whites

Frosting:

- 3 ounces unsweetened chocolate
- 14 ounces sweetened condensed milk
- 8 tablespoons unsalted butter, cut into bits
- 1 egg yolk, lightly beaten
- 1½ teaspoons vanilla

1. Mix the chocolate, ½ cup of the milk, the brown sugar, and 1 egg yolk in the top of a double boiler. Cook, stirring constantly, until the chocolate melts and a smooth mixture forms.
2. Sift the flour with the baking soda and salt.
3. Cream the butter until light. Beat in the sugar until light and fluffy. Beat in the remaining 2 egg yolks, one at a time, mixing well after each addition. Beat in the chocolate mixture.
4. Mix the water with the remaining ½ cup milk and the vanilla. Add this to the creamed mixture in thirds, alternating with the flour mixture.
5. Beat the egg whites until stiff. Fold them into the batter. Pour the batter into two 8-inch greased cake pans.
6. Bake at 375° for 25 minutes, or until a toothpick inserted in the center comes out clean. Allow to cool before frosting.
7. Prepare the frosting by melting the chocolate in the top of a double boiler over hot water. Blend in the condensed milk until smooth.
8. Stir in the butter, by bits, until smooth. Stir in the egg yolk and vanilla and cook until slightly thickened. Frost the cake with this mixture.

Comb Honey Cake

OHIO

Adapted from Macmillan, *In a Shaker Kitchen*

2½	cups flour	1¼	cups comb honey
1	teaspoon baking powder	¾	cup butter
½	teaspoon baking soda	3	eggs, lightly beaten
¼	teaspoon salt	¼	cup milk
½	teaspoon ground cinnamon	¼	cup sliced almonds
¼	teaspoon grated nutmeg		honey for glazing

1. Sift the flour, baking powder, baking soda, salt, and spices together into a bowl and set aside.
2. Warm the honey with the butter just until the butter has melted. Remove from the heat and beat in the eggs and milk.
3. Gradually add this to the dry ingredients, beating well after each addition.
4. Pour into a buttered 8-inch square pan lined with parchment paper. Scatter the almonds over the surface.
5. Bake at 325° for 1–1½ hours, or until browned and a wooden skewer comes out clean.
6. Remove the cake from the oven and prick the surface all over with a skewer or fork. Drizzle honey evenly over the surface to glaze.

Franklin Nut Cake

INDIANA

Adapted from *The Hoosier Cookbook*

1	pound butter	¼	teaspoon salt
2	cups sugar	½	pound candied cherries
6	eggs, beaten	1	pound pecans
4	cups flour, divided	½	pound candied pineapple
1	teaspoon baking powder	2	teaspoons vanilla

1. Cream the butter and sugar. Add the beaten eggs.
2. Add 3 cups of the flour sifted with the baking powder and salt.
3. Mix the remaining flour with the cherries, nuts, and pineapple. Stir into the batter.
4. Add the vanilla and pour into a greased and floured tube cake pan.
5. Bake at 250° for 3 hours.

SPICE, NUT, AND FRUIT CAKES

Cincinnati Cake

OHIO

Adapted from DuSablon, *Cincinnati Recipe Treasury*

1 pound fat salt pork	2 tablespoons cinnamon
1 pint boiling water	2 pounds raisins
2 cups light brown sugar	¼ pound citron
1 cup molasses	4 ounces brandy
1 tablespoon cloves	3 teaspoons baking powder
1 tablespoon nutmeg	7 cups flour, sifted

1. Chop the pork finely after removing the rind and pour the boiling water over. Allow to stand until cool.
2. Add the remaining ingredients in the order given. Stir to form a smooth batter.
3. Bake for 2 hours at 325°, or until a tester comes out clean.

"This is excellent, and requires neither butter nor eggs."

Hickory Nut Cake

ILLINOIS

Adapted from Linsenmeyer, *Cooking Plain*

2 cups sugar	¼ teaspoon salt
¾ cup butter	½ cup cream
5 eggs, separated	2 cups hickory nut meats,
3 cups cake flour, sifted	blanched and chopped
2 teaspoons baking powder	½ teaspoon almond extract

1. Cream the sugar with the butter until blended. Add the egg yolks and continue to beat.
2. Mix the flour, baking powder, and salt together. Add to the creamed mixture alternately with the cream.
3. Stir in the nut meats. Add the almond extract.
4. Whip the egg whites stiff. Fold into the batter. Pour into a 9-inch buttered loaf pan.
5. Bake at 350° for 20–25 minutes, or until a tester comes out clean from center of the cake. Cool on a wire rack.

Blueberry Crumb Cake

MICHIGAN

Adapted from Wilson, *American Cooking: The Eastern Heartland*

8 tablespoons butter, chilled and cut into ¼-inch bits	1 teaspoon salt
3¼ cups unsifted flour, divided	8 tablespoons butter, softened
2 cups sugar, divided	3 eggs
1 teaspoon ground cinnamon	¾ cup milk, divided
1 tablespoon baking powder	3 cups blueberries, washed, picked over, and dried
½ teaspoon ground nutmeg	
¼ teaspoon ground cloves	

1. Prepare the crumb topping by combining the chilled butter, ¾ cup of the flour, 1 cup of the sugar, and the cinnamon. Rub together until the mixture resembles coarse meal.
2. Sift the remaining flour, the baking powder, nutmeg, cloves, and salt together.
3. Cream the softened butter and 1 cup of sugar until light and fluffy. Beat in the eggs, one at a time.
4. Blend in 1 cup of the sifted flour mixture. Stir in ¼ cup of the milk. Repeat twice more, beating well after each addition.
5. Gently fold in the blueberries. Pour the batter into a 13-by-9-by-3-inch buttered and floured baking dish. Sprinkle the reserved crumb topping evenly over the cake.
6. Bake at 350° for 40–50 minutes, or until the top is crusty.

Rosewater Sponge Cake

OHIO

Adapted from Macmillan, *In a Shaker Kitchen*

4 eggs, separated	1 tablespoon rose water
⅛ teaspoon cream of tartar	¾ cup cake flour
¾ cup superfine sugar	powdered sugar

1. In a large bowl beat the egg whites until frothy. Add the cream of tartar and continue beating until the whites form soft peaks. Sprinkle in 2 tablespoons of the sugar and beat until the whites form stiff peaks.
2. In a separate bowl, beat the egg yolks until pale. Add the remaining sugar and continue beating until the mixture is very thick and pale. Add the rose water.
3. Sift the flour over the egg yolk mixture and fold it in gently but thoroughly.
4. Add a large spoonful of egg whites and mix in, then fold in the remainder of the whites.
5. Pour the batter into a buttered and floured 9-inch round cake pan lined with a disk of wax paper on the bottom.
6. Bake at 350° for 35–40 minutes.
7. Let the cake cool in the pan.
8. Unmold the cake and dust the top with a little powdered sugar before serving.

Sponge Cake Short Cake

ILLINOIS
Adapted from Linsenmeyer, *Cooking Plain*

1	cup cake flour, sifted	1½	tablespoons water
1	teaspoon baking powder	1	teaspoon vanilla
¼	teaspoon salt	2	quarts strawberries
1	cup sugar	2	cups sugar
3	eggs, lightly beaten	2	cups whipped cream

1. Resift flour with the remaining dry ingredients into a large bowl. Make a well in the center. Drop in the eggs, water, and vanilla.
2. Beat in the liquid ingredients until the batter is smooth. Turn into an 8-by-8-inch ungreased pan.
3. Bake at 350° for about 20 minutes. Cut into squares for serving.
4. Hull the berries and wash them quickly. Slice or crush with a masher. Add the sugar and allow to stand until sugar is dissolved.
5. Spoon plenty of fresh strawberries on top of a spongecake square and garnish with whipped cream.

Old Fashioned Scripture Cake

INDIANA
Adapted from *The Hoosier Cookbook*

2	cups Jeremiah 6:20	2	cups Numbers 17:8
6	Jeremiah 17:11	2	teaspoons Luke 13:21
2	cups Nahum 3:12	½	cup Judges 4:19
2	tablespoons I Samuel 14:25		(last clause)
4½	cups I Kings 4:22		pinch Leviticus 2:13
1	cup Isaiah 7:15		season to taste II Chron-
	(first word)		icles 9:9
2	cups I Samuel 30:12		

1. Cream the butter and sugar together. Add the eggs and beat the mixture smooth.
2. Dissolve the baking soda in the milk and add to the creamed mixture. Stir in the honey.
3. Reserve part of the flour to coat the fruit and nuts.
4. Add the flour sifted with the spices and salt and beat until smooth. Fold in the fruit and nuts.
5. Bake at 250° in a greased tube pan set in water for 2 hours.

"With Bible in hand you can easily bake this cake."

Two Strudels

OHIO

Adapted from DuSablon, *Cincinnati Recipe Treasury*

Dough:

½ cup milk	2 packages dry yeast
½ cup butter, room temperature	½ cup warm water
	2 eggs, beaten until thick
½ cup sugar	4½ cups white flour, divided
½ teaspoon salt	

Filling for nuss strudel (nut strudel):

½ cup honey	¼ teaspoon salt
1 tablespoon butter	dash cinnamon
2½ cups walnuts, ground	evaporated milk
rind of 1 lemon	

Filling for apfel strudel (apple strudel):

4 medium apples, peeled and sliced thin or shredded	1 cup walnuts, ground
	½ cup raisins
¾ cup sugar	1 teaspoon cinnamon

1. To make the dough, scald the milk, then add the butter, sugar, and salt.
2. In a large bowl, dissolve the yeast in the warm water.
3. Stir in the milk mixture. Add the eggs and 2 cups of the flour. Beat until smooth.
4. Stir in enough of the remaining flour to make the dough come away from the sides of the bowl. Knead the dough for 8–10 minutes.
5. Cover the bowl with plastic wrap and set aside to rise in a warm place until doubled. While the dough is rising, make the fillings.
6. For the nut strudel, heat the honey and butter together.
7. Add the walnuts, lemon rind, salt, cinnamon, and enough evaporated milk to make it a spreading consistency. Mix well.
8. For the apple strudel, mix all of the ingredients together well.
9. When the dough has risen sufficiently, punch it down and divide it in half. Roll out one half of the dough on a lightly floured towel to a 10-by-14-inch rectangle.
10. Spread with the nut filling. Roll up tightly, seal the edges and fold in the ends.
11. Repeat for the second strudel, using the apple filling.
12. Place the seam sides down on greased cookie sheets. Let the strudels rise until doubled.
13. Bake at 350° until lightly browned, about 30–40 minutes.

Mother's Brule Cake

KANSAS

Adapted from *The Centennial Treasury of Recipes*

Cake:

½ cup butter	1 cup cold water
1½ cups sugar	4 tablespoons burnt sugar
3 eggs, separated	½ teaspoon salt
2½ cups cake flour	1 teaspoon vanilla
2 teaspoons baking powder	

Frosting:

1 cup sugar	1¼ cups cream
1 cup light brown sugar	

1. For the cake, cream the butter until light. Add the granulated sugar and beat until light and fluffy. Add the egg yolks and beat until smooth.
2. Sift the flour and baking powder together. Add this in thirds to the creamed mixture, alternating with the water. Stir in the burnt sugar, salt, and vanilla. Mix well.
3. Whip the egg whites and fold them into the batter. Pour the batter into 2 greased 8-inch cake pans.
4. Bake at 350° until a toothpick comes out clean, about 20 minutes.
5. Prepare the frosting by cooking the sugars and cream together until thick and of spreading consistency. Beat well and spread on the cake.

WHITE CAKES

Minnehaha Cake

MINNESOTA

Adapted from Kreidberg, *Food on the Frontier*

Cake:

1½ cups sugar	5 eggs, separated
⅔ cup water	2½ cups flour
2 tablespoons melted butter	2½ teaspoons baking powder

Frosting:

1 coffee cup sugar	1 cup chopped raisins
¼ cup water	1 teaspoon vanilla

1. For the cake, dissolve the sugar in the water. Stir in the melted butter, egg yolks, 3 of the egg whites, and the flour, which has been sifted with the baking powder. Beat to form a smooth batter. Pour the batter into a greased 9-inch round cake pan.
2. Bake at 350° for 50 minutes, or until done. Allow the cake to cool.
3. Prepare the frosting by boiling the sugar and water together until a thick syrup forms.
4. Beat the reserved egg whites until stiff. Add the hot syrup, beating constantly. Stir in the raisins and vanilla.
5. Frost the cake with this mixture.

CHOCOLATE CAKES

Chocolate Potato Torte

WISCONSIN

Adapted from *St Paul's Centennial Cookbook*

1 cup instant potato flakes	1 cup sour cream
1⅔ cups milk	3 eggs
1 package devil's food cake mix	chopped nuts, optional

1. Mix the potato flakes with the milk. Stir in the cake mix.
2. Add the sour cream and eggs, one at a time, beating between additions. Stir until a smooth batter forms.
3. Pour the batter into a "potato torte pan" or a greased 10-by-15-inch pan. Bake at 350° for 20 to 30 minutes. "If you use the torte pan, it takes about 50 minutes."
4. Top with nuts, if desired "or make your own kind of frosting."

Miracle Whip Cake

MINNESOTA

Adapted from a personal communication.

2 cups flour	1 cup sugar
12 tablespoons cocoa	1 cup cold water
½ teaspoon salt	1 cup Miracle Whip
1 teaspoon baking soda	1 teaspoon Vanilla

1. Sift the flour, cocoa, salt, baking soda, and sugar together.
2. Add the water and mix. Stir in the Miracle Whip and vanilla to form a smooth batter. Pour batter into a greased 8-inch loaf pan.
3. Bake at 350° for 35 to 45 minutes or until done.

Buttermilk Spice Cake

KANSAS

Adapted from *The Centennial Treasury of Recipes*

2 cups flour	¾ teaspoon cinnamon
1 cup sugar	¾ cup light brown sugar
1 teaspoon salt	½ cup soft shortening
1 teaspoon baking powder	1 cup buttermilk
¾ teaspoon soda	3 eggs
¾ teaspoon cloves	

1. Sift the dry ingredients together.
2. Stir in the remaining ingredients except for the eggs and beat for 2 minutes. Add the eggs and beat 2 minutes more. Pour the batter into a greased 9-inch cake pan.
3. Bake at 350° for 35–40 minutes.

SPICE, NUT, AND FRUIT CAKES

White Nut Cake

IOWA

Adapted from *How Iowa Cooks*

¾ cup butter	1 cup walnuts, coarse
2 cups sugar	chopped
3 cups cake flour	1 teaspoon vanilla
2 teaspoons baking powder	6 egg whites
1 cup milk	

1. Cream the butter. Add the sugar gradually and cream together well.
2. Sift the flour before measuring. Add the baking powder, sifting together several times.
3. Add the flour mixture alternately with the milk to the butter mixture.
4. Add the nuts and vanilla.
5. Beat the egg whites until they form peaks, then fold into the batter.
6. Bake in a greased 9-by-13-inch pan at 350° for 35–45 minutes.

Poor Man's Cake (Depression Cake)

IOWA

Adapted from *How Iowa Cooks*

2 cups light brown sugar	1 teaspoon cinnamon
2 cups hot water	½ cup nut meats
2 tablespoons shortening	2 cups flour
1 cup raisins	1 teaspoon baking soda
1 teaspoon salt	1 teaspoon water
1 teaspoon cloves	

1. Boil the first 8 ingredients together for 5 minutes.
2. When cool, add the flour and the baking soda dissolved in the water. Pour into a greased 9-by-13-inch pan.
3. Bake at 350° for 25 minutes.

"Tastes like a fruit cake."

Butterless, Eggless, Milkless Cake

OKLAHOMA

Adapted from Wilhelm, *Smidgen of Honey*

1 cup sugar	1 cup nuts
1 cup raisins	1 teaspoon nutmeg
¾ cup lard	1 teaspoon cloves
1 teaspoon allspice	1¾ cups flour
1 teaspoon cinnamon	1 teaspoon baking soda
1 cup water	½ teaspoon salt

1. Add the first 9 ingredients to a saucepan and bring to a boil.
2. Allow to cool and add the flour to which have been added the baking soda and salt.
3. Bake at 350° for 20 minutes in a greased 10-inch cake pan.

Fig Cake

WISCONSIN

Adapted from *"The Four Hundred" Cook Book*

½ pound figs	1 cup sugar
1 cup raisins	½ cup butter
1 teaspoon baking soda dissolved in 1 cup boiling water	2 eggs
	2 cups flour
	1 teaspoon cinnamon

1. Chop the figs fine, add the raisins, and pour the boiling water, with the baking soda dissolved in it, over the fruit.
2. Mix the sugar, butter, eggs, flour, and cinnamon, then add the fig mixture while still hot. Pour into a greased 8-inch loaf pan.
3. Bake at 350° for 40 minutes.

SPICE, NUT, AND FRUIT CAKES

Moist Fruit Cake

WISCONSIN

Adapted from *"The Four Hundred" Cook Book*

1 cup sugar	1 teaspoon nutmeg
1 cup sour cream	½ cup butter
1 tablespoon grated un-	2 eggs
sweetened chocolate	1 cup raisins
1 cup dates	1 cup figs
1 cup English walnuts	1 teaspoon baking soda
1 teaspoon cinnamon	2 cups flour
1 teaspoon cloves	

1. Mix all the ingredients together in the order given to make a rich batter.
2. Bake in a greased 9-inch springform pan at 325° for 1 hour.

Grandma's Raisin Cake

KANSAS

Adapted from *The Centennial Treasury of Recipes*

2 cups raisins	3 cups flour
2 cups water	1 teaspoon cinnamon
2 cups butter	1 teaspoon nutmeg
1½ cups sugar	1 teaspoon baking soda
2 eggs, beaten	1 cup nuts
1 teaspoon vanilla	

1. Place the raisins and water in a saucepan. Bring the mixture to the boil and cook until the liquid has reduced to 1 cup. Reserve the liquid.
2. Cream the butter with the sugar until light and fluffy. Add the beaten eggs and vanilla. Stir to blend.
3. Sift the flour, cinnamon, nutmeg, and baking soda together. Add this mixture to the creamed mixture in thirds, alternating with the reserved raisin water. Stir in the raisins and nuts. Mix to form a smooth batter.
4. Bake in a greased 9-inch cake pan at 350° for 30 minutes, or until firm to the touch in the center.

Cherry Kringle

IOWA

Adapted from *How Iowa Cooks*

1 package dry yeast	¼ cup oil
¼ cup warm water	½ teaspoon salt
⅓ cup warm milk	2⅓ cups all-purpose flour
¼ cup sugar	1 can cherry pie filling
1 egg	1 tablespoon sugar

1. Dissolve the yeast in the warm water. Add the warm milk, sugar, egg, oil, and salt. Stir.
2. Add the flour 1 cup at a time. Allow the dough to rise.
3. Divide the dough in half and pat one piece into a buttered 12-by-16-inch pan. Cover with the pie filling.
4. Pat the remaining dough into a rectangle to cover the pie filling. Let rise and sprinkle with sugar.
5. Bake at 375° for 20–25 minutes.

One Cup Cake

KANSAS

Adapted from *The Centennial Treasury of Recipes*

1 cup flour	1 egg
1 cup sugar	¾ cup cream
2 teaspoons baking powder	1 teaspoon vanilla

1. Sift the dry ingredients together.
2. Mix the egg with the cream and vanilla. Stir the liquids into the dry ingredients to form a smooth batter.
3. Bake in a greased 8-inch square cake pan at 350° for 20 minutes.

Alva T.'s 7-Up Cake

TEXAS
Adapted from Ross, *Nanny's Texas Table*

¾ **pound butter or margarine, room temperature**
3 **cups sugar**
5 **eggs, room temperature**
3 **cups cake flour**

2 **tablespoons pure lemon extract**
¾ **cup 7-Up, room temperature**

1. Cream the butter until fluffy. Beat in the sugar and continue creaming for 3–4 minutes.
2. Add the eggs, one at a time, creaming after each addition. Fold the flour in gradually, about a third at a time, mixing gently.
3. Add the lemon extract and 7-Up. Pour the mixture into a greased and floured 10-inch tube pan.
4. Bake at 350° for 1¼ hours, or until firm in the center.

Sour Cream Cake

TEXAS
Adapted from Ross, *Nanny's Texas Table*

2 **eggs**
½ **cup sour cream**
1 **cup sugar**
1 **teaspoon vanilla**

1 **cup flour**
¼ **teaspoon baking soda**
1 **teaspoon baking powder**
⅛ **teaspoon salt**

1. Beat the eggs and sour cream together until well mixed. Add the sugar and beat for 1 minute. Add the vanilla and mix well.
2. Sift the flour, baking soda, baking powder, and salt together. Stir this into the egg mixture. Pour the batter into a greased 9-inch cake pan.
3. Bake at 350° for 25–30 minutes.

Josie Cake

TEXAS
Adapted from Ross, *Nanny's Texas Table*

¾ cup butter
1½ cups granulated sugar
4 eggs
3 cups cake flour

2½ teaspoons baking powder
1⅓ cups milk
1 recipe chocolate fudge
   frosting

1. Cream the butter for 30 seconds. Add the sugar and continue creaming until light and fluffy. Add the eggs, one at a time, beating well after each addition.
2. Sift the flour and the baking powder together. Fold about a third of it into the butter mixture. Stir in half the milk.
3. Continue alternating the flour and milk until all is added. Stir to form a smooth batter. Place the batter in 2 greased 9-inch cake pans or a greased 9-by-13-inch loaf pan.
4. Bake at 350° for 30–35 minutes for the layers. Add 10 minutes for the loaf pan.
5. When cool, frost with your favorite fudge frosting.

Auntie's Favorite White Cake

TEXAS
Adapted from Coleman and Coleman, *The Texas Cookbook*

½ cup vegetable shortening
2 cups sugar
3¼ cups cake flour
3¼ teaspoons baking powder

1 cup milk
5–6 egg whites
  water
1 teaspoon vanilla

1. Cream the shortening with the sugar until fluffy.
2. Sift the flour with the baking powder and add, alternating with the milk.
3. To the egg whites add enough water to measure 1 cup. Mix briefly. Add this to the cake batter along with the vanilla. Pour the batter into a greased 9-inch cake pan.
4. Bake at 350° for 40 minutes, or until done.

Postre Borracho (Drunken Cake)

ARIZONA
Adapted from *American Cooking: The Great West*

2⅓ cups flour	1 teaspoon vanilla extract
1½ teaspoons baking powder	1 teaspoon almond extract
10 ounces butter, softened	1 cup water
3⅓ cups sugar, divided	½ cup pure grain alcohol
7 eggs	

1. Sift the flour and the baking powder together.
2. Cream the butter with 1⅓ cups of the sugar until the mixture is light and fluffy. Beat in the eggs, one at a time, and add the vanilla and almond extracts.
3. Beat in the flour mixture ½ cup at a time, beating well after each addition. Pour the batter into a paper-lined, greased and sugared 9-inch square cake pan.
4. Bake at 350° for about 50 minutes, or until a toothpick inserted in the center comes out clean. Let the cake cool in the pan for about 5 minutes, then invert onto a serving plate.
5. Combine the remaining sugar and the water in a heavy saucepan. Cook over low heat until the mixture comes to a boil and the sugar dissolves. Stir in the alcohol.
6. With a wooden skewer, pierce the cake all over, pressing the skewer completely through the cake. Drizzle the syrup over the cake and set aside at room temperature for about an hour before serving.

Potato Cake

ARIZONA
Adapted from Weiner, *Arizona Territorial Cookbook*

⅔ cup butter or shortening,
   room temperature
2 cups sugar
4 eggs, separated
2–2½ cups flour
3½ teaspoons baking powder
½ teaspoon salt (if shortening
   is used in place of butter)
½ teaspoon nutmeg

½ teaspoon cinnamon
½ teaspoon allspice
½ teaspoon cloves
1 cup mashed potatoes
2 squares unsweetened
   chocolate, melted
½ cup milk
1 teaspoon vanilla extract
1 cup nuts, chopped

1. Cream the butter and sugar. Add the egg yolks one at a time.
2. Sift the flour, baking powder, salt (if using), and spices together.
3. Add the potatoes, chocolate, and flour mixture to the creamed mixture, alternating with the milk so it will mix together easily. Add the vanilla.
4. Beat the egg whites until stiff, fold in the nuts, and add this to the cake batter. Pour into a greased loaf pan.
5. Cook at 350° for about 1 hour, or until golden brown and springy to the touch.

Mix-in-the-Pan-Cake

TEXAS
Adapted from *Capitol Cook Book*

½ cup butter
1¼ cups flour
1 cup sugar
1 cup chopped walnuts
2 teaspoons cinnamon
1 teaspoon baking soda
½ teaspoon salt

1 egg
½ cup pureed sweet potato
8¾ ounces crushed pineapple,
   undrained
1 teaspoon vanilla
1 cup sour cream

1. Melt the butter in a 9-inch square cake pan.
2. Add the remaining ingredients, except the sour cream, to the pan and stir to form a batter. Spread evenly over the pan.
3. Bake at 325° for 40–45 minutes. Cool in the pan.
4. Spread the sour cream over the top and sprinkle lightly with additional cinnamon. Refrigerate at least 3 hours.

"This cake has a different and delicious flavor."

CHOCOLATE CAKES

Fudge Cake

TEXAS

Adapted from Ross, *Nanny's Texas Table*

½ cup butter
1 cup granulated sugar
2 eggs
1 cup cake flour
⅛ teaspoon salt

2 ounces unsweetened chocolate, melted
1 teaspoon vanilla extract
1½ cups coarsely chopped walnuts

1. Cream the butter for 1 minute. Add the sugar gradually and cream for 2 minutes. Add the eggs and cream for another minute.
2. Sift the flour and salt over the butter mixture and fold in. Add the melted chocolate.
3. Add the vanilla and nuts and fold in. Pour the batter into a buttered 8-inch square cake pan.
4. Bake at 350° for 30 minutes. Cool in the pan and cut into 2-inch squares.

Chocolate-Piñon Torte

NEW MEXICO
Adapted from Dent, *The Feast of Santa Fe*

Cake:

4	ounces bittersweet chocolate	3	tablespoons piñons (pine nuts)
4	tablespoons (½ stick) butter	6	tablespoons sugar, divided
1	grated orange rind (reserving a generous pinch for garnish)	2	tablespoons flour
		4	large eggs, separated
		2	tablespoons orange liqueur

Garnish:

½	cup heavy cream	2	tablespoons orange liqueur
2	tablespoons sugar		

1. Place the chocolate, butter, and orange rind in the top of a double boiler or in a microwave to melt the chocolate. Stir to combine. Set aside to cool.
2. Grind the piñons, 2 tablespoons of the sugar, and the flour together in a food processor to the consistency of fine meal. Do not overprocess.
3. Beat the egg yolks with 2 tablespoons of the sugar until pale and thick. Beat in the orange liqueur.
4. Whip the egg whites to form soft peaks. Whip in the remaining 2 tablespoons sugar until just combined.
5. Stir the piñon-flour mixture into the lukewarm melted chocolate and butter. Fold this mixture into the beaten egg yolks, blending thoroughly. Fold in the egg whites, forming a smooth batter.
6. Pour the batter into a 9-inch springform pan that has been greased and lined with parchment.
7. Bake at 350° for 25–30 minutes, or until the center is firm to the touch.
8. Whip the cream with the sugar and liqueur until stiff. Using a pastry bag, pipe rosettes onto the surface. Top each rosette with reserved orange peel.

Chocolate Chip Cake

TEXAS
Adapted from *Capitol Cook Book*

1 cup chopped dates	1 teaspoon vanilla
1 teaspoon baking soda	1¾ cups flour
1 cup boiling water	1 tablespoon cocoa
1 cup sugar	4 ounces semisweet chocolate
½ cup butter	chips
2 eggs	½ cup chopped pecans

1. Add the dates to the baking soda dissolved in the boiling water. Allow to cool.
2. Cream the sugar and butter until light and fluffy. Add the eggs, one at a time, beating after each addition. Add the vanilla.
3. Sift the flour with the cocoa and add it to the sugar mixture. Stir in the dates and date water and the chocolate chips. Pour into a well-greased and floured 9-by-13-inch baking pan. Sprinkle the chopped nuts over the top of the cake and press them down into the batter.
4. Bake at 350° for 30 minutes.

Hershey Pound Cake

TEXAS
Adapted from *Capitol Cook Book*

½ pound butter	¼ teaspoon baking soda
2 cups sugar	¾ cup buttermilk
4 eggs	2 teaspoons vanilla
2½ cups cake flour	14 Hershey's almond Kisses
¼ teaspoon salt	

1. Cream the butter and sugar until light and fluffy. Add the eggs, one at a time, beating well after each addition.
2. Sift the dry ingredients together and add them alternating with the buttermilk. Stir in the vanilla.
3. Melt the Hershey's Kisses in the top of double boiler over hot water. Add this to the batter and mix well. Pour the batter into a well-greased and floured tube pan.
4. Bake at 300° for 45 minutes.

Peanut Butter Fudge Cake

NEW MEXICO
Adapted from Cameron, *The Best from New Mexico Kitchens*

Cake:

¼ cup butter	½ cup cocoa
1 cup peanut butter, smooth or crunchy	3 cups sifted flour
2¼ cups sugar	1⅔ teaspoons baking soda
1½ teaspoons vanilla	¾ teaspoon salt
3 eggs	1½ cups ice water

Frosting:

2 cups sugar	2 tablespoons cocoa
1 cup light cream or evaporated milk	½ cup peanut butter

1. Cream the butter, peanut butter, sugar, and vanilla. Beat in the eggs one at a time.
2. Sift the dry ingredients together and add alternately with the water to the egg mixture. Pour into a greased and floured tube pan.
3. Bake at 350° for 1 hour.
4. To prepare the frosting, mix all the ingredients together in a heavy saucepan. Bring to a boil and cook until it reaches the soft-ball stage. Beat until creamy and spreadable.

Pearl's Special Cake

NEW MEXICO

Adapted from Cameron, *The Best from New Mexico Kitchens*

1 cup oil	2 teaspoons cinnamon
1 cup fruit juice	2 teaspoons nutmeg
2 cups light brown sugar	2 teaspoons allspice
3 eggs	2 teaspoons ground cloves
4 cups sifted flour	2 cups broken pecans
2 teaspoons baking soda	2 cups drained fruit cocktail
1 teaspoon salt	

1. Combine the oil and juice. Mix in the brown sugar. Beat in the eggs one at a time.
2. Sift the dry ingredients together and add to the egg mixture. Mix well. Stir in the nuts and fruit. Pour into a greased tube pan.
3. Bake at 325° for 1½ hours.

Pecan-and-Date Cake

TEXAS

Adapted from Coleman and Coleman, *The Texas Cookbook*

4 eggs	1 heaping teaspoon baking powder
1 cup sugar	
2 teaspoons vanilla	¼ teaspoon salt
½ cup sifted cake flour	2 pounds seeded dates
	1 pound pecans

1. Beat the eggs. Gradually add the sugar and the vanilla. Beat until smooth.
2. Sift the flour, baking powder, and salt over the dates and pecans. Pour the egg mixture over the pecan mixture. Mix well to form a smooth batter.
3. Grease a springform pan and pour in the batter.
4. Bake at 250° until a tester comes out clean from the center.

"This cake is chewy, and very good with tea."

Coriander Cake with Pecan Frosting

NEW MEXICO

Adapted from Dent, *The Feast of Santa Fe*

Cake:

1	cup unbleached white flour	1	cup sugar
¼	teaspoon salt	½	teaspoon vanilla
2	teaspoons ground coriander	¼	cup milk
		6	tablespoons butter, melted
2	eggs		

Frosting:

1	cup pecan halves	1	tablespoon flour
3	tablespoons butter	1	tablespoon milk
3	tablespoons sugar		

1. Sift the flour, salt, and coriander together.
2. Beat the eggs with the sugar until pale and light, about 3 minutes. Add the vanilla and continue to mix.
3. Add the flour in portions, alternating with the milk. Mix quickly to form a smooth batter. Carefully fold in the butter. Pour the batter into a greased 8-inch cake pan.
4. Bake at 350° for 30 minutes, or until set in the center.
5. For the frosting, chop the pecans coarsely and add the remaining ingredients. Cook over medium heat to boiling.
6. Top the cooled cake with this mixture and return it to the oven. Bake at 425° for 5 minutes.

SPICE, NUT, AND FRUIT CAKES

Drunken Prune Cake

NEW MEXICO
Adapted from Dent, *The Feast of Santa Fe*

Cake:

20	prunes, pitted	2	teaspoons baking powder
½	cup Madeira or ruby port	⅓	cup fresh orange juice
3	large eggs	1	teaspoon vanilla
1	cup sugar	¼	teaspoon nutmeg
¾	cup butter		scant ½ teaspoon salt (if
1½	cups unbleached white flour		the butter is unsalted)

Custard:

⅓	cup sugar	2	egg yolks
1	tablespoon plus 1 teaspoon cornstarch		grated peel of 1 orange
¾	cup scalded milk	1	teaspoon vanilla powdered sugar

1. Quarter the prunes and soak them in the wine overnight or simmer them in the wine for 1 hour.
2. Cream the eggs, sugar, and butter together until light and fluffy. Add the flour, baking powder, orange juice, vanilla, nutmeg, and salt (if using). Mix to form a smooth batter.
3. Prepare the custard by mixing the sugar and the cornstarch together in a small saucepan. Pour in the scalded milk, stirring constantly. Whisk in the egg yolks and cook over a low heat for 10 minutes, until the custard thickens.
4. Remove from the heat, stir in the grated orange peel and vanilla, and allow the custard to cool.
5. Spread half of the cake batter across the bottom of a preheated greased 9-inch springform pan. Drop the custard by spoonfuls over the surface of the batter and carefully spread it evenly. Leave a ½-inch border of batter. Dot the custard layer with the prunes and drizzle any remaining wine over all.
6. Finish the cake by topping the prune layer with the remaining batter. Smooth to cover all of the prunes.
7. Bake at 350° for about 1 hour. Dust with powdered sugar.

Mexican Pecan Cake

NEW MEXICO

Adapted from Butel, *Woman's Day Book of New Mexican Cooking*

Cake:

1½ cups sugar	1 tablespoon lemon juice
⅔ cup pecans, ground	5 eggs
¼ teaspoon salt	1¾ cups sifted all-purpose
1 cup butter	flour

Glaze:

¼ cup butter	2 tablespoons lemon juice
1 cup honey	¼ cup chopped pecans

1. Place the sugar, pecans, salt, butter, and lemon juice in a bowl and beat, using an electric mixer, until fluffy.
2. Add the eggs and beat thoroughly. Add the flour and mix well.
3. Bake in a greased and floured 10-inch springform pan at 325° for about an hour.
4. Prepare the glaze by warming the butter, honey, and lemon juice in a saucepan until the butter is melted. Stir in the pecans.
5. Serve with the warm glaze drizzled over the cake.

Navajo Puberty Cake

NEW MEXICO

Adapted from Cameron, *The Best from New Mexico Kitchens*

cornhusks	1½ quarts boiling water
2 pounds yellow stone-ground cornmeal	1 cup sprouted wheat flour
	1 pound raisins

1. Prepare a hole in the ground a little larger than the size of the cake you want and 5–6 inches deeper. Build a fire in the hole and keep it going for several hours.
2. Remove the ashes and embers and brush the cavity clean. Line the cavity with several layers of wet cornhusks.
3. Mix the cornmeal with boiling water, sprouted wheat flour and raisins. Pour the mixture into the lined cavity. Cover with several layers of wet cornhusks. Put 3–4 inches of damp earth above the cornhusks.
4. Build a fire on top of the earth. At the end of 8 hours take out the cake.

Ruby Thrash's Cup Cakes

TEXAS
Adapted from *The Texas Cookbook*

1 cup sugar	2 teaspoons baking powder
½ cup butter	¾ cup milk
2 eggs, separated	½ teaspoon vanilla
2 cups cake flour	

1. Cream the sugar with the butter until light and fluffy. Beat in the egg yolks.
2. Sift the flour with baking powder and add this in thirds to the creamed mixture, alternating with the milk. Stir in the vanilla.
3. Fold in the beaten egg whites to form a smooth batter. Pour this batter into paper-lined muffin tins and bake at 350° for 15 minutes or until cup cakes are firm to the touch in the centers.

Apple Rolly Polly

ARIZONA
Adapted from Weiner, *Arizona Territorial Cookbook*

1¾ cups flour, sifted	¾ cup heavy cream
1 tablespoon baking powder	1 egg white
1 teaspoon salt	5 – 6 large raw apples, sliced
1½ tablespoons sugar	1 cup light brown sugar
4 tablespoons butter, softened	½ teaspoon cinnamon or nutmeg

1. Blend the flour, baking powder, salt, sugar, butter, and cream quickly to form a biscuit-type dough.
2. Roll thin on a floured board. Brush with the egg white. Spread with slices of apple, sprinkle with brown sugar, and flavor with cinnamon or nutmeg. Roll up, jelly-roll fashion.
3. Bake the roll in a greased loaf pan at 400° for 30 – 40 minutes.

"This is also excellent with mince meat filling."

Cointreau Pound Cake

COLORADO

Adapted from *Nuggets, Recipes Good as Gold*

½	pound butter, softened	¼	cup fresh squeezed orange
2	cups sugar		juice
6	eggs	1	teaspoon almond extract
2	cups flour	1	teaspoon lemon extract
		⅓	cup Cointreau

1. Cream the butter and sugar together. Add the eggs, one at a time, mixing well after each addition. Add the flour in portions. Beat until smooth. Stir in the orange juice and the extracts.
2. Pour the batter into a greased and floured 12-cup bundt pan and bake at 350° for about 1 hour.
3. Remove the cake from the pan and allow to cool for 10 minutes. Pierce the surface with a skewer and drizzle the Cointreau over the cake, allowing it to be absorbed. Allow to cool thoroughly before serving.

CHOCOLATE CAKES

Never Fail Mahogany Cake

WYOMING

Adapted from *Cooking in Wyoming*

2	eggs, well beaten	¼	teaspoon salt
1½	cups sugar	1	teaspoon soda
2	squares melted un-sweetened chocolate	1	scant teaspoon baking powder
1	cup sour cream	½	teaspoon vanilla
2	cups flour	1	cup warm water

1. Beat the eggs, sugar, and chocolate together. Mix in the remaining ingredients, adding the water last.
2. Bake at 350° for 30 – 40 minutes in a greased tube pan.

CHOCOLATE CAKES

$100.00 Chocolate Cake

NEVADA

Adapted from *Nevada's Finest Western Cooking*

Cake:

2	cups sugar	4	ounces bitter chocolate,
½	cup butter		melted
2	eggs	1½	cups milk
2	cups flour	1	cup chopped pecans
2	teaspoons baking powder	2	teaspoons vanilla
½	teaspoon salt		

Icing:

1½	ounces bitter chocolate,	1	tablespoon vanilla
	melted	1	tablespoon lemon juice
2	tablespoons butter	1⅓	cups powdered sugar
1	egg, beaten	1	cup chopped nut meats

1. Cream the sugar with the butter until light and fluffy. Add the eggs, 1 at a time, beating well after each addition.
2. Stir in the remaining cake ingredients in the order given. Beat well to form a smooth batter. Pour the batter into a greased 9-inch loaf pan.
3. Bake at 350° for 1 hour, or until a tester comes out clean from the center. Allow the cake to cool before frosting.
4. Prepare the icing by mixing the melted chocolate and the butter together. Add the remaining ingredients and mix well. Frost the cake with this icing.

Sheath Cake

IDAHO
Adapted from *American Cooking: The Great West*

Cake:

2 cups flour
2 cups sugar
¼ cup cocoa powder
½ cup water
½ pound butter, cut into ¼-inch bits

1 cup buttermilk
2 eggs, lightly beaten
1 teaspoon baking soda
1 teaspoon vanilla extract

Frosting:

3½ cups powdered sugar
½ cup finely chopped pecans
¼ cup unsweetened cocoa
5 fluid ounces light cream

8 tablespoons butter, cut into ¼-inch bits
1 teaspoon vanilla extract

1. Sift the flour and the granulated sugar together.
2. Add the cocoa and water to a saucepan and whisk until smooth. Add the butter and cook over moderate heat until the mixture comes to a boil and the butter is completely melted. Allow to cool for 2 or 3 minutes.
3. Whisk the cocoa mixture into the flour mixture, beating to form a smooth batter. Stir in the buttermilk, eggs, baking soda, and vanilla extract. Pour the batter into a greased and floured jelly roll pan.
4. Bake at 325° for 20 minutes, or until done.
5. Prepare the frosting by mixing the powdered sugar and pecans together.
6. Combine the cocoa and cream in a saucepan and stir vigorously with a whisk until the mixture is smooth. Add the butter and cook over moderate heat until the mixture comes to a boil and the butter is melted.
7. Whisk the cocoa mixture into the sugar mixture, beating until smooth. Stir in the vanilla.
8. Use this frosting to top the cake while the cake is still warm.

Black Forest Cake

COLORADO

Adapted from *Nuggets: Recipes Good as Gold*

2½ cups flour
1⅔ cups sugar
⅔ cup cocoa
1½ teaspoons baking soda
1 teaspoon salt
¼ teaspoon baking powder
¾ cup shortening
2 eggs
1¼ cups water

1 teaspoon vanilla
1 16-ounce can pitted tart cherries
½ cup sugar
3 tablespoons cornstarch
¼ cup kirsch
3 cups whipping cream
⅔ cup powdered sugar
chocolate curls for garnish

1. Mix the flour, sugar, cocoa, baking soda, salt, and baking powder together.
2. Cream the shortening. Add the eggs, water, and vanilla. Add the dry ingredients. Beat on high speed for 3 minutes.
3. Bake in 2 greased 9-inch round cake pans at 350° for 30–35 minutes. Allow to cool.
4. Drain the cherries, reserving the juice. Add enough water to the juice to make ¾ cup. Heat in a saucepan with the ½ cup sugar and the cornstarch to boiling. Boil 2 minutes. Stir in the kirsch and cherries. Chill thoroughly.
5. Whip the cream stiff with the powdered sugar.
6. Assemble the cake by spreading half the cherry filling on the first cake layer. Top with 2 cups whipped cream. Add the second cake layer. Top with the remaining cherries. Ice the cake with the remaining whipped cream. Decorate with chocolate curls.

Pecan Cake

IDAHO

Adapted from *American Cooking: The Great West*

2½ cups seedless raisins	¾ cup butter, softened
1 cup bourbon	1½ cups sugar
3 cups flour	5 eggs
1½ teaspoons baking powder	3 cups coarsely chopped
1½ teaspoons ground nutmeg	pecans
1 teaspoon salt	

1. Plump the raisins in the bourbon, allowing them to stand for 30 minutes, stirring occasionally.
2. Sift 2½ cups of the flour with the baking powder, nutmeg, and salt.
3. Cream the butter and sugar together until light and fluffy. Beat in the eggs, 1 at a time, beating well after each addition.
4. Stir in the flour mixture in portions. Beat to form a smooth batter.
5. Stir in ¾ cup of the bourbon, straining out the raisins. Mix well.
6. Add the pecans and remaining ½ cup of flour to the raisins and toss then together. Add this to the batter, stirring to incorporate. Pour the batter into a greased and floured 10-inch tube pan.
7. Bake at 325° for 1 hour, or until firm to the touch in the center.

Webster Cake

WYOMING

Adapted from *Cooking in Wyoming*

1 cup butter	½ pound citron
¾ cup molasses	1½ cups raisins
½ cup milk	currants and spices [such as
¾ cup sugar	nutmeg, mace, cloves] to
2 eggs	taste
1 teaspoon baking soda	½ teaspoon cinnamon
3 cups flour	

1. Cream the butter. Beat in the molasses, milk, sugar, and eggs in order.
2. Mix the baking soda with the flour and add to the butter mixture. Add the fruits and spices. Mix to form a smooth batter.
3. Bake at 350° in a greased 10-inch loaf pan for 40 minutes, or until set in center.

Easy-Do Cake with Caramel Icing

WYOMING

Adapted from *Cooking in Wyoming*

Cake:

1½ cups all-purpose flour	1 cup milk
1 cup sugar	2 whole eggs
½ teaspoon salt	½ teaspoon vanilla
1 tablespoon baking powder	

Icing:

2 cups light brown sugar	1 tablespoon butter
¾ cup medium-thick cream	½ teaspoon vanilla

1. Sift the flour, sugar, salt, and baking powder together. Add the milk and beat for 2 minutes.
2. Add 1 egg at a time, beating for 2 minutes after each addition. Add the ½ teaspoon vanilla.
3. Bake in 2 well-greased and floured 8-inch layer pans at 350° until done "by the cake test."
4. For the icing, mix the brown sugar and cream and boil slowly until creamy. Stir constantly.
5. Remove from the heat and stir in the butter. Add the vanilla.
6. Beat until cool and spread over cake.

Grandma Alm's Shoebox Cake

UTAH

Adapted from Anderson, *Bounty: A Harvest of Food Lore and Country Memories from Utah's Past*

2 cups sugar	2 pound graham crackers,
2 teaspoons baking powder	crushed
6 eggs, beaten	½ pound grated coconut
2 cups milk	½ pound butter, melted and
2 cups chopped walnuts	cooled
1 cup pecans	

1. Mix the sugar and baking powder together. Stir in the eggs and milk. Beat until the sugar dissolves.
2. Stir in the nuts, graham crackers, coconut, and cooled, melted butter. Mix well. Pour the batter into a waxed paper–lined shoebox.
3. Bake at 250° for 3½ hours.

Lady Baltimore Cake

CALIFORNIA

Adapted from Berger and Custis, *Sumptuous Dining in Gaslight San Francisco 1875–1915*

Cake:

1	cup butter	1	cup milk
2	cups sugar	1	teaspoon vanilla
3½	cups flour	6	egg whites
1	tablespoon baking powder		

Lady Baltimore frosting:

3	cups sugar	1	cup chopped raisins
1	cup boiling water	5	figs, sliced
3	egg whites	1	cup chopped nut meats

1. Cream the butter and sugar together until light and fluffy.
2. Sift the flour and baking powder together and add this to the butter in thirds, alternating with the milk. Stir in the vanilla.
3. Whip the egg whites until stiff and fold them into the batter. Pour the batter into 3 well-buttered 8-inch cake pans.
4. Bake at 350° for 40 minutes, or until the cakes spring back lightly to the touch.
5. Prepare the frosting by heating the sugar and water to boiling and continue to cook to the soft ball stage.
6. Whip the egg whites to form soft peaks. Pour in the hot syrup and beat until stiff and glossy.
7. Add the fruits and the nuts and spread the frosting between the layers and over the Lady Baltimore Cake.

WHITE CAKES

Zucchini Cake

CALIFORNIA
Adapted from *The Los Angeles Times California Cookbook*

Cake:

2 cups sugar	1 tablespoon cinnamon
1 cup oil	2 cups shredded, unpeeled zucchini, packed
3 eggs	
2 cups flour	1 cup finely chopped nuts
1 teaspoon baking soda	1 tablespoon vanilla
1 teaspoon salt	

Cream cheese frosting:

3 cups powdered sugar, sifted	5 tablespoons butter or margarine
6 ounces cream cheese, softened	1 teaspoon lemon extract

1. Beat the sugar, oil, and eggs together for several minutes.
2. Sift the flour, baking soda, salt, and cinnamon together.
3. Fold the zucchini and nuts into the sugar mixture. Fold in the flour mixture and vanilla, mixing thoroughly.
4. Pour the batter into a well-greased 10-inch tube pan.
5. Bake at 350° for 1 hour. Allow to cool before icing.
6. For the frosting, beat the powdered sugar, cream cheese, butter or margarine, and lemon extract until thoroughly blended and of spreading consistency.

Grapefruit Cake

CALIFORNIA
Adapted from *The Los Angeles Times California Cookbook*

Cake:

1½ cups sifted cake flour	¼ cup oil
¾ cup sugar	3 eggs, separated
1½ teaspoons baking powder	3 tablespoons grapefruit juice
1 teaspoon salt	½ teaspoon grated lemon peel
¼ cup water	¼ teaspoon cream of tartar

Cream cheese frosting:

6 ounces cream cheese, softened	¾ cup powdered sugar, sifted
	6 – 8 drops yellow food color
2 teaspoons lemon juice	1 grapefruit, sectioned
1 teaspoon grated lemon peel	

1. Sift the flour, sugar, baking powder, and salt together. Make a well in the center and add the water, oil, egg yolks, grapefruit juice, and lemon peel. Beat until very smooth.
2. Beat the egg whites with the cream of tartar until stiff but not dry. Fold gently into the egg yolk mixture until just blended. Pour the batter into an ungreased 9-inch springform pan.
3. Bake at 350° for 30 minutes, or until top springs back. Invert onto a rack and cool thoroughly.
4. Prepare the frosting by beating the cream cheese until fluffy. Add the lemon juice and peel. Gradually blend in the sugar and beat until well blended. Stir in the food color. Crush one grapefruit section and blend it into the frosting.
5. With a serrated knife, cut the cake crosswise to make 2 layers. Fill with most of the grapefruit sections and half of the frosting. Ice the cake with the remaining frosting and top with grapefruit sections.

Maggie Inouye's 50th State Cake

HAWAII

Adapted from Toupin, *Hawaii Cookbook & Backyard Luau*

Cake:

1	cup butter		pinch salt
2	cups sugar	1	cup milk
5	large eggs	1	teaspoon lemon extract
3	cups cake flour	1	teaspoon vanilla extract
4½	teaspoons baking powder		

Filling:

1 4-ounce box lemon pie filling

Frosting:

2	egg whites	1	teaspoon vanilla
1	cup white corn syrup	½	cup grated fresh coconut
	pinch salt		

1. Cream the butter with the sugar and beat until light and fluffy. Add the eggs, 1 at a time, beating well after each addition.
2. Sift the dry ingredients together and add them in thirds, alternating with the milk, to the creamed mixture. Stir in the extracts and pour the batter into a buttered 10-by-15-inch baking pan.
3. Bake at 350° for 40 minutes, or until done. Allow the cake to cool before filling.
4. Prepare the filling by following the box directions.
5. For the frosting, beat the egg whites until frothy.
6. Heat the corn syrup and salt until the mixture begins to boil. Stir in the vanilla. Slowly add the hot syrup to the egg whites and beat until a smooth, stiff frosting forms.
7. Spread the entire cake with the lemon filling. Allow it to set for a few minutes and ice the entire cake with the frosting. Sprinkle with the coconut.

Fudge Pudding Cake

CALIFORNIA
Adapted from *The Los Angeles Times California Cookbook*

1 cup sifted flour	2 tablespoons melted
2 teaspoons baking	shortening
powder	1 ounce unsweetened
½ teaspoon salt	chocolate, melted
½ cup sugar	¼ cup cocoa
¾ cup chopped walnuts	¾ cup light brown sugar,
½ cup milk	packed
1 teaspoon vanilla	1¾ cups hot water

1. Sift the flour, baking powder, salt, and sugar together. Add the nuts, then the milk, vanilla, shortening, and chocolate. Stir to blend. Pour the batter into a greased 8-inch square pan.
2. Mix the cocoa with the brown sugar. Stir in the hot water, and pour this over the batter.
3. Bake at 375° for 40 minutes.

Golf Cake

OREGON
Adapted from *The Portland Woman's Exchange Cook Book, 1913*

¾ cup butter	1 teaspoon cinnamon
1½ cups sugar	1 teaspoon cloves
4 eggs	1 teaspoon allspice
1 cup milk	3 ounces baking chocolate,
1¾ cups flour	grated
3 teaspoons baking powder	1 cup chopped walnuts

1. Cream the butter with the sugar until light and fluffy. Beat in the eggs. Add the milk and beat until smooth.
2. Sift the flour with the baking powder and spices. Stir this mixture into the creamed mixture. Add the chocolate and nuts and stir to form a smooth batter.
3. Bake in a greased 9-inch cake pan at 350° for 30 minutes, or until firm to the touch in the center.

CHOCOLATE CAKES

Potato Caramel Cake

OREGON

Adapted from *The Portland Woman's Exchange Cook Book, 1913*

⅔ cup butter	1 teaspoon nutmeg
2 cups granulated sugar	1 cup grated baking
4 eggs, separated	chocolate
½ cup milk	2 teaspoons baking powder
1 cup hot mashed potatoes	2 cups flour
1 teaspoon cinnamon	1 cup chopped walnuts
1 teaspoon cloves	

1. Cream the butter, sugar, and egg yolks together. Add the milk, mashed potatoes, spices, and chocolate. Blend until smooth.
2. Sift the baking powder with the flour and resift over the creamed mixture. Stir to incorporate.
3. Beat the whites to a stiff froth. Fold them into the batter. Fold the flour into the batter. Gently stir in the nuts. Pour the batter into a greased 9-inch loaf pan.
4. Bake at 350° for 20 minutes, or until done.

SPICE, NUT, AND FRUIT CAKES

Dumbarton Cake

OREGON

Adapted from *The Portland Woman's Exchange Cook Book, 1913*

½ pound butter	½ pound sultana raisins
1 cup sugar	½ pound candied cherries
6 eggs	grated rind of 1 lemon
3 cups flour	1 teaspoon baking powder

1. Cream the butter with the sugar until light and fluffy. Add the eggs, 2 at a time, beating well after each addition.
2. Add the flour, fruit, lemon rind, and baking powder. Beat to form a smooth batter.
3. Bake in a greased 10-inch bread tin at 300° for 2 hours.

Mountain Bartlett Pear Cake

CALIFORNIA

Adapted from Berger and Custis, *Sumptuous Dining in Gaslight San Francisco 1875–1915*

2 cups sugar	2 teaspoons cinnamon
½ cup oil	1 teaspoon allspice
2 eggs, beaten	1 teaspoon nutmeg
4 cups diced Bartlett pears	2 teaspoons baking soda
2 cups sifted flour	1 teaspoon cream of tartar
1 teaspoon salt	

1. Beat the sugar, oil, and eggs together. Stir in the pears.
2. Sift the flour with the salt, cinnamon, allspice, nutmeg, baking soda, and cream of tartar. Stir this into the pear mixture briefly and pour the batter into a greased 9-by-13-inch pan.
3. Bake at 350° for at least an hour, or until it tests done.

Royal Rhubarb Cake

WASHINGTON

Adapted from Brown, *American Cooking: The Northwest*

1 pound rhubarb, trimmed, washed, and cut into ½-inch pieces	2 teaspoons baking powder
	4 tablespoons butter, chilled and cut into ¼-inch bits
¾ cup sugar, divided	1 egg, lightly beaten
1 cup all-purpose flour	3 tablespoons milk
1 tablespoon freshly grated orange peel	3 tablespoons orange juice concentrate
1 teaspoon ground cinnamon	

1. Arrange the rhubarb on the bottom of a greased and floured 8-inch square baking dish.
2. Mix ½ cup of the sugar, 2 tablespoons of the flour, the orange peel, and the cinnamon together and sprinkle the mixture over the rhubarb.
3. Sift the remaining flour and sugar with the baking powder. Rub in the butter to form coarse meal.
4. Mix the egg with the milk and add it to the flour mixture to form a smooth, thick batter. Spoon this mixture over the rhubarb, covering completely.
5. Bake at 350° for 25 minutes.
6. Brush the top of the cake with the orange juice concentrate and bake for 15 minutes longer, or until the top is brown and a toothpick inserted in the center comes out clean.

SPICE, NUT, AND FRUIT CAKES

Pineapple Nut Cake

HAWAII
Adapted from Toupin, *Hawaii Cookbook & Backyard Luau*

¾ cup flour
¼ teaspoon baking soda
1 teaspoon salt
½ cup butter, melted
1 cup sugar
2 eggs, beaten

6 ounces crushed pineapple, drained
½ cup chopped nuts
1 cup sweetened whipped cream

1. Sift the flour, baking soda, and salt together.
2. Beat the melted butter with the sugar. Add the beaten eggs and mix well.
3. Beat in the flour mixture, stirring until well blended. Add the pineapple and nuts and mix well.
4. Pour the batter into a greased 9-inch square cake pan.
5. Bake at 325° for 1 hour. Allow to cool.
6. Top with the whipped cream before serving.

Paradise Fruit Cake

HAWAII
Adapted from Toupin, *Hawaii Cookbook & Backyard Luau*

2 cups flour
1 teaspoon baking powder
½ teaspoon salt
1 cup dried, grated coconut
2 cups currants
6–8 slices candied pineapple cut into narrow wedges
½ pound whole red candied cherries

½ cup chopped unsalted macadamia nuts
½ cup citron, chopped
½ cup orange peel
½ cup lemon peel
1 cup butter
1 cup sugar
3 medium-size eggs, beaten
½ cup sherry

1. Sift the flour, baking powder, and salt together. Resift these ingredients over the fruit, nuts, and peels.
2. Cream the butter with the sugar until light and fluffy. Add the beaten eggs and blend thoroughly. Fold this into the floured fruits and nuts. Mix well and add the sherry. Pour the batter into a greased and parchment-lined 10-inch springform pan.
3. Bake in a pan of water at 300° for 1½–2 hours, or until set.

Old-Time San Francisco Sponge Cake

CALIFORNIA

Adapted from Berger and Custis, *Sumptuous Dining in Gaslight San Francisco 1875–1915*

1	teaspoon vanilla	6	eggs, separated
1	teaspoon grated orange peel	1	cup sifted cake flour
½	cup water	½	teaspoon salt
1	cup sugar	½	teaspoon cream of tartar

1. Mix the vanilla, orange peel, water, and sugar together. Beat in the egg yolks until the mixture is light and fluffy. Fold in the flour.
2. Whip the egg whites until foamy. Add the salt and the cream of tartar and continue to beat until the whites are stiff but not dry. Fold them into the batter to form a smooth mixture.
3. Bake the cake in an ungreased 10-inch tube pan at 350° for 50 minutes, or until it is firm to the touch in the center. Invert the pan to cool.

Carrot-Raisin Sourdough Cake

ALASKA

Adapted from *Cooking Alaskan*

1	cup flour	½	cup vegetable oil
1	teaspoon baking powder	½	cup sourdough starter
½	teaspoon salt	1	cup coarsely grated carrots
1	teaspoon cinnamon	½	cup seedless raisins
½	teaspoon baking soda	2	tablespoons grated lemon peel
4	eggs, separated		
½	cup light brown sugar		

1. Combine the flour, baking powder, salt, cinnamon, and baking soda and set aside.
2. Beat the egg whites until soft peaks forms. Set aside.
3. Combine the egg yolks, sugar, oil, and starter. Mix in the carrots, raisins, and lemon peel.
4. Stir in the dry ingredients, then fold in the beaten egg whites. Pour the batter into a well-greased and lightly floured tube pan.
5. Bake at 350° for 30 minutes, or until the cake springs back in the center.

Pistache Cake

OREGON

Adapted from *The Portland Woman's Exchange Cook Book, 1913*

12 eggs, separated	1 cup grated pistachio nuts
2 tablespoons sugar	2 cups sweetened whipped
1 teaspoon almond extract	cream
¾ pound grated walnuts	

1. Beat the egg yolks until pale and thick. Beat in the sugar and almond extract. Add the walnuts and pistachio nuts while beating.
2. Whip the egg whites stiff, but not dry. Fold them into the nut mixture.
3. Pour the batter into 3 greased 8-inch cake pans.
4. Bake at 325° for 30 minutes, or until set.
5. When cool, fill and frost the cake with the whipped cream.

Bread Cake

OREGON

Adapted from *The Portland Woman's Exchange Cook Book, 1913*

½ cup butter, softened	1½ cups flour
1 cup risen bread dough	½ teaspoon baking soda
1 egg, beaten	1 teaspoon cinnamon
1 cup light brown sugar	¼ teaspoon cloves
½ cup buttermilk	¼ teaspoon mace
1 cup raisins, seeded and	¼ teaspoon nutmeg
chopped	1 teaspoon salt

1. Beat the butter into the bread dough. Add the egg, brown sugar, and buttermilk. Beat until smooth.
2. Toss the raisins with 2 tablespoons of the flour. Stir this into the dough.
3. Sift the remaining flour with the baking soda, spices, and salt. Beat this mixture into the batter.
4. Place the dough into a buttered 10-inch loaf pan and allow to rise 1 hour.
5. Bake at 350° for 1 hour.

The Techau Torte

CALIFORNIA

Adapted from Berger and Custis, *Sumptuous Dining in Gaslight San Francisco 1875–1915*

Cake:

6 eggs	4 ounces flour
4 ounces sugar	4 ounces melted butter

Mocha filling:

6 ounces butter	¼ cup water
4 egg whites	coffee extract
½ cup sugar	

1. Beat the eggs and sugar together over hot water until warm. Remove the pan from the water and continue to beat until the mixture is cool and light.
2. Fold in the flour, mixing gently, and add the butter, mixing until light.
3. Bake in a greased 10-inch cake pan at 350° for 25 minutes. When cool, cut the cake into 3 layers.
4. Prepare the filling by creaming the butter until light.
5. Beat the egg whites to a stiff froth.
6. Dissolve the sugar in the ¼ cup water and boil it until a syrup forms at the soft ball stage. Pour the syrup into the beaten egg whites and beat until stiff and glossy.
7. Beat in the butter and coffee extract to taste. Spread it generously between the torte layers.

Marionberry Cheesecake with Walnut Crust

OREGON

Adapted from Brooks, *Oregon's Cuisine of the Rain*

Cake:

1½	cups flour	6	tablespoons unsalted
1½	cups walnuts,		butter, chilled
	ground	1	teaspoon vanilla

Filling:

2½	pounds cream cheese	¼	cup heavy cream
1	cup sugar	¼	cup all-purpose flour
4	eggs	1	teaspoon salt
2	egg yolks	1	cup marionberry conserve

1. Add the flour and walnuts to a food processor. Add the butter and pulse. Add the vanilla and mix until a dough just forms.
2. Press into the bottom of a 10-inch springform pan. Chill until ready for use.
3. Bake the chilled crust in a 400° oven for 15 minutes, or until lightly browned.
4. To make the filling, mix the cream cheese with the sugar until dissolved. Add the eggs and yolks, 1 at a time, each being incorporated before the next addition. Add the cream.
5. Gently mix in the flour and salt. Fold in the conserve until uniformly blended.
6. Pour the filling into the crust. Wrap the bottom of the springform pan with foil and place it into a pan with water to come up half the height of the springform.
7. Bake at 400° for 1½ hours, or until set in the middle. Allow to cool to room temperature.

Chocolate Mayonnaise Cupcakes

CALIFORNIA
Adapted from *The Los Angeles Times California Cookbook*

Cupcakes:

3 cups sifted flour	½ tablespoon baking soda
1½ cups sugar	1½ cups mayonnaise
⅓ cup cocoa	1½ cups water
2 teaspoons baking powder	1½ teaspoons vanilla

Chocolate frosting:

3 tablespoons butter or margarine	2 cups powdered sugar
2 ounces semisweet chocolate	2–4 tablespoons hot milk
	½ teaspoon vanilla

1. Sift the flour with the sugar, cocoa, baking powder, and baking soda.
2. Stir in the mayonnaise until smooth. Stir in the water and vanilla.
3. Fill 2 greased or paper-lined muffin pans half full with batter.
4. Bake at 350° for 25–30 minutes.
5. Prepare the frosting by melting the butter or margarine and chocolate in the top of a double boiler.
6. Sift the powdered sugar and add to the chocolate mixture. Stir to blend. Beat in enough hot milk to make a spreadable consistency. Beat in the vanilla.
7. Spread on cooled cakes.

ROLL CAKE

Baked in Pineapple Cake Roll

HAWAII

Adapted from Toupin, *Hawaii Cookbook & Backyard Luau*

2½	cups crushed pineapple	4	egg whites
⅔	cup light brown sugar	¾	cup sifted flour
2	tablespoons chopped nuts	1	teaspoon baking powder
1	tablespoon butter	½	teaspoon salt
4	egg yolks	1	cup heavy cream, whipped
⅔	cup sugar, divided		and sweetened
½	teaspoon vanilla		

1. Drain the pineapple thoroughly and spread it over the bottom of an ungreased 10-by-15-inch pan.
2. Cover the pineapple with the brown sugar and nuts. Dot the surface with butter.
3. Beat the egg yolks until thick and pale. Beat in ¼ cup of the sugar and the vanilla.
4. Beat the egg whites to form soft peaks. Add the remaining sugar and beat to form stiff peaks. Fold this into the egg yolk mixture.
5. Sift the flour, baking powder, and salt together. Gradually fold the flour mixture into the egg mixture. Spread the batter over the pineapple base in the pan.
6. Bake at 375° for 20 minutes. Loosen the edges and invert the cake onto a towel and roll it up. Allow it to cool.
7. Unroll, spread with the whipped cream, and reroll. Dust the cake with powdered sugar.

Cookies

Cookies

Wendy's Lemon Drop Cookies

NEW HAMPSHIRE
Adapted from Berquist, *The High Maples Farm Cookbook*

2 cups sugar
½ cup (1 stick) butter
2 large eggs
1 cup sour cream
½ teaspoon baking soda

¼ cup lemon juice
   grated peel of 1 lemon
3 cups sifted flour
   sugar

1. Cream the sugar and butter together until light and fluffy. Beat in the eggs.
2. Add the sour cream, baking soda, lemon juice, and peel and beat until smooth. Add the flour and mix well.
3. Drop the dough by teaspoonfuls onto a greased cookie sheet.
4. Bake at 350° for 15–18 minutes. Sprinkle with sugar while warm.

Twiddie's Molasses Cookies

MAINE
Adapted from Roux, *What's Cooking Down in Maine*

1 cup shortening
1 cup sugar
2 eggs
1 cup molasses
3½ cups flour

2 teaspoons baking soda
1 teaspoon salt
1 teaspoon ginger
1 teaspoon cinnamon
½ cup cold water

1. Cream the shortening and sugar together. Add the eggs and molasses.
2. Sift the flour, baking soda, salt, ginger, and cinnamon together. Add alternately with the cold water to the creamed mixture.
3. Drop large spoonfuls on a greased cookie sheet.
4. Bake at 350° for 10 minutes, or until nicely done.

DROP AND SHAPED COOKIES

Lilies

VERMONT

Adapted from *Out of Vermont Kitchens*

2 eggs, lightly beaten	1 teaspoon vanilla
pinch salt	¼ cup boiling water
1 cup sugar	1 cup whipping cream
1 cup flour	¼ cup sugar
1 teaspoon baking powder	½ cup orange marmalade

1. Mix the eggs, salt, and sugar together, then beat in ½ cup of the flour.
2. Add the other ½ cup flour with the baking powder. Continue to beat while adding the vanilla and boiling water. The batter will be thin.
3. Drop tablespoons of the batter on buttered cookie sheets.
4. Bake at 375° for 3–5 minutes.
5. Remove immediately and shape over custard cups to produce a lily shape.
6. Whip the cream with the sugar and fill the lilies just before serving. Add a bit of orange marmalade to the center to imitate the spadix.

Makes about 3 dozen

Cranberry Oatmeal Cookies

MASSACHUSETTS

Adapted from Hawkins, Havemeyer, and Havemeyer, *Nantucket and Other New England Cooking*

2 cups flour	2 eggs
2 cups sugar	juice and grated rind of 1
4 teaspoons baking powder	orange
1 teaspoon salt	3 cups rolled oats
1 teaspoon grated nutmeg	1 cup cranberries, halved
1 cup vegetable shortening	

1. Sift the flour, sugar, baking powder, salt, and nutmeg together.
2. Add the shortening, eggs, orange juice and rind. Mix well.
3. Stir in the oats and cut cranberries. Drop by tablespoons onto greased cookie sheets.
4. Bake at 375° for 10–12 minutes.

Original Nestlé Toll House Chocolate Chip Cookies

MASSACHUSETTS
Adapted from *Best-Loved Cookies*

2¼ cups flour	¾ cup light brown sugar
1 teaspoon baking soda	1 teaspoon vanilla
1 teaspoon salt	2 eggs
8 ounces (2 sticks) unsalted butter	2 cups (1 12-ounce package) semisweet chocolate chips
¾ cup sugar	1 cup chopped walnuts

1. Mix the flour, baking soda, and salt together.
2. Cream the butter with both sugars until light and fluffy.
3. Stir in the vanilla and add the eggs 1 at a time, beating well after each addition. Gently stir in the flour mixture to form a smooth dough. Fold in the chocolate chips and nuts.
4. Drop by heaping tablespoonsful onto an ungreased or parchment-lined baking sheet.
5. Bake at 375° for 20–30 minutes, or until golden brown. Cool on wire racks.

Cry-Baby Cookies

NEW HAMPSHIRE
Adapted from Berquist, *The High Maples Farm Cookbook*

2½ cups all-purpose flour	¾ cup softened butter
2 teaspoons baking powder	1 cup sugar
½ teaspoon ground cloves	1 egg
½ teaspoon allspice	4 tablespoons light molasses
½ teaspoon cinnamon	sugar
¼ teaspoon ginger	

1. Sift the flour, baking powder, and spices together twice.
2. Cream the butter and sugar together until light and fluffy. Beat in the egg.
3. Mix in portions of the flour mixture alternating with the molasses. Chill the dough thoroughly.
4. Roll the dough into ½-inch balls. Dip each in sugar and place the balls, sugar side up, on a greased cookie sheet.
5. Bake at 375° degrees for 10 minutes.

ROLL, SLICE, AND CUT COOKIES

Mother's Maple Icebox Cookies

NEW HAMPSHIRE
Adapted from Berquist, *The High Maples Farm Cookbook*

3½ cups all purpose-flour	¾ cup softened butter
¼ teaspoon salt	1 egg, beaten
1 teaspoon cream of tartar	½ teaspoon vanilla
½ teaspoon baking soda	1 cup broken walnuts
1 cup soft maple sugar	

1. Sift the flour, salt, cream of tartar, and baking soda together.
2. Cream the sugar and butter until light and fluffy. Add the egg and vanilla. Mix briefly. Stir in the flour mixture, roll the dough into a cylinder, and chill until firm.
3. Slice into thin cookies. Press a few walnut pieces into each cookie and place them on an ungreased cookie sheet.
4. Bake at 350° for 10 minutes, or until nicely browned.

Grandmother Smith's Shin-Plasters

NEW HAMPSHIRE
Adapted from Berquist, *The High Maples Farm Cookbook*

3 cups all-purpose flour	½ cup dark molasses
1 teaspoon ginger	½ cup sugar
½ teaspoon salt	½ cup butter
1 teaspoon baking soda	1 large egg

1. Sift the flour, ginger, salt, and baking soda together.
2. Heat the dark molasses, sugar, and butter in a saucepan to boiling. Allow to cool. Add the egg and beat well.
3. Stir in the flour mixture to form a soft dough. Chill overnight.
4. Roll the dough very thin and cut with a large cookie cutter. Place on a greased cookie sheet.
5. Bake at 350° degrees for 3–5 minutes.

Butterscotch Ice Box Cookies

CONNECTICUT
Adapted from *The Neighborhood Cook Book*

2 cups light brown sugar	3 cups flour
½ cup shortening	1½ teaspoons cream of tartar
2 eggs, beaten	1 teaspoon baking soda
2 teaspoons vanilla	1 teaspoon salt

1. Cream the sugar and shortening together. Add the eggs and vanilla. Mix well.
2. Sift the dry ingredients together. Add them to the creamed mixture. Mix to form a dough. Form into an oblong shape and refrigerate overnight.
3. Slice into ½-inch pieces and place on an ungreased cookie sheet.
4. Bake at 350° for 10 minutes, or until done.

Marshmallow Gnomes

MASSACHUSETTS
Adapted from *Boston Chapter, No. 28 Order of Eastern Star Cook Book*

2 heaping cups sugar	1 egg yolk
1 cup butter	1 tablespoon candied caraway
2 eggs, well beaten	seeds
4 cups flour	marshmallows

1. Cream the sugar and butter together until fluffy. Add the beaten eggs and the flour. Mix until smooth.
2. Roll into thin sheets and cut into large discs. Brush each with the egg yolk and sprinkle with candied caraway seeds.
3. Fold the edges over to form triangles, placing a marshmallow in the center of each.
4. Bake on greased cookie sheets at 400° until brown.

ROLL, SLICE, AND CUT COOKIES

Joe Froggers

MASSACHUSETTS
Adapted from *Recipes, American Cooking: New England*

3½ cups flour
2 teaspoons ground ginger
½ teaspoon ground cloves
½ teaspoon ground nutmeg,
   fresh if possible
¼ teaspoon ground allspice
1½ teaspoons salt

1 cup molasses
1 teaspoon baking soda
4 ounces butter
1 cup sugar
2 tablespoons dark rum
6 fluid ounces water

1. Sift the flour with the spices and salt.
2. Mix the molasses with the baking soda. Stir until foaming subsides.
3. Cream the butter with the sugar until light and fluffy. Beat in the molasses mixture. Mix the rum with the water and add it to the creaming mixture. Mix to incorporate.
4. Stir in the flour mixture a little at a time to form a smooth dough. Wrap the dough in plastic and refrigerate overnight.
5. Roll out the dough to a thickness of 1/3 to 14-inch on a floured surface. Cut 3-inch circles and place them two inches apart on grease cookie sheets.
6. Bake at 375° for 10 to 15 minutes, or until the edges are crisp and the centers are firm to the touch.

Mae's Overnight Cookies (Tried and True)

MASSACHUSETTS
Adapted from *Boston Chapter, No. 28 Order of Eastern Star Cook Book*

1 cup light brown sugar
½ cup melted butter
1 egg
¼ teaspoon salt

1 teaspoon vanilla
1¾ cups pastry flour
½ teaspoon baking soda
½ cup chopped nuts

1. Mix all the ingredients together thoroughly.
2. Line a bread tin with wax paper and press the dough in and pat it down. Refrigerate overnight.
3. Remove the dough from the refrigerator and slice into cookies. Place on greased cookie sheets.
4. Bake at 350° for 10 minutes, or until done.

"Very nice for children's lunches."

Dorothy's Blond Brownies

NEW HAMPSHIRE
Adapted from Berquist, *The High Maples Farm Cookbook*

1½ cups all-purpose flour
2 teaspoons baking powder
½ teaspoon salt
½ cup butter, melted

2 cups light brown sugar
2 eggs
2 teaspoons vanilla
1 cup broken pecan meats

1. Sift the flour, baking powder, and salt together.
2. To the melted butter, add the brown sugar. Beat in the eggs and vanilla until smooth. Stir in the flour mixture and nut meats.
3. Spread the batter into a greased 9-inch square baking pan.
4. Bake at 350° for 20 minutes, or until set.

Butterscotch Meringue Bars

NEW HAMPSHIRE
Adapted from Berquist, *The High Maples Farm Cookbook*

2 cups all-purpose flour
1 teaspoon baking powder
¼ teaspoon salt
½ cup softened butter
½ cup sugar
2 eggs, separated

2 teaspoons vanilla, divided
4 tablespoons heavy cream
1 cup broken pecan meats
1 cup sifted light brown sugar

1. Sift the flour, baking powder, and salt together.
2. Cream the butter and the sugar until light and fluffy. Beat in the egg yolks and 1 teaspoon of the vanilla.
3. Stir in the flour mixture and the cream. Mix in the pecans.
4. Spread the mixture evenly into a greased 8-by-11-inch pan.
5. Bake at 350° for 15 minutes. Allow to cool while preparing the top layer.
6. Beat the egg whites until shiny. Whisk in the remaining vanilla. Fold in the brown sugar. Spread this meringue over the baked layer.
7. Bake at 275° for 45 minutes. Cut into bars.

BARS AND BROWNIES

Maple Butternut Bars

NEW HAMPSHIRE
Adapted from Berquist, *The High Maples Farm Cookbook*

1 cup all-purpose flour	2 large eggs, beaten until
½ teaspoon baking powder	light
¼ teaspoon salt	½ cup broken butternut
½ cup soft maple sugar	meats (or walnuts)
½ cup softened butter	

1. Sift the flour, baking powder, and salt together.
2. Cream the maple sugar and butter until light and fluffy. Add the eggs and mix well.
3. Stir in the flour mixture. Add the nut meats.
4. Spread the batter in a greased 9-inch square baking pan.
5. Bake at 375° for 30–35 minutes. Cut into squares.

North Atlantic

DROP AND SHAPED COOKIES

Warts

DELAWARE
Adapted from *Winterthur's Culinary Collection*

1 cup sugar	½ teaspoon salt
½ cup butter or lard	¼ teaspoon cloves, ground
1 egg	¼ teaspoon ginger, ground
½ cup molasses	¼ teaspoon mace, ground
⅓ cup cold water	1 cup raisins
3 cups flour	1 cup walnuts
1 teaspoon baking soda	

1. Cream the sugar and butter or lard. Add the egg, molasses, and water.
2. Sift the flour with the baking soda, salt, and spices. Add to the butter mixture. Fold in the raisins and walnuts.
3. Drop the mixture onto greased and floured cookie sheets to form small balls.
4. Bake at 350° for 12–15 minutes.

Aunt Anna's Cream Cheese Cookies

NEW YORK

Adapted from *A Library of Favorite Recipes from New York State*

½ pound cream cheese	5 teaspoons baking powder
½ pound Crisco	4 teaspoons vanilla
2 cups sugar	7 cups flour
4 eggs	

1. Cream the cream cheese and Crisco well. Add the sugar, 1 cup at a time, and beat until fluffy. Add the eggs, 1 at a time, and mix well.
2. Add the baking powder and vanilla. Add the flour, 1 cup at a time, mixing well.
3. Drop by teaspoons onto a greased cookie sheet.
4. Bake at 350° for 10–15 minutes, until light brown.

Italian Chocolate Cookies

NEW YORK

Adapted from *A Library of Favorite Recipes from New York State*

Cookies:

6 cups flour	2 teaspoons vanilla
1 cup cocoa	1½ cups hot water
2 cups sugar	3 eggs
5 teaspoons baking powder	1 cup grape jelly
1 teaspoon cloves	1 cup chopped walnuts
1 teaspoon cinnamon	

Glaze:

1 cup powdered sugar	milk
1 teaspoon vanilla	

1. For the cookies, sift the dry ingredients together. Make a well in the center and add the vanilla, water, eggs, jelly, and nuts. Mix well.
2. Roll into balls, using 1 tablespoon dough for each cookie. Place on greased cookie sheets.
3. Bake at 375° for 10 minutes. Cool on a rack.
4. Mix the powdered sugar and vanilla. Add milk by tablespoons to make a thin glaze. Drizzle over the cookies.

Honey Cakes

PENNSYLVANIA
Adapted from Lestz, *The Pennsylvania Dutch Cookbook*

1 quart honey	2 pounds and 5 ounces bread
½ cup butter	flour
2 tablespoons baking soda	4 egg whites
4 egg yolks, well beaten	

1. Boil the honey and skim the surface.
2. Add the butter and allow to cool until the mixture is lukewarm. Add the baking soda dissolved in a little warm water.
3. Add the egg yolks, then stir in the flour.
4. Beat the egg whites until stiff and fold into the batter. Refrigerate for 1½ hours before baking.
5. Drop by the teaspoonful on a greased and floured cookie sheet.
6. Bake at 375° for 10 minutes.

Makes 200 cookies

Chocolate Hermits

PENNSYLVANIA
Adapted from *Choice Recipes*

½ cup butter	2 teaspoons baking powder
⅔ cup sugar	¼ teaspoon salt
2 eggs	¼ cup grated chocolate,
½ cup seeded raisins	melted
2 cups flour	1 teaspoon cinnamon

1. Cream the butter and sugar. Add the eggs and raisins.
2. Sift the flour, baking powder, and salt together and add it, stirring to form a smooth mixture.
3. Add the chocolate and cinnamon. Drop by spoonfuls onto a greased cookie sheet.
4. Bake at 350° for 10–12 minutes, or until done.

Lepp Cookies

PENNSYLVANIA

Adapted from Lestz, *The Pennsylvania Dutch Cookbook*

1¾ cups shortening	1 tablespoon baking soda
2 pounds light brown sugar	6 tablespoons baking powder
3 eggs	1 teaspoon cream of tartar
1 pint sour cream	½ teaspoon salt
8½ cups flour	

1. Cream the shortening. Add the sugar and continue to beat until fluffy.
2. Add the eggs, mixing well. Add the sour cream.
3. Sift all the dry ingredients and add them to form a smooth dough("more flour may be needed").
4. Drop by tablespoonfuls onto a greased cookie sheet.
5. Bake at 350° for 10–12 minutes.

Krunchy Drop Cookies

NEW YORK

Adapted from *A Library of Favorite Recipes from New York State*

1 cup margarine, melted	1 teaspoon baking soda
1 cup light brown sugar	½ teaspoon salt
1 cup white sugar	2 cups Rice Krispies
2 eggs	2 cups oatmeal (regular or
1 teaspoon vanilla	quick)
2 cups flour	

1. Mix the melted margarine, both sugars, eggs, and vanilla together until smooth.
2. Add the dry ingredients. Add the Rice Krispies and oatmeal.
3. Drop by spoonfuls onto ungreased cookie sheets.
4. Bake at 350° until lightly brown, about 10 minutes.

Jumbo Fruit Cookies

NEW YORK

Adapted from *A Library of Favorite Recipes from New York State*

2	cups muscat raisins	1	teaspoon baking powder
1	cup water	1	teaspoon salt
2	cups sugar	1½	teaspoons cinnamon
1	cup shortening	¼	teaspoon nutmeg
3	eggs	¼	teaspoon allspice
1	teaspoon vanilla	¼	teaspoon mace
4	cups flour		beaten egg
1	teaspoon baking soda		

1. Cook the raisins in the water for 5 minutes. Drain. Allow to cool.
2. Cream the sugar and shortening together. Add the eggs and vanilla.
3. Mix the dry ingredients together and stir in the raisins. Drop by large spoonfuls on a greased cookie sheet. Pat each cookie thin and brush with beaten egg.
4. Bake at 350° for 20 minutes.

The Practically Perfect Cookie

NEW YORK

Adapted from *A Library of Favorite Recipes from New York State*

2¼	cups flour	2	sticks unsalted butter, soft
1	teaspoon baking soda	1	teaspoon vanilla extract
1	teaspoon salt	2	large eggs
¾	cup sugar	12	ounces semisweet chocolate
¾	cup light brown sugar, packed		chips

1. Sift the flour, baking soda, and salt together.
2. Mix the two sugars together. Cream with the butter until fluffy. Beat in the vanilla.
3. Add the eggs and beat 1 minute.
4. Add the dry ingredients ½ cup at a time, mixing to form a smooth dough. Scrape down the bowl and add the chocolate chips. Mix briefly.
5. Put tablespoons of the dough on an ungreased cookie sheet.
6. Bake at 375° until the cookies are pale golden brown, about 10 minutes.

Sugar and Spice Cookies

NEW JERSEY
Adapted from *Chicken Foot Soup and Other Recipes from the Pine Barrens*

¾ cup vegetable shortening	2 teaspoons baking soda
1 cup sugar	¼ teaspoon salt
1 egg	1 teaspoon cinnamon
¼ cup molasses	¾ teaspoon cloves
2 cups flour	powdered sugar

1. Cream the shortening, sugar, egg, and molasses together until smooth.
2. Sift the flour, baking soda, salt, cinnamon, and cloves together and stir into the creamed mixture.
3. Form the dough into 1-inch balls and place them 2 inches apart on greased cookie sheets.
4. Bake at 350° for 10–12 minutes.
5. Roll the cookies in powdered sugar while still warm.

Hard Ginger Cookies

PENNSYLVANIA
Adapted from Lestz, *The Pennsylvania Dutch Cookbook*

1 cup dark molasses	1 teaspoon baking soda
1 cup lard	1 tablespoon vinegar
1 cup light brown sugar	6 cups sifted flour
1 egg	2 tablespoons cinnamon
2 teaspoons ginger	sugar

1. In the top of a double boiler melt the molasses, lard, and brown sugar.
2. Allow the mixture to cool and add the egg, ginger, and baking soda dissolved in the vinegar.
3. Add the flour to form a stiff dough. Roll out very thin. Cut and sprinkle with cinnamon sugar.
4. Bake at 375° for 7–10 minutes.

ROLL, SLICE, AND CUT COOKIES

Grandma's Christmas Biscuits

PENNSYLVANIA
Adapted from Lestz, *The Pennsylvania Dutch Cookbook*

½ pound butter
1 pound sugar
1 cup milk
1 teaspoon cream of tartar

1 teaspoon baking soda
¼ cup hot water
flour

1. Cream the butter and beat in the sugar, milk, and cream of tartar.
2. Dissolve the baking soda in the hot water and add it to the mixture.
3. Add enough flour to make a stiff dough. Mix until smooth. Refrigerate overnight.
4. Roll out and cut into circles. Place on greased cookie sheets.
5. Bake at 375° for 15 minutes.

Poppy Seed Nut Slices

DELAWARE
Adapted from *Winterthur's Culinary Collection*

1 cup butter, softened
1 cup sugar
1 egg
1 teaspoon vanilla
½ teaspoon cinnamon

½ cup poppy seeds
1½ cups walnuts or pecans
2 cups flour
¼ teaspoon salt
2 tablespoons sugar

1. Cream the butter with the 1 cup sugar. Add the egg, vanilla, and cinnamon. Beat 2–3 minutes. Stir in the poppy seeds and nuts.
2. Stir in the flour and salt gradually. Chill the dough until firm.
3. Roll the dough into 2 logs of 2-inch diameter. Roll the logs in the 2 tablespoons sugar to coat them. Slice into ¼-inch thick cookies. Arrange on an ungreased cookie sheet.
4. Bake at 325° for 20 minutes, or until just browned.

Rose's Rogelach

NEW YORK

Adapted from *A Library of Favorite Recipes from New York State*

½ pound cream cheese	1½ cups sugar
½ pound butter	1½ cups ground walnuts
2 cups flour	

1. Combine the cream cheese and butter. Cream for 2 minutes.
2. Add the flour. Mix until smooth, then work it into a ball and refrigerate overnight.
3. Divide the dough into 4 parts. Roll each section into an oblong shape, as thin as possible, between sheets of waxed paper.
4. Spread equal amounts of sugar and walnuts on the dough. Roll them up, jelly-roll fashion, and place on an unbuttered baking sheet.
5. Bake at 350° for 15–20 minutes, until lightly browned.
6. Remove from the oven and cut into 1-inch pieces while warm.

Refrigerator Cookies

NEW JERSEY

Adapted from *Chicken Foot Soup and Other Recipes from the Pine Barrens*

2 cups sugar	½ cup smooth peanut butter
½ cup milk	1 teaspoon vanilla
¼ pound butter	2¾ cups rolled oats
4 heaping tablespoons cocoa	

1. Cook the sugar with the milk, butter, and cocoa over low heat until the butter has melted. Beat in the peanut butter, vanilla, and oats, mixing well.
2. When cool, form the dough into 2 cylinders, wrap them in plastic film, and refrigerate overnight.
3. Slice the dough into cookies with a sharp knife dipped in hot water. Place the cookies onto ungreased cookie sheets.
4. Bake at 375° for 10 minutes, or until slightly browned.

ROLL, SLICE, AND CUT COOKIES

Russian Poppy Seed Cookies

NEW YORK

Adapted from *A Library of Favorite Recipes from New York State*

¾ cup sugar
¾ cup vegetable oil
2 eggs, beaten
4 cups flour
1 teaspoon baking powder

¼ teaspoon baking soda
    dash salt
⅓ cup poppy seeds, plus additional for sprinkling
¼ cup water

1. Mix the sugar and oil together. Add the beaten eggs.
2. Add the flour, baking powder, baking soda, salt, ⅓ cup poppy seeds, and water. Mix together to form a smooth dough. Divide into 3 balls.
3. Roll out the dough and cut out with cookie cutters or a glass. Place on a greased cookie sheet. Sprinkle with poppy seeds.
4. Bake at 350° for 10–12 minutes, or until light brown.

Rolled Almond Wafers

PENNSYLVANIA

Adapted from Reed, *The Philadelphia Cook Book of Town and Country*

9 egg whites
½ pound almonds, blanched and chopped

10 ounces sugar
2 ounces flour
    pinch ground cinnamon

1. Whip the egg whites until stiff but not dry. Stir in the almonds, sugar, flour, and cinnamon.
2. Spread the batter in 2-inch squares on greased cookie sheets.
3. Bake at 400° until golden brown.
4. Remove the pans from the oven and immediately roll the cookies around small wooden sticks and press the seams together.

Cinnamon Stars

PENNSYLVANIA
Adapted from *Choice Recipes*

8 egg whites	2 teaspoons grated lemon
2 cups granulated sugar	rind
6 teaspoons cinnamon	2 cups powdered sugar
2 cups finely ground almonds	

1. Whip the egg whites until frothy. Mix the sugar with the cinnamon and add it to the egg whites. Beat the mixture until it becomes very stiff. Reserve ½ cup of this mixture.
2. Add the almonds and lemon rind to the remaining mixture. Thoroughly mix in the powdered sugar.
3. Roll out to ½-inch thickness and cut into cookies with a star-shaped cutter. Brush the tops with the reserved egg white mixture.
4. Place the cookies on greased cookie sheets.
5. Bake at 350° for about 20 minutes, or until very lightly browned.

Sand Tarts

PENNSYLVANIA
Adapted from Reed, *The Philadelphia Cook Book of Town and Country*

½ pound butter	4 cups flour
2 cups light brown sugar	1 teaspoon baking powder
3 eggs, beaten lightly	sugar and cinnamon mixed
4 tablespoons milk	

1. Cream the butter and brown sugar until light and fluffy.
2. Mix the beaten eggs and milk and add this to the creamed mixture.
3. Sift the flour with the baking powder and beat this in to form a smooth dough. Refrigerate for several hours.
4. Roll the dough out as thinly as possible. Cut the dough with a cookie cutter and place the cookies on a greased cookie sheet.
5. Sprinkle the tops of the cookies with a mixture of sugar and cinnamon.
6. Bake at 375° for 10 –12 minutes.

Adirondack Brownies

NEW YORK
Adapted from *A Library of Favorite Recipes from New York State*

½	cup butter	¼	teaspoon salt
4	ounces unsweetened chocolate	1	teaspoon vanilla
		1	cup flour
4	eggs	1	cup nut meats
2	cups sugar		

1. Melt the butter and chocolate together. Beat until creamy. Add the eggs, sugar, salt, and vanilla.
2. Add the flour and beat until smooth. Add the nuts.
3. Bake in a 13-by-9-inch greased pan at 350° for 30 minutes.

Chocolate Walnut Wafers

PENNSYLVANIA
Adapted from *Choice Recipes*

¼	cup butter	¼	cup milk
½	cup powdered sugar	½	teaspoon vanilla
2	ounces grated chocolate	1	cup chopped walnuts
1	cup flour		

1. Cream the butter until light. Add the dry ingredients, milk, and vanilla.
2. Spread on greased and floured cookie sheets. Sprinkle with the chopped nuts.
3. Bake at 350° for 8 minutes.

Brown Sugar Bars

PENNSYLVANIA
Adapted from *Choice Recipes*

4	tablespoons butter or lard	1	teaspoon baking powder
1	cup dark brown sugar	1	cup flour
1	teaspoon vanilla	½	cup broken nut meats
	a little salt		

1. Mix all the ingredients together and beat for 1 minute.
2. Press into a greased 8-inch square cake pan.
3. Bake at 350° for 15 minutes, or until set.

Pumpkin Bars

NEW JERSEY

Adapted from *Chicken Foot Soup and Other Recipes from the Pine Barrens*

2 cups cooked pumpkin	1 teaspoon cinnamon
¾ cup brown sugar	1 teaspoon pumpkin pie
3 eggs	spices
¼ teaspoon ginger	½ cup evaporated milk

1. Mix all of the ingredients together in the order given, varying the amount of evaporated milk to form a stiff mixture.
2. Pour the batter into a greased and floured 8-inch square pan.
3. Bake at 375° for about an hour, or until a knife inserted in the center comes out clean.
4. Cut into squares or bars.

South Atlantic

DROP COOKIES

Oatmeal Crisp Cookies

WEST VIRGINIA

Adapted from *The Foxfire Book of Appalachian Cookery*

1 cup shortening	1½ cups flour
1 cup dark brown sugar	1 teaspoon salt
1 cup granulated sugar	1 teaspoon baking soda
2 eggs	3 cups quick-cooking oats
1 teaspoon vanilla	½ cup chopped nuts

1. Cream the shortening and both sugars together until light and smooth. Add the eggs and vanilla and beat well.
2. Sift the flour, salt, and baking soda together and add this to the creamed mixture. Beat until smooth.
3. Stir in the oatmeal and nuts.
4. Drop the dough by teaspoonfuls onto a greased cookie sheet.
5. Bake at 350° for 8–10 minutes.

Pecan Sandies

KENTUCKY
Adapted from *The Foxfire Book of Appalachian Cookery*

1 cup butter	2 teaspoons vanilla
⅓ cup sugar	2 cups sifted flour
2 teaspoons water	1 cup chopped pecans

1. Cream the butter and sugar together until light and fluffy. Add the water and vanilla and beat until smooth.
2. Blend in the flour and pecans.
3. Drop by teaspoonfuls onto an ungreased cookie sheet.
4. Bake at 325° for 15 minutes, or until lightly browned.

Pie Crust Cookies

NORTH CAROLINA
Adapted from *Pass the Plate*

4 cups flour	1 cup buttermilk
2½ cups sugar	1½ teaspoons baking soda
½ teaspoon salt	2 teaspoons vanilla
1 cup shortening	½ teaspoon cinnamon
2 eggs, beaten	

1. Sift the flour, 2 cups of the sugar, and the salt together. Cut in the shortening until fine and crumbly.
2. Combine the beaten eggs and the buttermilk. Add the baking soda to the buttermilk mixture and stir until foamy.
3. Combine the buttermilk mixture with the shortening mixture, add the vanilla, and mix to form a smooth dough.
4. Drop by heaping teaspoons onto greased baking sheets and flatten a bit.
5. Mix the remaining ½ cup sugar with the cinnamon and sprinkle this on top of the cookies.
6. Bake at 375° for about 7 minutes, or until the edges are lightly browned.

Fruit Drop Biscuits

SOUTH CAROLINA
Adapted from *The South Carolina Cook Book*

2 cups sifted flour	¾ cup milk (scant)
2½ teaspoons baking powder	1 cup apples, pared, cored,
2 tablespoons sugar	and finely chopped
4 tablespoons butter or	½ cup raisins, finely chopped
shortening	1½ teaspoons grated orange
½ teaspoon salt	rind

1. Mix the flour, baking powder, and sugar together. Stir in the shortening. Add the salt.
2. Beat in the milk to form a smooth dough. Stir in the fruit and the orange rind.
3. Drop by teaspoons on an ungreased baking sheet.
4. Bake at 450° for 12 minutes.

Billy Goat Cookies

TENNESSEE
Adapted from Dalsass, *Miss Mary's Down-Home Cooking*

⅓ cup butter, softened	1 teaspoon baking powder
⅔ cup sugar	½ teaspoon cinnamon
1 egg	¼ teaspoon ground cloves
1 tablespoon milk	8 ounces (about 1½ cups)
½ teaspoon vanilla extract	chopped dates
1⅓ cups flour	⅔ cup chopped walnuts or
¼ teaspoon baking soda	pecans

1. Cream the butter and sugar together until fluffy. Beat in the egg, milk, and vanilla.
2. Stir the flour, baking soda, baking powder, cinnamon, and cloves together. Beat into the creamed mixture and then stir in the dates and nuts.
3. Drop the batter by heaping teaspoonfuls onto greased cookie sheets.
4. Bake the cookies at 375° for 20 minutes, or until lightly browned.

Banana Oatmeal Cookies

SOUTH CAROLINA
Adapted from *A Taste of South Carolina*

¾	cup shortening	1½	cups all-purpose flour
1	cup sugar	½	teaspoon baking soda
1	egg	½	teaspoon baking powder
1	cup mashed banana	¼	teaspoon salt
1	cup quick-cooking oats, uncooked	¾	teaspoon ground cinnamon
		¼	teaspoon ground nutmeg

1. Cream the shortening and sugar until light and fluffy. Beat in the egg. Stir in the bananas and oats.
2. Combine the remaining ingredients and stir into the creamed mixture.
3. Drop by teaspoonfuls onto greased cookie sheets.
4. Bake at 400° for 13 minutes.

Squaws

VIRGINIA
Adapted from *The Junior League Cook Book*

⅔	cup butter	¼	cup flour
1	ounce bitter chocolate	1	teaspoon vanilla
1	egg	⅔	cup chopped walnuts
⅔	cup sugar		

1. Melt the butter with the chocolate and allow it to cool.
2. Beat the egg and sugar together. Stir in the flour and vanilla.
3. Stir in the chocolate mixture to form a smooth dough. Add the nuts and allow the dough to stand until firm.
4. Drop the dough by teaspoonfuls onto a greased cookie sheet.
5. Bake at 350° until just firm, about 10 minutes.

Fruit Jumbles

VIRGINIA
Adapted from *The Junior League Cook Book*

1	cup butter	½	cup milk
2	cups light brown sugar	½	teaspoon nutmeg or
3	eggs		cinnamon
3½	cups flour	1	cup currants or raisins

1. Cream the butter with the brown sugar until light. Add the eggs, 1 at a time, beating well after each addition.
2. Add the flour in thirds, alternating with the milk. Stir in the spice and currants.
3. Drop by teaspoonfuls onto a greased baking sheet.
4. Bake at 350° until done.

"Sugar and chopped almonds on top make them very nice."

Rock Cakes

VIRGINIA
Adapted from *The Junior League Cook Book*

3	eggs, separated	1½	pounds dates
1	cup butter	1½	pounds walnuts
2	cups light brown sugar	1	teaspoon cinnamon
3	cups flour	1	teaspoon baking soda
½	pound raisins	½	cup water

1. Blend the egg yolks with the butter until smooth. Beat in the brown sugar.
2. Beat in the flour, reserving 2 tablespoons to toss with the fruit. Add the fruit, nuts, and cinnamon.
3. Dissolve the baking soda in the water and add it to the dough.
4. Beat the egg whites stiff and fold them in.
5. Drop by teaspoonfuls onto greased baking sheets.
6. Bake at 325° for 30 minutes, or until done.

DROP COOKIES

Old-Fashioned Orange Drop Cookies

FLORIDA

Adapted from Nickerson, *Florida Cookbook*

3 cups sifted flour	2 teaspoons grated orange
½ teaspoon cinnamon	rind
4 teaspoons baking powder	1 egg, lightly beaten
½ cup butter, softened	½ cup orange juice
1 cup sugar	

1. Sift the flour, cinnamon, and baking powder together.
2. Cream the butter, sugar, and orange rind together until light and fluffy. Beat in the egg and orange juice.
3. Add the dry ingredients, mixing to form a smooth dough.
4. Drop by teaspoonfuls onto an ungreased cookie sheet.
5. Bake at 375° for 10 minutes, or until pale brown.

ROLL, SLICE, AND CUT COOKIES

Ice Box Tea Cakes

VIRGINIA

Adapted from *The Junior League Cook Book*

1 cup butter	4 cups flour
2 cups light brown sugar	¾ teaspoon baking soda
2 eggs	¾ teaspoon baking powder

1. Cream the butter with the brown sugar until light and fluffy. Beat in the eggs, 1 at a time.
2. Sift the flour, baking soda, and baking powder and add to the creamed mixture.
3. Roll the dough into a cylinder, wrap in plastic, and refrigerate until firm.
4. Slice the dough into ½-inch cakes and place them on a greased cookie sheet.
5. Bake at 375° for 10 minutes, or until golden brown.

Eggless Cookies

VIRGINIA
Adapted from *Marion Cook Book*

1	teaspoon baking soda	½	teaspoon salt
1	cup buttermilk	½	teaspoon grated nutmeg
1	cup vegetable shortening		flour
2	cups sugar		

1. Add the baking soda to the buttermilk. Let stand 1 minute.
2. Cream shortening with the sugar. Add the buttermilk, salt, and nutmeg.
3. Add enough flour to make a soft dough.
4. Roll out, cut into shapes, and bake on a parchment-lined cookie sheet at 425° for 8 minutes, or until browned on edge.

Miss Kate Hanes' Tea Cakes

NORTH CAROLINA
Adapted from *Pass the Plate*

2	cups light brown sugar	2	tablespoons buttermilk
¾	cup butter	1½	tablespoons lemon
2	eggs		flavoring
½	tablespoon baking soda	5½	cups flour

1. Cream the brown sugar and butter until light and fluffy. Add the eggs, mixing well after each addition.
2. Dissolve the baking soda in the buttermilk. Add this to the butter mixture along with the lemon flavoring. Mix well.
3. Add the flour, mixing to form a soft, smooth dough.
4. Roll out thinly and cut out shapes with cookie cutters. Place on ungreased cookie sheets.
5. Bake at 350° until golden.

ROLL, SLICE, AND CUT COOKIES

Kourambiades (Greek Butter Cookies)

FLORIDA

Adapted from Nickerson, *Florida Cookbook*

½ pound (2 sticks) unsalted,   1 teaspoon baking powder
    sweet butter   2⅓ cups sifted flour
¼ cup powdered sugar   powdered sugar
1 egg

1. Heat the butter until it starts to turn brown. Remove from the heat and allow to stand 5 minutes. Pour off the liquid from the solids in the pan and allow the liquid to cool until solidified.
2. Cream this butter until very fluffy. Add the sugar, creaming well, about 3 minutes. Beat in the egg.
3. Sift the baking powder with the flour and add it to the creamed mixture, beating to form a smooth dough.
4. Roll the dough into cylinders 5-inches long and ½ inch in diameter.
5. Cut each cylinder in thirds and arrange on an ungreased cookie sheet.
6. Bake at 350° for 15–20 minutes, or until the cookies are lightly colored.
7. When cool, sprinkle heavily with powdered sugar.

Caramel Cookies

KENTUCKY

Adapted from *The Foxfire Book of Appalachian Cookery*

4 cups dark brown sugar   1 tablespoon baking soda
1 cup lard   1 teaspoon cream of tartar
4 large or 5 small eggs   1 cup seedless raisins
6–7 cups flour   1 teaspoon vanilla

1. Cream the brown sugar and lard together. Add the eggs, one at a time, beating well after each addition.
2. Sift the flour with the baking soda and cream of tartar. Beat into the creamed mixture. Add the raisins and vanilla and beat until smooth.
3. Form the dough into cylinders and refrigerate for an hour.
4. Slice into thin cookies and place them on a greased cookie sheet. Leave plenty of room between each cookie, as they will spread.
5. Bake at 350° for 10–15 minutes. Remove the cookies from the pan while hot.

Molasses Wafers

APPALACHIA

Adapted from *The Foxfire Book of Appalachian Cookery*

1 cup molasses	1½ teaspoons salt
¼ cup butter	1 tablespoon baking soda
¼ cup shortening	2 tablespoons milk
1 tablespoon ginger	3 cups flour

1. Heat the molasses to boiling. Stir in the butter and shortening.
2. Mix in the ginger and salt.
3. Dissolve the baking soda in the milk and add it to the molasses mixture.
4. Stir in the flour in portions, beating until smooth.
5. Roll the dough thin and cut out 2-inch circles. Place the cookies on greased cookie sheets.
6. Bake at 350° until done.

Peanut Wafers

VIRGINIA

Adapted from *Marion Cook Book*

2 tablespoons butter, softened	1 pint shelled peanuts, crushed
1 cup sugar	2 tablespoons milk
3 eggs	all-purpose flour

1. Cream the butter with the sugar. Add the eggs and beat 1 minute.
2. Stir in the peanuts and milk. Add enough flour to make a rollable dough.
3. Roll to ⅛-inch thick.
4. Cut and bake on a parchment-lined baking sheet at 425° for 10 minutes.

South Carolina Finger Chews

SOUTH CAROLINA
Adapted from *A Taste of South Carolina*

Cookies:

1	cup light brown sugar	1	cup grated coconut
1	cup butter	2	cups coarsely chopped
2	cups plain flour		pecans
4	eggs, lightly beaten	1	teaspoon salt
¼	cup flour	½	teaspoon vanilla
3	cups dark brown sugar		

Orange glaze:

1	cup powdered sugar	½	teaspoon orange rind
1	tablespoon orange juice		

1. Mix the first 3 ingredients together and spread evenly over a greased 8-by-12-inch pan.
2. Bake at 350° for 15 minutes. Remove from the oven and cool.
3. Mix the rest of the cookie ingredients together and spread on the cooled layer.
4. Bake at 325° for 35–40 minutes, or until cookie is firm.
5. For the orange glaze, mix the powdered sugar with the orange juice and orange rind. Dribble the glaze over the top while the cookie is still warm.
6. When cold, cut into fingers.

Marshmallow–Chocolate Chip Bars

NORTH CAROLINA
Adapted from *Pass the Plate*

½	cup margarine	¼	teaspoon salt
½	cup sugar	1	cup pecans
1	whole egg	½	cup chocolate chips
2	eggs, separated	1	cup miniature
½	cup flour		marshmallows
1	teaspoon baking powder	1	cup light brown sugar

1. Cream the margarine and sugar together until light and fluffy. Add the whole egg and 2 egg yolks, beating well.
2. Add the flour, baking powder, and salt. Mix to form a smooth dough. Spread the dough into a greased 9-by-13-inch pan. Sprinkle on the pecans and chocolate chips, followed by the marshmallows.
3. Beat the egg whites until firm. Add the brown sugar and beat to form stiff peaks. Spread this over the marshmallows, maintaining the layers as carefully as possible.
4. Bake at 350° for 30 – 40 minutes.
5. Slice into bars when cooled.

Brownies

VIRGINIA
Adapted from *The Junior League Cook Book*

1	cup sugar	2	ounces unsweetened choco-
¼	cup melted butter		late, melted
1	egg, beaten	½	cup flour
¾	teaspoon vanilla	½	cup nuts, chopped

1. Mix the ingredients together in the order given. Beat until smooth.
2. Pour the batter into a parchment-lined 7-inch square pan.
3. Bake at 325° until done, about 40 minutes.
4. Cut in squares while hot.

Cheesecake Bars

FLORIDA

Adapted from *Palm Beach Entertains Then and Now*

5	tablespoons butter	8	ounces softened cream cheese
⅓	cup light brown sugar	1	egg
1	cup sifted flour	2	tablespoons milk
¼	cup chopped walnuts	1	tablespoon lemon juice
½	cup sugar	½	teaspoon vanilla

1. Cream the butter and the brown sugar together until light and fluffy. Add the flour and nuts, mixing well. Set aside 1 cup of this mixture for the topping.
2. Press the remaining dough into the bottom of a greased 8-inch square pan.
3. Bake at 350° for 12–15 minutes.
4. Beat the sugar and the cream cheese together until smooth. Add the egg, milk, lemon juice, and vanilla. Beat until smooth.
5. Spread this over the baked bottom crust. Sprinkle with the reserved topping and continue to bake 25 minutes longer.
6. Allow to cool and cut into bars.

Benne Seed Cookies

GEORGIA

Adapted from DeBolt, *Savannah Sampler Cookbook*

6 ounces butter
1½ cups packed light brown
   sugar
2 eggs
1¼ cups flour

½ cup benne seeds [sesame
   seeds]
1 teaspoon vanilla
¼ teaspoon baking powder

1. Cream the butter and sugar.
2. Add the remaining ingredients in the order given, to form a dough.
3. Drop teaspoons of cookie dough onto a parchment-lined cookie sheet.
4. Bake at 325° for 15–20 minutes.

Makes 36
"These cookies burn easily."

Pecan Lace Cookies

LOUISIANA

Adapted from *Feibleman, American Cooking: Creole and Acadian*

½ cup flour
1 teaspoon baking powder
⅛ teaspoon salt
2 tablespoons butter,
   softened

2 cups sugar
2 eggs, well beaten
1 teaspoon vanilla extract
2 cups coarsely chopped
   pecans

1. Sift the flour, baking powder, and salt together.
2. Cream the butter with the sugar. Beat in the eggs and the vanilla extract.
3. Stir in the flour mixture. Mix to form a smooth dough. Stir in the pecans.
4. Drop the dough by the heaping teaspoonful onto greased and floured baking sheets, spacing the cookies about 3 inches apart.
5. Bake at 400° for 5 minutes, or until the cookies have a lacelike appearance and are golden brown.

Lizzies

GEORGIA

Adapted from DeBolt, *Savannah Sampler Cookbook*

3 cups white seedless raisins	½ cup light brown sugar, firmly packed
½ cup bourbon	
1½ cups sifted flour	2 eggs
1½ teaspoons baking soda	4 cups pecan halves
1½ teaspoons cinnamon	½ pound chopped citron
½ teaspoon nutmeg	1 pound whole candied cherries
½ teaspoon cloves	
¼ pound (1 stick) butter, room temperature	

1. Soak the raisins in the bourbon until plump.
2. Sift the flour, baking soda, and spices together.
3. Cream the butter with the brown sugar until fluffy. Beat in the eggs, 1 at a time, until smooth.
4. Stir in the flour mixture to form a smooth dough. Add the raisins and their liquid. Stir in the pecans and candied fruit.
5. Drop by spoonfuls onto a greased cookie sheet.
6. Bake at 400° until done, about 10 minutes.

Golden Delights

MISSISSIPPI

Adapted from *Tunica County Tasty Treats*

½ cup shortening	1 teaspoon lemon juice
¾ cup sugar	2 cups sifted flour
1 egg	1½ teaspoons baking powder
1 cup carrots, cooked and mashed	½ teaspoon salt

1. Cream the shortening and sugar together until light and fluffy. Add the egg and beat well.
2. Stir in the carrots and lemon juice and blend until smooth.
3. Sift the flour, baking powder, and salt together. Stir this into the creamed mixture.
4. Drop by teaspoonfuls onto greased baking sheets.
5. Bake at 325° for 20–25 minutes.

Lizzie's Hermits

MISSISSIPPI
Adapted from *Tunica County Tasty Treats*

½ cup shortening
1½ cups light brown sugar
2 eggs, well beaten
2¼ cups flour
1 teaspoon baking soda
½ teaspoon cinnamon
1 teaspoon allspice

⅛ teaspoon salt
1 cup chopped dates
½ teaspoon vanilla
1 cup seedless raisins
1 cup currants
½ cup nuts, chopped
3 tablespoons milk

1. Cream the shortening with the brown sugar until light. Add the eggs and beat until smooth.
2. Sift the flour, baking soda, cinnamon, allspice, and salt together. Beat this mixture into the creamed mixture.
3. Add the remaining ingredients and mix thoroughly.
4. Drop by teaspoonfuls onto greased cookie sheets.
5. Bake at 400° for 10–12 minutes.

Pecan Cocoons

MISSISSIPPI
Adapted from *Tunica County Tasty Treats*

6 tablespoons powdered sugar
2½ cups flour
2 cups chopped pecans

½ teaspoon salt
½ pound butter, melted
1 teaspoon vanilla
powdered sugar for garnish

1. Mix the 6 tablespoons powdered sugar, flour, pecans, and salt together.
2. Stir in the melted butter and vanilla. Beat until smooth.
3. Shape into "cocoons" and place on a greased cookie sheet.
4. Bake at 375° until lightly browned.
5. Roll in powdered sugar while still warm.

Peanut Butter Cross-Bar Cookies

MISSISSIPPI
Adapted from *Tunica County Tasty Treats*

1 cup white sugar	½ teaspoon salt
1 cup light brown sugar	1 teaspoon vanilla
1 cup shortening	2½ cups flour
1 cup smooth peanut butter	1½ teaspoons baking soda
2 eggs, beaten	¼ teaspoon baking powder

1. Cream the sugars, shortening, and peanut butter together until smooth.
2. Beat in the eggs, salt, and vanilla.
3. Sift the flour with the baking soda and baking powder. Stir this into the creamed mixture and beat until a smooth dough forms.
4. Form the dough into small balls and place them 2 inches apart on greased baking sheets. With the back of a fork, press the tines across the top at right angles to flatten the cookies and make a cross-bar design.
5. Bake at 375° for 10–15 minutes.

Kisses

MISSISSIPPI
Adapted from *Tunica County Tasty Treats*

4 egg whites	2 cups chopped nuts
1¼ cups sugar	1 package chopped dates
1 teaspoon vinegar	

1. Beat the egg whites stiff.
2. Stir in the sugar and vinegar. Fold in the nuts and dates.
3. Drop onto parchment-lined cookie sheets by teaspoonfuls.
4. Bake at 275° for 40 minutes.

Mary Telfair's Derby Cakes

GEORGIA
Adapted from DeBolt, *Savannah Sampler Cookbook*

½	pound butter	1	cup milk
2	cups sugar	4	cups sifted flour
1	egg	½	pound raisins

1. Cream the butter and sugar. Add the egg and beat until smooth.
2. Stir in the milk, alternating with the flour. Add the raisins and mix until smooth.
3. Roll out thin and cut with a round cutter. Place on an ungreased cookie sheet.
4. Bake at 375° for 5 minutes.

Grand Mudder's Cookies

MISSISSIPPI
Adapted from *Tunica County Tasty Treats*

2	cups sugar	1	tablespoon water
1	cup shortening	1	tablespoon vanilla or
3	eggs		almond flavoring
1	teaspoon baking soda		flour
2	teaspoons cream of tartar		milk

1. Cream the sugar, shortening, and eggs together until smooth.
2. Mix the baking soda and cream of tartar with the water and add it. Stir in the vanilla.
3. Add enough flour to make a soft dough. Refrigerate overnight.
4. Roll the dough thin, cut into cookies, and place them on a greased cookie sheet. Brush the tops with milk.
5. Bake at 325° until done, about 15 minutes.

Thimble Cookies

ARKANSAS
Adapted from Marshall, *Cooking Across the South*

Cookies:

1 cup sugar	1 teaspoon vanilla extract
1 cup molasses	5 cups flour
1 tablespoon baking soda	1 teaspoon ground ginger
1 teaspoon cream of tartar	1 teaspoon ground cinnamon
1 cup shortening	1 teaspoon salt
⅔ cup hot water	

Filling:

1 cup raisins	dash cream of tartar
¾ cup lard	1 cup warm water
2 tablespoons all-purpose flour	

1. Mix the sugar, molasses, baking soda, and cream of tartar together until the mixture is foamy. Beat in the shortening, hot water, and vanilla.
2. Sift the dry ingredients together and add this to the molasses mixture. Beat to form a smooth dough. Refrigerate the dough overnight.
3. Prepare the filling by cooking all of the ingredients together over low heat until thickened. Allow the filling to cool.
4. Roll the dough out ¼-inch thick. Cut the dough into 2-inch circles.
5. Cut a thimble-size hole in the center of half the cookies. Place a teaspoonful of filling in center of the uncut cookies and top each one with a cookie that has a hole in its center.
6. Press the edges together and place them on greased cookie sheets.
7. Bake at 400° for 10 minutes.

Girl Scout Brownies

GEORGIA
Adapted from DeBolt, *Savannah Sampler Cookbook*

4 ounces unsweetened chocolate	1 teaspoon vanilla extract
⅔ cup vegetable shortening	1¼ cups flour
2 cups sugar	1 teaspoon baking powder
4 eggs	¼ teaspoon salt
	1 cup chopped nuts

1. Melt the chocolate and shortening together in a large saucepan over low heat. Stir in the sugar, eggs, and vanilla.
2. Sift the dry ingredients together and stir into the chocolate mixture. Stir in the nuts. Mix until smooth.
3. Spread into an oiled and floured 9-inch square baking pan.
4. Bake at 350° for 30 minutes, or until brownies start to pull away from the sides of the pan.

Savannah Nut Bars

GEORGIA
Adapted from DeBolt, *Savannah Sampler Cookbook*

Cookies:

⅔ cup vegetable shortening	2 cups sifted flour
1 cup light brown sugar	½ teaspoon cinnamon
1 egg	pinch salt

Topping:

1 egg, lightly beaten	¾ cup chopped pecans
½ cup light brown sugar	

1. Cream the shortening and sugar together until fluffy. Add the egg and beat until light.
2. Sift the dry ingredients together and fold into the creamed mixture. Press onto the bottom of an oiled 11-by-16-by-½-inch pan.
3. Top by brushing the dough with the egg. Sprinkle evenly with the brown sugar and pecans.
4. Bake at 350° for 20–25 minutes.

Caramel Cuts

MISSISSIPPI
Adapted from *Tunica County Tasty Treats*

¼ cup butter	¾ cup flour
1 cup light brown sugar	1 teaspoon baking powder
1 egg	½ teaspoon salt
½ teaspoon vanilla	½ cup chopped pecans

1. Melt the butter and stir in the brown sugar, blending well. Add the egg and beat well. Stir in the vanilla.
2. Sift the flour, baking powder, and salt together and add to the first mixture, beating to form a smooth dough. Stir in the chopped pecans.
3. Pour the batter into a greased and parchment-lined 8-inch square baking pan.
4. Bake at 350° for 30 minutes.
5. Cut into squares when cool.

Mrs. Still's Good Lemon Sours

MISSISSIPPI
Adapted from *Tunica County Tasty Treats*

¾ cup flour	⅛ teaspoon baking powder
½ cup butter	½ teaspoon vanilla
2 eggs	1 teaspoon grated lemon rind
1 cup light brown sugar	1½ tablespoons fresh lemon
¾ cup shredded coconut	juice
½ cup chopped nuts	⅔ cup powdered sugar

1. Rub the flour and butter together to a fine meal.
2. Sprinkle into an 11-by-7-inch pan and bake at 350° for 10 minutes.
3. Beat the eggs with the brown sugar and stir in the coconut, nuts, baking powder, and vanilla. Add this to the baked layer in the pan while still warm.
4. Return the pan to the oven and bake an additional 20 minutes.
5. Mix the lemon rind, lemon juice, and powdered sugar until smooth and spread this over the top as soon as the pan is taken from the oven.
6. Cut into squares when cool.

Aunt Julia's Macaroons

ILLINOIS
Adapted from Linsenmeyer, *Cooking Plain*

2	egg whites
2	tablespoons all-purpose flour
2	cups powdered sugar, sifted

¼	teaspoon salt
1	teaspoon vanilla
1	cup grated coconut

1. Beat the egg whites until foamy.
2. Sift the flour, sugar, and salt together and add gradually to the egg whites, beating constantly. Add the vanilla.
3. Fold in the coconut and drop teaspoons of dough onto a greased and floured cookie sheet.
4. Bake at 300° for about 20 minutes. Cookies should be done but not browned.
5. Allow to cool on a cookie sheet for a few minutes before removing to a wire rack.

Cinnamon Sour Cream Cookies

OHIO
Adapted from Macmillan, *In a Shaker Kitchen*

½	cup soft butter
1	cup packed light brown sugar
1	egg
½	cup sour cream
½	teaspoon baking soda

2½	cups flour
1	teaspoon baking powder
¼	teaspoon salt
½	tablespoon ground cinnamon

1. Beat the butter with the brown sugar until well blended, then beat in the egg.
2. Mix the sour cream and the baking soda together and add to the butter mixture.
3. Sift the flour, baking powder, salt, and cinnamon together and add to the butter mixture.
4. Beat well to make a soft dough. Cover and chill 1 hour.
5. Place large walnut-sized pieces of dough on lightly greased baking sheets, leaving space for spreading. Flatten each with a floured fork.
6. Bake at 375° until golden brown and still slightly soft in the center, 10–15 minutes.
7. Allow to cool 1–2 minutes on the baking sheets before removing.

Pecan Balls

OHIO
Adapted from Macmillan, *In a Shaker Kitchen*

2   cups flour
½   teaspoon salt
1   cup soft butter
1   teaspoon pure vanilla
    extract

½   cup powdered sugar, plus
    additional for dusting
1   cup pecans, finely chopped

1. Sift the flour with the salt.
2. Beat the butter, vanilla, and powdered sugar until well blended and creamy.
3. Gradually beat in the flour, then mix in the pecans.
4. Take pieces of dough and roll into walnut-sized balls. Arrange on ungreased baking sheets.
5. Bake at 350° until set and "very nicely browned," about 15–20 minutes.
6. Let cool 1 minute on the baking sheets, then transfer to wire racks.
7. While still warm, dust with powdered sugar.

Applesauce-Nut Cookies

ILLINOIS
Adapted from Linsenmeyer, *Cooking Plain*

2   cups all-purpose flour,
    sifted
½   teaspoon salt
½   teaspoon cinnamon
½   teaspoon nutmeg
½   teaspoon allspice
1   cup chopped hickory nuts
    or pecans

1   cup chopped raisins
½   cup lard
1   cup sugar
1   teaspoon baking soda
1   cup applesauce
1   egg, well beaten

1. Sift the flour, salt, and spices together. Mix with the nuts and raisins and set aside.
2. Cream the lard until fluffy, add the sugar gradually, and continue creaming until very light.
3. Stir the baking soda into the applesauce and combine with the creamed mixture. Add the beaten egg.
4. Blend in the flour-nut mixture. Drop by teaspoonfuls onto a greased baking sheet.
5. Bake at 350° for 15–20 minutes.

Yankee Doodle Cookies

INDIANA
Adapted from *The Hoosier Cookbook*

6 ounces semisweet chocolate
  bits
6 ounces butterscotch bits

6 ounces chow mein noodles
½ cup peanuts, chopped

1. Melt the chocolate and butterscotch bits in the top of a double boiler. Remove from the heat.
2. Stir in the noodles and nuts to coat evenly.
3. Drop by teaspoonfuls onto waxed paper. Chill.
4. Store in the refrigerator until ready to serve.

Yummies

INDIANA
Adapted from *The Hoosier Cookbook*

1 stick butter or margarine
1 cup sugar
½ teaspoon salt
1 egg, beaten

¾ cup dates, chopped
2 cups Rice Krispies
½ cup pecans, chopped
2–3 cups shredded coconut

1. Melt the butter. Add the sugar, salt, and egg. Cook until thick.
2. Add the dates and continue cooking about 4–5 minutes, stirring constantly.
3. Pour the date mixture over the Rice Krispies and nuts. Stir until well blended.
4. Drop by teaspoonfuls into a bowl of coconut.
5. Roll the balls to cover with coconut and place on waxed paper. Chill 30 minutes. (Cookies may be rolled in chopped pecans instead of coconut.)
6. Store in an airtight metal container.

Applescotch Cookies

INDIANA

Adapted from *The Hoosier Cookbook*

1¼ cups light brown sugar, packed	1 teaspoon cinnamon
½ cup butter	1 teaspoon nutmeg
3 tablespoons milk	1½ cups apples, diced
1 egg	1 cup nuts, chopped
2 cups flour	1 cup white raisins
1 teaspoon baking powder	1 6-ounce package butter-
1 teaspoon baking soda	scotch bits

1. Cream the brown sugar, butter, milk, and egg together.
2. Sift the flour, baking powder, baking soda, cinnamon, and nutmeg together. Add to the creamed mixture.
3. Add the apples, nuts, white raisins, and butterscotch bits. Drop by teaspoonfuls onto a greased cookie sheet.
4. Bake at 375° for 12–15 minutes.

Archway Cookies

INDIANA

Adapted from *The Hoosier Cookbook*

½ cup crushed pineapple	1 cup nuts, chopped
½ cup white sugar	2 teaspoons baking soda
2 cups shortening	2 teaspoons molasses
3 cups light brown sugar	8 cups flour
6 eggs	2 teaspoons cinnamon
1 cup strawberry jam	2 teaspoons nutmeg
1 pound chopped dates	2 teaspoons ground cloves
1 pound raisins	1 teaspoon salt

1. Combine the pineapple with white sugar. Cook to a thick syrup.
2. Cream the shortening and brown sugar. Add the eggs, 1 at a time, beating well after each addition.
3. Add the pineapple, jam, dates, raisins, and nuts to the creamed mixture. Dissolve the baking soda in the molasses and add it to the mixture.
4. Sift the flour, spices, and salt together, then add to the mixture. Chill 1 hour.
5. Drop by teaspoonfuls on an ungreased cookie sheet.
6. Bake at 350° for 15 minutes.

Makes 12 dozen

Buckaroon Cookies

INDIANA
Adapted from *The Hoosier Cookbook*

2	cups flour	1	cup light brown sugar
1	teaspoon baking soda	2	eggs
½	teaspoon salt	2	cups rolled oats
½	teaspoon baking powder	1	teaspoon vanilla
1	cup shortening	6	ounces chocolate chips
1	cup sugar	½	cup nuts, chopped

1. Sift the flour, baking soda, salt, and baking powder together.
2. Blend the shortening and sugars until creamed.
3. Beat the eggs until light and fluffy and add them to the shortening mixture. Add the flour mixture.
4. Stir in the oats, vanilla, chocolate chips, and nuts.
5. Drop by spoonfuls onto a greased cookie sheet.
6. Bake at 350° for 10–12 minutes.

Old-Fashioned Wine Cookies

INDIANA
Adapted from *The Hoosier Cookbook*

1	cup butter	1	teaspoon baking soda
1	cup sugar	2	teaspoons cinnamon
2	tablespoons preserves or jelly	1	teaspoon salt
4	eggs, beaten	3	cups oats
3	cups flour	2	ounces red wine

1. Cream the butter, sugar, jelly, and eggs together.
2. Add the flour, baking soda, cinnamon, and salt. Mix thoroughly. Add the oats and wine.
3. Drop by teaspoonfuls onto a greased cookie sheet.
4. Bake at 375° until set.

ROLL, SLICE, AND CUT COOKIES

Log House Cookies

OHIO

Adapted from DuSablon, *Cincinnati Recipe Treasury*

1 cup sugar	2½ cups flour
½ cup (1 stick) butter, room temperature	½ teaspoon baking soda
	1 teaspoon cream of tartar
1 egg	1 tablespoon cold water
2½ tablespoons sour milk or buttermilk	1 tablespoon molasses or sorghum
¾ teaspoon vanilla extract	sugar for dusting
¾ teaspoon salt	

1. Cream the sugar and butter. Beat in the egg, milk, vanilla, and salt.
2. Sift the flour, baking soda, and cream of tartar together. Mix with the butter mixture. Blend into a fairly stiff dough.
3. Roll out to about ¼-inch thickness on a floured board with a floured rolling pin.
4. Cut into log houses and carefully place on a greased cookie tin.
5. In a small cup, mix the cold water and molasses. Brush each cookie lightly with this mixture, and then sprinkle with sugar.
6. Bake at 350° for about 10 minutes, or until lightly browned.

Peppernuts

ILLINOIS

Adapted from Linsenmeyer, *Cooking Plain*

¾ cup dark brown sugar, firmly packed
¾ cup white sugar
2 eggs
1 lemon, rind only (grated)
1 tablespoon citron, minced
1 tablespoon candied orange peel, minced
½ teaspoon ground cloves
½ teaspoon allspice
1 teaspoon cinnamon
¼ teaspoon cardamom
½ teaspoon freshly ground black pepper
3½ cups all-purpose flour
1 teaspoon baking soda
¼ cup grated unblanched almonds
1 cup powdered sugar
¼ cup brandy

1. Combine the brown and white sugar, add the eggs, and beat until the mixture is very thick and light colored.
2. Add the lemon rind, citron, orange peel, and spices and mix thoroughly.
3. Sift the flour with the baking soda and stir into the egg mixture. Add the grated almonds.
4. Turn onto a well-floured board and knead until smooth. Shape into long rolls 1 inch in diameter and cut into ½- to ¾-inch slices.
5. Place on a buttered cookie sheet and let set overnight to dry at room temperature.
6. Bake at 300° for about 20 minutes.
7. Sprinkle the cookies with brandy and roll in powdered sugar.

Yields about 9 dozen

ROLL, SLICE, AND CUT COOKIES

Honey Spice Cookies

OHIO

Adapted from DuSablon, *Cincinnati Recipe Treasury*

1	cup butter or margarine	¼	teaspoon nutmeg
1	cup salad oil	6–7	cups flour, sifted
½	cup sugar	1	teaspoon baking powder
	rind from 1 orange, grated	½	teaspoon baking soda
2	teaspoons cinnamon	½	cup orange juice
1½	teaspoons ground cloves	1	cup warmed honey

1. Melt the butter or margarine and then cool slightly. Add the oil and beat with a mixer until creamy.
2. Add the sugar and continue beating.
3. Mix the orange rind with the spices, flour, baking powder, and baking soda. Add to the creamed mixture. Stir in the juice and honey to form a stiff dough.
4. Roll out to ¼-inch thickness. Cut and place on an ungreased cookie sheet.
5. Bake at 325° for 10 minutes, or until browned.

BARS AND BROWNIES

Honey Brownies

INDIANA

Adapted from *The Hoosier Cookbook*

½	cup butter or margarine	1	cup sugar
4	ounces unsweetened chocolate	1	cup honey
		1	cup plus 2 tablespoons flour, sifted
4	eggs		
½	teaspoon salt	1	cup chopped nuts

1. Melt the butter and chocolate over low heat in a heavy saucepan.
2. Beat the eggs and salt in a mixing bowl until light. Add the sugar and honey gradually and continue beating the mixture until very light. Add the melted chocolate and butter.
3. Stir in the flour and the nuts. Pour into a greased 9-inch square pan.
4. Bake at 325° for 50–60 minutes.
5. Allow to cool and cut into squares.

Mint Brownies

INDIANA
Adapted from *The Hoosier Cookbook*

Brownies:

1	cup butter	1½	cups flour
4	squares baking chocolate	½	cup nuts
2	cups sugar	2	teaspoons vanilla
4	whole eggs		

Mint topping:

1	egg white		dash salt
2	cups powdered sugar	1½	teaspoons mint flavoring
2	tablespoons butter, melted		green food coloring
1	tablespoon cream		

Fudge frosting:

2	ounces semisweet chocolate	1	pound powdered sugar
3	tablespoons butter		cream as needed

1. For the brownies, melt the butter and chocolate. Cool. Add the sugar and eggs. Mix well.
2. Add the flour, nuts and vanilla. Pour into a buttered 9-by-13-inch pan.
3. Bake at 350° for 20–25 minutes. Allow to cool.
4. For the mint topping, beat the egg white, adding the sugar gradually. Add the melted butter, cream, salt, mint flavoring, and coloring. Spread on the brownies.
5. For the fudge frosting, melt the chocolate and butter. Mix with the sugar and enough cream to make a soft frosting. Spread on the brownies. Cut into squares.

Peanut Bars

OHIO

Adapted from DuSablon, *Cincinnati Recipe Treasury*

Cookies:

4 eggs	½ teaspoon salt
2 cups sugar	½ teaspoon vanilla extract
2 cups cake flour	1 cup milk, scalded
2 teaspoons baking powder	

Icing:

1 pound powdered sugar	milk as needed
½ cup (1 stick) butter	1 pound white salted pea-
1 teaspoon vanilla extract	nuts, ground
½ teaspoon salt	

1. Beat eggs and sugar until light and fluffy. Beat several minutes more.
2. Mix the flour, baking powder, and salt together and gradually fold into the egg mixture.
3. Add the vanilla and the warm milk and blend well.
4. Pour into an ungreased 13-by-16-inch pan lined with wax paper.
5. Bake at 350° for 35 minutes.
6. To make the icing, mix the powdered sugar, butter, vanilla, and salt with enough milk to make a thin icing.
7. When cake is cool, cut into oblong pieces. Dip each piece into the icing and roll in the ground peanuts. Place on wax paper until firm.

Midwest

DROP AND SHAPED COOKIES

Potato Chip Cookies

IOWA

Adapted from *How Iowa Cooks*

1 cup margarine	2 cups flour
1 cup sugar	1 teaspoon baking soda
1 cup light brown sugar	2 cups crushed potato chips
2 eggs, well beaten	6 ounces butterscotch chips

1. Cream the margarine with the sugar until fluffy.
2. Add the remaining ingredients and stir to mix thoroughly.
3. Form into balls and place on greased cookie sheets.
4. Bake at 325° for 10 minutes.

Angel Cookies

IOWA

Adapted from *How Iowa Cooks*

½ cup butter	½ teaspoon salt
½ cup lard	1 teaspoon cream of tartar
½ cup light brown sugar	½ cup nuts
½ cup white sugar	cold water
1 egg	sugar
2 cups flour	

1. Cream the butter, lard, and sugars together.
2. Add the egg and mix well.
3. Sift the flour, salt, and cream of tartar together. Add this to the sugar mixture and add the nuts.
4. Roll into balls the size of a walnut or smaller. Dip the top half in cold water then sugar. Place them on a greased cookie sheet sugar side up.
5. Bake at 350° for 10–12 minutes.

Butterscotch Drop Cookies

IOWA

Adapted from *How Iowa Cooks*

1 cup white sugar	1 teaspoon salt
1 cup light brown sugar	1 teaspoon baking soda
1 cup shortening	2 cups flour
2 eggs	1 cup quick oats
1 teaspoon burnt sugar	6 ounces butterscotch chips
½ teaspoon vanilla extract	½ cup walnuts

1. Stir the ingredients together, in the order given, to form a smooth dough.
2. Drop by spoonfuls onto an ungreased cookie sheet.
3. Bake at 350° for 10–12 minutes.

Raisin Rocks

OKLAHOMA

Adapted from Wilhelm, *Smidgen of Honey*

1	cup butter	1	teaspoon salt
1	cup light brown sugar	4–5	cups flour
2	cups molasses	2	teaspoons baking soda
1	teaspoon ginger	1	cup seeded raisins

1. Cook the butter, brown sugar, molasses, ginger, and salt together. Stir the mixture until it boils and boil 5 minutes.
2. Stir in most of the flour and baking soda sifted together. Add additional until the dough is stiff enough to drop from a spoon.
3. Add the raisins and drop from a spoon onto a greased cookie sheet.
4. Bake at 350° for 10 minutes, or until done.

Honey Hermits

OKLAHOMA

Adapted from Wilhelm, *Smidgen of Honey*

1⅓	cups strained honey	1	cup chopped raisins
⅓	cup shortening	1½	teaspoons cinnamon
2	eggs	½	teaspoon ground cloves
½	cup milk	3	teaspoons baking powder
½	teaspoon salt	3½	cups flour

1. Mix the strained honey and melted shortening. Add the eggs, milk, salt, and raisins.
2. Sift the cinnamon, cloves, and baking powder with the flour. Add this to the honey mixture and beat well.
3. Drop by teaspoonfuls onto a greased cookie sheet.
4. Bake at 375° until golden brown.

Rolled Oats Macaroons

WISCONSIN
Adapted from *"The Four Hundred" Cook Book*

1 egg	1 cup rolled oats
½ cup sugar	⅓ teaspoon salt
⅔ teaspoon butter, melted	¼ teaspoon vanilla

1. Beat the egg very light, gradually add the sugar, then stir in the remaining ingredients.
2. Drop mixture by teaspoons on a well-greased cookie sheet, 1 inch apart.
3. Spread each with a knife first dipped into cold water.
4. Bake at 350° "till delicately browned."
5. To give variety, use only ⅔ cup of oats and fill the cup with shredded coconut.

Almond and Date Cookies

WISCONSIN
Adapted from *"The Four Hundred" Cook Book*

5 egg whites	flour
1 cup granulated sugar	½ pound almonds, sliced
½ pound dates	

1. Beat the whites to a stiff froth, then add the sugar and beat to form stiff peaks.
2. Seed and shred the dates. Toss in a little flour and add them and the almonds to the egg whites.
3. Drop on a waxed baking sheet some distance apart.
4. Bake at 350° until golden brown.

Beeswax is recommended by the author of the original recipe.

Sorghum Chewies

KANSAS
Adapted from Carey and Naas, *The Kansas Cookbook*

1	cup plus 2 tablespoons sugar	¾	teaspoon salt
¾	cup shortening	1½	teaspoons baking soda
1	egg	6	ounces chocolate chips
⅓	cup sorghum	1	cup flaked coconut
1	teaspoon vanilla extract	1	cup quick cooking rolled oats
2¼	cups flour		

1. In a large bowl, cream the sugar and shortening together. Add the egg, sorghum, and vanilla. Beat until smooth.
2. Sift the flour, salt, and baking soda together and add it to the creamed mixture, forming a smooth dough. Stir in the chocolate chips, coconut, and oats.
3. Drop by teaspoonfuls onto greased cookie sheets.
4. Bake at 375° for 10 minutes, or until done.

Breakfast Drop Cakes

WISCONSIN
Adapted from *"The Four Hundred" Cook Book*

2	cups molasses	3	teaspoons baking soda
1	cup shortening	1	tablespoon ginger
1	cup milk (sweet or sour)	4½	cups flour

1. Mix all ingredients together to form a smooth dough. Refrigerate overnight.
2. Drop walnut-sized pieces on greased cookie sheets.
3. Bake at 375° for 8–10 minutes.

Hot Lard Cookies

KANSAS

Adapted from *The Centennial Treasury of Recipes*

2 eggs
2 cups sugar
1 cup lard, melted and hot
1 cup milk

3½ cups flour
1 teaspoon baking soda
1 teaspoon vanilla

1. Whisk the eggs with the sugar, beating well. Beat in the lard. Stir in the milk.
2. Sift the flour with the baking soda and beat this into the egg mixture. Add the vanilla and beat well to form a smooth dough.
3. Roll the dough out and cut as desired. Place cookies on a greased cookie sheet.
4. Bake at 375° for 10–15 minutes, or until done.

Hard-Boiled Egg Cookies

MINNESOTA

Adapted from Kreidberg, *Food on the Frontier*

½ pound butter
½ pound sugar
8 hard-boiled egg yolks, chopped

1 pound flour
1 lemon, grated rind only
1 whole egg

1. Cream the butter, sugar, and eggs yolks together. Add the flour and lemon rind gradually. Beat to form a smooth dough.
2. Roll the dough thin and cut into "fancy shapes." Glaze the top of each cookie with beaten egg and place them on greased cookie sheets.
3. Bake at 375° for 10 minutes, or until nicely browned.

ROLL, SLICE, AND CUT COOKIES

Aunt Miranda's Sour Cream Tea Biscuits

KANSAS
Adapted from Carey and Naas, *The Kansas Cookbook*

3	eggs	6	cups flour
2	cups sugar	1	teaspoon baking soda
1	teaspoon vanilla extract	1	teaspoon baking powder
1	cup butter, softened	1	teaspoon nutmeg
1	cup sour cream		sugar

1. Beat the eggs with the sugar, mixing well. Stir in the vanilla and butter, creaming the mixture, then add the sour cream. Beat well.
2. Sift the remaining dry ingredients (except the sugar) together and gradually add them to the creamed mixture. Refrigerate the dough for an hour.
3. Roll the cookie dough out to ¼-inch thickness. Cut the cookies out with a 2-inch biscuit cutter. Place the biscuits on a greased cookie sheet and sprinkle them lightly with sugar.
4. Bake at 375° for 8–10 minutes.

Soft Sorghum Cookies

KANSAS
Adapted from *The Centennial Treasury of Recipes*

2	eggs	½	teaspoon ginger
1½	cups sugar	¼	teaspoon salt
½	cup lard	1	cup sour cream
½	teaspoon cinnamon	1	cup sorghum
½	teaspoon allspice	2	teaspoons soda
½	teaspoon nutmeg	6	cups flour
½	teaspoon cloves		

1. Whip the eggs and sugar together until light. Beat in the lard and stir in the spices and salt.
2. Add the sour cream and sorghum and blend until smooth.
3. Sift the baking soda with the flour and add this to the mixture. Beat to form a smooth dough.
4. Roll out the dough to ¼-inch thickness and cut with a cookie cutter. Place the cookies on an ungreased cookie sheet.
5. Bake at 400° for 10–15 minutes.

Rhubarb Oatmeal Bars

WISCONSIN

Adapted from *St. Paul's Centennial Cookbook*

Crust:

½ cup chopped nuts	¼ teaspoon baking soda
1½ cups rolled oats, instant	1½ cups flour
1 cup brown sugar	1 cup shortening
¼ teaspoon salt	

Filling:

4 cups rhubarb, chopped	¼ cup water
1½ cups sugar	1 teaspoon vanilla
2 tablespoons cornstarch	

1. Mix the dry ingredients for the crust. Cut in the shortening to make a crumbly mixture.
2. Prepare the filling by cooking the rhubarb with the sugar, cornstarch, and water. Stir until the mixture is no longer cloudy. Stir in the vanilla.
3. Pat half of the crust mixture into the bottom of a 9-by-13-inch rectangular pan that has been greased and floured. Pour the filling over the crust. Sprinkle the remaining crust over the filling.
4. Bake at 375° for 20 minutes. Allow to cool and cut into bars.

Raisin Sheet Cookies

KANSAS

Adapted from *The Centennial Treasury of Recipes*

1 cup seedless raisins	1 cup sugar
1 cup water	1 teaspoon cinnamon
1 teaspoon baking soda	½ teaspoon cloves
½ cup vegetable shortening	¼ teaspoon baking powder
2 cups flour	2 cups powdered sugar

1. Bring the raisins to a boil in the water. Remove them from the heat and add the baking soda and shortening.
2. Sift the dry ingredients (except the powdered sugar) together and stir this into the raisin mixture. Beat to form a smooth dough. Spread the dough onto a greased cookie sheet.
3. Bake at 375° for 15 minutes.
4. Mix the powdered sugar with enough water to form a thin icing and glaze the sheet cookie while still warm. Cut into squares for serving.

Piñon Cookies

NEW MEXICO
Adapted from Cameron, *The Best from New Mexico Kitchens*

4 eggs	¼ teaspoon salt
1½ cups sugar	¼ cup powdered sugar
½ teaspoon grated lemon zest	1 cup piñon nuts (pine nuts
2½ cups flour, sifted	or pignolis)

1. Place the eggs and sugar in the top of a double boiler over hot water and mix to dissolve the sugar. Remove the pan from the water and continue to beat until cool and foamy.
2. Add the lemon zest. Stir in the flour, salt, powdered sugar, and nuts. Drop by teaspoonfuls onto a greased and floured cookie sheet.
3. Bake at 375° for about 10 minutes.

Makes about 60

Sweet Rocks

ARIZONA
Adapted from Weiner, *Arizona Territorial Cookbook*

1 cup sugar	1 teaspoon baking soda
1 cup light brown sugar	2 tablespoons water
1 cup butter, softened	2½ cups flour, sifted
3 eggs, lightly beaten	1 pound dates or raisins,
1 teaspoon ground cloves	seeded and chopped
1 teaspoon cinnamon	1½ pounds walnuts, broken

1. Cream the sugar, brown sugar, and butter together.
2. Add the eggs, cloves, cinnamon, baking soda dissolved in the water, flour, dates or raisins and the walnuts.
3. Drop the batter in small lumps on buttered cookie sheets.
4. Bake at 375° until golden brown, about 12–15 minutes.

Pumpkin Cookies

NEW MEXICO
Adapted from Dent, *The Feast of Santa Fe*

Cookies:

½ cup honey
⅔ cup light brown sugar
¾ (1½ sticks) butter, cut into small chunks
1 cup cooked pumpkin
2 teaspoons baking soda
1 teaspoon salt
½ teaspoon ground cinnamon

½ teaspoon grated nutmeg
¼ teaspoon ground cloves
1 teaspoon vanilla
 grated rind of 1 orange
2 large eggs
2 cups flour
⅔ cup raisins

Glaze:

1 cup powdered sugar
2 tablespoons milk
 few drops vanilla

dash cinnamon
24–48 pecan halves

1. Combine the first 12 ingredients. Mix thoroughly until smooth.
2. Mix in the flour, 1 cup at a time. Do not overmix. Stir in the raisins.
3. Drop the dough by large tablespoons onto lightly greased cookie sheets.
4. Bake at 375° for 12–15 minutes, or until just lightly colored. Allow to cool.
5. Prepare the glaze by mixing together all of the ingredients, reserving the pecans. Drizzle the glaze over the cookies and press a pecan half firmly onto each one.

DROP COOKIES

Piñon Tiles

NEW MEXICO
Adapted from Dent, *The Feast of Santa Fe*

6 tablespoons sweet butter, cut into 12 pieces	⅓ cup flour
	1 grated lemon peel
½ cup sugar	1 cup shelled piñons (pine nuts)
2 egg whites	

1. Cream the butter with the sugar. Add the egg whites and beat until light. Stir in the flour and lemon peel.
2. Chop the piñons coarsely and stir them into the dough. Drop the dough by teaspoonfuls onto lightly greased cookie sheets, about 2 inches apart.
3. Bake at 400° for 8–10 minutes, or until the edges of the cookies are golden brown.
4. While still warm, bend each cookie over a rolling pin, giving the cookies a delicate curve.

ROLL, SLICE, AND CUT COOKIES

Nanny's Sugar Cookies

TEXAS
Adapted from Ross, *Nanny's Texas Table*

1 cup butter	2 tablespoons heavy cream
2 cups granulated sugar	2 cups all-purpose flour
2 eggs	2 teaspoons baking powder
2 teaspoons vanilla extract	sugar

1. Cream the butter and the 2 cups sugar until fluffy. Add the eggs, vanilla, and cream and mix well.
2. Sift the flour with the baking powder twice and add it to the batter, mixing well. Chill the dough thoroughly.
3. Divide the dough into workable amounts. On a well-floured board, roll out one dough piece at a time to ⅛-inch thickness, keeping the rest of the dough chilled. Cut the cookies with a 2½-inch cutter and place on greased cookie sheets. Sprinkle with sugar.
4. Bake at 375° for 10–12 minutes, until browned and crisp.

Bizcochitos (Aniseed Cookies)

NEW MEXICO
Adapted from Dent, *The Feast of Santa Fe*

½ cup lard	1½ cups flour
⅔ cup sugar	1 teaspoon baking powder
1 egg	¼ teaspoon salt
1 teaspoon aniseed	¼ cup sugar
1 tablespoon brandy	¼ teaspoon cinnamon

1. Cream the lard with the ⅔ cup sugar. Beat in the egg until light and fluffy. Stir in the aniseed and brandy.
2. Sift the flour, baking powder, and salt together. Add this to the creamed mixture and mix to form a smooth dough. Chill the dough thoroughly.
3. Roll the dough to a thickness of ¼ inch and cut cookies with a cutter.
4. Mix the ¼ cup sugar with the cinnamon and dredge each cookie in this mixture. Place them on ungreased cookie sheets.
5. Bake at 350° for 10 minutes.

Whoopie Pies

COLORADO
Adapted from *Nuggets: Recipes Good as Gold*

Cookies:

½ cup shortening
1 cup sugar
2 eggs
2 cups flour
⅔ cup cocoa

¼ teaspoon salt
1 teaspoon baking soda
⅔ cup buttermilk
½ cup water

Filling:

¼ cup butter, softened
½ cup shortening

1 teaspoon vanilla
2 cups sifted powdered sugar

1. For the cookies, beat ½ cup of the shortening and the sugar until creamy. Add 1 egg and 1 egg yolk, reserving the white.
2. Combine the flour, cocoa, salt, and baking soda. Add alternately to the creamed mixture with the buttermilk and water. Stir to form a smooth batter.
3. Drop batter by small teaspoonfuls onto a greased baking sheet.
4. Bake at 350° for 8–10 minutes. Cool.
5. To prepare the filling, combine the butter, shortening, reserved egg white, and the vanilla. Gradually beat in the powdered sugar until light.
6. To assemble the cookies, spread the filling on the bottom side of 1 cookie and top with a second cookie.

Cowboy Cookies

COLORADO
Adapted from *Nuggets: Recipes Good as Gold*

½ cup margarine
½ cup light brown sugar
½ cup sugar
½ cup vegetable oil
1 egg
1 teaspoon vanilla
1¾ cups flour
½ teaspoon salt

½ teaspoon baking soda
½ teaspoon cream of tartar
½ cup chopped pecans
½ cup flaked coconut
½ cup old fashioned oats
½ cup Rice Krispies
6 ounces semisweet chocolate
  chips

1. Cream the margarine with both sugars and the oil. Beat in the egg and vanilla.
2. Add the remaining ingredients and mix well. Drop by teaspoonfuls onto a greased baking sheet.
3. Bake at 350° for 8–10 minutes.

24 Karat Cookies

COLORADO
Adapted from *Nuggets: Recipes Good as Gold*

Cookies:

1 cup shortening
¾ cup sugar
1 cup cooked, mashed carrots
1 egg
1 teaspoon vanilla

2 cups flour
2 teaspoons baking powder
¼ teaspoon salt
¾ cup flaked coconut

Frosting:

2 cups powdered sugar
1 tablespoon butter, softened

zest and juice of 1 orange

1. Cream the shortening and sugar. Beat in the carrots, egg, and vanilla.
2. Stir in the flour, baking powder, salt, and coconut. Mix well. Drop by teaspoonfuls onto a greased and floured cookie sheet.
3. Bake at 375° for 12–15 minutes. Frost when cool.
4. Prepare frosting by combining the powdered sugar, butter, orange zest, and enough orange juice for an icing consistency.

Pecan Cookies

WYOMING

Adapted from *Cooking in Wyoming*

¼ pound butter	1 cup cake flour
1 cup dark brown sugar	½ teaspoon baking powder
1 egg	¾ cup pecan pieces
1 teaspoon vanilla	

1. Cream the butter and sugar. Add the unbeaten egg and blend well. Add the vanilla.
2. Sift the flour. Measure and sift again with the baking powder.
3. Add the flour gradually to the creamed mixture.
4. Add the broken nut meats and blend well.
5. Drop by teaspoonfuls onto an ungreased cookie sheet. Place fairly far apart.
6. Bake at 325° for 12–15 minutes.

Kifflings (A Scotch Cookie)

COLORADO

Adapted from *Pioneer Potluck*

1 stick butter, cubed	2 teaspoons vanilla
½ cup sugar	1½ cups ground almonds
3½ cups flour	powdered sugar

1. Mix the butter with the sugar. Add the flour, vanilla, and almonds and knead well.
2. Take a small ball of dough in your hand and flatten to a cookie shape. Place on an ungreased cookie sheet.
3. Bake at 375° for 10–12 minutes, or until brown. Roll in powdered sugar while hot.

Makes 12 dozen

Golden Pecan Tassies

WYOMING

Adapted from *Cooking in Wyoming*

Cookies:

1 cup soft butter	2 cups sifted flour
6 ounces cream cheese, room temperature	

Pecan filling:

2 eggs	dash salt
1½ cups light brown sugar, firmly packed	½ teaspoon vanilla
2 tablespoons melted butter	1 cup coarsely chopped pecans

1. Blend the butter and cream cheese.
2. Add the flour gradually, mixing thoroughly. Work into a smooth dough with your fingers.
3. Shape into balls about 1¼ inches in diameter. Put each in a small muffin cup and press dough to the bottom and on the sides with your thumb, making a shell.
4. Make the pecan filling by beating the eggs slightly, gradually beating in the brown sugar, butter, salt, and vanilla.
5. Sprinkle ½ cup chopped pecans over the bottom of the dough-lined muffin cups. Spoon in the brown sugar mixture, filling cups not quite full. Sprinkle with the remaining nuts.
6. Bake at 350° for about 15 minutes. Reduce heat to 250° and bake 10 minutes longer, or until filling is firm.

DROP AND SHAPED COOKIES

Cherry Winks

WYOMING
Adapted from *Cooking in Wyoming*

1 cup sugar	1 teaspoon vanilla
¾ cup butter	1 cup chopped dates
2 eggs, beaten	1 cup chopped pecans
2 tablespoons milk	½ cup chopped maraschino
2½ cups flour	cherries
1 teaspoon baking powder	2½ cups crushed cornflakes
½ teaspoon soda	maraschino cherry halves
½ teaspoon salt	

1. Mix all the ingredients, except the cornflakes, to make a smooth dough. Form into 1½-inch balls.
2. Roll each ball of dough in the flakes and place them on a greased cookie sheet. Top each with a half cherry.
3. Bake at 375° for 10 –12 minutes.

Swedish Heirloom Cookies

WYOMING
Adapted from *Cooking in Wyoming*

1 cup powdered sugar	1 tablespoon water
1 cup shortening	1 tablespoon vanilla
1¼ cups ground almonds	powdered sugar for dusting
2 cups sifted flour	

1. Cream the sugar and shortening together. Add the almonds.
2. Blend in the flour. Add the water and vanilla.
3. Shape into balls using 1 level tablespoon dough for each cookie. Place on ungreased cookie sheets and flatten slightly.
4. Bake at 325° for 12 –15 minutes. Roll in powdered sugar while still warm.

Pecan-stuffed Date Cookies

MONTANA

Adapted from *American Cooking: The Great West*

Cookies:

45 (12 ounces) pitted dates	6 tablespoons butter,
45 (4 ounces) shelled pecan	softened
halves	¾ cup light brown sugar
2 cups flour	2 eggs
½ teaspoon baking powder	½ cup sour cream
½ teaspoon baking soda	1 teaspoon vanilla extract
½ teaspoon salt	

Icing:

8 tablespoons butter	1 tablespoon vanilla extract
3 cups powdered sugar	3 – 4 tablespoons milk

1. Gently open each date along the slit in its side, insert a pecan half, and press the date closed.
2. Sift the flour, baking powder, baking soda, and salt together.
3. Cream the butter with the brown sugar until the mixture is light and fluffy. Beat in the eggs 1 at a time. Add the flour mixture in thirds, alternating with the sour cream. Beat well after each addition. Stir in the vanilla extract.
4. Dip each pecan-stuffed date into the batter and swirl to coat the surface evenly. Arrange the dates about 1 inch apart on buttered baking sheets.
5. Bake at 350° for about 10 minutes, until delicately browned. Allow to cool before icing.
6. Prepare the icing by melting the butter over low heat. Sift in the powdered sugar and stir in the vanilla and milk. Beat until smooth. Ice each date with this mixture.

DROP AND SHAPED COOKIES

Cherry Cookies

UTAH

Adapted from Anderson, *Bounty: A Harvest of Food Lore and Country Memories from Utah's Past*

1¼	cups sugar	¼	cup cherry juice
¾	cup shortening	1	teaspoon baking soda
2	eggs	½	teaspoon salt
1	cup sour cherries	3	cups flour

1. Cream the sugar with the shortening until smooth and light. Beat in the eggs, 1 at a time, mixing well after each addition. Stir in the cherries and the juice.
2. Sift the baking soda with the salt and flour and add it in portions to the cherry mixture.
3. Drop the dough by tablespoonfuls onto greased cookie sheets.
4. Bake at 400° until done, about 10 minutes.

Persimmon Cookies

NEVADA

Adapted from *Nevada's Finest Western Cooking*

½	cup butter	1	cup persimmon pulp
1	cup sugar	1	egg
1	cup nuts, ground	½	teaspoon cinnamon
1	cup raisins, ground	½	teaspoon cloves
2	cups flour	½	teaspoon nutmeg
1	teaspoon baking soda		

1. Cream the butter and sugar together until light and fluffy.
2. Toss the nuts and raisins with the flour.
3. Add the baking soda to the persimmon pulp with the egg. Beat this into the creamed mixture.
4. Add the flour mixture and the spices and beat until a smooth dough forms. Drop by teaspoonfuls onto greased baking sheets.
5. Bake at 350° for 10 minutes.

Honey Cookies

COLORADO

Adapted from *Pioneer Potluck*

1⅓ cups honey	1 grated lemon peel
4 ounces butter	1½ teaspoons cloves
4 cups flour	2 teaspoons baking soda
4 ounces almonds	

1. Heat the honey and butter in a saucepan. When the mixture is melted and at the point of boiling, remove from the fire and cool.
2. When cold, stir in the flour slowly, followed by the almonds, lemon peel, and cloves.
3. Dissolve the baking soda in a little water and stir it into the mixture. Cover with a cloth and let stand in a cool place overnight.
4. Roll out ¼- to ½-inch thick and cut into squares. Place on a greased cookie sheet.
5. Bake at 350° for 10 minutes, or until nicely browned.

Filled Cookies

DENVER

Adapted from *Pioneer Potluck*

Cookies:

1 cup sugar	3½ cups flour
½ cup shortening	2 teaspoons cream of tartar
1 egg	1 teaspoon baking soda
½ cup milk	1 teaspoon vanilla

Filling:

1 cup chopped raisins	½ cup water
½ cup sugar	1 teaspoon flour

1. Cream the sugar, shortening, and egg. Add the milk.
2. Sift the flour with the cream of tartar and baking soda. Add to the creamed mixture. Add the vanilla.
3. Roll thin and cut with a large round cookie cutter. Place cookies on an ungreased cookie sheet.
4. Prepare filling by cooking all of the ingredients together.
5. Put 1 teaspoon of filling on each cookie, cover with a second cookie, sealing around each.
6. Bake at 375° until browned.

ROLL, SLICE, AND CUT COOKIES

Mary Duncan's Receipt for Cookies

COLORADO

Adapted from *Pioneer Potluck*

2   cups sugar
1   cup shortening
    a little salt

1   cup sour milk
1   teaspoon baking soda
    flour

1. Cream the sugar with the shortening. Add the salt, sour milk, and baking soda.
2. Use enough flour to make a dough stiff enough to roll. Cut into shapes.
3. Bake on a greased cookie sheet at 350° until done.

BARS AND BROWNIES

Mud Pie Bars

COLORADO

Adapted from *Nuggets: Recipes Good as Gold*

Pecan coconut brownie:

1   cup margarine
2   cups sugar
4   eggs
2   tablespoons cocoa
1½ cups flour

1   tablespoon vanilla
1   cup chopped pecans
1   cup flaked coconut
1   7-ounce jar marshmallow
    cream

Chocolate frosting:

½   cup margarine
¼   cup cocoa
5   tablespoons milk

1   tablespoon vanilla
1   pound powdered sugar

1. Prepare the brownie by creaming the margarine and sugar until fluffy. Add the eggs and beat until smooth.
2. Mix in the cocoa, flour, and vanilla. Fold in the pecans and coconut. Pour into a greased 9-by-13-inch pan.
3. Bake at 350° for 30–40 minutes.
4. Cool slightly then spread the marshmallow cream on top of the brownie. Place in the freezer for 30 minutes.
5. Prepare the frosting by combining the margarine, cocoa, and milk over low heat in a saucepan until the margarine is melted. Remove from the heat and beat in the vanilla and powdered sugar.

Three-Layer Brownies

COLORADO

Adapted from *Nuggets: Recipes Good as Gold*

Brownie:

2 ounces unsweetened
   chocolate
½ cup margarine
2 eggs
1 cup sugar

½ cup flour
1 teaspoon vanilla
½ cup chopped walnuts
   (optional)

Filling:

2 tablespoons butter, melted
1 cup powdered sugar

1½ tablespoons half-and-half
1   teaspoon vanilla

Glaze:

½ ounce unsweetened
   chocolate

1 tablespoon butter

1. For the brownie, melt the chocolate with the margarine over hot water or in a microwave. Stir in the remaining ingredients. Pour into a greased 8-inch square baking pan.
2. Bake at 350° for 25–30 minutes.
3. Combine the filling ingredients, spread over the cooled brownie. Chill for 10 minutes.
4. For the glaze, melt the chocolate with the butter in a microwave. Drizzle over the filling. Chill.

Hazelnut and Frangelico Cookies

OREGON

Adapted from Brooks, *Oregon's Cuisine of the Rain*

1   cup roasted and skinned hazelnuts
2   cups unbleached flour
1   cup butter, softened

1   cup powdered sugar
1   tablespoon Frangelico
1   teaspoon almond extract

1. Grind the hazelnuts with the flour in a food processor.
2. Cream the butter with the sugar until fluffy. Add the liqueur and extract. Beat thoroughly.
3. Slowly mix in the flour-hazelnut mixture.
4. Scoop out ½-inch balls and place them on a greased cookie sheet.
5. Bake at 350° for 10 minutes, or until bottoms are golden.

Grandma's Whoppers

WASHINGTON

Adapted from *The Seattle Classic Cookbook*

1   cup butter
1   cup sugar
1   cup light brown sugar
2   eggs
1   teaspoon vanilla extract
2   cups flour

1   teaspoon baking soda
1   teaspoon baking powder
¼   teaspoon salt
1   cup cornflakes
1   cup rolled oats

1. Beat the butter, sugar, brown sugar, eggs, and vanilla together.
2. Sift the flour, baking soda, baking powder, and salt together. Stir this into the butter mixture. Beat until smooth. Mix in the cornflakes and oats.
3. Drop the dough by heaping tablespoons onto greased cookie sheets, about 3 inches apart.
4. Bake at 325° for 20 minutes.

Chocolate Chip Butter Cookies

CALIFORNIA
Adapted from *The Los Angeles Times California Cookbook*

1 pound butter or margarine	4½ cups flour
2 cups powdered sugar	12 ounces semisweet chocolate
½ teaspoon salt	pieces
2 teaspoons vanilla	powdered sugar for dusting

1. Cream the butter and powdered sugar together until smooth. Add the salt, vanilla, and flour. Mix until blended. Stir in the chocolate pieces.
2. Roll into 1-inch balls and flatten each with a fork on an ungreased baking sheet.
3. Bake at 350° for 15 minutes. Sprinkle with additional powdered sugar while hot.

Haystacks

CALIFORNIA
Adapted from *The Los Angeles Times California Cookbook*

13 egg whites, lightly beaten	1 cup chopped walnuts
2 cups sugar	½ teaspoon salt
6½ cups flaked coconut	1½ teaspoons vanilla
1½ cups chopped dates	

1. Combine the egg whites and sugar. Cook in the top of a double boiler over simmering water until the mixture feels hot to the touch.
2. Combine the coconut, dates, walnuts, salt, and vanilla. Add the hot egg white mixture and blend well.
3. Using an ice cream scoop, form the stiff mixture into balls and place on a lightly greased baking sheet.
4. Bake at 350° for 20 minutes, or until golden brown.

DROP AND SHAPED COOKIES

Turtle Cookies

CALIFORNIA
Adapted from *The Los Angeles Times California Cookbook*

Cookies:

1½	cups sifted flour		pecan halves
¼	teaspoon baking soda	2	eggs
½	teaspoon salt	¼	teaspoon vanilla
½	cup butter or margarine		
½	cup light brown sugar, packed		

Chocolate frosting:

2	ounces unsweetened chocolate	1	tablespoon butter or margarine
¼	cup milk	1	cup sifted powdered sugar

1. Sift the flour with the baking soda and salt.
2. Cream the butter and brown sugar together until light. Add 1 egg, 1 egg yolk. Stir in the vanilla. Add the dry ingredients and mix well.
3. Arrange pecan halves in groups of 3 to 5 on greased baking sheets to resemble the head and legs of turtle. Roll rounded teaspoons of dough into balls. Dip the bottom of each ball into the remaining unbeaten egg white and press lightly into the nuts, allowing the tips of the nuts to show.
4. Bake at 350° for 10–12 minutes. Allow to cool.
5. Combine the chocolate, milk, and butter in the top of a double boiler over simmering water. Stir and cook until smooth.
6. Remove from the heat and beat in the sugar until smooth and glossy, adding more sugar if needed. Frost.

Garden-Fresh Cookies

WASHINGTON
Adapted from *The Seattle Classic Cookbook*

⅔ cup butter, softened
1¼ cups light brown sugar
2 eggs
1 teaspoon vanilla extract
1 tablespoon grated lemon zest
½ cup buttermilk or sour milk
2 cups flour
1 teaspoon baking powder

1 teaspoon baking soda
1 teaspoon salt
1 teaspoon cinnamon
½ teaspoon nutmeg
¼ teaspoon cream of tartar
2 cups rolled oats
1 cup currants
½ cup chopped walnuts
2 cups grated carrots or zucchini

1. Cream the butter and brown sugar together until light an fluffy. Stir in the eggs, vanilla, lemon zest, and buttermilk. Mix until well blended.
2. Sift the flour, baking powder, baking soda, salt, cinnamon, nutmeg, and cream of tartar together. Add this to the creamed mixture and stir in the oats, currants, nuts, and grated carrots or zucchini. Mix until well blended.
3. Drop by tablespoons onto greased cookie sheets.
4. Bake at 400° for 12 minutes, or until lightly browned.

Waterford Crystal Cookies

WASHINGTON
Adapted from *The Seattle Classic Cookbook*

1	cup butter	4	cups flour
1	cup vegetable oil	1	teaspoon baking soda
1	cup sugar	1	teaspoon cream of tartar
1	cup powdered sugar	½	teaspoon salt
2	eggs	1	tablespoon vanilla extract

1. Cream the first 4 ingredients together. Add the remaining ingredients, mixing well to form a smooth dough. Refrigerate 2 hours.
2. Form the dough into small balls and place them on greased cookie sheets. Flatten each cookie with the greased bottom of a Waterford crystal glass (or any glass with a pattern in its base) dipped in sugar.
3. Bake at 350° for 10–12 minutes.

Oatmeal Cookies

OREGON
Adapted from *The Portland Woman's Exchange Cook Book, 1913*

1⅓	cups butter	2	eggs
1⅓	cups light brown sugar	2	teaspoons baking powder
1½	cups rolled oats	1	teaspoon cinnamon
1½	cups flour		

1. Cream the butter with the brown sugar until light and fluffy. Stir in the remaining ingredients. Beat to form a smooth dough.
2. Drop by teaspoonfuls onto a greased cookie sheet.
3. Bake at 375° for 10 minutes, or until cookies are lightly browned.

Chinese Almond Cookies

CALIFORNIA
Adapted from *The Los Angeles Times California Cookbook*

2 cups flour	½ cup granulated sugar
½ teaspoon baking soda	½ teaspoon almond extract
¾ teaspoon baking powder	3 dozen blanched whole
1 egg	almonds
½ pound lard	2 egg yolks, beaten
½ cup light brown sugar, packed	

1. Sift the flour with the baking soda and baking powder.
2. Beat the egg and lard together. Add the sugars and almond extract. Gradually mix in the dry ingredients until well blended.
3. Roll tablespoons of dough into balls. Place them on ungreased cookie sheets and press an almond into the middle of each. Brush with beaten egg yolk.
4. Bake at 350° for 15–20 minutes.

Ghiradelli's Chocolate Chip Cookies

CALIFORNIA
Adapted from Berger and Custis, *Sumptuous Dining in Gaslight San Francisco 1875–1915*

½ cup sugar	1½ cups sifted flour
½ cup light brown sugar	½ teaspoon baking soda
⅓ cup butter, softened	salt
⅓ cup shortening	½ cup chopped nuts or raisins
1 egg	6 ounces semisweet chocolate
1 teaspoon vanilla	chips

1. Mix the sugars, butter, shortening, egg, and vanilla together. Beat until light and smooth. Stir in the remaining ingredients.
2. Drop the dough by heaping teaspoonfuls about 2 inches apart onto an ungreased cookie sheet.
3. Bake at 375° until light brown, about 8–10 minutes.

Dreams

OREGON
Adapted from Brown, *American Cooking: The Northwest*

1⅓ cups flour	½ cup sugar
½ teaspoon baking soda	1 egg
⅛ teaspoon ground cardamom	¼ cup shelled hazelnuts
8 tablespoons butter, softened	

1. Sift the flour, baking soda, and cardamom together.
2. Cream the butter and the sugar together until light and fluffy. Beat in the egg and add the flour mixture a little at a time, beating well after each addition.
3. Form 1-inch balls from the dough and place them on buttered cookie sheets 2 inches apart. Press a hazelnut into the center of each cookie.
4. Bake at 350° for about 10 minutes, or until the cookies are firm to the touch and lightly browned.

Sesame Seed Wafers

HAWAII
Adapted from Toupin, *Hawaii Cookbook & Backyard Luau*

¾ cup butter	¼ teaspoon baking powder
1½ cups light brown sugar	1 teaspoon vanilla
2 large eggs	¾ cup toasted sesame seeds
2 cups flour	

1. Cream the butter with the brown sugar until light and fluffy. Add the eggs, 1 at a time, beating well after each addition.
2. Sift the flour and baking powder together and add to the butter mixture. Mix well. Stir in the vanilla and sesame seeds.
3. Drop the dough by teaspoonfuls about 2 inches apart on greased cookie sheets.
4. Bake at 350° for 10 minutes, or until the edges are brown.

Almond Cookies

HAWAII

Adapted from Toupin, *Hawaii Cookbook & Backyard Luau*

3 cups sifted flour	1 cup shortening
1 cup sugar	1 egg, well beaten
1 teaspoon baking soda	1 tablespoon almond extract
¼ teaspoon salt	1 cup blanched almonds

1. Sift the flour, sugar, baking soda, and salt together. Cut in the shortening until the mixture resembles coarse meal.
2. Add the egg and the flavoring. Beat well to form a smooth dough.
3. Form the dough into 1-inch balls. Flatten each ball and place them on a greased cookie sheet. Press an almond on top of each cookie.
4. Bake at 350° for 15 minutes.

Ginger Crisps

ALASKA

Adapted from *Cooking Alaskan*

½ cup molasses	½ teaspoon salt
¼ cup granulated sugar	½ teaspoon nutmeg
3 tablespoons margarine	½ teaspoon cinnamon
1 tablespoon milk	½ teaspoon cloves
2 cups flour	¾ teaspoon ginger
½ teaspoon baking soda	1 tablespoon lemon juice

1. Heat the molasses to boiling. Add the sugar, margarine, and milk.
2. Sift the dry ingredients together and stir into first mixture, adding more flour if needed to make a thick enough dough to roll out. Add the lemon juice and beat to form a smooth dough. Chill the dough for several hours.
3. Roll out portions of dough and cut into favorite shapes. Place the cookies on an ungreased cookie sheet.
4. Bake at 400° until crisp.

ROLL, SLICE, AND CUT COOKIES

Napoleon Cakes

OREGON

Adapted from *The Portland Woman's Exchange Cook Book, 1913*

3	ounces butter	1	ounce ground almonds
1	cup flour	1	egg yolk
2	tablespoons sugar	½	cup raspberry preserves

1. Rub the butter into the flour. Stir in the sugar and almonds, mixing well.
2. Beat in the egg yolk to make a very stiff paste. Refrigerate 1 hour.
3. Divide the dough in half and roll each out to a thin rectangle. Place the first sheet of dough onto a greased baking sheet and spread the raspberry preserves on it. Place the second sheet of dough over it.
4. Bake at 350° until very pale brown. Cut into strips while hot.

BARS AND BROWNIES

Hardtack

ALASKA

Adapted from *Cooking Alaskan*

2	level teaspoons baking powder	4	eggs, well beaten
	pinch salt	12	ounces orange marmalade
1½	cups flour	1	pound finely chopped walnuts
2	cups sugar	1	pound finely chopped dates

1. Sift the dry ingredients together. Add the remaining ingredients and mix well.
2. Spread this batter about 1-inch thick on a greased cookie sheet.
3. Bake at 375° for 45 minutes. Cut into squares while warm.

Lemon-Glazed Shortbread

WASHINGTON
Adapted from *The Seattle Classic Cookbook*

First layer:

1½ cups flour	½ cup butter
½ cup light brown sugar	

Second layer:

2 eggs	2 tablespoons flour
1 cup light brown sugar	½ teaspoon baking powder
½ cup coconut	½ teaspoon vanilla extract
1 cup chopped nuts	¼ teaspoon salt

Frosting:

1 cup powdered sugar	juice and grated zest of
1 tablespoon butter, melted	1 lemon

1. Combine the ingredients for the first layer and mix until crumbly. Press this mixture into a 9-by-13-inch baking pan.
2. Bake at 350° for 10 minutes. Remove the pan from the oven and reduce the heat to 325°.
3. For the second layer, beat the eggs lightly and add the brown sugar, mixing well. Stir in the remaining ingredients, and spread this over the baked layer. Bake for 15 minutes.
4. Prepare the frosting by combining the ingredients and beating smooth. Ice the second layer while still warm.
5. Cut the cookies into bars and refrigerate.

Disappearing Marshmallow Brownies

WASHINGTON
Adapted from *The Seattle Classic Cookbook*

½ cup butterscotch chips	1 egg
¼ cup butter	1 cup miniature
¾ cup flour	marshmallows
⅓ cup light brown sugar	1 cup semisweet chocolate
1 teaspoon baking powder	chips
¼ teaspoon salt	¼ cup chopped nuts
½ teaspoon vanilla extract	

1. Melt the butterscotch chips and butter in the top of a double boiler. Remove from the heat and cool to lukewarm.
2. Add the flour, brown sugar, baking powder, salt, vanilla, and egg to the butterscotch mixture. Mix well to form a smooth dough.
3. Fold in the marshmallows, chocolate chips, and nuts until just combined.
4. Spread the batter into a 9-inch square cake pan and bake for 20 minutes at 350°. Do not overbake. Cut when cool.

Lollies

CALIFORNIA
Adapted from *American Cooking: The Great West*

8 tablespoons butter, softened	½ teaspoon baking powder
	½ teaspoon vanilla extract
1½ cups dark brown sugar, divided	1 cup finely chopped pecans
	1 cup canned shredded
1 cup sifted flour	coconut
2 eggs	

1. Cream the butter and ½ cup of the dark brown sugar together until light and fluffy. Beat in the flour ½ cup at a time. Pat the dough into a buttered 9-by-12-inch pan.
2. Bake at 350° for 15 minutes.
3. Beat the eggs, baking powder, and vanilla extract together lightly. Stir in the remaining brown sugar and mix well. Stir in the pecans and coconut.
4. Pour the egg batter over the baked sheet cookie and bake 15 minutes, or until the top is golden brown and firm.
5. Allow to cool and cut into squares.

Guava Crisps

HAWAII

Adapted from Toupin, *Hawaii Cookbook & Backyard Luau*

Filling:

¼ cup butter	¼ teaspoon salt
⅓ cup guava jelly	1 egg yolk, slightly beaten
2 tablespoons lemon juice	¼ cup chopped macadamia
2 tablespoons sugar	nuts

Pastry:

1 cup flour	½ cup butter
½ teaspoon salt	½ cup light brown sugar
½ teaspoon baking soda	1 cup quick rolled oats

1. Heat the butter, guava jelly, lemon juice, sugar, and salt in the top of a double boiler until the guava jelly has melted and dissolved.
2. Beat 2 tablespoons of this hot mixture into the egg yolk and add this back to the double boiler. Cook until thick. Add the nuts and allow the filling to cool.
3. To prepare the pastry, sift the flour, salt, and baking soda over the butter and brown sugar. Cut the butter in with a pastry blender until coarse crumbs form. Stir in the oats and mix well.
4. Pat half of the mixture into the bottom of a 9-inch square cake pan. Spread the filling over the pastry layer. Top this with the remaining pastry.
5. Bake at 350° for 25 minutes. Cool and cut into 1½-inch squares.

Coconut-Macadamia Nut Bars

HAWAII
Adapted from Toupin, *Hawaii Cookbook & Backyard Luau*

Pastry:

½ cup butter	1¼ cups flour, sifted
½ cup light brown sugar	¼ teaspoon salt
1 egg	

Filling:

2 eggs	½ teaspoon baking powder
1 cup light brown sugar	1½ cups shredded coconut
1 teaspoon vanilla	1 cup chopped unsalted
2 tablespoons flour	macadamia nuts
¼ teaspoon salt	

Glaze:

1½ cups powdered sugar	1 tablespoon lemon juice
2 tablespoons pineapple juice	

1. Cream the butter and brown sugar together. Add the egg and beat until light and fluffy.
2. Add the flour and salt and blend well. Pat the dough into the bottom of a 9-by-12-inch pan.
3. Bake at 350° for 15 minutes. Allow the pastry to cool.
4. Prepare the filling by combining all of the ingredients, mixing well. Pour this over the cooled pastry.
5. Bake at 350° for 20 minutes. Allow the pastry to cool before frosting.
6. Spread with a glaze made by beating the powdered sugar with pineapple and lemon juices until smooth.
7. Cut into 1-by-2-inch bars.

BIBLIOGRAPHY

Starred cookbooks are historical; that is, they contain recipes originally published before 1900.

American Cooking: The Great West. New York: Time-Life Books, 1974.

Anderson, Janet Alm. *Bounty: A Harvest of Food Lore and Country Memories from Utah's Past.* Boulder: Pruett Publishing Company, 1990.

*Beecher, Catharine. *Miss Beecher's Domestic Receipt Book.* N.p., n.d.

*Beecher, Catharine, and Harriet Beecher Stowe. *The American Woman's Home.* New York: J. R. Ford and Co., 1869.

*Beldon, Louise Conway. *The Festive Tradition: Table Decoration and Desserts in America, 1650–1900.* New York: W. W. Norton, 1983.

*Berger, Frances De Talavera, and John Parke Custis. *Sumptuous Dining in Gaslight San Francisco 1875–1915.* Garden City: Doubleday & Company, 1985.

Berquist, Edna Smith. *The High Maples Farm Cookbook.* New York: Collier Books, 1971.

Best-Loved Cookies. Des Moines, Ia.: Meredith Publishing Services, 1995.

The Best of Shaker Cooking. Edited by A. B. W. Miller and P. W. Fuller. New York: Macmillan, 1970.

*Booth, Sally Smith. *Hung, Strung, & Potted: A History of Eating in Colonial America.* New York: Clarkson N. Potter, 1971.

Boston Chapter, No. 28 Order of Eastern Star Cook Book. N.p., n.d.

Brack, Fred, and Tina Bell. *The Tastes of Washington.* Seattle: Evergreen Publishing Company, 1986.

Brooks, Karen. *Oregon's Cuisine of the Rain.* New York. Addison-Wesley, n.d.

Brown, Dale. *American Cooking: The Northwest.* New York: Time-Life Books, 1970.

*Bullock, Helen. *The Williamsburg Art of Cookery or Accoplish'd Gentlewoman's Companion.* Williamsburg, Va.: Colonial Williamsburg, Inc., 1942.

Butel, Jane. *Woman's Day Book of New Mexican Cooking.* New York: Pocket Books, n.d.

Cameron, Shiela MacNiven. *The Best from New Mexico Kitchens.* Santa Fe: New Mexico Magazine, n.d.

Capitol Cook Book: Favorite Family Recipes of Texas Governors, Senators and Other State Officials. Edited by Sue Creighton. Waco: Texian Press, 1973.

Carey, Frank, and Jayni Naas. *The Kansas Cookbook.* Lawrence: University Press of Kansas, 1989.

*Carson, Jane. *Colonial Virginia Cookery: Procedures, Equipment, and Ingredients in Colonial Cooking.* Williamsburg, Va.: Colonial Williamsburg Foundation, 1985.

* *The Centennial Treasury of Recipes: Swiss Mennonites.* Edited by Harley J. Stucky. North Newton, Kansas: The Mennonite Press, n.d.

Chicken Foot Soup and Other Recipes from the Pine Barrens. Edited by A. M. Ridgway. New Brunswick, N.J.: Rutgers University Press, 1980.

Choice Recipes. Compiled by The E. S. Gerberich Bible Class. Middletown, Pennsylvania: St. Peter's Lutheran Sunday-School, n.d.

Coleman, Arthur, and Bobbie Coleman. *The Texas Cookbook.* New York: A. A. Wyn, 1949.

A Colonial Plantation Cookbook: The Receipt Book of Harriott Pinkney Horry, 1770. Edited by R. J. Hooker. Columbia: University of South Carolina Press, 1984.

Cooking Alaskan. Anchorage: Alaska Northwest Publishing Company, 1983.

Cooking in Wyoming. Basin, Wy.: Bighorn Book Company, 1965.

Curye on Inglysch: English Culinary Manuscripts of the Fourteenth Century. Edited by C. B. Hieatt and S. Butler. London: Oxford University Press, 1985.

Dalsass, Diana. *Miss Mary's Down-Home Cooking: Traditional Recipes from Lynchburg, Tennessee.* New York: New American Library Books, 1984.

DeBolt, Margaret Wayt. *Savannah Sampler Cookbook.* Norfolk, Virginia: Donning Company, 1978.

DeMasters, Carol. *Dining In—Milwaukee.* Mercer Island, Washington: Peanut Butter Publishing, 1981.

Dent, Huntley. *The Feast of Santa Fe.* New York: Simon & Schuster, 1985.

Dining in America 1850–1900. Edited by K. Grover. Amherst: University of Massachusetts Press, 1987.

DuSablon, Mary Anna. *Cincinnati Recipe Treasury.* Cincinnati: Ohio University Press, 1989.

Dyer, Ceil. *The Newport Cookbook.* New York: Hawthorn Books, 1972.

Early American Cooking: Recipes from America's Historic Sites. Edited by E. L. Beilenson. White Plains, N.Y.: Peter Pauper Press, 1985.

*Farmer, Fannie Merritt. *The Boston Cooking-School Cook Book.* New ed. Boston: Little, Brown, and Company, [1896] 1928.

*Farrington, Doris E. *Fireside Cooks & Black Kettle Recipes.* Indianapolis: Bobbs-Merrill, 1976.

Feibleman, Peter S. *American Cooking: Creole and Acadian.* New York: Time-Life Books, 1971.

"The Four Hundred" Cook Book: 400 Choice Recipes. Madison, Wis.: N.p., n.d.

The Foxfire Book of Appalachian Cookery. Edited by L. G. Page and E. Wiggington. New York: E. P. Dutton, 1984.

*Glasse, Hannah. *The Art of Cookery Made Plain and Easy.* London: n.p., 1796.

Gulf City Cook Book. Compiled by The Ladies of the St. Francis Street Methodist Episcopal Church, 1878. Tuscaloosa: University of Alabama Press, 1990.

Hawkins, Nancy, Arthur Havemeyer, and Mary Allen Havemeyer. *Nantucket and Other New England Cooking.* New York: Hastings House, n.d.

Hawkins, Nancy, and Arthur Hawkins. *The American Regional Cookbook.* New York: Prentice-Hall, 1976.

*Hechtlinger, Adelaide. *The Seasonal Hearth: The Woman at Home in Early America.* Woodstock, N.Y.: Overlook Press, 1977.

Hemingway, Joan, and Russell Armstrong. *Dining In—Sun Valley.* Seattle: Peanut Butter Publishing, 1982.

*Hooker, Margaret Huntington. *Early American Cookery or Yᵉ Gentlewoman's Housewifery.* Dodd, Mead, and Company, 1896.

The Hoosier Cookbook. Edited by Elaine Lumbra. Bloomington: Indiana University Press, n.d.

How Iowa Cooks. Compiled by Tipton's Woman's Club. N.p., n.d.

Huber, E. *Bier und Bierbereitung bei den Volkernder Urzeit.* N.p., 1926.

Jackson, Michael. *The New World Guide to Beer.* Philadelphia: Running Press, 1988.

The Junior League Cook Book. Roanoke, Va. N.p., ca. 1922.

Kellner, Lyn. *The Taste of Appalachia: A Collection of Traditional Recipes Still in Use Today.* Boone, N.C.: Simmer Pot Press, 1987.

*Kreidberg, Marjorie. *Food on the Frontier: Minnesota Cooking from 1850– 1900 with Selected Recipes.* St. Paul: Minnesota Historical Society Press, 1975.

*Langseth-Christensen, Lillian. *The Mystic Seaport Cookbook: 350 Years of New England Cooking.* New York: Funk & Wagnalls, 1970.

*Lee, Hilde Gabriel. *Taste of the States.* Charlottesville, Virginia: Howell Press, 1992.

*Leslie, Eliza. *New Receipts for Cooking.* Philadelphia: n.p., 1846.

*———. *Seventy Five Receipts, for Pastry, Cakes, and Sweetmeats.* London: n.p., 1828.

Lestz, Gerald S. *The Pennsylvania Dutch Cookbook.* New York: Grosset & Dunlap, 1970.

A Library of Favorite Recipes from New York State. Edited by 1984 Vitality Fund Committee, New York Library Association. Leawood, N.Y.: Circulation Service, 1985.

Linsenmeyer, Helen Walker. *Cooking Plain.* Carbondale: Southern Illinois University Press, n.d.

The Los Angeles Times California Cookbook. Edited by Betsy Balsley. New York: Harry N. Abrams, 1981.

*MacDonald, Margaret F. *Whistler's Mother's Cook Book.* 2nd ed. San Francisco: Pomegranate Art Books, 1995.

Macmillan, Norma. *In a Shaker Kitchen: 100 Recipes from the Shaker Tradition.* New York: Simon & Schuster, 1995.

Marion Cook Book. N.p., 1921.

*Markham, Gervase. *The English Housewife.* Edited by M. R. Best. Montreal: McGill–Queens University Press, 1986.

Marshall, Lillian Bertram. *Cooking Across the South.* Birmingham: Oxmoor House, 1980.

*May, Robert. *The Accomplisht Cook, or the Art and Mystery of Cookery.* London: Nathan Brooke, 1671.

Nebraska Pioneer Cookbook. Compiled by Kay Graber. Lincoln: University of Nebraska Press, 1974.

The Neighborhood Cook Book. Compiled by the Women's Guild of the First Congregational Church. Greenwich, Conn.: N.p., 1931.

Nevada's Finest Western Cooking. Compiled by Nevada Federation of Women's Clubs. Lenexa, Nev.: Cookbook Publishers, 1982.

Nickerson, Jane. *Florida Cookbook.* Gainesville: University of Florida Press, n.d.

Nuggets: Recipes Good as Gold. Compiled by The Junior League of Colorado Springs. Memphis, Tenn.: S. C. Toof & Co., 1983.

Out of Vermont Kitchens. Compiled by Trinity Mission of Trinity Church (Rutland, Vermont) and The Women's Service League of St. Paul's Church (Burlington, Vermont). N.p., [1939] 1947.

Palm Beach Entertains Then and Now. Edited by The Junior League of the Palm Beaches. New York: Coward, McCann & Geoghegan, 1976.

Pass the Plate. New Berne, N.C.: Episcopal Churchwomen and Friends of Christ Episcopal Church, 1981.

Patterson, Charles. *Kentucky Cooking.* New York: Harper & Row, 1988.

Pioneer Potluck: Stories and Recipes of Early Colorado. Edited by The Volunteers of the State Historical Society of Colorado. N.p., n.d.

Pixley, Aristene. *Vermont Country Cooking.* New York: Dover Publications, 1979.

The Pocumtuc Housewife. N.p., 1805.

The Portland Woman's Exchange Cook Book, 1913. Portland, Ore.: Glass-Dahlstrom Printers, 1973.

*Raffald, Elizabeth. *The Experienced English Housekeeper.* London: R & W Dean, 1807.

*Randolph, Mary. *The Virginia Housewife.* 1824 ed. Commentaries by Karen Hess. Columbia: University of South Carolina Press, 1985.

*————. *The Virginia Housewife: or Methodical Cook.* Philadelphia: E. H. Butler and Co., 1860.

Recipes Collected by the Woman's Exchange of Memphis, Tennessee. Memphis: Jno. R. Kinnie Printing Co., 1967.

Reed, Anna Wetherhill. *The Philadelphia Cook Book of Town and Country.* New York: Bramhall House, 1963.

Ross, Larry. *Nanny's Texas Table.* New York: Simon & Schuster, 1987.

Roux, Willan C. *What's Cooking Down in Maine.* Lewiston, Me.: Twin City Printery, 1964.

Schultz, Philip Stephen. *As American as Apple Pie.* New York: Simon & Schuster, 1990.

*Scully, Terence. *The Art of Cookery in the Middle Ages.* Woolbridge, England: The Boydel Press, 1995.

The Seattle Classic Cookbook. Compiled by The Junior League of Seattle. Seattle: Madrona Publishers, 1983.

Selected Receipts of a Van Rensselaer Family 1785–1835. Edited by J. C. Kellar, E. Miller, and P. Stambach. Cherry Hill, N.Y.: Historic Cherry Hill Corp., 1964.

Shenton, James P., et al. *American Cooking: The Melting Pot.* New York: Time-Life Books, 1971.

*Simmons, Amelia. *American Cookery 1796.* Introduction and Updated Recipes by Iris Ihde Frey. Green Farms, Conn.: Silverleaf Press, 1984.

*Smith, Eliza. *The Compleat Housewife; or, Accomplished Gentlewoman's Companion.* Williamsburg, Va.: William Parks, 1742.

The South Carolina Cook Book. Edited by South Carolina Homemakers Council. Columbia: University of South Carolina Press, 1990.

St. Paul's Centennial Cookbook (Lake Mills, Wis.). Olathe, Kansas: Cookbook Publishers, 1992.

A Taste of South Carolina. Edited by The Palmetto Cabinet. Orangeburg, S.C.: Sandlapper Publishing, 1983.

Tested Maryland Recipes. 2nd ed. Compiled by The Ladies of the Presbyterian Church. Chesapeake City, Md.: The Ladies of the Presbyterian Church, 1900.

Toupin, Elizabeth Ann. *Hawaii Cookbook & Backyard Luau.* New York: Bantam Books, 1967.

Tunica County Tasty Treats. Tunica, Miss.: Tunica Times-Democrat, 1953.

Waldemar, Carla. *Dining In—Minneapolis/St. Paul.* Mercer Island, Wash.: Peanut Butter Press, 1982.

*Washington, Martha. *Booke of Cookery.* Transcribed by Karen Hess. New York: Columbia University Press, 1981.

*———. *A Booke of Sweetmeats.* Transcribed by Karen Hess. New York: Columbia University Press, 1981.

*Weaver, William Woys. *Thirty Five Receipts from "The Larder Invaded."* Philadelphia: The Library Company of Philadelphia, 1986.

Weiner, Melissa Ruffner. *Arizona Territorial Cookbook.* Norfolk, Va.: Donning Company, 1982.

Whitehill, Walter Muir. *The Best of Shaker Cooking.* N.p., n.d.

Wilhelm, Maxine. *Smidgen of Honey.* N.p., n.d.

Wilson, José. *American Cooking: The Eastern Heartland.* New York: Time-Life Books, 1971.

Winterthur's Culinary Collection. Compiled by A. B. Coleman. Baum Printing Company, 1983.

*Woolley, Hannah. *The Gentlewoman's Companion.* London: A. Maxwell for D. Newman, 1673.

Indexes

BREADS

PIES

CAKES

COOKIES